Jane's

WARSHIP

RECOGNITION GUIDE

In the USA for information address:
HarperCollins*Publishers* Inc
10 East 53rd Street
New York
NY 10022
www.**fire**and**water**.com

In the UK for information address:
HarperCollins*Publishers*
77-85 Fulham Palace Road
Hammersmith
London W6 8JB
everything clicks at www.collins.co.uk

First published by HarperCollins*Publishers* 2002

ISBN 0 00 713722 2

Design: Rod Teasdale
Additional illustrations: Ian Sturton

Printed in England by Bath Press

A M Pitman
Fall, 2003.
$20.00

WARSHIP

RECOGNITION GUIDE

2002

Revised and edited by
Robert Hutchinson

HarperCollins*Publishers*

CONTENTS

CONTENTS

CONTENTS

CONTENTS

CONTENTS

CONTENTS

CONTENTS

FOREWORD

For some time, some voices in the world of defence have been raised to warn of the dangers of "asymmetric warfare" facing the West. As normal with military speak, the meaning of this phrase may seem obscure, if not a misuse of the English language. Sadly, we all now have a clarification. Look to the attacks on homeland USA, on New York and Washington DC, in September, 2001, for a terrifyingly graphic definition of what asymmetric warfare really means: the ability of an enemy to outwit superior military might by unconventional means.

Nine months before the attacks, Dan Goure, a senior fellow with the Washington-based think tank, the Lexington Institute, wrote in *Jane's Defence Weekly* of some of the continuing crises faced by the west in a world of disorder – Somalia, Bosnia, Liberia, Haiti, Rwanda, Iraq and the Taiwan Straits. "Some might call this period an age of chaos," he added.

So none of this should come as a complete shock to Western politicians. The US Special Forces have recognised the nature of the new threats for some time. Lieut. Gen. William Tangney, deputy commander in chief of the US Special Operations Command, said in October 2001: "In Beirut, 1984, we had the loss of the marines; the Khobar Towers, the USS *Cole*, the (US) Embassy in Nairobi. These are not acts of terrorism. These are.... rational acts of war by non-traditional actors using asymmetric means to get at what is perceived to be our largest national vulnerability, which is an unwillingness to accept casualties."

But September 11 was a numbing shock. Aside from the audacity of the attacks on the very symbols of American life, the horrific loss of life, and the scale of destruction, the West was *unprepared*. Not only culturally, but militarily as well. It was unprepared because corporately, it lacked accurate, timely intelligence on the intentions and capabilities of potential adversaries.

Sadly, this was not a new phenomenon.

A year earlier, the suicide attack on the 'Arleigh Burke' class guided missile destroyer USS *Cole* in Aden harbour, Yemen, in which 17 sailors died, occurred because "protection was inadequate through a lack of timely intelligence," according to the Pentagon's subsequent investigating commission.

Rear Admiral Rick Porterfield, director of US naval intelligence, says the attack on the *Cole*, which inflicted $240 million of damage, demonstrated how terrorism "provides a constant concern for our military commanders.... We have many ships forward-deployed and they are making port visits, they are doing exercises and they are transiting choke points. We have to be especially mindful when our ships and units are in a limited manoeuvring situation in restricted waters."Admiral Porterfield says the USA's reliance on high technology and information and therefore its vulnerability to information warfare – or cyber attacks – is of particular concern. "The cyber terrorism we have heard about, such as the 'Melissa' [computer] virus, are just the tip of the iceberg of the potential the entire world faces." In conventional warfare, there is a growing trend towards weapons such as sea mines that are accessible to a host of countries because of their low cost. "Russia and China are key suppliers of mines and have sophisticated mines with many and multiple effects," says Admiral Porterfield. Relatively cheap mines can cause a disproportionate amount of damage, he adds, citing the incident in 1988 when "the USS *Samuel B Roberts* struck a $1,500 Iranian mine in the Persian Gulf, causing $96 million in damage." In an overview of the development of naval threats, the naval intelligence staff indicated that many coastal nations "are developing – either by buying outright or developing them indigenously – the military capabilities intended to deny the USA access to waters that are on their periphery." These countries "have read our naval strategy documents and those of our allies and have responded to them."

For example, China's perception that threats have historically originated from off the coast has led Beijing to develop strategies and "buying and building capabilities designed to keep any potential adversary in a band they described as the first island chain and the second island chain.

"Their plan involves mines, submarines, the deployment of anti-ship cruise missile-equipped surface combatants and asymmetric portions such as the use of small boats to provide a rudimentary but effective surveillance network," said Admiral Porterfield.

"The Chinese certainly are developing a

USS COLE ARRIVES HOME AFTER REFIT FOLLOWING THE TERRORIST ATTACK IN ADEN.

capability designed as an anti-access strategy. It could be used against the USA, Taiwan, or anybody else."

For two years the US Navy has been examining the possible nature of asymmetric threats and the tactics needed to counter them.

In January, 1999, Vice Adm. Dennis McGinn, commander of the US Third Fleet, said some of these threats included "bomb-laden suicide jet skis" and other fast-moving, small craft such as light aircraft.

In the light of the *Cole* attack, how prophetic his words were! But again, unsurprising: the Tamil Tigers have been successfully using small, fast and high manoeuvrable boats in massed attacks against the Sri Lankan navy for some years.

As we have seen in Afghanistan, hunting down the terrorist and destroying the network, root and

FOREWORD

branch, is a long and costly business involving combined operations, deploying high technology air-dropped munitions with special forces on the ground. In most potential theatres of operation, it will be naval assets that will play a key role in the war against terrorism.

Let's take a look at developments in naval capability around the world in this "age of chaos."

UNITED STATES

The percentage of the fleet deployed operationally has risen from 21% in the early 1990s to around 30% in early 2001, taking a toll not only on the hulls, but also on the hard-pressed crews in a service that is some 14,000 sailors short of establishment. Requirements, as in the Afghan air strikes, continue to mount, but without the necessary rates of build. In attack submarines alone, recent studies have indicated a need for a force of 68 by 2015, compared with 2001's 55. By 2025, the number required will inflate to 76.

The US Navy's latest carrier, *Ronald Reagan* was christened on March 4, 2001 and will replace the 40 year old *Constellation* when she commissions in 2003, thereby maintaining a 12 carrier force. A $161 million contract for research and design development of the next generation of nuclear-powered carriers, the CVNX, has been awarded to Newport News Shipbuilding. The new

class could be eventually 10 strong with a building rate of one every five years. Construction of the first, based on the 'Nimitz' class, is expected to begin in 2006 to meet an in-service date of 2013.

The DD (X) class is planned to replace the 'Oliver Hazard Perry' (FFG 7) and 'Spruance' (DD 963). This class will be a part of a new family of surface combatants.

The new 'San Antonio' class of transport dock ships, the first of which is launching in 2002, will replace several classes of ageing vessels and will augment the existing 'Wasp' and 'Tarawa' classes to form the core of the US Navy's future amphibious warfare capability. It's 25,000 sq. ft of deck space will be used for vehicles, in addition to the 34,000 cu. ft of cargo below decks; accommodation for 720 embarked Marines, two air cushion vehicles and hangar space for two Sikorsky CH-53 Super Stallion helicopters.

Mine counter-measures have now been directed to become a core competency, particularly in shallow water operations.

The insertion of special forces has become a new priority with the addition of dry deck shelters in the 'Benjamin Franklin' class submarine *Kamehameha* as an experiment, followed by the fitting of these features (carrying swimmer deliver vehicles) on five 'Ohio' class SSBNs. A further four 'Ohios' are being equipped with the Advanced

KAMEHAMEHA VISITING PEARL HARBOUR

RUSSIA STILL RELIES ON ELDERLY DELTA IVS FOR HER SEABORNE STRATEGIC MISSILE CAPABILITY.

Swimmer Delivery system, a dry submersible, capable of deploying from the mother boat to a hostile shore, with a range of 125 nms at 8 kts.

RUSSIA

Lack of funding continues to afflict the Russian fleet. The modernisation of the ballistic missile submarine force has been further delayed. The cancellation of the new SLBM, the SS-N-28, has paused construction of the new 'Borey' class SSBN while planners make up their mind on the size and shape of the new strategic weapon. Meanwhile, as the leviathan 'Typhoon' class is phased out, because of high running and maintenance costs, the burden of maintaining the Russian strategic deterrent sea rests on the 20 and 30 year old Delta IVs and IIIs. These operate on a low patrol level, indicating perhaps, the Russian Navy's adoption of a policy of maintaining high readiness alongside for reasons of cash shortages.

Although operations by the increasingly quiet attack submarine force continue, reports suggest that it is doubtful that many more than half the 24 'Oscar II' and 'Akula' boats are fully operational at any one time.

There remains the question of what is going to happen to the decommissioned hulls of nuclear

boats a major environmental issue, and one hardly resolved by Western navies with their own retired boats. Japan has paid for a new facility to process dangerous low-grade radioactive waste from old Russian Pacific Fleet nuclear submarines. The Tokyo government launched the $34 million project in November 1993, following concerns over potential leakage of radioactive waste into the Sea of Japan from submarines laid up at Vladivostock. Now the material will be processed on a barge based at the Russian shipyard of Zvedza. Full operations will begin when safety regulations on its discharge of water have been finalised.

Japan has proposed a plan for the disposal of decommissioned Russian nuclear submarines. Moscow has yet to reveal how many await dismantling but it believed that 150 boats have been retired from service. The US government meanwhile has been helping Russia break up two nuclear missile submarines a year at Zvedza.

The loss of the highly proficient Oscar II submarine *Kursk* due to an accident involving its munitions, indicated, to some, the decline of the Russian Navy. Let no-one doubt that while it's operational readiness has been considerably reduced from Cold War levels, existing capabilities remain impressive.

FOREWORD

SOVREMENNY - CHINA HAS PROCURRED THESE SHIPS TO PROVIDE AREA AIR DEFENCE.

CHINA

China has chosen to use its naval forces to emphasise its new-found position as a world power through modest naval deployments to Australia, South Africa and the United States. These deployments demonstrate the transition of the navy from the brown water force of a decade ago to one with aspirations (and the growing ability to fulfil them,) to act both regionally and internationally.

The strategic aim, as we have seen, is the ability to defend the homeland, or influence events as far as the "first island chain" off the coast – which stretches from Japan to the Indonesian archipelago and covering the East China Seas, the Yellow Sea and the Sea of Japan. The need for "strategic depth" means this area of military interest probably extends another 1,000 miles out, including the "second island chain."

The pace of Chinese naval activity in the first zone is quickening: Chinese naval vessels repeatedly make incursions into Japan's Exclusive Economic Zone. According to Japan's Self Defence Agency, 31 Chinese naval vessels were sighted in Japanese waters during 2000, compared with the one or two of previous years. Most of these operations involve hydrographic and oceanographic surveys of the region, indicating Chinese interest in the nature of the seabed – a

firm pointer to submarine operations in the future.

Submarines occupy a key role in Chinese naval procurement, because of the strategic importance that these platforms may play in any operations around Taiwan, such as a naval blockade or the deterrence of US naval deployments to the area.

Beijing is currently running five submarine programmes, but many are beset with problems - with the average time taken to complete a boat now averaging six years. The Type 094 SSBN, with first of class laid down in 2001, awaits satisfactory development of the new strategic missile, JL-2, before work can proceed further. The first 'Han' class took nine years to build, the new Type 093 attack submarine 11 years and the first of the 'Song' class SSKs has experienced major design problems on sea trials.

Similar problems with surface ship construction has led to procurement of four Russian 'Sovremenny' class destroyers to help rectify the Chinese navy's chronic lack of area air defence. Much speculation has focused on Beijing's undoubted firm ambitions for organic air at sea, its attempts to buy-in technology and expertise, and what shape a Chinese aircraft carrier would eventually take. At this stage, it looks more likely to go down the route of a smaller hull of around 25,000 tons for local sea control.

UNITED KINGDOM

One of the key elements, if not battlegrounds, of the UK's 1998 Strategic Defence Review was whether the current ageing carriers should be replaced. The commitment to the USA's Joint Strike Fighter as the solution to the UK requirement for a Future Carrier Borne Aircraft brought with it plans for two new aircraft carriers. If they survive successive Treasury attacks on funding, (and what fat spending targets they make!) the decision for the demonstration and manufacture of the new class is expected in late 2003 with contracts to follow in spring 2004. The new ships, which will accommodate around 50 aircraft each, are planned to enter service in 2012 and 2015.

Two other areas of current and future capability shortfall remain in the Royal Navy – amphibious warfare and the destroyer and frigate force. *Fearless*, the only landing platform left in service, will be around 40 years old when she pays off in 2003. She will be replaced by two new assault ships, *Albion* and *Bulwark*, under construction, in addition to the helicopter carrier *Ocean*, now in service. In 2001, four landing ships were ordered to replace the elderly 'Sir Bedivere' class LSLs, (based on the revolutionary Dutch 'Rotterdam' class), and will have twice the military lift capacity of their predecessors.

Turning to British destroyers and frigates, the sad story of delay continues. After abandoning the 'Horizon' project with France and Italy, the Royal Navy pressed ahead with the Type 45 destroyer. The first of class is now not expected to enter service before 2008. By that time the hulls they were planned to replace (in the 1990s) will be 30 years old with a growing obsolescent missile air defence system. The Type 23 frigate is now approaching the end of its construction phase and decisions on the successor Future Surface Combatant are not too far away. Contenders for the design are likely to include a tri-maran hull, based on the small-scale test bed *Triton* now being trialled.

ABOVE; TRITON TEST BED ON TRIALS

BELOW; COMPUTER IMAGE OF TYPE 45 (BAE SYSTEMS)

FOREWORD

The keel of *Astute*, the Royal Navy's new class of SSN has been laid, with a planned in-service date of 2005. Two further boats will follow by 2008 and an order for a second batch of two or three is likely to be made in 2002.

JAPAN

Japan, increasingly concerned about the growth of Chinese naval power and North Korean ballistic missile development, continues to enhance the capabilities of the Maritime Self-Defence force. A new class of 13,500 ton destroyers will be aviation capable, and despite official denials, the 'Oosumi' class amphibious warfare ships already have some aircraft carrier characteristics. Some observers have pointed to the "unfinished" look of the forward end of these ships' flight decks, as though a ski-jump ramp for aircraft operations may be planned in due course.

The new 30 kt. destroyers, authorised in the Fiscal Year 2001-2005 programme, may fulfil a shallow-water ASW role, together with ballistic missile detection, when they enter service in 2009 and 2010. They will be able to carry SH-60J and MH-53 helicopters with minesweeping equipment and may also be capable of operating a V-22 Osprey tilt-rotor aircraft.

New diesel-electric submarines are also entering service. The 'Oyashio' class, which first commissioned in 1998, will eventually total eight strong. The increase in displacement over the earlier 'Harushio' class is due to the fitting of large flank array sonar arrays.

FRANCE

Power projection capabilities continue to be developed. The 'Horizon' class destroyers, due to enter service in 2006, will boost area air defence. Two new classes of destroyer, with a common hull and machinery, will replace the 'Tourville' and 'Georges Leygues' classes, as well as augmenting the 'La Fayette' hulls. First of the 17-strong class is likely to begin sea trials in 2008. A new SSN, displacing about 4,000 tons, and armed with vertical launch tubes for surface-to-surface missiles, will be ordered in 2003 to eventually replace the 'Rubis' class, hull for hull. Two 'Mistral' class assault ships will replace the two 'Ouragan' class from 2004.

GERMANY

The German Navy plans to commission the first of its Type 212A submarines with air-independent propulsion in May 2004 after tests of the system in a Type 205 boat in 1988/89. These four boats, displacing 1,830 tons dived, will have greater diving depth and improved living conditions than their predecessors. (Italy plans two identical boats).

In surface combatants, *Sachsen* first-of-class of three new air defence frigates, will enter service at the end of 2002 and the 'K130' corvette, although mainly designed for coastal duties, are large enough to operate further away, emphasising a trend towards blue water operations. The introduction of the first two 'Berlin' class oilers in 2001, confirm this trend

GERMANY'S CLASS OF AIR DEFENCE FRIGATES, SASCHSEN

KILO CLASS

ITALY

Italy has begin construction of a new carrier, the *Andrea Doria* class, combining the ability to mount fixed wing operations off a 12° ski-jump with the support of amphibious landings and a Ro-Ro capability. Laid down in 2001, she will enter service in 2007.

INDIA

The Indian Navy, for so long starved of funds, has at last received substantial increases in its budget to support its mission to extend New Delhi's aspirations of power projection throughout the region. The elderly Russian carrier *Admiral Gorshkov* looks like being finally procured after a substantial refit, equipped with 20 MiG 29 aircraft, for service around 2004. An "air defence ship," of 32,000 tons, probably based on Russian design expertise, will replace the recently refitted *Vikrant* in 2007.

In submarines, the long saga of an indigenous SSN, the Advanced Technology Vessel or ATV continues, with construction planned to begin in 2002. The 6,000 ton boat is based on a development of a Russian design with an Indo/Russian reactor, and is due to enter service after 2007. Leasing two Akula class Russian SSNs to gain operational experience in the meantime has been agreed. The Indian Navy has placed a high priority on a sea-launched nuclear deterrent and in late 2001, a large submersible barge was commissioned with a vertical missile launcher, designed to develop expertise in cruise and ballistic missile operations. (India has already tested an anti-ship cruise missile, the PJ-10, based on the Russian SS-N-26 Oniks). The Indian 'Kilo' class are being upgraded with the installation of the SS-N-27 Klub cruise missile system. Elsewhere, earlier plans to build more Type 1500 submarines seem to have been abandoned, and India is now pursuing the possibility of building up to six new boats with French assistance, based on the 'Scorpene' design as Project 75.

Robert Hutchinson

ABOUT THIS BOOK

Jane's Warship Recognition Guide has been published to help readers identify any one of more than 2,200 ships featured; to provide information on the physical characteristics of the ships and the main weapons and to indicate which helicopters and fixed wing aircraft are embarked.

The most important feature of recognition is the visual impact of hulls, masts, radar aerials, funnels and major weapons systems. To help the reader to identify a particular ship, two different types of visual aid have been included:-

- Each entry has a photograph that has been chosen, where possible, for its clarity and the detail it shows.
- At the top of every page is a silhouette which can be used in the traditional way to help with horizon or sun-backed views.

Composite diagrams of a theoretical warship and submarine are printed in the front of the book to help the less experienced reader identify parts of a ship's structure and to become familiar with the terminology used in the text.

Despite the sophistication of modern electronic sensors, visual ship recognition remains as important as ever and is still taught to armed forces in most countries.

This book is intended to be a lead-in to the subject of recognition for the student and is not a comprehensive volume of ship types with full data on equipment and systems.

Jane's Information Group publishes a series of authoritative titles in electronic or book formats covering ships and associated equipment in great detail. Examples are *Jane's Fighting Ships, Jane's Naval Weapons Systems, Jane's Underwater Warfare Systems,* and *Jane's Radar and Electronic Warfare Systems* . The journal, *Jane's Navy International* covers maritime developments with news and articles on designs, ships, weapons systems, and tactical and strategic issues.

Ship classes for *Jane's Warship Recognition Guide* have been selected for reasons ranging from those ships which may be the most numerous, the most heavily armed, the most tactically important, to those which are most likely to be seen away from their home country's territorial waters.

Navies' orders of battle constantly change with deletions from the strength of the fleet, sales to other countries, refits, and the arrival of new designs and constructions. This edition of *Jane's Warship Recognition Guide* includes details of 58 classes new to the book. A few classes have been deleted, because they are about to disappear; others remain, as whilst the country of origin may be paying them off, they stay in the service of other navies.

The book has been structured to make its use as easy as possible. There are nine sections which cover the major types of warships, namely:-

- Aircraft carriers
- Cruisers
- Destroyers
- Frigates
- Corvettes
- Patrol forces
- Mine warfare forces
- Amphibious warfare
- Submarines

There is no significance to a ship's strategic or tactical importance indicated by its position in the book.

Each section is now presented in alphabetical order; firstly, by those navies including specific ships in their orders of battle - and then by the country where the design originated (and often where the hull was constructed as well). In this way, many more classes of warships and hulls are covered and the reader is able, for the first time, to compare the differences within classes and different navies.

GENERAL NOTES

In the **Name (Pennant Number)** section of each entry, the names and pennant numbers of relevant ships will only be included where applicable. Some countries do not use pennant numbers, or change them so frequently that the information would soon be of little value. In the case of submarines, pennant numbers are included where often they are not displayed on the boat's hull.

There are some cases where the ships fall into the **Patrol Forces** category with one country and are designated as **Corvettes** by another, and *vice versa*. This also can apply in some cases to **Frigates** and **Corvettes** and **Mine Warfare** vessels. To avoid confusion, this has been pointed out in the text.

There are a few instances where a silhouette may not display exactly the same weapons fit as the photograph. This occurs when there are different versions of that class within a navy or a group of navies operating that class of ship.

COMPOSITE WARSHIP

STARBOARD SIDE

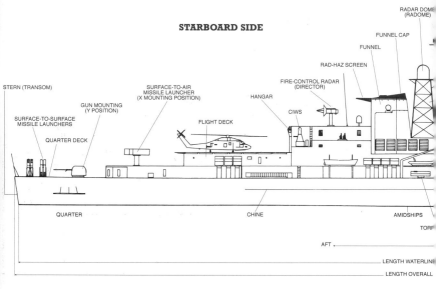

STERN (TRANSOM)

SURFACE-TO-SURFACE MISSILE LAUNCHERS

QUARTER DECK

GUN MOUNTING (Y POSITION)

SURFACE-TO-AIR MISSILE LAUNCHER (X MOUNTING POSITION)

FLIGHT DECK

HANGAR

CIWS

FIRE-CONTROL RADAR (DIRECTOR)

RAD-HAZ SCREEN

FUNNEL

FUNNEL CAP

RADAR DOME (RADOME)

QUARTER

CHINE

AMIDSHIPS

TORP

AFT

LENGTH WATERLINE

LENGTH OVERALL

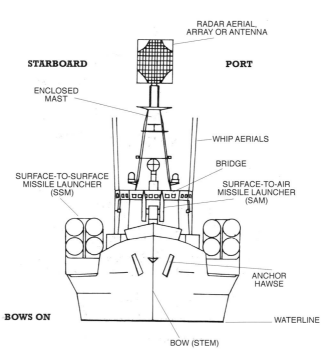

RADAR AERIAL, ARRAY OR ANTENNA

STARBOARD

PORT

ENCLOSED MAST

WHIP AERIALS

BRIDGE

SURFACE-TO-SURFACE MISSILE LAUNCHER (SSM)

SURFACE-TO-AIR MISSILE LAUNCHER (SAM)

ANCHOR HAWSE

BOWS ON

WATERLINE

BOW (STEM)

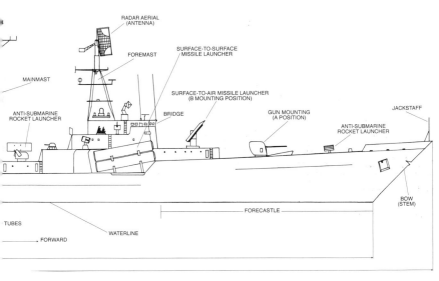

RADAR AERIAL (ANTENNA)

FOREMAST

SURFACE-TO-SURFACE MISSILE LAUNCHER

SURFACE-TO-AIR MISSILE LAUNCHER (B MOUNTING POSITION)

MAINMAST

GUN MOUNTING (A POSITION)

JACKSTAFF

ANTI-SUBMARINE ROCKET LAUNCHER

BRIDGE

ANTI-SUBMARINE ROCKET LAUNCHER

BOW (STEM)

FORECASTLE

TUBES

WATERLINE

FORWARD

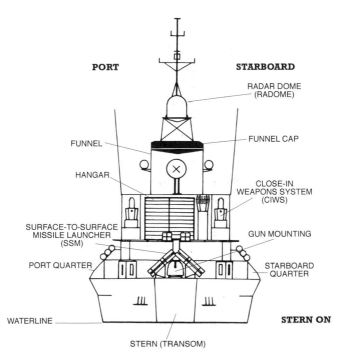

PORT

STARBOARD

RADAR DOME (RADOME)

FUNNEL

FUNNEL CAP

HANGAR

CLOSE-IN WEAPONS SYSTEM (CIWS)

SURFACE-TO-SURFACE MISSILE LAUNCHER (SSM)

GUN MOUNTING

PORT QUARTER

STARBOARD QUARTER

WATERLINE

STERN ON

STERN (TRANSOM)

TYPES OF WARSHIP MASTS

AFT ⟶ FWD

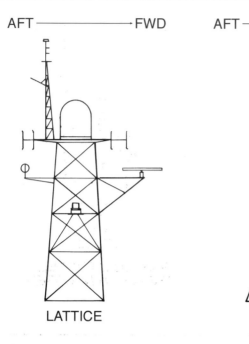

LATTICE

AFT ⟶ FWD

TRIPOD

AFT ⟶ FWD

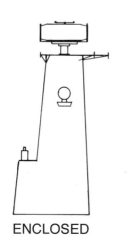

ENCLOSED

AFT ⟶ FWD

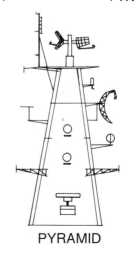

PYRAMID

TYPES OF WARSHIP MASTS

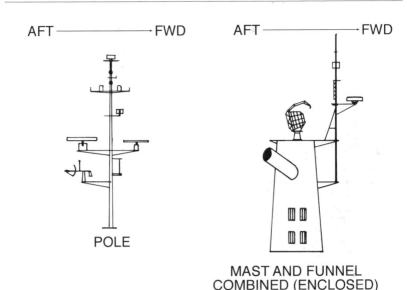

AFT ⟶ FWD

AFT ⟶ FWD

POLE

MAST AND FUNNEL
COMBINED (ENCLOSED)

COMPOSITE SUBMARINE

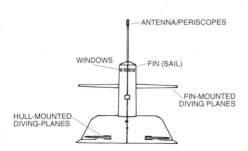

ANTENNA/PERISCOPES

WINDOWS — FIN (SAIL)

FIN-MOUNTED
DIVING PLANES

HULL-MOUNTED
DIVING-PLANES

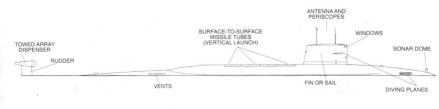

TOWED ARRAY
DISPENSER

RUDDER

VENTS

SURFACE-TO-SURFACE
MISSILE TUBES
(VERTICAL LAUNCH)

ANTENNA AND
PERISCOPES

WINDOWS

SONAR DOME

FIN OR SAIL

DIVING PLANES

AIRCRAFT CARRIERS

Säo Paolo (Clemenceau)

SÄO PAOLO

H. M. Steele

Country:	BRAZIL
Country of origin:	FRANCE
Ship type:	AIRCRAFT CARRIERS
Class:	CLEMENCEAU (CV)
Active:	1

Name (Pennant Number): SÄO PAULO (ex-*Foch*) (A-12, ex-R 99)

SPECIFICATION

Displacement, tons: 27,307 standard; 32,780, full load.
Length, feet (metres): 869.4 oa (265).
Beam, feet (metres): 104.1 (31.7) hull, 168 (51.2) oa.
Draught, feet (metres): 28.2 (8.6).
Flight deck length, feet (metres): 543 (165.5).
Flight deck width, feet (metres): 96.8 (29.5).
Speed, knots: 32.
Range, miles: 7,500 at 18 kts., 4,800 at 24 kts.

ARMAMENT

Guns: 12.7 mm M2 machine-guns

RADARS

Air search – Thomson-CSF DRBV 23B.
Air/surface search - 2 DRBI 10; Thomson-CSF DRBV 15.

Navigation - Racal Decca 1226.
Landing approach control - NRBA 51.

AIR SUPPORT

Fixed wing aircraft: 15 A-4 Skyhawk strike fighters (of 23 acquired from Kuwaiti Air Force in 1998).
Helicopters: 4-6 Agusta-Sikorsky SH-3A/D Sea Kings; 3 Eurocopter UH-12 Esquilo (liaison/ patrol), 2 Eurocopter UH-14 Cougar (SAR).

KEY RECOGNITION FEATURES

- Large thin island just forward of midships, starboard side (three bridges, flag, command and aviation).
- Black-capped, raked funnel atop centre of island.
- Spherical landing approach control (NRBA 51) dome at after end of island.
- Crane aft of island.
- Single pole mainmast supporting air/surface search radar aerial forward and air search radar aerial aft.
- Foldable mini ski-jump fitted to both deck catapults.

MINAS GERAIS

Country:	BRAZIL
Country of Origin:	UK
Ship type:	AIRCRAFT CARRIERS
Class:	COLOSSUS
Active:	1

Name (Pennant Number): MINAS GERAIS
(ex-HMS *Vengeance*) (A 11)

SPECIFICATION

Displacement, tons: 15,890 standard,
    19,890 full load.
Length, feet (metres): 695 (211.8).
Beam, feet (metres): 80 (24.4).
Draught, feet (metres): 24.5 (7.5).
Flight deck length, feet (metres): 690 (210.3).
Flight deck width, feet (metres): 119.6 (36.4).
Speed, knots: 24.
Range, miles: 12,000 at 14 kts; 6,200 at 23 kts.

ARMAMENT

Missiles: SAM – 2 Matra Sadral twin launchers;
    Mistral.
Guns: 2 - 47 mm saluting guns.
Decoys: Plessey Shield chaff launcher.

RADARS

Air search - Lockheed SPS-40E.
Air/surface search - Plessey AWS 4.
Navigation - Scanter Mil and Furuno

AIR SUPPORT

Helicopters: 4-6 Agusta SH-3A/D Sea Kings; 2
    Europcopter UH-12 Esquilo (liaison/patrol), 2
    Eurocopter UH-14 Cougar (SAR).

Note: Expected to be paid off in 2002.

KEY RECOGNITION FEATURES:

- Lattice catapult spur at bows.
- Island forward of midships, starboard side.
- Lattice mainmast immediately forward of
  funnel supporting large air search radar
  aerial on platform at half mast.
- Short tapered funnel atop island, sloping
  aft.
- Angled flight deck.

Charles de Gaulle

CHARLES DE GAULLE

Country: FRANCE
Country of origin: FRANCE
Ship type: AIRCRAFT CARRIERS
Class: CHARLES DE GAULLE (CVN)
Active: 1
Name (Pennant Number): CHARLES DE GAULLE
(R 91)

SPECIFICATION

Displacement, tons: 36,600 standard,
    40,600 full load.
Length, feet (metres): 857.7 (261.5).
Beam, feet (metres): 211.3 (64.4).
Draught, (metres): 27.8 (8.5).
Flight deck length (metres): 857.7 (261.5).
Flight deck width (metres): 211.3 (64.4).
Speed, knots: 28.

ARMAMENT

Missiles: SAM - 4 EUROSAM VLS octuple
    launchers; Aerospatiale Aster 15 anti-missile
    system; 2 - Matra Sadral PDMS sextuple
    launchers: Mistral.
Guns: 8 - Giat 20F2 20 mm.
Decoys: 4 - CSEE Sagaie 10-barrel launchers.
    Dassault LAD offboard decoys. SLAT torpedo
    decoys from 2002.

RADARS:

Air search - Thomson-CSF DRBJ 11B; Thomson
    DRBV 26D Jupiter
Air/Surface search - Thomson-CSF DRBV 15D Sea
    Tiger Mk 2.
Navigation - 2 Racal 1229 (DRBN 34A)

Fire control - Thomson-CSF Arabel 3D (SAM).
Sonars: To include SLAT torpedo attack warning.

AIR SUPPORT

Fixed wing aircraft: 24 Super Étendard strike
    fighters; 2 E-2C Hawkeye Group 2, (AEW), 10
    Rafale F1 air defence/strike fighters from 2002.
Helicopters: 2 Eurocopter AS 565MB Panther, or
    2 Eurocopter AS 532A2 Cougar Mk II (SAR).

KEY RECOGNITION FEATURES

- Sweeping bow with near vertical stern.
- Very distinctive, clean superstructure,
  angled surfaces for reduced radar
  signature.
- Large angular island starboard side, well
  forward of midships.
- Sturdy enclosed mainmast atop island,
  supporting tall pole mast and prominent
  fire control radar dome forward
- Large spherical air-search radar dome atop
  after end of bridge roof.
- Angled flight deck terminating port side
  just forward of island.
- Two VLS EUROSAM SAM launchers
  outboard of flight deck sited amidships,
  just forward of island, starboard side.

Jeanne d'Arc

JEANNE D'ARC

Country: FRANCE
Country of origin: FRANCE
Ship type: AIRCRAFT CARRIERS (HELICOPTERS)
Class: JEANNE D'ARC (CVH)
Active: 1
Name (Pennant Number): JEANNE D'ARC (ex-*La Résolue*) (R 97)

SPECIFICATION

Displacement, tons: 10,000, standard,
     13,270, full load.
Length, feet (metres): 597.1 (182).
Beam, feet (metres): 78.7 (24) (hull).
Draught, feet (metres): 24. (7.3).
Flight deck length, feet (metres): 203.4 (62).
Flight deck width, feet (metres): 68.9 (21).
Speed, knots: 26.5.
Range, miles: 6,000 at 15 kts.

ARMAMENT

Missiles: SSM – 6 - Aerospatiale MM 38 Exocet,
     (2 triple launchers.)
Guns: 2 - DCN 3.9 in (100 mm)/55 Mod 1964
     CADAM automatic. 4 - 12.7 mm machine-guns.
Decoys: 2 - CSEE/VSEL Syllex 8-barrel trainable
     chaff launchers. (May not be fitted.)

RADARS

Air search – Thomson-CSF DRBV 22D.
Air/surface search - DRBV 51
Navigation – 2 DRBN 34A (Racal-Decca)
Fire control - 3 Thomson-CSF DRBC 32A.

Sonars: Thomson Sintra DUBV 24C, hull-mounted,
     active search.

AIR SUPPORT

Helicopters: 4 SA 365F Dauphin (SAR); war
     inventory includes 8 Super Frelon and Mk 4
     Lynx (ASW).
Note: Used for training officer cadets. After rapid
     modification, could be used as a commando
     ship, helicopter carrier or troop transport with
     a 700-strong battalion. In service until possibly
     2010.

KEY RECOGNITION FEATURES

- Long forecastle.
- SSM launcher immediately forward of
  bridge.
- Main superstructure one third of ship's
  length from bow.
- Pole mainmast forward of funnel
  supporting air/surface search and air
  search radar aerials.
- Very tall black-capped funnel at after end
  of bridge structure.
- Flight deck extending from bridge aft to
  break at short quarterdeck.
- Four 3.9 in mountings, two on flight deck
  level in line with forward edge of bridge,
  port and starboard, two on quarterdeck,
  port and starboard.

Modified Kiev

ADMIRAL GORSHKOV

Country: INDIA
Country of origin: RUSSIA
Ship type: AIRCRAFT CARRIERS
Class: MODIFIED KIEV (KRECHYET) (TYPE 1143.4) (CVG)
Active: 0 (In refit.)
Name (Pennant Number): ———, (ex-*Admiral Gorshkov*, ex-*Baku*)

SPECIFICATION

Displacement, tons: 45,400, full load.
Length, feet (metres): 928.5 (283) oa.
Beam, feet (metres): 167.3 (51) oa.
Draught, feet (metres): 32.8 (10) (screws).
Flight deck length, feet (metres): 640 (195).
Flight deck width, feet (metres): 68 (20.7).
Speed, knots: 28.
Range, miles: 13,800 at 18 kts.

ARMAMENT

Missiles: SAM – 6 - Altair CADS-N-1 (Kortik/Kashtan) each with twin 30 mm Gatling combined with 8 - SA-N-11 Grisson and Hot Flash/Hot Spot fire control radar/optronic director.
Decoys: 2 - PK 2 twin chaff launchers. 2 towed torpedo decoys.

RADARS

Air search –Plate Steer.
Surface search - 2 Strut Pair.
Aircraft control - Cake Stand.
Sonars: Horse Jaw MG 355; hull-mounted, active search and attack;

AIR SUPPORT

Fixed wing aircraft: Up to 24 MiG-29MTK 2002 Fulcrum air defence/strike fighters or Sea Harrier FRS Mk 51.
Helicopters: 6 Kamov Ka-27/28/31 Helix (ASW); or Westland Sea King 42A/42B.

KEY RECOGNITION FEATURES

- Raked bow, square stem.
- Angled flight deck only.
- 14° ski jump
- Massive, tall island just forward of midships, starboard side.
- Distinctive cylindrical Tacan Cake Stand radar aerial housing centrally sited atop island.
- Squat, low funnel.

Viraat (Hermes)

VIRAAT

Country: INDIA
Country of Origin: UK
Ship type: AIRCRAFT CARRIERS
Class: HERMES
Active: 1
Name (Pennant Number): VIRAAT (Ex-HMS *Hermes*) (R 22)

SPECIFICATION

Displacement, tons: 23,900, standard; 28,700 full load.
Length, feet (metres): 685 (208.8) wl.
Beam, feet (metres): 90 (27.4).
Draught, feet (metres): 28.5 (8.7).
Speed, knots: 28.

ARMAMENT

Missiles/Guns: 2- Raphael Barak VLS/CIWS.
Guns: 4 - Oerlikon 20 mm; 4 30 mm; 2 - USSR 30 mm AK 230 Gatlings on aft sponsons.
Decoys: 2 - Knebworth Corvus chaff launchers.

RADARS:

Air search – Bharat RAWL-02 Mk II (PLN 517)
Air/surface search – Bharat RAWS (PFN 513)
Navigation – Bharat Rashmi.
Sonars: Graseby Type 184M; hull-mounted, active search and attack.

AIR SUPPORT

Fixed wing aircraft: 12 Sea Harriers FRS Mk 51/60 air defence/strike fighters (capacity for 30).
Helicopters: 7 Sea King Mk 42B/C (ASW/ASV) and Ka-28/31 Helix. (ASW/AEW).

Note: Completed refit at Mazagon Dock 2001. Ship planned in service until ?2010.

KEY RECOGNITION FEATURES

- Fitted with 12° ski jump ramp over bulbous bows.
- Large midships island, starboard side.
- Medium height, enclosed mast at forward end of island with air search radar aerial atop.
- Squat square profile funnel, mid-island.
- Tall lattice mainmast at after end of island supporting air/surface search radar and communications aerials.
- Crane derrick immediately aft of island, starboard side.

Garibaldi

GARIBALDI

Country:	ITALY
Country of origin:	ITALY
Ship type:	AIRCRAFT CARRIERS
Class:	GARIBALDI (CVS)
Active:	1

Name (Pennant Number): GIUSEPPE GARIBALDI (C 551)

SPECIFICATION

Displacement, tons: 10,100 standard, 13,850 full load.
Length, feet (metres): 591 (180).
Beam, feet (metres): 110.2 (33.4).
Draught, feet (metres): 22 (6.7).
Flight deck length, feet (metres): 570.2 (173.8).
Flight deck width, feet (metres): 99.7 (30.4).
Speed, knots: 30.
Range, miles: 7,000 at 20 kts.

ARMAMENT

Missiles: SSM - 8 - OTO MELARA Teseo Mk 2 (TG 2). SAM - 2 Selenia Elsag Albatros octuple launchers: Aspide. Upgrade to Aster 15 missiles planned.
Guns: 6 - Breda 40 mm/70 (3 twin) MB.
Torpedoes: 6 - 324 mm B-515 (2 triple) tubes. Honeywell Mk 46 anti-submarine. (Being replaced by A 290.)
Decoys: AN/SLQ-25 Nixie noisemaker torpedo decoy. 2 - Breda SCLAR 105 mm 20-barrel trainable chaff launchers. SLAT torpedo defence system planned.

RADARS

Long range air search - Hughes SPS-52C, 3D.
Air search - Selenia SPS-768 (RAN 3L). SMA SPN-728. (RAN-40S planned).
Air/surface search - Selenia SPS-774 (RAN 10S).
Surface search/target indication - SMA SPS-702

UPX; 718 beacon.
Navigation - SMA SPN-749(V)2.
Fire control - 3 Selenia SPG-75 (RTN 30X). 3 Selenia SPG-74 (RTN 20X).
Sonars: Raytheon DE 1160 LF; bow-mounted, active search.

AIR SUPPORT

Fixed wing aircraft: 16 AV-8B Harrier II Plus.
Helicopters: 18 Agusta-Sikorsky SH-3D Sea King helicopters or EH Industries' EH 101 Merlin Mk 110 (ASW/anti-surface vessel). (12 in hangar, 6 on deck). Capacity is either 16 Harriers or 18 Sea Kings, but this leaves no space for movement.

Note: Fleet flagship, equipped for joint task force command and control.

KEY RECOGNITION FEATURES

- 6.5° ski jump ramp.
- Large, long midships island.
- Short mast forward of funnel supporting square profile, long-range air search radar aerial.
- Air search radar aerial atop forward end of bridge with 2 low fire control radar domes immediately forward.
- Integral, short, black-capped funnel after end of island with four aerials.
- Two tall pole masts, after one supporting air/surface search radar aerial.
- Angled SSM launchers, two port, two starboard, below after end of flight deck.
- Three 40 mm/70 mountings, one port, one starboard below flight deck just aft of ski jump ramp, one centre-line aft quarterdeck.

Andrea Doria

ANDREA DORIA

Country: ITALY	
Country of origin: ITALY	
Ship type: AIRCRAFT CARRIERS	
Class: ANDREA DORIA (CV)	
Building: 1*	
*Expected to be commissioned – 2007.	
Name (Pennant Number): ANDREA DORIA (C 552)	

SPECIFICATION

Displacement, full load, tons: 26,500
Length, feet, (metres): 769 (234.4) oa.
Beam, feet (metres): 120 (39).
Draught, feet, (metres): 24.6 (7.5).
Flight deck length, feet (metres): 603.7 (184).
Flight deck width, feet (metres): 111.5 (34).
Speed, knots: 30
Range, miles: 7,000 at 16 kts.

ARMAMENT

Missiles: SAM - 4 - Sylver VLS, Aster 15.
Guns: 2 - CIWS and 3 small calibre.
Decoys: 2 - Breda SCLAR-H 20-barrel trainable chaff.

RADARS

Long range air search – RAN-40S or S-1850M
Air search and missile guidance – EMPAR
Surface search – SPS-791
Navigation – SPN-753G(V)
Sonars: SNA-2000 mine avoidance.

AIR SUPPORT

Fixed wing aircraft: 8 AV-8B Harrier II or Joint Strike Fighter.
Helicopters: 12 EH Industries EH 101 Merlin.

KEY RECOGNITION FEATURES

- Main deck continuous from stem to stern, with 12° ski jump.
- Low island superstructure with funnels with twin exhausts at forward and aft ends.
- Large deck-crane forward of superstructure; smaller one aft.
- Large enclosed mast above bridge, topped by bulbous EMPAR air search and missile guidance radome.
- Slim enclosed mast at forward edge of aft funnel, topped by short pole mast.

Admiral Kuznetsov

ADMIRAL KUZNETSOV

Country: RUSSIA
Country of origin: RUSSIA
Ship type: AIRCRAFT CARRIERS
Class: ADMIRAL KUZNETSOV (OREL)
(TYPE 1143.5/6) (CV)
Active: 1
Name (Pennant Numbers): ADMIRAL KUZNETSOV
(ex-*Tbilisi*, ex-*Leonid Brezhnev*. (063)

SPECIFICATION

Displacement, tons: 45,900 standard,
58,500 full load.
Length, feet (metres): 918.6 (280) wl., 999
(304.5) oa.
Beam, feet (metres): 121.4 (37) wl., 229.7 (70) oa.
Draught, feet (metres): 34.4 (10.5).
Flight deck length, feet (metres): 999 (304.5).
Flight deck width, feet (metres): 229.7 (70).
Speed, knots: 30.
Range, miles: 3,850 at 29 kts., 8,500 at 18 kts.

ARMAMENT

Missiles: SSM – 12 - Chelomey SS-N-19
Shipwreck (Granit 4K-8) launchers (flush
mounted).
SAM - 4 - Altair SA-N-9 Gauntlet (Klinok)
sextuple vertical launchers.
SAM/Guns - 8 - Altair CADS-N-1
(Kortik/Kashtan); each with twin 30 mm
Gatling combined with 8 SA-N-11 Grisson and
Hot Flash/Hot Spot fire control radar/optronic
director.
Guns: - 6 - 30 mm/65 AK 630; 6 barrels per
mounting.
A/S mortars: 2 - RBU 12000.
Decoys: 19 - PK 10 and 4 - PK 2 chaff launchers.

RADARS

Air search - Sky Watch, 4 planar phased arrays,
3D.
Air/surface search - Top Plate B
Surface search - 2 Strut Pair.
Navigation - 3 Palm Frond.
Fire control - 4 Cross Sword (SAM); 8 Hot Flash.
Aircraft control - Fly Trap B.
Sonars: Bull Horn and Horse Jaw; hull-mounted,
active search and attack.

AIR SUPPORT

Fixed wing aircraft: 18 Sukhoi Su-27K/Su-33
Flanker D air defence fighters; 4 Sukhoi Su-
25UTG Frogfoot ground attack fighters.
Helicopters: 15 Kamov Ka-27PL Helix, (ASW); 2
Kamov Ka-31 RLD Helix (AEW.)

KEY RECOGNITION FEATURES

- Typical high, sweeping bow profile.
- 14° ski jump ramp.
- 7° angled flight deck.
- SSM launchers forward end of flight deck
  in centre, with flush deck covers.
- SAM VLS port and starboard, forward of
  angled deck.
- High freeboard of 16.5 m.
- Large island aft of midships, starboard side.
- Distinctive cylindrical Tacan 'Cake Stand'
  radar aerial housing forward of funnel atop
  island/bridge.
- Short, slightly raked funnel at after end of
  island structure.
- Square stem with clear flight deck
  overhang.

Príncipe de Asturias

PRÍNCIPE DE ASTURIAS

Country: SPAIN

Country of origin: SPAIN

Ship Type: AIRCRAFT CARRIERS

Class: PRINCIPE DE ASTURIAS (CVS)

Active: 1

Name (Pennant Number): PRÍNCIPE DE ASTURIAS
(ex-*Almirante Carrero Blanco*, (R 11).

SPECIFICATION

Displacement, tons: 17,188, full load.
Length, feet (metres): 642.7 (195.9) oa.
Beam, feet (metres): 79.7 (24.3).
Draught, feet (metres): 30.8 (9.4).
Flight deck length, feet (metres): 575.1 (175.3).
Flight deck width, feet (metres): 95.1 (29).
Speed, knots: 25.
Range, miles: 6,500 at 20 kts.

ARMAMENT

Guns: 4 - Bazán Mod 2A/2B Meroka 12-barrel 20
mm/120; 2 - Rheinmetall 37 saluting guns on
port quarter.
Decoys: Loral Hycor SRBOC 6-barrel fixed
Mk 36; SLQ-25 Nixie noisemaker towed
torpedo decoy; US Prairie/Masker; hull
noise/blade rate suppression.

RADARS

Air search - Hughes SPS-52 C/D, 3D.
Surface search - ISC Cardion SPS-55.
Aircraft control – ITT SPN-35A
Fire control - 1 Selenia RAN 12L (target
designation); 4 Sperry/Lockheed VPS 2,
(Meroka); 1 RTN 11L/X, (missile warning.)

AIR SUPPORT

Fixed wing aircraft: 6-12 BAe/McDonnell Douglas
EAV-8B Harrier II/Harrier Plus.
Helicopters: 6-10 Sikorsky SH-3D/G Sea Kings,
(ASW/AEW); 2-4 Agusta AB 212EW; 2 Sikorsky
SH-60B Seahawks.

CHAKRI NARUEBET

Country: THAILAND	
Country of origin: SPAIN	
Ship type: AIRCRAFT CARRIER	
Class: CHAKRI NARUEBET (CVS)	
Active: 1	
Name (Pennant Number): CHAKRI NARUEBET (911)	

SPECIFICATION

Displacement, full load, tons: 11,485.
Length, feet (metres): 599.1 (182.6) oa.
Beam, feet (metres): 73.8 (22.5) wl., 100.1 (30.5) oa.
Draught, (metres): 20.3 (6.2).
Flight deck length (metres): 572.8 (174.6).
Flight deck width (metres): 90.2 (27.5).
Speed, knots: 26; 16 (diesels).
Range, miles: 10,000 at 12 kts.

ARMAMENT

Missiles: SAM - 1 Mk 41 LCHR 8 cell VLS launcher, Sea Sparrow, (to be fitted.) 3 - Matra Sadral sextuple launchers, Mistral.
Guns: 4 - Vulcan Phalanx CIWS; 2 30 mm (to be fitted.)
Decoys: 4 - Tracor Mk 137 chaff launchers.

RADARS

Air search – Hughes SPS-52C.
Surface search – SPS-64.

Fire control - Signaal STIR.
Navigation - Kelvin Hughes.
Aircraft control – Kelvin Hughes.
Sonars: Type not known; hull-mounted, active search.

AIR SUPPORT

Fixed wing aircraft: 6 BAe/McDonnell Douglas AV-8S Matador, (supplied to Spain and transferred in 1996.)
Helicopters: 6 Sikorsky S-70B7 Seahawk, (multi-mission.) Chinook capable.

KEY RECOGNITION FEATURES

- 12° ski jump ramp.
- Squared, 'chunky' island aft of midships, starboard side.
- Crane gantry forward end of island, starboard side.
- One of two aircraft lifts at after end of flight deck.
- Enclosed mainmast part of funnel structure
- Air search radar, Hughes SPS-52C, atop bridge.

Note: Similarities with Spanish carrier, *Principe de Asturias.*

Invincible

INVINCIBLE

Country: UNITED KINGDOM
Country of origin: UK
Ship type: AIRCRAFT CARRIERS
Class: INVINCIBLE (CVG)
Active: 3
Name (Pennant Number): INVINCIBLE (R 05),
ILLUSTRIOUS (R 06), ARK ROYAL (R 07)

SPECIFICATION

Displacement, full load, tons: 20,600.
Length, feet (metres): 685.8 (209.1) oa.
Beam, feet (metres): 118 (36) oa.
Draught, feet (metres): 26 (8).
Flight deck length, feet (metres): 550 (167.8).
Flight deck width, feet (metres): 44.3 (13.5).
Speed, knots: 28.
Range, miles: 7,000 at 19 kts.

ARMAMENT

Guns: 3 - 30 mm 7-barrel Gatling Goalkeeper
(R 05/R 06) ; 3 Vulcan Phalanx Mk.15 (R 07);
2 - Oerlikon/BMARC 20 mm GAM-B01.
Decoys: Outfit DLJ - 8 - Sea Gnat 6-barrel 130/102
mm dispensers; Prairie/Masker noise suppression.

RADARS

Air search - Marconi/Signaal Type 1022.
Surface search - Plessey Type 996(2) (R 05 and
06); Marconi Type 996.
Navigation - 2 Kelvin Hughes Type 1007
Sonars: Plessey Type 2016; hull-mounted, active
search and attack.

AIR SUPPORT

Fixed wing aircraft: 8 British Aerospace Sea
Harrier FA 2 air defence/strike fighters and 8
Harrier GR 7 ground attack fighters.
Helicopters: 2 Westland Sea King HAS 6 or EH
101 Merlin HM Mk 1 (ASW); 4 Westland Sea
King AEW 2. Chinook capable.

Note: *Illustrious* to begin two-year refit in
autumn 2002.
LPH *Ocean* based on 'Invincible' design but with
modified superstructure with prominent angled
bridge for flight operations.

KEY RECOGNITION FEATURES

- 12° ski jump ramp fitted on offset, port
  side deck, (*Invincible*); 13° on *Illustrious*,
  and *Ark Royal.*
- Very long and low island situated
  amidships, starboard side.
- Twin funnels, one immediately aft of
  bridge, one aft of mainmast, forward
  funnel taller. Both funnels have twin, black
  painted exhausts atop.
- Large fire control radar dome(s) aft
  extreme of island.
- Central, enclosed mainmast supporting
  surface search radar aerial, 992R (R 07) or
  996(2) (R 05 and R 06). *Illustrious* has
  SATCOM terminals midway mast.
- Goalkeeper CIWS mountings fitted at bows,
  port side aft and immediately forward of
  after funnel.

ENTERPRISE

Country: UNITED STATES OF AMERICA
Country of origin: USA
Ship type: AIRCRAFT CARRIERS
Class: ENTERPRISE (CVN)
Active: 1
Name (Pennant Number): ENTERPRISE (CVN 65)

SPECIFICATION

Displacement, tons: 75,700 standard,
  93,970 full load.
Length, feet (metres): 1123 (342.3).
Beam, feet (metres): 133 (40.5).
Draught, feet (metres): 39 (11.9).
Flight deck length, feet (metres): 1088 (331.6).
Flight deck width, feet (metres): 252 (76.8).
Speed, knots: 33.

ARMAMENT

Missiles: SAM - 3 Raytheon GMLS Mk 29 octuple
  launchers, NATO Sea Sparrow.
Guns: 3 - GE/GD 20 mm Vulcan Phalanx 6-barrel
  Mk 15.
Decoys: 4 - Loral Hycor SRBOC 6-barrel fixed Mk
  36; SSTDS; SLQ-36 Nixie noisemaker torpedo
  decoy.

RADARS

Air search - ITT SPS-48E, 3D; Raytheon SPS-
  49(V)5; Hughes Mk 23 TAS.
Surface search - Norden SPS-67.
Navigation - Raytheon SPS 64(V)9; Furuno 900.
Fire control - 6 Mk 95, (SAM).

AIR SUPPORT

Fixed wing aircraft: 50 TACAIR wing, depending
  on mission, includes up to 20 Grumman F-
  14A/B/D Tomcat air defence fighters; 36
  McDonnell Douglas F/A-18A/B/C/D Hornet
  (strike/interdiction) ; 4 Grumman EA-6B
  Prowler (EW) ; 4 Grumman E-2C Hawkeye
  (AEW); 6 Lockheed S-3B Viking (ASW/ASV) ; 2
  Lockheed ES-3A Shadow (ELINT).
Helicopters: 4 Sikorsky SH-60F Seahawk (ASW)
  and 2 HH-60H Seahawk (strike/special warfare
  support/SAR).

KEY RECOGNITION FEATURES

- Angled flight deck.
- Island aft of midships, starboard side.
- Island comprises unusual box shaped
  bridge supported on significantly narrower
  pedestal structure.
- Square profile air search radar aerial
  mounted atop the bridge, forward.
- SAM launchers mounted port and
  starboard, at after end of flight deck. Third
  launcher situated starboard side forward,
  approximately quarter of ship's length
  from bows.
- CIWS mountings situated right aft below
  flight deck overhang and on sponson on
  port side, forward of angled deck.

CONSTELLATION

Country: UNITED STATES OF AMERICA
Country of origin: USA
Ship type: AIRCRAFT CARRIERS
Class: KITTY HAWK and JOHN F KENNEDY (CV)
Active: 3
Name (Pennant Number): KITTY HAWK (CV 63),
CONSTELLATION (CV 64), JOHN F KENNEDY (CV 67)

SPECIFICATION

Displacement, full load, tons: 83,960 full load;
(81,430, CV 67).
Length, feet (metres): 1062.5 (323.6) (CV 63),
1072.5 (326.9) (CV 64), 1052 (320.6) (CV 67).
Beam, feet (metres): 130 (39.6).
Draught, feet (metres): 37.4 (11.4).
Flight deck length, feet (metres): 1046 (318.8).
Flight deck width, feet (metres): 252 (76.8).
Speed, knots: 32.
Range, miles: 4,000 at 30 kts., 12,000 at 20 kts.

ARMAMENT

Missiles: SAM - 3 Raytheon GMLS Mk 29 octuple
launchers, NATO Sea Sparrow.
Guns: 3 or 4 - GE/GD 20 mm Vulcan Phalanx 6-
barrel Mk 15. (Two mountings to be replaced by
RAM in CV 63 and CV 67).
Decoys: 4 - Loral Hycor SRBOC 6-barrelled fixed
Mk 36. SSTDS; SLQ-36 Nixie noisemaker
torpedo decoy.

RADARS

Air search - ITT SPS-48E, 3D; Raytheon SPS-
49(V)5, Hughes Mk 23 TAS.
Surface search - Norden SPS-67.
Navigation - Raytheon SPN-64(V)9; Furuno 900.
Fire control - 6 Mk 95, (SAM).
Sonar: Fitted for SQS-23.

AIR SUPPORT

Fixed wing aircraft: 50 TACAIR air wing,
depending on mission, including up to 20
Grumman F-14A/B/D Tomcat air defence
fighters; 36 McDonnell Douglas F/A-18 Hornet
(strike/interdiction); 4 Grumman EA-6B
Prowler (EW); 4 Grumman E-2C Hawkeye; 6
Lockheed S-3B Viking (ASW/ASV);2 ES-3A
Shadow (ELINT).
Helicopters. 4 Sikorsky SH-60F (ASW), 2 HH-60H
Seahawk (strike/special forces/SAR).
Note: Constellation to pay off in 2003.

KEY RECOGNITION FEATURES

- Angled flight deck.
- Complex thin pole mast on central island,
  fitted with air search radar, WT and EW
  aerials, (topped by radome in CV67 alone)
- Funnel at rear of island structure, flush
  with top of bridge.
- Tall lattice mast immediately aft of bridge
  supporting square profile air search radar
  aerial.
- Crane derrick starboard, aft of island,
  outboard of flight deck.
- CIWS mountings, one port side aft below
  flight deck overhang, (one halfway up
  island structure starboard side,CV 64) and
  one port side forward sited on platform
  below round of angled flight deck. CV 64
  has further CIWS at stern, on starboard
  sponson below flightdeck.
- Two deck-edge lifts fitted forward of island
  superstructure, a third aft of the island,
  and a fourth port side quarter.

Nimitz

9+

Country: UNITED STATES OF AMERICA
Country of origin: USA
Ship type: AIRCRAFT CARRIERS
Class: NIMITZ (CVN)
Active: 8
Building: 2 (RONALD REAGAN CVN 76); ---- ,
(CVN 77) ---- (CVN 78)
Name (Pennant Number): NIMITZ (CVN 68),
DWIGHT D EISENHOWER (CVN 69), CARL VINSON
(CVN 70), THEODORE ROOSEVELT (CVN 71),
ABRAHAM LINCOLN (CVN 72), GEORGE
WASHINGTON (CVN 73), JOHN C STENNIS (CVN 74),
HARRY S. TRUMAN, (ex-*United States*) (CVN 75).

Ronald Reagn (CVN78) G.A.Ford 8-H.Bush

SPECIFICATION

Displacement, full load, tons:, 91,487 (CVN 68-
70), 96,386 (CVN 71), 102,000 (CVN 72-76)
Length, feet (metres): 1040 (317).
Beam, feet (metres): 134 (40.8).
Draught, feet (metres): 37 (11.3) CVN 68-70; 38.7
(11.8) CVN 71; 39 (11.9) CVN 72-76.
Flight deck length, feet (metres): 1092 (332.9).
Flight deck angled, feet (metres): 779.8 (237.7).
Flight deck width, feet (metres): 252 (76.8).
Speed, knots: 30.0+

ARMAMENT

Missiles: SAM - 2 or 3 - Raytheon GMLS Mk 29
octuple launchers, NATO Sea Sparrow.
Guns: 4 - GE/GD 20 mm Vulcan Phalanx 6-barrel
Mk 15 (3 in CVN 68 and 69). To be replaced by
RAM from 2002 onwards.
Decoys: 4 - Loral Hycor SRBOC 6-barrel fixed Mk
36. SSTDS; SLQ-36 Nixie (Phase I) noisemaker
torpedo decoy.

RADARS

Air search - ITT SPS-48E, 3D; Raytheon SPS-
49(V)5; Hughes Mk 23 TAS.
Surface search - Norden SPS- 67(V)1.
Navigation - Raytheon SPS-64(V)9; Furuno 900.
Fire control - 6 Mk 95, (SAM).

AIR SUPPORT

Fixed wing aircraft: 50 TACAIR air wing,
depending on mission, includes, up to 20
Grumman F-14D Tomcat, air defence fighter;
36 McDonnell Douglas F/A-18E Super Hornet
strike/interdiction; 4 Grumman EA-6B Prowler

NIMITZ

(EW); 4 Grumman E-2C Hawkeye; 6 Lockheed
S-3B Viking (ASW/ASV); 2 ES-3A Shadow,
(ELINT).
Helicopters: 4 Sikorsky SH-60F Seahawk (ASW)
and 2 HH-60H Seahawk (strike, special warfare
support and SAR.)

KEY RECOGNITION FEATURES

- Large island well aft of midships. (Reshaped island in CVN 69 from 2002)
- Square profile air search radar aerial mounted atop forward end of island, above bridge.
- Tall thin complex pole mainmast atop central bridge supporting array of radar, EW and WT aerials.
- Enclosed isolated mast immediately aft of island supporting curved lattice bedstead air search radar aerial.
- Two CIWS mountings fitted right aft, one port, one starboard below flight deck overhang.
- Second two CIWS mountings, port and starboard, immediately forward of where flight deck narrows.
- Octuple SAM missile launch boxes right after, port and starboard on sponsons and on port side where flight deck narrows.
- Large radome on narrow sponson, port side, forward of weapons mountings.

CRUISERS

Vittorio Veneto

VITTORIO VENETO   C D Yaylali

Country: ITALY
Country of origin: ITALY
Ship type: CRUISERS
Class: VITTORIO VENETO (CGH)
Active: 1
Name (Pennant Number): VITTORIO VENETO (C 550)

SPECIFICATION

Displacement, tons: 7,500 standard,
9,500 full load.
Length, feet (metres): 589 (179.6).
Beam, feet (metres): 63.6 (19.4).
Draught, feet (metres): 19.7 (6).
Flight deck length, feet (metres): 131 (40.6).
Flight deck width, feet (metres): 61 (18.6).
Speed, knots: 32.
Range, miles: 5,000 at 17 kts.

ARMAMENT

Missiles: SSM - 4 OTO MELARA Teseo Mk 2 (TG 2).
SAM - GDC Pomona Standard SM-1ER; Aster twin
Mk 10 Mod 9 launcher.
A/S - Honeywell ASROC launcher.
Guns: 8 - OTO MELARA 3 in (76 mm)/62 MMK.
6 - Breda 40 mm/70 (3 twin).
Torpedoes: 6 - 324 mm US Mk 32 (2 triple) tubes;
Honeywell Mk 46; anti-submarine.
Decoys: 2 - Breda SCLAR 105 mm 20-barrel
trainable chaff. SLQ-25 Nixie towed torpedo
decoy.

RADARS

Long range air search - Hughes SPS-52C, 3D.
Air search - Selenia SPS-768 (RAN 3L).

Surface search/target indication - SMA SPS-702.
Navigation - SMA SPS-748.
Fire control - 4 Selenia SPG-70 (RTN 10X).
2 Selenia SPG-74 (RTN 20X).
2 Sperry/RCA SPG-55C (Standard).
Sonars: Sangamo SQS-23G; bow-mounted, active
search and attack.

AIR SUPPORT

Helicopters: 6 Agusta-Bell AB 212 (ASW).
Note: Will be replaced by new carrier *Andrea
Doria* in 2007.

KEY RECOGNITION FEATURES

- Two large enclosed masts just forward and
aft of midships.
- Twin funnels in 'V' formation at after end
of each mast.
- Forward mast supports distinctive, square,
SPS-52C long-range air search radar aerial.
- Lattice crane derrick and ship's boat sited
between masts.
- Very unusual break in deck level, just aft of
bridge, up from main deck to flight deck.
- Breda 40 mm/70 gun mountings situated
port and starboard at forward end of long
flight deck.
- SAM launcher at after end of forecastle.
- Four SSM launchers amidships, two port
two starboard, adjacent to forward funnel.

De Ruyter

ALMIRANTE GRAU

Country: PERU
Country of origin: NETHERLANDS
Ship type: CRUISERS
Class: DE RUYTER (CG)
Active: 1
Name (Pennant Number): ALMIRANTE GRAU (ex-
De Ruyter) (CLM 81)

SPECIFICATION

Displacement, full load, tons: 12,165.
Length, feet (metres): 624.5 (190.3).
Beam, feet (metres): 56.7 (17.3).
Draught, feet (metres): 22 (6.7).
Speed, knots: 32.
Range, miles: 7,000 at 12 kts.

ARMAMENT

Missiles: SSM - 8 OTO MELARA Otomat Mk 2 (TG
1). (To be replaced by Exocets from 'Daring'
class.
Guns: 8 - Bofors 6 in (152 mm)/53 (4 twin); 4
OTO BREDA 40mm/70 (2 twin); 4 - Bofors 40
mm/70.
Decoys: 2 - Dagaie and 1 - Sagaie chaff
launchers.

RADARS

Air search - Signaal LW08.

Surface search/target indication - Signaal DA00.
Navigation - Racal Decca 1226.
Fire control - Signaal WM25 (6 in guns), Signaal
STIR.
Sonars: Removed.

Note: Sister ship Aguirre deleted in 1999.

KEY RECOGNITION FEATURES

- Two 6 in gun mountings only forward of
bridge in 'B' and 'A' mounting positions.
- Cylindrical after funnel close to midships,
sloped slightly aft with lattice mast built
around it.
- Forward funnel at after end of tall forward
superstructure with mast above.
- Dome-shaped Signaal WM25 fire control
radar on pylon immediately forward of
main mast.
- Upper deck superstructure sited astern of
after funnel with fire control director atop.
- Two 6 in gun mountings on afterdeck in 'Y'
and 'X' mounting positions
- No flight deck but long, low quarterdeck.
- Spherical SATCOM dome aft of
superstructure.

Kara

KERCH

Harmut Ehlers

Country:	RUSSIA
Country of origin:	RUSSIA
Ship type:	CRUISERS
Class:	KARA (BERKOT-B) (TYPE 1134B/BF) (CG)
Active:	1
Name (Pennant Number):	KERCH (713, ex-711).

SPECIFICATION

Displacement, tons: 7,650, standard, 9,900 full load.
Length, feet (metres): 568 (173.2).
Beam, feet (metres): 61 (18.6).
Draught, feet (metres): 22 (6.7).
Speed, knots: 32.
Range, miles: 9,000 at 15 kts, 3,000 at 32 kts.

ARMAMENT

Missiles: SAM - 2 SA-N-3 Goblet twin launchers; 2 SA-N-4 Gecko twin launchers. A/S - 2 Raduga SS-N-14 Silex (Rastrub) quad launchers.
Guns: 4 - 3 in (76 mm)/60 (2 twin). 4 - 30 mm/65; 6 barrels per mounting.
Torpedoes: 10 - 21 in (533 mm) (2 quin) tubes.
A/S mortars: 2 - RBU 6000 12-tubed, trainable. 2 - RBU 1000 6-tubed.
Decoys: 2 - PK 2 chaff launchers. 1 - BAT-1 torpedo decoy.

RADARS

Air search - Flat Screen.
Air/surface search - Head Net C, 3D.
Navigation - 2 Don Kay, Don 2 or Palm Frond

Fire control - 2 Head Light B/C (for SA-N-3 and SS-N-14); 2 Pop Group, (SA-N-4); 2 Owl Screech, (76 mm guns);   2 Bass Tilt, (30 mm guns).
Sonars: Bull Nose, (Titan 2-MG 332) hull-mounted, active search and attack; Mare Tail; VDS.

AIR SUPPORT

Helicopters: 1 Kamov Ka-27 Helix (ASW).

KEY RECOGNITION FEATURES

- SAM (twin) SA-N-3 Goblet launcher on raised forecastle structure forward of bridge.
- 'Head Light C' fire control director mounted on bridge roof.
- Forward tripod mast aft of bridge supporting air/surface search radar aerial.
- Large pyramid mainmast sited amidships supporting square profile Flat Screen air search radar.
- Two 3-in gun mountings, port and starboard, sited between forward and aftermasts.
- Large, slightly tapered, square section funnel situated immediately aft of mainmast.
- 'Head Light C' fire control director sited aft of funnel.

Kirov

PYOTR VELIKIY (old pennant number)

Country: RUSSIA

Country of origin: RUSSIA

Ship type: CRUISERS

Class: KIROV (ORLAN) (TYPE 1144.1/1144.2) (CGN)

Active: 2

Name (Pennant Number): ADMIRAL NAKHIMOV
(ex-*Kalinin*), (080) PYOTR VELIKIY (ex-*Yuri
Andropov*) (099, ex-183)

SPECIFICATION

Displacement, tons: 19,000 standard, 24,300 full
load.

Length, feet (metres): 826.8 (252).

Beam, feet (metres): 93.5 (28.5).

Draught, feet (metres): 29.5 (9.1).

Speed, knots: 30.

Range, miles: 14,000 at 30 kts.

ARMAMENT

Missiles: SSM - 20 Chelomey SS-N-19 Shipwreck
(Granit); SAM - 12 SA-N-6 Grumble (Rif)
vertical launchers; 12 SA-NX-20 VL (099 only).
2 SA-N-4 Gecko twin launchers; 2 SA-N-9
Gauntlet (Klinok) octuple vertical launchers.

SAM/Guns - 6 CADS-N-1 (Kortik/Kashtan) with
twin 30 mm Gatling, combined with 8 SA-N-11
Grisson missiles on Hot Flash/Hot Spot fire
control radar/optronic director. A/S – Novator
SS-N-15 (Starfish) fired from fixed torpedo
tubes behind shutters in superstructure.

Guns: 2 - 130 mm/70 (twin) AK 130.

Torpedoes: 10 - 21 in (533 mm) (2 quin) tubes.

A/S mortars: 1 - RBU 12000; 10 tubes per
launcher; 2 - RBU 1000 6-tubed.

Decoys: 2 - twin PK 2 150 mm chaff launchers;
towed torpedo decoy.

RADARS

Air search - Top Pair (Top Sail + Big Net) 3D.

Air/surface search - Top Plate 3D.

Navigation - 3 Palm Frond.

Fire control - Cross Sword (SA-N-9); 1 (*Velikiy*) or
2 Top Dome for SA-N-6; Tomb Stone (*Velikiy*
only) (SA-NX-20); 2 Pop Group, (SA-N-4);
Kite Screech (130 mm guns); 6 Hot Flash
(CADS-N-1)

Aircraft control - Flyscreen B.

Sonars: Horse Jaw; hull-mounted, active search
and attack; Horse Tail; VDS active search.

AIR SUPPORT

Helicopters: 3 Kamov Ka-27PL Helix (ASW).

KEY RECOGNITION FEATURES

- Very large tall mast and funnel combined
  sited amidships supporting Top Pair air
  search radar aerials.
- Raised raked bows, sloping forecastle, break
  in deck aft of superstructure.
- Secondary masts and upper deck structures
  aft of mainmast supporting (from forward
  to aft) Top Plate air/surface search and Top
  Dome fire control radar aerials.
- 130mm/70 gun mounting fitted
  immediately forward of flight deck.
- CADS-N-1 SAM/gun mounting and Hot
  Flash/Hot Spot fire control radar/optronic
  director on raised platforms each side of
  SS-N-19 launch silos; four more on after
  superstructure.

Kynda

ADMIRAL GOLOVKO

Country: RUSSIA
Country of origin: Russia
Ship Type: CRUISERS
Class: KYNDA (TYPE 58) (CG)
Active: 1
Name (Pennant Number): ADMIRAL GOLOVKO (118)

SPECIFICATION

Displacement, tons: 4,265 standard, 5,412 full load.
Length, feet (metres): 468.2 (142.7).
Beam, feet (metres): 52.5 (16).
Draught, feet (metres): 13.5 (4.1).
Speed, knots: 34.
Range, miles: 3,610 at 18 kts.

ARMAMENT

Missiles: SSM – 8 SS-N-3B Sepal (2 quad) launchers; SAM – SA-N-1 Goa twin launcher.
Guns: 4 - 3in (76mm)/60 (2 twin); 4 - 30mm/65, 6-barrels per mounting.
Torpedoes: 6 - 21 in (533mm) (2 triple) tubes.
A/S mortars: 2 - RBU 6000 12-tube trainable.

RADARS

Air search – 2 Head Net A.
Surface search and navigation – 2 Don 2.

Fire control – 2 Scoop Pair (SS-N-3B); Peel Group (SA-N-1 SAM); Owl Screech (76mm gun); Bass Tilt, (30 mm guns).
Sonars: Herkules-2N (GS 372) hull-mounted, active search and attack.

AIR SUPPORT

Helicopters: Platform only.

Note: Replaced by 'Slava' class CG Moskva as Black Sea flagship in 2001.

KEY RECOGNITION FEATURES

- Heavy tubular SS-N-39 Sepal SSM launchers fore and aft of superstructure.
- Twin 3 in mountings in 'X' and 'Y' positions.
- Twin level deckhouse alongside forward funnel - large flat rectangular area.
- Two pylon masts forward of funnels, both with 'Head Net A' air search radar aerials atop.
- Triple torpedo tubes between funnels.
- Distinctive Scoop Pair fire control radar aerials midway up both masts.

Slava

MARSHAL USTINOV

Country:	RUSSIA, UKRAINE
Country of origin:	RUSSIA
Ship type:	CRUISERS
Class:	SLAVA (ATLANT) (TYPE 1164) (CG)
Active:	3 (Russia) Building 1 Ukraine

RUSSIA – Name (Pennant Number): MOSKVA (ex-*Slava*) (121), MARSHAL USTINOV (055), VARYAG (ex-*Chervona Ukraina*,) (011).

UKRAINE – Name (Pennant Number): UKRAINA (ex-*Admiral Lobov*) (–)

SPECIFICATION

Displacement, tons: 9,380 standard, 11,490 full load.
Length, feet (metres): 611.5 (186.4).
Beam, feet (metres): 68.2 (20.8).
Draught, feet (metres): 27.6 (8.4).
Speed, knots: 32.
Range, miles: 7,500 at 15 kts., 2,200 at 30 kts.

ARMAMENT

Missiles: SSM – 16 Chelomey SS-N-12 (8 twin) Sandbox (Bazalt) launchers.   SAM - 8 SA-N-6 Grumble (Rif) vertical launchers;   2 SA-N-4 Gecko twin launchers.
Guns: 2 - 130 mm/70 (twin) AK 130; 6 - 30 mm/65 AK 650; 6-barrels per mounting.
Torpedoes: 10 - 21 in (533 mm) (2 quin).
A/S mortars: 2 - RBU 6000 12-tubed, trainable.
Decoys: 2 - PK 2 chaff launchers. (Russian units) 2 - PK 10, (Ukraine)

RADARS

Air search - Top Pair (Top Sail + Big Net), 3D.
Air/surface search - Top Steer or Top Plate, (*Varyag* and *Ukraina*) 3D.

Navigation - 3 Palm Frond.
Fire control - Front Door, (SS-N-12); Top Dome, (SA-N-6 SAM); 2 Pop Group, (SA-N-4 SAM); 3 Bass Tilt, (30 mm guns); Kite Screech, (130 mm gun).
Sonars. Bull Horn and Steer Hide; hull-mounted, active search and attack.

AIR SUPPORT

Helicopters: 1 Kamov Ka-27PL Helix, (ASW).

KEY RECOGNITION FEATURES

- High raked bow, sloping forecastle.
- 130 mm/70 gun mounting at after end of forecastle.
- Distinctive angled SSM launchers adjacent to the bridge structure, four pairs port and four pairs starboard.
- Large pyramid mainmast at after end of bridge structure with lattice gantry protruding horizontally astern at the top. Mainmast supports the air/surface search Top Steer or Top Plate radar aerial.
- Smaller aftermast supporting the Top Pair air search radar aerials.
- Short, squat twin funnels, side by side, immediately astern of aftermast.
- Single funnel casing in Ukraine unit
- Notable gap abaft the twin funnels (SA-N-6 area) is traversed by a large crane which stows between the funnels, (Russia)
- Prominent Top Dome fire control director aft situated just forward of small flight deck.

Ticonderoga

Country:	UNITED STATES OF AMERICA
Country of origin:	USA
Ship type:	CRUISERS
Class:	TICONDEROGA (AEGIS) (CG)
Active:	27

Name (Pennant number): TICONDEROGA (CG 47) (ex-DDG 47), YORKTOWN (CG 48), VINCENNES (CG 49), VALLEY FORGE (CG 50), THOMAS S GATES (CG 51), BUNKER HILL (CG 52), MOBILE BAY (CG 53), ANTIETAM (CG 54), LEYTE GULF (CG 55), SAN JACINTO (CG 56), LAKE CHAMPLAIN (CG 57), PHILIPPINE SEA (CG 58), PRINCETON (CG 59), NORMANDY (CG 60), MONTEREY (CG 61), CHANCELLORSVILLE (CG 62), COWPENS (CG 63), GETTYSBURG (CG 64), CHOSIN (CG 65), HUE CITY (CG 66), SHILOH (CG 67), ANZIO (CG 68), VICKSBURG (CG 69), LAKE ERIE (CG 70), CAPE ST GEORGE (CG 71), VELLA GULF (CG 72), PORT ROYAL (CG 73)

SPECIFICATION

Displacement, full load, tons: 9,590 (CG 47-48); 9,407 (CG 49-51); 9,516 (remainder).
Length, feet (metres): 567 (172.8).
Beam, feet (metres): 55 (16.8).
Draught, feet (metres): 31 (9.5) (sonar).
Speed, knots: 30+.
Range, miles: 6,000 at 20 kts.

ARMAMENT

Missiles: SLCM/SSM - GDC Tomahawk (CG 52 onwards). 8 McDonnell Douglas Harpoon (2 quad).   SAM - GDC Standard SM-2MR.
A/S - Honeywell ASROC, (CG 47-51) and Loral ASROC VLA (CG 52 onwards).
(SAM and A/S missiles are fired from 2 twin Mk 26 Mod 5 launchers (CG 47-51) and 2 Mk 41 Mod 0 vertical launchers (CG 52 onwards). Tomahawk is carried in CG 52 onwards with 8 missiles in each VLS launcher.)
Guns: 2 - FMC 5 in (127 mm)/54 Mk 45 Mod 0 (CG 47-50); Mod 1 (CG 51 onwards); 2 -GE/GD 20 mm/76 Vulcan Phalanx 6-barrel Mk 15 Mod 2; 2 - McDonnell Douglas 25 mm; 4 - 12.7 mm machine-guns.
Torpedoes: 6 - 324 mm Mk 32 (2 triple) Mk 14 tubes with Honeywell Mk. 46 Mod 5.
Decoys: Up to 8 Loral Hycor SRBOC 6-barrel fixed Mk 36, firing IR flares and chaff; SLQ-25 Nixie; towed torpedo decoy.

RADARS

Air search/fire control - RCA SPY-1A phased arrays, 3D. Raytheon SPY-1B phased arrays, 3D (CG 59 on).
Air search - Raytheon SPS-49(V)7 or 8.
Surface search - ISC Cardion SPS-55.
Navigation - Raytheon SPS-64(V)9.
Fire control - Lockheed SPQ-9A/B. 4 Raytheon/RCA SPG-62.
Sonars: General Electric/Hughes SQS-53A/B (CG 47-51); bow-mounted, active search and attack. Gould SQR-19 (CG 54-55); passive towed array. Gould/Raytheon SQQ-89(V)3 (CG 52 onwards); combines hull-mounted SQS-53B (CG 56-67) or SQS-53C (CG 68-73) and passive towed array SQR-19.

AIR SUPPORT

Helicopters: 2 Sikorsky SH-60B Seahawk LAMPS III; 2 Kaman SH-2F LAMPS I (CG 47-48).

VINCENNES

KEY RECOGNITION FEATURES

- High raked bow with unusual raised solid sides surrounding forecastle.
- 5 in gun mounting on forecastle at break in maindeck profile.
- Two SAM or A/S Mk 26 Mod 5 launchers (CG 47-51), or two Mk 41 Mod 0 vertical launchers (CG 52 onwards), one between forward turret and bridge structure and one at the after break to quarterdeck. This is the clearest way to differentiate between the two versions of the class.
- Large, boxlike forward superstructure just forward of midships. Bridge at forward end, small lattice mast on bridge roof supporting dome for SPQ-9A fire control radar.
- Twin funnels, both with three exhausts. Forward funnel has two larger diameter exhausts forward of a smaller one, after funnel has smaller diameter exhaust of three at the forward end.
- Tall lattice mainmast supporting radar aerials situated between funnels, exactly amidships. CG 49 and later hulls have lighter tripod mainmast instead of the square quadruped of CG 47-48.
- Both versions of class have 5 in mounting on quarterdeck.

DESTROYERS

Meko 360

SARANDI

Country: ARGENTINA, NIGERIA
Country of origin: GERMANY
Ship type: DESTROYERS
Class: ALMIRANTE BROWN (MEKO 360) (DDG/FFG)
Active: 4 Argentina, 1 Nigeria (under repair)
ARGENTINA – Name (Pennant Number):
ALMIRANTE BROWN (D 10), LA ARGENTINA (D 11),
HEROINA (D 12), SARANDI (D 13).
NIGERIA – Name (Pennant Number): ARADU (ex-
Republic) (F 89)

SPECIFICATION

Displacement, tons: 2,900 standard,
3,360 full load.
Length, feet (metres): 413.1 (125.9).
412 (126.6), *Aradu.*
Beam, feet (metres): 46 (14). 49.2 (15), *Aradu*
Draught, feet (metres): 19 (5.8) (screws)
Speed, knots: 30.5.
Range, miles: 4,500 at 18 kts.

ARMAMENT

Missiles: SSM - 8 Aerospatiale MM 40 Exocet (2
quad) launchers, (Argentine units). 8 OTO
MELARA/Matra Otomat Mk.1, (*Aradu*). SAM -
Selenia/Elsag Albatros octuple launcher; Aspide.
Guns: 1 - OTO MELARA 5 in (127 mm)/54
automatic. 8 - Breda/Bofors 40 mm/70 (4 twin).
Torpedoes: 6 - 324 mm ILAS 3 (2 triple) tubes;
Whitehead A 244, (Argentine hulls); 6 – 324
mm Plessey SWTWS-1B (2 triple) tubes,
Whitehead A244S, (*Aradu*).
Depth charges: 1 rack, (*Aradu*).
Decoys: CSEE Dagaie double mounting. Graseby
G1738 towed torpedo decoy system. (Argentine
hulls only) 2 Breda 105 mm SCLAR chaff
launchers.

RADARS

Air/surface search - Signaal DA08A. (Plessey AWS
5, *Aradu*)
Surface search - Signaal ZW06 Argentine hulls only.
Navigation - Decca 1226.
Fire control - Signaal STIR.
Sonars: Atlas Elektronik 80 DSQS-21BZ; hull-
mounted, active search and attack.

AIR SUPPORT

Helicopters: Aerospatiale AS 555 Fennec,
(ASW/ASV), (Argentine hulls). 1 Lynx Mk 89
(*Aradu*).

KEY RECOGNITION FEATURES

- Short forecastle, 5 in gun mounting in 'A'
  position.
- 40 mm/70 gun mountings immediately
  forward of bridge in 'B' position.
- Short, stubby pyramid mast at after end of
  bridge structure with WM25 fire control
  radome atop.
- Exocet SSM launchers, port and starboard,
  immediately forward of funnels.
- Two side-by-side funnels angled outboard
  in 'V' formation with pole 'T' mast at
  forward edge.
- DA08A Air/surface search and STIR fire
  control radars on raised superstructure aft
  of funnels.
- Short flight deck right aft with open
  quarterdeck below.
- Nigerian hull has solid deckhouse supporting
  lattice pylon aft of funnels with prominent
  Albatros octuple launcher further aft.

Iroquois

ATHABASKAN

Country:	CANADA
Country of origin:	CANADA
Ship type:	DESTROYERS
Class:	IROQUOIS (DDG)
Active:	4

Name (Pennant Number): IROQUOIS (280), HURON (281), ATHABASKAN (282), ALGONQUIN (283)

SPECIFICATION

Displacement, full load, tons: 5,300.
Length, feet (metres): 426 (129.8) oa.
Beam, feet (metres): 50 (15.2).
Draught, feet (metres): 15.5 (4.7).
Speed, knots: 27.
Range, miles: 4,500 at 15 kts.

ARMAMENT

Missiles: SAM - 1 Martin Marietta Mk 41 VLS, Standard SM-2MR Block III.
Guns: 1 - OTO MELARA 3 in (76 mm)/62 Super Rapid. 1 - GE/GD 20 mm/76 6-barrel Vulcan Phalanx Mk 15.
Torpedoes: 6 - 324 mm Mk 32 (2 triple) tubes. Honeywell Mk 46, Mod 5.
Decoys: 4 - Plessey Shield Mk 2 6-tubed trainable launchers.; chaff or IR flares. SLQ-25 Nixie torpedo decoy.

RADARS

Air search - Signaal SPQ-502 (LW08).
Surface search - Signaal SPQ-501 (DA08).
Navigation - 2 Raytheon Pathfinder. Koden MD 373 (Iroquois only, on hangar roof).
Fire control - 2 Signaal SPG-501 (STIR 1.8).
Sonars: 2 Westinghouse SQS-510; combined VDS and hull-mounted, active search and attack.

AIR SUPPORT

Helicopters: 2 Sikorsky CH-124A Sea King (ASW).

KEY RECOGNITION FEATURES

- SAM VLS at after end of forecastle.
- 3 in gun mounting ('B' position).
- Distinctive, curved, Signaal SPQ-502 air search radar aerial atop short pylon after end of bridge structure.
- Tall lattice mainmast immediately forward of funnel.
- Unusual, large, square funnel amidships.
- Distinctive break in superstructure alongside lattice mast with ship's boat.
- Large SATCOM domes alongside funnel.
- CIWS mounting immediately aft of funnel, atop after superstructure.
- Helicopter flight deck raised above quarterdeck level with torpedo tubes visible below.

Prat

COCHRANE

Maritime photographic

Country:	CHILE
Country of origin:	UK
Ship type:	DESTROYERS
Class:	PRAT (Ex-COUNTY)
Active:	3

Name (Pennant Number): PRAT (ex-*Norfolk*) (11), COCHRANE (ex-*Antrim*) (12), BLANCO ENCALADA (ex-*Fife*) (15)

SPECIFICATION

Displacement, full load, tons: 6,200.
Length, feet (metres): 520.5 (158.7).
Beam, feet (metres): 54 (16.5).
Draught, feet (metres): 20.5 (6.3).
Speed, knots: 30.
Range, miles: 3,500 at 28 kts.

ARMAMENT

Missiles: SSM - 4 Aerospatiale MM 38 Exocet. SAM - 2 octuple IAI/Rafael Barak 1
Guns: 2 - Vickers 4.5 in (115 mm) Mk 6 semi-automatic twin mounting. 2 or 4 - Oerlikon 20 mm Mk 9.
Torpedoes: 6 - 324 mm Mk 32 (2 triple) tubes. Honeywell Mk 46 Mod 2.
Decoys: 2 - Corvus 8-barrel trainable launchers; 2 - Wallop Barricade double layer chaff launchers.

RADARS

Air search - Marconi Type 965 or 966 (15); Elta LM 2228S (for Barak).
Surface search - Marconi Type 992 Q or R.
Navigation - Decca Type 978/1006.
Fire control - Plessey Type 903 (guns); 2 Elta EL/M-2221GM.
Sonars: Kelvin Hughes Type 162 M; hull-mounted. Graseby Type 184 M hull-mounted; active search and attack.

AIR SUPPORT

Helicopters: 2 Nurtanio NAS 332C Cougar (ASW/ASV).

KEY RECOGNITION FEATURES

- High freeboard.
- 4.5 in gun mounting ('A' position) immediately forward of SSM launchers in 'B' mounting position.
- Slim pyramid mast aft of bridge.
- Squat funnels with pyramid mainmast centrally situated between them. Double bedstead air search radar aerial atop.
- Enlarged hangar and flight deck continued right aft, making hulls effectively flush-decked. Obsolete Seaslug system has been removed.

Luda I/II

LUDA 1

Country: CHINA
Country of origin: CHINA
Ship type: DESTROYERS
Class: LUDA I/II (TYPE 051) (DDG)
Active: 15

Name (Pennant Number): JINAN (105) (Type II), XIAN (106), YINCHUAN (107), XINING (108), KAIFENG (109), DALIAN (110) (Type II), NANJING (131), HEFEI (132), CHONGQING (133), ZUNYI (134), CHANGSHA (161), NANNING (162), NANCHANG (163), GUILIN (164), ZHANJIANG (165).

SPECIFICATION

Displacement, tons: 3,250, standard.
   3,670, full load.
Length, feet (metres): 433.1 (132).
Beam, feet (metres): 42 (12.8).
Draught, feet (metres): 15.1 (4.6).
Speed, knots: 32.
Range, miles: 2,970 at 18 kts.

ARMAMENT

Missiles: SSM - 6 HY-2 (C-201) (CSS-C-3A Seersucker) (2 triple) launchers. 8 C-802 (CSS-N-8 Saccade) in *Kaifeng*. SAM - Thomson-CSF Crotale octuple launcher (*Kaifeng, Dalian* and *Xian*).
Guns: 4 - (Type I) or 2 - (Type II) USSR 5.1 in (130 mm)/58; (2 twin) (Type I). 8 - China 57mm/70 4 twin) fitted in some Type I hulls, the others have 37mm. 8 - China 37mm/63 (4 twin). 8 - USSR 25mm/60 (4 twin).
Torpedoes: 6 - 324mm Whitehead B5 15 (2 triple tubes) (fitted in some Type I). Yu-2 (Mk 46 Mod 1).
A/S mortars: 2 - FQF 2500 12-tubed launchers. Similar in design to the RBU 1200.
Depth charges: 2 or 4 - BMB projectors; 2 or 4 racks. (Type I).
Mines: 38 can be carried.
Decoys: Chaff launchers (fitted to some).

RADARS

Air search - Knife Rest or Cross Slot, or Bean Sticks or Pea Sticks. Rice Screen, 3D (on mainmast in some).

Surface search - Eye Shield or Thomson-CSF TSR 3004 Sea Tiger. Square Tie (not in all).
Navigation - Fin Curve or Racal Decca 1290.
Fire control - Wasp Head (Wok Won) or Type 343 Sun Visor B (Series 2). 2 Rice Lamp (series 2) or 2 Type 347G. Thomson-CSF Castor II (Crotale)
Sonars: Pegas 2M and Tamir 2; hull-mounted, active search and attack.

AIR SUPPORT

Helicopters: 2 Harbin Zhi-9A Haitun (Dauphin 2) (Type II). (ASW/ASV).

Luda III

Country:	CHINA
Country of origin:	CHINA
Ship type:	DESTROYERS
Class:	LUDA III (DDG)
Active:	1

Name (Pennant Number): ZHUHAI (166 – 168 when out of area)

SPECIFICATION

Displacement, tons: 3,250, standard, 3,730, full load.
Length, feet (metres): 433.1 (132).
Beam, feet (metres): 42 (12.8).
Draught, feet (metres): 15.3 (4.7).
Speed, knots: 32.
Range, miles: 2,970 at 18 kts.

ARMAMENT

Missiles: SSM – 8 YJ-1 Eagle Strike (C-801) (CSS-N-4 Sardine) (4 twin launchers). A/S – The after set of launchers may also be used for CY-1 anti-submarine missile in the future.
Guns: 4 - USSR 5.1 in (130 mm)/58; (2 twin). 8 - China 37 mm/63 Type 76A (4 twin).
Torpedoes: 6 - 324 mm Whitehead B5 15 (2 triple tubes) Yu-2 (Mk 46 Mod 1).
A/S mortars: 2 - FQF 2500 12-tubed fixed launchers. Similar in design to the RBU 1200.
Decoys: 2 -15-tubed fixed Chaff /IR flare launchers

RADARS

Air search - Rice Screen, 3D. (Similar to Hughes SPS-39A).

Surface search – China ESR 1.
Navigation - Racal Decca 1290.
Fire control - Type 343 Sun Visor B; 2 Type 347G.
Sonars: DUBV 23; hull-mounted, active search and attack. DUBV 43 VDS, active search and attack.

ZHUHAI

Luhai

SHENZHEN

Country: CHINA
Country of origin: CHINA
Ship type: DESTROYERS
Class: LUHAI (DDG)
Active: 1
Planned : 1
Name (Pennant Number): SHENZHEN (167).

SPECIFICATION

Displacement, full load, tons: 6,000.
Length, feet (metres): 505 (154).
Beam, feet (metres): 54.1 (16.5).
Draught, feet (metres): 55.8 (17).
Speed, knots: 29.
Range, miles: 14,000 at 15 kts.

ARMAMENT

Missiles: SSM – C-802 (CSS-N-8 Saccade), 2
    octuple box launchers. SAM – 1- HQ-7
    (Crotale) octuple launcher.
Guns: 2 - 3.9 in (100 mm)/56 (twin); 8 - 37
    mm/63 Type 76A (4 twin).
Torpedoes: 6 - 324 mm B5 15 (2 triple) tubes
    with Yu-2/5/6.
Decoys: 2 - MK 35 SBROC chaff launchers.

RADARS

Air search – Rice Screen 3D.
Air/surface search – China Type 363.
Fire control – Type 347G (SSM/100 mm guns); 2

EFR-1 Rice Lamp. China Castor II (Crotale).
Sonars: DUBV-23; hull-mounted, active search
    and attack.

AIR SUPPORT

Helicopters: 2 Harbin Zhi-9A Haitun (Dauphin 2)
    (ASW/ASV) or Kamov Ka-28 Helix.

KEY RECOGNITION FEATURES

- Raised bow with one maindeck level
  through to stern
- 3.9 in gun twin turret in 'A' position.
- HQ-7 (Crotale) SAM launcher in 'B'
  mounting position.
- Tall superstructure, forward and helicopter
  hangar aft of midships with two funnels
  separated by aft pylon mast and two C-802
  SSM missile box launchers
- Short forward mast atop bridge
  superstructure with low vertical lattice
  pylon behind Type 363 air/surface search
  radar aerial. Two low pylons with fire
  control radars forward of mast.
- 4 Twin 37 mm/63 Type 64A gun turret
  mountings atop hangar superstructure.
- Triple torpedo tubes just aft of forward
  funnel.

Luhu

QINGDAO

Country: CHINA
Country of origin: CHINA
Ship type: DESTROYERS
Class: LUHU (TYPE 052) (DDG)
Active: 2
Name (Pennant Number): HARBIN (112), QUINGDAO (113)

SPECIFICATION
Displacement, full load, tons: 4,600.
Length, feet (metres): 472.4 (144).
Beam, feet (metres): 52.5 (16).
Draught, feet (metres): 16.7 (5.1).
Speed, knots: 31.
Range, miles: 5,000 at 15 kts.

ARMAMENT
Missiles: SSM - 8 YJ-1 (Eagle Strike) (C-801)
  (CSS-N-4 Sardine). SAM - 1 HQ-7 (Crotale)
  octuple launcher.
Guns: 2 - 3.9 in (100 mm)/56 (twin). 8 - 37
  mm/63 Type 64A (4 twin).
Torpedoes: 6 - 324 mm Whitehead B5 15 (2
  triple) tubes. YU-2 (Mk 46 Mod 1).
A/S mortars: 2 -FQF 2500 12-tubed fixed launchers.
Decoys: 2 - SRBOC Mk 36 6-barrel chaff
  launchers. 2 - China 26-barrel chaff launchers

RADARS:
Air search - Hai Ying or God Eye.
Air/surface search - Thomson-CSF TSR 3004 Sea
  Tiger.
Surface search – China ESR 1.
Navigation – Racal Decca 1290.
Fire control - Type 347G, (for SSM and 100 mm
  gun); 2 EFR 1 Rice Lamp (37 mm gun);
  Thomson-CSF Castor II (Crotale).

Sonars: DUBV-23. Hull-mounted, active search
  and attack. DUBV-43 VDS, active attack.

AIR SUPPORT
Helicopters: 2 Harbin Zhi-9A Haitun (Dauphin 2)
  (ASW/ASV).

KEY RECOGNITION FEATURES
- Acute angled high bow. Single maindeck
  level from stem to stern.
- Sloping forecastle with 3.9 in gun
  mounting ('A' position).
- Crotale SAM octuple launcher ('B'
  mounting position).
- 2 - 37 mm/63 gun turret mountings
  immediately forward of bridge.
- Short, tapered, lattice mainmast at after
  end of main superstructure.
- Single funnel amidships with black, wedge-
  shaped, Rad-Haz screen at after end.
- Two SSM missile launchers. One set
  between enclosed aftermast and funnel,
  second aft of aftermast.
- Square after superstructure supports large
  curved Hai Ying air search radar aerial at
  forward end and 37 mm/63 gun mounting
  at after end.
- Helicopter flight deck aft with open
  quarterdeck below.
Note: Forecastle gun and SAM mounting may
  cause confusion with 'Luhai' class. But 'Luhu'
  has single funnel and prominent, raised
  37mm gun turrets immediately forward of
  bridge as quick distinguishing features.

Cassard

JEAN BART

Country: FRANCE
Country of origin: FRANCE
Ship type: DESTROYERS
Class: CASSARD (TYPE F 70(A/A)) (DDG)
Active: 2
Name (Pennant Number): CASSARD (D 614),
JEAN BART (D 615)

SPECIFICATION

Displacement, tons: 4,230, standard, 5,000, full
load.
Length, feet (metres): 455.9 (139).
Beam, feet (metres): 45.9 (14).
Draught, feet (metres): 21.3 (6.5) (sonar).
Speed, knots: 29.
Range, miles: 5,800 at 14 kts.

ARMAMENT

Missiles: SSM - 8 Aerospatiale MM 40 Exocet.
SAM - GDC Pomona Standard SM-1MR; Mk 13
Mod 5 launcher. 2 Matra Sadral PDMS sextuple
launchers; Mistral.
Guns: 1 - DCN 3.9 in (100 mm)/55 Mod 68
CADAM automatic. 2 - Oerlikon 20 mm. 4 -
12.7 mm. machine-guns
Torpedoes: 2 - fixed launchers model KD 59E.
ECAN L5 Mod 4.
Decoys: 2 - CSEE Dagaie and 2 - AMBL Sagaie
10-barrel Chaff/IR launchers. SLQ-25 Nixie;
towed torpedo decoy.

RADARS

Air search - Thomson-CSF DRBJ 11B, 3D.
Air/surface search - DRBV 26C.

Navigation - 2 Racal DRBN 34A.
Fire control - Thomson-CSF DRBC 33A, (guns). 2
Raytheon SPG-51C (missiles).
Sonars: Thomson-Sintra DUBA 25A (D 614) or
DUBV 24C (D 615); hull-mounted, active search
and attack.

AIR SUPPORT

Helicopters: 1 Aerospatiale AS 565MA Panther
(SSM targeting).

Georges Leygues

Country: FRANCE
Country of origin: FRANCE
Ship type: DESTROYERS
Class: GEORGES LEYGUES (TYPE F 70 (ASW)) (DDG)
Active: 7
Name (Pennant Number): GEORGES LEYGUES (D 640), DUPLEIX (D 641), MONTCALM (D 642), JEAN DE VIENNE (D 643), PRIMAUGUET (D 644), LA MOTTE-PICQUET (D 645), LATOUCHE-TRÉVILLE (D 646).

SPECIFICATION

Displacement, full load, tons: 4,300 (D 640-643), 4,580 (D 644-646).
Length, feet (metres): 455.9 (139).
Beam, feet (metres): 45.9 (14).
Draught, feet (metres): 18.7 (5.7).
Speed, knots: 30; 21on diesels.
Range, miles: 8,500 at 18 kts. on diesels.

ARMAMENT

Missiles: SSM - 4 Aerospatiale MM 38 Exocet (MM 40 in D 642-646). SAM - Thomson-CSF Crotale Naval EDIR octuple launcher. 2 Matra Sadral/Mistral sextuple launchers being fitted to D 640-643. (2 Matra Simbad twin launchers may be mounted in place of 20 mm guns in D 644-646).
Guns: 1 - DCN/Creusot-Loire 3.9 in (100 mm)/55 Mod 68 CADAM automatic. 2 - Breda/Mauser 30 mm guns being fitted to D 640-643. 2 - Oerlikon 20 mm, (see note under 'Missiles.') 4 - M2HB 12.7 mm machine-guns.
Torpedoes: 2 fixed launchers, ECAN L5; Honeywell Mk 46 or Eurotorp Mu 90 for helicopters in due course.
Decoys: 2 - CSEE Dagaie Mk 1 or 2 10-barrel double trainable chaff/IR flare launcher.

RADARS

Air search - Thomson-CSF DRBV 26A (not in D 644-646).
Air/surface search - Thomson-CSF DRBV 51C (DRBV 15A in D 644-646).
Navigation - 2 Decca 1226.
Fire control - Thomson-CSF Vega with DRBC 32E (D 640-643), DRBC 33A (D 644-646),(Crotale.)
Sonars: Thomson-Sintra DUBV 23D (DUBV 24C in D 644-646); bow-mounted active search and attack. DUBV 43B (43C in D 643-646) VDS;

JEAN DE VIENNE

paired with DUBV 23D/24. DSBV 61B (in D 644 onwards) passive linear towed array.

AIR SUPPORT

Helicopters: 2 Westland Lynx Mk 4 (FN). (ASW) except D 640.

KEY RECOGNITION FEATURES

- Long forecastle with 3.9 in gun mounting ('A' position) close to superstructure.
- Tall lattice mainmast at after end of bridge with vertical after edge and sloping forward edge. Tall pole mast with ESM array further forward on lattice mainmast in D 645.
- Tall funnel amidships with vertical forward edge and sloping after edge, funnel cap angled down at after end.
- Two Exocet SSM launchers atop forward end of after superstructure immediately aft of funnel.
- Crotale SAM launcher atop after superstructure.
- Flight deck aft of hangar.
- VDS towing equipment on quarterdeck.

Note - Bridge raised one deck in the last three of the class. INMARSAT aerial can be fitted forward of the funnel or between the Syracuse SATCOM domes.

Horizon

Country: FRANCE, ITALY

Country of origin: FRANCE, ITALY

Ship type: DESTROYERS

Class: HORIZON

Building : 2 France. 2 Italy.

Planned: 2 France. 1 Italy.

FRANCE – Name (Pennant Number): FORBIN (D 616); CHEVALIER PAUL (D 617)

ITALY – Name (Pennant Number): ––– (-), ––– .

SPECIFICATION

Displacement, full load, tons: 6,700.

Length, feet (metres): 494.2 (150.6) oa, (French hulls); 497.4 (151.6) oa, (Italian hulls).

Beam, feet (metres): 65.3 (19.9) (French); 57.4 (17.5) (Italian).

Draught, feet (metres): 15.7 (4.8), (French); 16.7 (5.1), (Italian).

Speed, knots: 29.

Range, miles: 7,000 at 18 kts.

ARMAMENT

Missiles: SSM – 4 Aerospatiale MM 40 Block II Exocet, (French hulls); 8 (2 quad) Teseo Mk 2 (Italian hulls). SAM – DCN Sylver A50 VLS, with Aster 15 and 30 weapons. (2 Sadral launchers France only).

Guns: 2 - OTOBreda 76 mm)/62 Super Rapid (3 in Italian hulls). 2 - GIAT, (France), 2 - Breda Oerlikon 25mm/80 (Italy).

Torpedoes: 2 launchers, Eurotorp Mu 90.

Decoys: 2 - OTOBreda SCHLAR H chaff launchers, (Italy); 4 - Matra Defense chaff/IR, (France). SLAT torpedo decoy

RADARS

Air/surface search - Thomson-CSF/Marconi DRBV 27 (S 1850M).

Surveillance/fire control – Alenia EMPAR

Surface search – Alenia RASS. (Not known, French ships).

Navigation – Alenia SPN 753(v)4 (Not known, French ships).

Fire control – 2 Alenia Marconi RTN 25X. (Italy). Alenia Marconi NA25 (French hulls).

Sonars: Thomson-Marconi 4110CL; hull-mounted, active search/attack.

AIR SUPPORT

Helicopters: 1 Marine Nationale NH 90 (France). 1 EH Industries' EH 101 Merlin. (ASW).

Note: First French hull to be delivered December 2006. First French pair to replace 'Suffren' class; second, 'Cassard'class. Italian first of class scheduled for delivery 2007.

KEY RECOGNITION FEATURES

- Sylver VLS SAM in forecastle in 'A' position
- 2 - 76 mm gun turrets in 'B' position.
- Tall pyramid mast above bridge superstructure with Alenia EMPAR surveillance/fire control radar atop.
- Low, squat funnel with integral narrow pyramid mast, topped by pole mast with Electtronica JANEWS ESM array.
- SSM box launchers between forward and after superstructure.
- Short pyramid mast on forward edge of after superstructure with air surface radar atop.
- 76 mm gun turret (Italian hulls) Sadral SAM launchers (French hulls) atop helicopter hanger.
- Short helicopter landing deck on quarterdeck.

Suffren

DUQUESNE

Country:	FRANCE
Country of origin:	FRANCE
Ship type:	DESTROYERS
Class:	SUFFREN (DDG)
Active:	1
Name (Pennant Number):	DUQUESNE (D 603)

SPECIFICATION

Displacement, tons: 5,335 standard,
6,780 full load.
Length, feet (metres): 517.1 (157.6).
Beam, feet (metres): 50.9 (15.5).
Draught, feet (metres): 20 (6.1).
Speed, knots: 34.
Range, miles: 5,100 at 18 kts., 2,400 at 29 kts.

ARMAMENT

Missiles: SSM - 4 Aerospatiale MM 38 Exocet.
SAM - ECAN Ruelle Masurca twin launcher.
Guns: 2 - DCN/Cruesot-Loire 3.9 in (100 mm)/55
Mod 1964 CADAM automatic. 4 or 6 - Oerlikon
20 mm. 2 - 12.7 mm machine-guns.
Torpedoes: 4 launchers (2 each side). 10 ECAN L5.
Decoys: 2 - CSEE Sagaie 10-barrel trainable
chaff/IR flare launchers. 2 -Dagaie launchers.

RADARS

Air search (radome) - DRBI 23.
Air/surface search - DRBV 15A.
Navigation - Racal Decca 1226 (DRBN 34A)
Fire control - 2 Thomson-CSF DRBR 51, (Masurca).
    Thomson-CSF DRBC 33A, (guns.)
Sonars: Thomson-Sintra DUBV 23; hull-mounted,
    active search/attack. DUBV 43 VDS.

Tourville

DEGRASSE

Country: FRANCE
Country of origin: FRANCE
Ship type: DESTROYERS
Class: TOURVILLE (TYPE F 67) (DDG)
Active: 2
Name (Pennant Number): TOURVILLE (D 610); DE GRASSE (D 612)

SPECIFICATION

Displacement, tons: 4,580 standard, 5,950 full load.
Length, feet (metres): 501.6 (152.8).
Beam, feet (metres): 52.4 (16).
Draught, feet (metres): 18.7 (5.7).
Speed, knots: 32.
Range, miles: 5,000 at 18 kts.

ARMAMENT

Missiles: SSM - 6 Aerospatiale MM 38 Exocet. SAM - Thomson-CSF Crotale Naval EDIR octuple launcher.
Guns: 2 - DCN/Creusot-Loire 3.9 in (100 mm)/55 Mod 68 CADAM automatic. 2 - Giat 20 mm.
Torpedoes: 2 launchers, 10 ECAN L5.
Decoys: 2 - CSEE/VSEL Syllex 8-barrel trainable chaff launchers.

RADARS

Air search - DRBV 26.
Air/surface search - Thomson-CSF DRBV 51B.

Navigation - 2 Racal Decca Type 1226.
Fire control - Thomson-CSF DRBC 32D, (Crotale.)
Sonars. Thomson-Sintra DUBV 23; bow-mounted, active search/attack. DSBX 1A (ATBF) active VDS; DSBV 62C, passive linear towed array.

AIR SUPPORT

Helicopters: 2 Westland Lynx Mk 4 (FN). (ASW).

Modified Charles F Adams

Country: GERMANY, GREECE
Country of origin: USA
Ship type: DESTROYERS
Class: LÜTJENS (MODIFIED CHARLES F ADAMS - TYPE 103B), KIMON (CHARLES F ADAMS) (DDG).
Active: 2 'Lütjens' Germany. 4 'Kimon' Greece.
GERMANY - Name (Pennant Number): LÜTJENS (D 185, ex-DDG 28), MÖLDERS (D 186, ex-DDG 29),
GREECE - Name (Pennant Number): KIMON (ex-*Semmes*) (D 218, ex-DDG 18), NEARCHOS (ex-*Waddell*) (D 219, ex-DDG 24), FORMION (ex-*Miltiadis*, ex-*Strauss*) (DDG 220, ex-DDG 16), THEMISTOCLES (ex-*Konon*, ex-*Berkeley*) (DDG 221, ex-DDG 15).

SPECIFICATION

Displacement, full load, tons: 4,500, German, 4,825 Greek.
Length, feet (metres): 437 (133.2).
Beam, feet (metres): 47.1 (14.3)
Draught, feet (metres): 20.1 (6.1) 21, (6.0) Greek (sonar).
Speed, knots: 30, (Greek), 32, (German).
Range, miles: 6,000 at 15 kts, 4,500 miles at 20 kts.

KEY RECOGNITION FEATURES

- High bow, sweeping forecastle to 5 in mounting ('A' position).
- High bridge structure with SATCOM dome atop Australian ship only, SATCOM atop short lattice pylon in German ships.
- Twin funnels sloped aft. Tripod mainmast astride forward funnel.
- Distinctive SPS-52C air search radar aerial (SPS-39 in Greek ships) mounted on aftermast and funnel combined.
- Two Raytheon SPG-51C/D fire control radar aerials immediately aft of after funnel.
- Standard SAM launcher immediately forward of quarterdeck, aft of 5 in gun mounting in 'X' position. RAM launchers on quarterdeck in German hulls.
- Unusual tapered black tops to funnels.
- ASROC box launcher between funnels.

ARMAMENT

Missiles: SAM - GDC Pomona Standard SM-1MR; Mk 13 Mod 6 launcher. (Dual capability launcher for SSM.) (Mod 0 launcher, German ships). RAM 21 cell Mk 49 launchers (German ships only). SSM – McDonnell Douglas Harpoon. Honeywell ASROC Mk 16 octuple launcher (Greek ships only). Mk 112 in German ships.
Guns: 2 - FMC 5 in (127 mm)/54 Mk 42 Mod 10. 4 - 12.7mm machine guns in Greek ships, none in German ships). 2 - Rheinmetall 20 mm Rh 202 (German ships only).
Torpedoes: 6 - 324 mm Mk 32 Mod 5 (2 triple) tubes; Honeywell Mk 46 Mod 2 or 5.
Decoys: 2 - Loral Hycor SRBOC 6-barrel fixed Mk 36. (4 in Greek ships.) T Mk-6 Fanfare torpedo decoy, (Greek ships only).

MÖLDERS

RADARS

Air search - SPS-39, SPS-40B/D in Greek ships, SPS-40/SPS-52 in German.

Surface search - SPS-64 or SPS-67; SPS 10D/F in German and Greek ships).

Navigation – Marconi LN66 (Greek ships).

Fire control - SPG-51, Lockheed SPQ-9 and SPG-60 in German ships. (SPG-51D, SPG-53A, Greek ships).

Sonars: Sangamo or Raytheon DE 1191 (Greek). Atlas Elektronik DSQS-21B hull-mounted, (German ships).

Note: Greek ships leased by USA and then gifted by grant aid in 1999 D221 and D220 will be decommissioned in 2002. German ships expected to pay off in December 2003.

Delhi

MUMBAI

Country: INDIA
Country of origin: INDIA
Ship type: DESTROYERS
Class: DELHI (DDG)
Active: 3
Planned : 3
Name (Pennant Number): DELHI (D 61), MYSORE (D 60), MUMBAI (D 62).

SPECIFICATION

Displacement, full load, tons: 6,700.
Length, feet (metres): 534.8 (163).
Beam, feet (metres): 55.8 (17).
Draught, feet (metres): 21.3 (6.5).
Speed, knots: 32.
Range: 4,500 at 18 kts.

ARMAMENT

Missiles: SSM – 16 Zvezda SS-N-25 (4 quad) (KH 35 Uran). SAM – 2 SA-N-7 Gadfly (KashmirUragan).
Guns: 1 - USSR 3.9 in (100 mm)/59 AK 100. 4 - USSR 30 mm/65 AK 630, 6-barrels per mounting.
Torpedoes: 5 - 533 mm PTA 21 in (533 mm) (quin) tubes.
A/S mortars: 2 -RBU 6000, 12 tubed trainable.
Depth charges: 2 rails.
Decoys: 2 - PK 2 chaff launchers. Towed torpedo decoy.

RADARS

Air search – Bharat/Signaal RALW (LW08).

Air/surface search – Half Plate.
Navigation – Bharat Rashmi.
Fire control – 6 Front Dome (SAM), Kite Screech (100 mm gun), 2 Bass Tilt (30 mm guns), Plank Shave, (Granit Harpun B) (SSM).
Sonars: Bharat HUMVAD, hull mounted, active search. India/Garden Reach Model 15-750 VDS.

AIR SUPPORT

Helicopters: 2 Westland Sea King Mk 42B (ASV) or 2 Hindustan Aeronautics ALH, (ASW/ASV).

KEY RECOGNITION FEATURES

- High bow with sweeping forecastle aft to bridge. One maindeck level through to stern.
- Squat 3.9 in gun mounting in 'A' position.
- SA-N-7 SAM launcher in 'B' position with 2 RBU 6000 A/S launchers aft.
- Four angled, tubular quad launcher tubes for SS-N-25 SSM, (two port, two starboard) alongside and forward of bridge superstructure.
- Prominent square Half Plate air/surface search radar aerial at top of short mainmast atop bridge superstructure.
- Second low pyramid mast between two squared funnels, with Bharat/Signaal RALW (LW08) air search aerial atop.
- Long, low helicopter hangar aft of second funnel.

ARDITO

Country: ITALY

Country of origin: ITALY.

Ship type: DESTROYERS

Class: AUDACE (DDG)

Active: 2

Name (Pennant Number): ARDITO (D 550),
AUDACE (D 551).

SPECIFICATION

Displacement, tons: 3,600 standard,
4,400 full load.

Length, feet (metres): 448 (136.6).

Beam, feet (metres): 46.6 (14.2).

Draught, feet (metres): 15.1 (4.6).

Speed, knots: 34.

Range, miles: 3,000 at 20 kts.

ARMAMENT

Missiles: SSM - 8 OTO MELARA/Matra Teseo Mk 2
(TG 2) (4 twin). SAM - GDC Pomona Standard
SM-1MR; Mk 13 Mod 4 launcher. Selenia
Albatros octuple launcher for Aspide.

Guns: 1 - OTO MELARA 5 in (127 mm)/54. 3 - OTO
MELARA 3 in (76 mm)/62 Compact (*Ardito*) and
1 (*Ardito*) or 4 (*Audace*) Super Rapid.

Torpedoes: 6 - 324 mm US Mk 32 (2 triple)
tubes. Honeywell Mk 46.

Decoys: 2 - Breda 105 mm SCLAR 20-barrel chaff
launchers. SLQ-25 Nixie towed torpedo decoy.

RADARS

Long range air search - Hughes SPS-52C, 3D.

Air search - Selenia SPS-768 (RAN 3L).

Air/surface search - Selenia SPS-774 (RAN 10S).

Surface search - SMA SPQ-2D.

Navigation - SMA SPN-748.

Fire control - 3 Selenia SPG-76 (RTN 30X), 2
Raytheon SPG-51, (Standard SAM).

Sonars: CWE 610; hull-mounted, active search
and attack.

AIR SUPPORT

Helicopters: 2 Agusta-Bell AB 212 (ASW) or 1 EH
Industries' EH 101 Merlin.

KEY RECOGNITION FEATURES

- Continuous maindeck from stem to stern.
- 5 in gun mounting ('A' position) with
  Albatros SAM launcher ('B' position).
- Unusually high forward superstructure.
- Forward mast and funnel, combined at
  after end of forward superstructure,
  supports air search radar aerial. Twin
  exhausts in 'V' protruding aft.
- Aftermast and funnel combined has
  sloping forward edge supporting large,
  angled square-shaped long-range air
  search radar aerial.
- Ship's boat alongside after funnel and mast.
- Teseo SSM launchers sited between
  funnels, above 76 mm gun mountings.
- Two prominent fire control radars on
  pylons aft of after funnel/mast.
- Standard SAM launcher atop forward end
  of hangar which rises at an angle aft.
- Flight deck right aft with open quarterdeck
  below.

De la Penne

Country: ITALY
Country of origin: Italy
Ship type: DESTROYERS
Class: DE LA PENNE (ex-ANIMOSO) (DDG)
Active: 2
Name (Pennant Number): LUIGI DURAND DE LA PENNE (ex-Animoso) (D 560), FRANCESCO MIMBELLI (ex-Ardimentoso) (D 561).

SPECIFICATION

Displacement, tons: 4,330 standard, 5,400 full load.
Length, feet (metres): 487.4 (147.7).
Beam, feet (metres): 52.8 (16.1).
Draught, feet (metres): 28.2 (8.6) (sonar).
Speed, knots: 31.
Range, miles: 7,000 at 18 kts.

ARMAMENT

Missiles: SSM - 4 or 8 OTO MELARA/Matra Teseo Mk 2 (TG 2) (2 or 4 twin). SAM - GDC Pomona Standard SM-1MR; Mk 13 Mod 4 launcher.

KEY RECOGNITION FEATURES

- High bow, continuous maindeck from stem to stern.
- 5 in gun mounting ('A' position) with Albatros SAM octuple box launcher ('B' mounting position).
- Slim pyramid foremast atop forward superstructure.
- Slightly shorter, enclosed aftermast supporting square long range air search radar aerial on platform protruding aft. Pole mast atop aftermast with air/surface search radar atop.
- Three square section funnels, one at after end of forward superstructure and twin 'V' funnels just abaft aftermast. Both sets slightly tapered towards top.
- Teseo SSM launchers amidships between forward funnel and after mast.
- Prominent fire control arrays on pylons aft of after mast.
- Standard SAM launcher and 3 in gun mounting atop after superstructure.
- Flight deck right aft with open quarterdeck below.

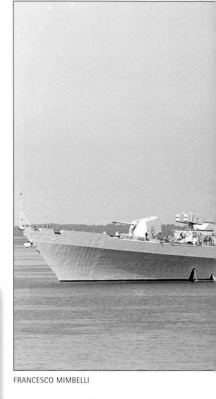

FRANCESCO MIMBELLI

Selenia Albatros Mk 2 octuple launcher for Aspide. A/S - OTO MELARA/Matra Milas launcher with Mk 46 Mod 5 or Mu 90 torpedoes planned to be fitted by 2002.
Guns: 1 - OTO MELARA 5 in (127 mm)/54. 3 - OTO MELARA 3 in (76 mm)/62 Super Rapid.
Torpedoes: 6 - 324 mm B5 15 (2 triple) tubes. Honeywell Mk 46.
Decoys: 2 - CSEE Sagaie chaff launchers. 1 - SLQ-25 Nixie anti-torpedo system.

RADARS

Long range air search - Hughes SPS-52C, 3D.
Air search - Selenia SPS-768 (RAN 3L).
Air/surface search - Selenia SPS-774 (RAN 10S).
Surface search - SMA SPS-702.
Navigation - SMA SPN-748.
Fire control - 4 Selenia SPG-76 (RTN 30X). 2 Raytheon SPG-51D. (SAM).
Sonars: Raytheon DE 1164 LF-VDS; integrated hull and VDS, active search/attack.

AIR SUPPORT

Helicopters: 2 Agusta-Bell AB 212 (ASW); SH-3D Sea King and EH 101 capable.

Asagiri

UMIGIRI

Country: JAPAN
Country of origin: JAPAN
Ship type: DESTROYERS
Class: ASAGIRI (DDG/DD)
Active: 8
Name (Pennant Number): ASAGIRI (DD 151), YAMAGIRI (DD 152), YUUGIRI (DD 153), AMAGIRI (DD 154), HAMAGIRI (DD 155), SETOGIRI (DD 156), SAWAGIRI (DD 157), UMIGIRI (DD 158).

SPECIFICATION
Displacement, full load, tons: 4,200.
Length, feet (metres): 449.4 (137).
Beam, feet (metres): 48 (14.6).
Draught, feet (metres): 14.6 (4.5).
Speed, knots: 30.

ARMAMENT
Missiles: SSM - 8 McDonnell Douglas Harpoon (2 quad) launchers. SAM - Raytheon Sea Sparrow Mk 29 (Type 3/3A) octuple box launcher. A/S - Honeywell ASROC Mk 112 octuple launcher; payload, Mk 46 Mod 5 Neartip torpedoes.
Guns: 1 - OTO MELARA 3 in (76 mm)/62 Compact. 2 - GE/GD 20 mm Phalanx Mk 15 CIWS.
Torpedoes: 6 - 324 mm Type 68 (2 triple) HOS 301 tubes. Honeywell Mk 46 Mod 5 Neartip.
Decoys: 2 - Loral Hycor SRBOC 6-barrel Mk 36 chaff launchers. 1 - SLQ-51 Nixie or Type 4 towed anti-torpedo decoy.

RADARS
Air search - Melco OPS-14C (DD 151-154). Melco OPS-24 (DD 155-158), 3D.
Surface search - JRC OPS-28C. (DD 151, 152, 155-158). JRC OPS-28C-Y (DD 153-154.)

Fire control - Type 2-22, (guns). Type 2-12E (DD 151-154). Type 2-12G (for SAM), (DD 155-158).
Sonars: Mitsubishi OQS-4A (II); hull-mounted, active search/attack. OQR-1 towed array.

AIR SUPPORT
Helicopters: 1 Sikorsky/Mitsubishi SH-60J Sea Hawk (ASW).

Haruna

HIEI

Country: JAPAN
Country of origin: JAPAN.
Ship type: DESTROYERS
Class: HARUNA (DD/DDH)
Active: 2
Name (Pennant Number): HARUNA (DDH 141),
HIEI (DDH 142).

SPECIFICATION

Displacement, standard, tons: 4,950 (5,050, DD
142).
Length, feet (metres): 502 (153).
Beam, feet (metres): 57.4 (17.5).
Draught, feet (metres): 17.1 (5.2).
Speed, knots: 31.

ARMAMENT

Missiles: SAM - Raytheon Sea Sparrow Mk 29
(Type 3A) octuple box launcher. A/S -
Honeywell ASROC Mk 112 octuple launcher;
payload, Mk 46 Mod 5 Neartip torpedoes.
Guns: 2 - FMC 5 in (127 mm)/54 Mk 42
automatic. 2 - GE/GD 20 mm Phalanx Mk 15
CIWS.
Torpedoes: 6 - 324 mm Type 68 (2 triple) tubes.
Honeywell Mk 46 Mod 5 Neartip.
Decoys: 4 - Loral Hycor SRBOC 6-barrel Mk 36
chaff launchers.

RADARS

Air search - Melco OPS-11C.
Surface search - JRC OPS-28C/28C-Y.

Navigation: Koden OPN-11.
Fire control - 1 Type 1A, (guns); 1 Type 2-12,
(SAM).
Sonars: Sangamo/Mitsubishi OQS-3; bow-
mounted, active search/attack.

AIR SUPPORT

Helicopters: 3 Sikorsky/Mitsubishi SH-60J
Seahawk, (ASW).

KEY RECOGNITION FEATURES

- Continuous maindeck line from bows to
stern.
- Forecastle identical to *Shirane* class.
- Similar large, slab-sided central
superstructure to *Shirane* class. Main
difference is single mast funnel combined
offset slightly to port.
- Lattice mast and curved Melco OPS-11C air
search radar aerial atop funnel.
- Prominent fire control radome aft of
mainmast and funnel.
- Aft of funnel almost identical to *Shirane*
class.
Note: A heavy crane is fitted atop the
hangar, starboard side.
Note 2: Appearance of weapons fit on
forecastle is very similar in appearance to
Shirane class.

Hatakaze

SHIMAKAZE

Country: JAPAN
Country of origin: JAPAN
Ship type: DESTROYERS
Class: HATAKAZE (DDG)
Active: 2
Name (Pennant Number): HATAKAZE (DDG 171),
SHIMAKAZE (DDG 172).

SPECIFICATION

Displacement, full load, tons: 5,500.
Length, feet (metres): 492 (150).
Beam, feet (metres): 53.8 (16.4).
Draught, feet (metres): 15.7 (4.8).
Speed, knots: 30.

ARMAMENT

Missiles: SSM - 8 McDonnell Douglas Harpoon.
  SAM - GDC Pomona Standard SM-1MR; Mk 13
  Mod 4 launcher. A/S - Honeywell ASROC Mk
  112 octuple box launcher; payload Mk 46 Mod
  5 Neartip torpedoes.
Guns: 2 - FMC 5 in (127 mm)/54 Mk 42
  automatic. 2 - GE/GD 20 mm Phalanx Mk 15
  CIWS.
Torpedoes: 6 - 324 mm Type 68 (2 triple) tubes.
  Honeywell Mk 46 Mod 5 Neartip.
Decoys: 2 - Loral Hycor SRBOC 6-barrel Mk 36
  chaff launchers.

RADARS

Air search - Hughes SPS-52C, 3D. Melco OPS-11C.
Surface search – JRC-OPS 28B.

Fire control - 2 Raytheon SPG-51C. Melco 2-21.
  Type 2-12.
Sonars: Nec OQS-4 Mod 1; bow-mounted, active
  search/attack.

AIR SUPPORT

Helicopters: Platform for 1 Sikorsky/Mitsubishi
  SH-60J Seahawk, (ASW).

KEY RECOGNITION FEATURES

- Break in upper deck profile just aft from
  bow, continuous maindeck from stem to
  stern.
- Three weapons fitted on long forecastle,
  from forward to aft, Standard SAM
  launcher, raised 5 in gun mounting, ASROC
  A/S missile launcher.
- Central superstructure with lattice
  mainmast atop after end supporting square
  profile SPS-52C air search radar aerial.
- Thin break in superstructure just after of
  mainmast.
- Black-capped, slightly tapered single funnel
  just aft of midships.
- Short lattice aftermast supporting curved,
  OPS-11C air search radar.
- 5 in gun mounting forward end flight deck
  ('Y' position).
- Long flight deck with open quarterdeck
  below.

Hatsuyuki

Country: JAPAN
Country of origin: JAPAN
Ship type: DESTROYERS
Class: HATSUYUKI (DDG/DD)
Active: 11
Name (Pennant Number):
HATSUYUKI (DD 122),
SHIRAYUKI (DD 123),
MINEYUKI (DD 124),
SAWAYUKI (DD 125),
HAMAYUKI (DD 126),
ISOYUKI (DD 127),
HARUYUKI (DD 128),
YAMAYUKI (DD 129),
MATSUYUKI (DD 130),
SETOYUKI (DD 131),
ASAYUKI (DD 132).

HATSUYUKI

SPECIFICATION

Displacement, full load, tons: 3,700 (3,800 DD
129 onwards).
Length, feet (metres): 426.4 (130).
Beam, feet (metres): 44.6 (13.6).
Draught, feet (metres): 13.8 (4.2), (14.4 (4.4) DD
129 onwards).
Speed, knots: 30.

ARMAMENT

Missiles: SSM - McDonnell Douglas Harpoon (2
quad) launchers. SAM - Raytheon Sea Sparrow
Type 3A launcher. A/S - Honeywell ASROC Mk
112 octuple box launcher; payload Mk 46 Mod
5 Neartip torpedoes.
Guns: 1 - OTO MELARA 3 in (76 mm)/62 Compact.
2 - GE/GD 20 mm Phalanx Mk 15 CIWS.
Torpedoes: 6 - 324 mm Type 68 (2 triple) tubes.
Honeywell Mk 46 Mod 5 Neartip.
Decoys: 2 - Loral Hycor SRBOC 6-barrel Mk 36
chaff launchers.

RADARS

Air search - Melco OPS-14B.
Surface search - JRC OPS-18.
Fire control - Type 2-12 A, (SAM).
2 Type 2-21/21A (guns).
Sonars: Nec OQS-4A (II) (SQS-23 type); bow-
mounted active search/attack. OQR-1 TACTASS
(in some) passive.

AIR SUPPORT

Helicopters: 1 Sikorsky/Mitsubishi SH-60J
Seahawk, (ASW).

KEY RECOGNITION FEATURES

- Continuous maindeck with break down to
quarterdeck.
- 3 in gun mounting ('A' position).
- ASROC A/S missile box launcher
immediately forward of bridge.
- Large black-capped funnel, slightly tapered,
amidships.
- Lattice mainmast at after end of bridge
structure supporting several radar aerials,
most prominent, OPS-14B air search on
forward gantry. CIWS mountings at base of
mainmast.
- Fire control radome mounted atop hangar,
offset to starboard.
- Flight deck aft raised above maindeck level.
- Sea Sparrow SAM launcher just forward of
quarterdeck.
Note: Last of class, Shimayuki converted to
training ship (TV 35 13) March, 1999.
Lecture room added to helicopter hanger.

Kongou

KIRISHIMA

Country:	JAPAN
Country of origin:	JAPAN
Ship type:	DESTROYERS
Class:	KONGOU (DDG)
Active:	4

Name (Pennant Number): KONGOU (DDG 173), KIRISHIMA (DDG 174), MYOUKOU (DDG 175), CHOUKAI (DDG 176).

SPECIFICATION

Displacement, tons: 7,250 standard, 9,485 full load.
Length, feet (metres): 528.2 (161)
Beam, feet (metres): 68.9 (21).
Draught, feet (metres): 20.3 (6.2), 32.7 (10) sonar.
Speed, knots: 30.
Range, miles: 4,500 at 20 kts.

ARMAMENT

Missiles: SSM - 8 McDonnell Douglas Harpoon (2 quad) launchers. SAM - GDC Pomona Standard SM-2MR, FMC Mk 41 VLS (29 cells) forward, Martin Marietta Mk 41 VLS (61 cells) aft. A/S - Vertical launch ASROC; payload Mk 46 torpedoes.
Guns: 1 - OTO MELARA 5 in (127 mm)/54 Compatto. 2 - GE/GD 20 mm/76 Mk 15 Vulcan Phalanx.
Torpedoes: 6 - 324 mm (2 triple) HOS tubes. Honeywell Mk 46 Mod 5 Neartip.
Decoys: 4 -Loral Hycor SRBOC 6-barrel Mk 36 chaff launchers. SLQ-25 towed torpedo decoy.

RADARS

Air search - RCA SPY-1D, 3D.

Surface search – JRC OPS-28D.
Navigation - JRC OPS-20.
Fire control - 3 SPG-62; 1 Mk 2/21.
Sonars: Nec OQS-102 (SQS-53B/C) bow-mounted, active search/attack; Oki OQR-2 (SQR- 19A(V)) TACTASS towed array, passive.

AIR SUPPORT

Helicopters: Platform and refuelling facilities for Sikorsky/Mitsubishi SH-60J Seahawk.

KEY RECOGNITION FEATURES

- Continuous maindeck line from stem to stern.
- Sole visible armament on long foredeck 5 in gun mounting ('A 'position).
- CIWS mounting immediately forward of bridge and at after end of after superstructure.
- High forward superstructure topped by lattice mast sloping aft.
- SPY 1D panels on forward face of bridge superstructure.
- Two unusually large angular funnels, close together amidships. Funnels tapered and with several black exhausts protruding at top.
- Harpoon SSM launchers between funnels.
- Standard SAM VLS cells at after end of foredeck and forward end of flight deck; not obvious from side aspect of ship.
- Long flight deck aft.

Note: This is an enlarged and improved version of the US *Arleigh Burke* class with a lightweight version of the Aegis system.

HARUSAME

Country: JAPAN
Country of origin: JAPAN
Ship type: DESTROYERS
Class: MURASAME (DDG/DD)
Active: 9
Name (Pennant Number): MURASAME (DD 101),
HARUSAME (DD 102), YUUDACHI (DD 103),
KIRISAME (DD 104), INAZUMA (DD 105),
SAMIDARE (DD 106), IKAZUCHI (DD 107),
AKEBONO (DD 108), ARIAKE (DD 109).

SPECIFICATION

Displacement, tons: 4,550 standard,
5,100 full load.
Length, feet (metres): 495.4 (151).
Beam, feet (metres): 57.1 (17.4).
Draught, feet (metres): 17.1 (5.2).
Speed, knots: 30.
Missiles: SSM - 8 SSM-1B Harpoon. SAM -
Raytheon Mk 48 VLS Sea Sparrow. A/S - Mk 41
VL ASROC.
Guns: 1 - OTO MELARA 3 in (76 mm)/62 Compact.
2 - GE/GD 20 mm Vulcan Phalanx Mk 15.
Torpedoes: 6 - 324 mm Type 68 (2 triple) tubes
Mk 46 Mod 5 Neartip.
Decoys: 4 - Mk 36 SRBOC chaff launchers, SLQ-
25 Nixie towed torpedo decoy.

RADARS

Air search - Melco OPS-24, 3D.
Surface search - JRC OPS-28D.

Navigation - OPS-20.
Fire control - 2 Type 2-31.
Sonars: Mitsubishi OQS-5; hull-mounted, active
search/attack. OQR-1 towed array, passive
search.

AIR SUPPORT

Helicopters: 1 Sikorsky/Mitsubishi SH-60J
Seahawk ASW).

KEY RECOGNITION FEATURES

- Curved, sweeping bow, square, near vertical
stern.
- 3 in gun mounting sited at mid-forecastle.
- VL ASROC abaft forward gun mounting.
- CIWS mounting on raised platform
immediately forward of bridge.
- Slab-like forward superstructure has winged
bridge; large lattice mainmast at after end.
- Two large, twin, square profile funnels, one
at after end of forward superstructure and
one at forward end of after superstructure.
- Break in superstructure between funnels.
Harpoon launchers immediately forward of
this break.
- Large flight deck at after end of
superstructure.
- CIWS mounting on helicopter hangar.
Note: See entry on 'Improved Murasame' class.

Takanami (Improved Murasame)

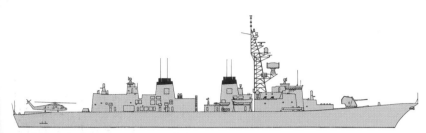

IMPROVED MURASAME

Country: JAPAN
Country of origin: JAPAN
Ship type: DESTROYERS
Class: IMPROVED MURASAME (DDG/DD)
Building: 4
Planned: 1
Name (Pennant Number): TAKANAMI (DD 110),
OONAMI (DD 111), ––––– (DD 112), ––––(DD
113), ––––(DD 114).

SPECIFICATION

Displacement, tons: 4,600 standard,
5,150 full load.
Length, feet (metres): 495.4 (151).
Beam, feet (metres): 57.1 (17.4).
Draught, feet (metres): 17.1 (5.2).
Speed, knots: 30.

ARMAMENT

Missiles: SSM - 8 SSM-1B Harpoon. (2 quad)
SAM - Raytheon Mk 41 VLS Sea Sparrow. A/S –
Mk 41 VL ASROC.
Guns: 1 - OTOBreda 5 in (127 mm)/54. 2 - GE/GD
20 mm Vulcan Phalanx Mk 15.
Torpedoes: 6 - 324 mm Type 68 (2 triple) tubes
Mk 46 Mod 5 Neartip.
Decoys: 4 - Mk 36 SRBOC chaff launchers, SLQ-25
Nixie towed torpedo decoy.

RADARS

Air search - Melco OPS-24, 3D.
Surface search - JRC OPS-28D.
Navigation – OPS-20.
Fire control - 2 FCS 3
Sonars: Hull-mounted, active search/attack. OQR-
1 towed array, passive search.

AIR SUPPORT

Helicopters: 1 Sikorsky/Mitsubishi SH-60J
Seahawk (ASW).

Note: First two hulls due to be commissioned in
March, 2003.

KEY RECOGNITION FEATURES

- Curved, sweeping bow, square, near vertical
  stern.
- Larger, 5 in gun mounting sited at mid-
  forecastle (compared with low rounded
  turret of 3 ins in 'Murasame' class.
- SAM VLS abaft forward gun mounting on
  low superstructure, with CIWS mounting
  above, on platform immediately forward of
  bridge.
- Slab-like forward superstructure has
  winged bridge; large lattice mainmast at
  after end, very similar to 'Murasame' class.
- Two large, twin, square profile funnels, one
  at after end of forward superstructure and
  one at forward end of after superstructure,
  as 'Murasame' class.
- Wider break in superstructure between
  funnels. Harpoon launchers immediately
  forward of after funnel.
- Large flight deck at after end of
  superstructure.
- CIWS mounting on helicopter hangar.

Shirane

SHIRANE

Hachiro Nakai

Country: JAPAN
Country of origin: JAPAN
Ship type: DESTROYERS
Class: SHIRANE (DD/DDH)
Active: 2
Name (Pennant Number): SHIRANE (DDH 143), KURAMA (DDH 144).

SPECIFICATION

Displacement, standard, tons: 5,200.
Length, feet (metres): 521.5 (159).
Beam, feet (metres): 57.5 (17.5).
Draught, feet (metres): 17.5 (5.3).
Speed, knots: 31.

ARMAMENT

Missiles: SAM - Raytheon Sea Sparrow Mk 25 octuple launcher. A/S - Honeywell ASROC Mk 112 octuple box launcher; payload Mk 46 Mod 5 Neartip torpedoes.
Guns: 2 - FMC 5 in (127 mm)/54 Mk 42 automatic. 2 - GE/GD 20 mm Phalanx Mk 15 CIWS.
Torpedoes: 6 - 324 mm Type 68 (2 triple) tubes. Honeywell Mk 46 Mod 5 Neartip.
Decoys: 4 - Mk 36 SBROC chaff launchers. Prairie Masker blade rate suppression system.

RADARS

Air search - Nec OPS-12, 3D.
Surface search - JRC OPS-28.
Navigation - Koden OFS-2D.
Fire control - Signaal WM 25. Two Type 72-1A FCS.
Sonars: EDO/Nec SQS-35(J); VDS active/passive

search. EDO/Nec OQS-101; bow-mounted. EDO/Nec SQR-18A; towed array, passive.

AIR SUPPORT

Helicopters: 3 Sikorsky/Mitsubishi SH-60J Sea Hawk, (ASW).

KEY RECOGNITION FEATURES

- High bow, sweeping continuous maindeck line from stem to stern.
- Two 5 in gun mountings ('A' and 'B' positions) with ASROC A/S missile octuple box launcher between after mounting and bridge. 'B' position on raised platform.
- High, slab-sided centrally sited superstructure, similar to 'Haruna' class.
- Two funnels and masts combined with distinctive black, wedge-shaped exhaust diffusers/RAD-HAZ screens atop. The after funnel is set to starboard and the forward one to port.
- Lattice mast mounted atop forward funnel and WM25 fire control radar dome atop after one.
- Long flight deck with open quarterdeck below.
- Sea Sparrow SAM octuple box launcher atop hangar.

Note: Almost identical to and easily confused with Haruna class from bow to bridge. Number and type of funnels distinguish.

TACHIKAZE

Country: JAPAN
Country of origin: JAPAN
Ship type: DESTROYERS
Class: TACHIKAZE (DDG)
Active: 3
Name (Pennant Number): TACHIKAZE (DDG 168), ASAKAZE (DDG 169), SAWAKAZE (DDG 170)

SPECIFICATION

Displacement, standard, tons: 3,850 (3,950, DD 170).
Length, feet (metres): 469 (143).
Beam, feet (metres): 47 (14.3).
Draught, feet (metres): 15.4 (4.7).
Speed, knots: 32.

ARMAMENT

Missiles: SSM - 8 McDonnell Douglas Harpoon. (DDG 170 only). SAM - GDC Pomona Standard SM-1MR; Mk 13 Mod 1 or 4 launcher. A/S - Honeywell ASROC Mk 112 octuple launcher; payload Mk 46 Mod 5 Neartip torpedoes.
Guns: 1 (DDG 168) or 2 - FMC 5 in (127 mm)/54 Mk 42 automatic. 2 - GE/GD 20 mm Phalanx CIWS Mk 15.
Torpedoes: 6 - 324 mm Type 68 (2 triple) tubes. Honeywell Mk 46 Mod 5 Neartip.
Decoys: 4 - Loral Hycor SRBOC 6-barrel Mk 36 chaff launchers. SLQ-25 Nixie towed torpedo decoy.

RADARS

Air search - Melco OPS-11C. Hughes SPS-52B or C (DDG 170), 3D.
Surface search - JRC OPS-16D. (DDG 168) JRC OPS-28 (DD 170). JRC OPS-18-3, (DDG 169).
Fire control - 2 Raytheon SPG 51. Type 2 FCS.
Sonars: Nec OQS-3A (Type 66); bow-mounted, active search/attack.

KEY RECOGNITION FEATURES

- High bow, continuous sweeping maindeck line from stem to stern.
- 5 in gun mounting ('A' position).
- ASROC A/S missile octuple box launcher immediately forward of bridge.
- Forward mast and funnel combined at after end of main superstructure topped by lattice mast with air search radar on forward gantry.
- Wide break in superstructure between funnels.
- Aftermast and tall funnel combined has SPS-52B/C square profile radar aerial mounted atop.
- Two sets of triple torpedo tubes mounted between funnels.
- After 5 in gun mounting ('X' position). (Removed from *Tachikaze* to allow increased Flag accommodation.)
- Standard SAM launcher on long afterdeck.

Takatsuki

TAKATSUKI

Country:	JAPAN
Country of origin:	JAPAN
Ship type:	DESTROYERS
Class:	TAKATSUKI (DDG/DDA)
Active:	2

Name (Pennant Number): TAKATSUKI (DDA 164), KIKUZUKI (DDA 165).

SPECIFICATION

Displacement, standard, tons: 3,250.
Length, feet (metres): 446.1 (136).
Beam, feet (metres): 44 (13.4).
Draught, feet (metres): 14.8 (4.5).
Speed, knots: 31.
Range, miles: 7,000 at 20 kts.

ARMAMENT

Missiles: SSM – McDonnell Douglas Harpoon (2 quad) launchers. SAM – Raytheon Sea Sparrow Type 3 or 3A octuple launchers. A/S – Honeywell ASROC Mk 112 octuple launcher with payload Mk 46 Mod 5 Neartip torpedo.
Guns: 1 - FMC 5 in (127 mm)/54 Mk 42 automatic. 1 - GE/GD 20 mm Phalanx CIWS.
Torpedoes: 6 - 324 mm Type 68 (2 triple) tubes. Honeywell Mk 46 Mod 5 Neartip.
A/S mortars: 1 - 375 mm Bofors Type 71 4-barrel trainable rocket launcher.
Decoys: 2 - Loral Hycor SBROC 6-barrel Mk 36 chaff launchers.

RADAR

Air search – Melco OPS-11B-Y.
Surface search – JRC OPS-17.
Fire control – Type 2-12B. 2 GE Mk 35.
Sonars: Nec SQS-35J, hull-mounted active search/attack. EDO SQR-18 TACTASS, passive.

KEY RECOGNITION FEATURES

- High bow, continuous sweeping maindeck line from stem to stern.
- 5 in gun mounting ('A' position), with Bofors 375 mm A/S mortar forward on forecastle.
- Lattice platform on forward face of bridge superstructure
- ASROC A/S missile octuple box launcher immediately forward of bridge
- Tall forward bridge superstructure with forward mast and short funnel combined at after end, topped by lattice mast.
- Two black-topped funnels, with Harpoon SSM quad launchers aft of second funnel.
- Wide gap between forward and aft superstructures, with triple torpedo tubes between.
- Large Type 2-12B fire control radome atop tall raised platform on after superstructure.
- Sea Sparrow SAM octuple box launcher in 'Y' position.

Yamagumo

YUUGUMO

Country:	JAPAN
Country of origin:	JAPAN
Ship type:	DESTROYERS
Class:	YAMAGUMO (DD/DDK)
Active:	1
Name (Pennant Number):	YUUGUMO (DDK 121).

SPECIFICATION

Displacement, standard, tons: 2,150.
Length, feet (metres): 377.2 (114.9).
Beam, feet (metres): 38.7 (11.8).
Draught, feet (metres): 13.1 (4).
Speed, knots: 27.
Range, miles: 7,000 at 20 kts.

ARMAMENT

Missiles: A/S Honeywell ASROC Mk 112 octuple
launcher with payload, Mk 46 Mod 5 Neartip.
Guns: 4 - USN 3 in (76mm)/50 Mk 33 (2 twin).
Torpedoes: 6 - 324 mm Type 68 (2 triple) tubes
with Honeywell Mk 46 Mod 5 Neartip.
A/S mortars: 1 - Bofors 375 mm Type 71 4-barrel
trainable rocket launcher.

RADARS

Air search – Melco OPS-11B/11C.

Surface search – JRC OPS-118-3
Fire control – 2 GE Mk 35.
Sonars: Nec OQS-3A, hull-mounted, active
search/attack. EDO SQS-35(J).

KDX-2   *Hyundai 1996 (Computer graphic)*

Country: KOREA, SOUTH
Country of origin: KOREA, SOUTH
Ship type: DESTROYERS
Class: KDX-2 (DDG)
Building: 3
Planned: 3
Name (Pennant Number): ––– (DDG 975), –––
(DDG 976), ––– (DDG 977)

SPECIFICATION

Displacement, full load, tons: 4,800.
Length, feet (metres): 506.6 (154.4).
Beam, feet (metres): 55.5 (16.9).
Draught, feet (metres): 14.1 (4.3).
Speed, knots: 29.
Range, miles: 4,000 at 18 kts.
Missiles: SSM – Harpoon (Block 1C) (2 quad).
   SAM – Standard SM-2MR (Block IIIA); Lockheed
   Martin Mk 4 VLS Launcher. Raytheon RAM Mk
   31 Mk 1 with Mk 116 Block 1 missiles.
Guns: 1 - United Defense 5 in (127 mm)/62 Mk
   45 Mod 4. 1 – OTOBreda 3 in (76 mm)/62; 1 –
   Signaal Goalkeeper 30 mm, 7-barrels.
Decoys: 4 chaff launchers

RADARS

Air search –Raytheon SPS-49(V)5
Surface search –Signaal MW08
Fire control – 2 Signaal STIR 240

Sonars: DSQS-23, hull-mounted, active
   search/attack. Daewoo Telecom towed array.

AIR SUPPORT

Helicopters: 1 Westland Super Lynx Mk 99.

KEY RECOGNITION FEATURES

- High bow, continuous sweeping maindeck
  line from stem to stern.
- 5 in gun mounting in 'A' position.
- VLS SAM system in raised platform
  immediately after of forward gun.
- 3 in gun on raised platform immediately
  forward of superstructure.
- Slab sided bridge superstructure supporting
  pyramid mast with surface search radar.
- Wide, clear break between bridge
  superstructure and funnel (wider than
  'Okpo' class)
- Low squat tapering funnel aft of midships.
- Two pylons supporting air search and fire
  control radars atop aft superstructure.
- Helicopter landing deck aft ('Okpu' class
  landing deck above open quarterdeck).
Note: See entry on 'Okpu' class which has
   hull and superstructure similarities

OKPO (KDX-1)

EULJIMUNDOK

Sattler/Steele

Country: KOREA, SOUTH
Country of origin: KOREA, SOUTH
Ship type: DESTROYERS
Class: OKPO (KDX-1) (DDG)
Active: 3
Name (Pennant Number): KWANAGGAETO THE GREAT (DDG 971), EULJIMUNDOK (DDG 972), YANGMANCHUN (DDG 973)

SPECIFICATION
Displacement, full load, tons: 3,855.
Length, feet (metres): 444.2 (135.4).
Beam, feet (metres): 46.6 (14.2).
Draught, feet (metres): 13.8 (4.2).
Speed, knots: 30.
Range, miles: 4,000 at 18 kts.

ARMAMENT
Missiles: SSM – Harpoon (Block 1C) (2 quad). SAM – Raytheon Sea Sparrow Mk 48 Mod 2 VLS launcher
Guns: 1 - OTOBreda 5 in (127 mm)/54; 2 – Signaal Goalkeeper 30 mm, 7-barrels per mounting.
Decoys: 4 - CSEE Dagaie Mk 2 chaff launchers

RADARS
Air search –Raytheon SPS-49(V)5
Surface search –Signaal MW08
Navigation – Daewoo DTR 92 (SPS-55M)
Fire control – 2 Signaal STIR 180

Sonars: Atlas Elektronik DSQS-218Z hull-mounted, active search/attack. Daewoo Telecom towed array.

AIR SUPPORT
Helicopters: 1 Westland Super Lynx Mk 99.

KEY RECOGNITION FEATURES
- High bow, continuous sweeping maindeck line from stem to stern.
- 5 in gun mounting in 'A' position.
- VLS SAM system in raised platform immediately aft of forward gun.
- *No* 3 in turret forward of bridge as in KDX-2 class.
- CIWS mounting atop bridge
- Slab sided bridge superstructure supporting lattice mast with surface search radar atop, and navigation radar on forward gantry
- Clear break between bridge superstructure and funnel – narrower than KDX-2 class.
- Low squat tapering funnel aft of midships.
- Separate squat lattice mast supporting air search radar, and pylon with fire control radars atop aft superstructure.
- Helicopter deck above open quarterdeck.

Note: Hull and superstructure has similarities with KDX-2 class.

NETZAHUALCOYOTL

Country: SOUTH KOREA, MEXICO, PAKISTAN, TAIWAN

Country of origin: USA.

Ship type: DESTROYERS

Class: GEARING (FRAM I) (WU CHIN III CONVERSION) (DD)

Active: 5 (South Korea); 2 (Mexico); 1 (Pakistan, Maritime Safety Agency), 7 (Taiwan, Wu Chin III)

SOUTH KOREA – Name (Pennant Number):
JEONG BUK (ex-*Everett F Larson*) (DD 916 ex-DD 830), TAEJON (ex-*New*) (DD 919, ex-DD 818), KWANG JU (ex-*Richard E Kraus*) (DD 921 ex DD 849); KANG WON (ex-*William R Rush*) (DD 922 ex-DD 714); JEON JU (ex-*Rogers*) (DD 925 ex-DD 876).

MEXICO – Name (Pennant Number):
ILHUICAMINA (ex-*Quetzalcoatl*, ex-*Vogelgesang*) (E 10, ex-E 03, ex-DD 862); NETZAHUALCOYOTL (ex-*Steinaker*) (E 11, ex-E 04, ex-DD 863).

PAKISTAN (Maritime Safety Agency) – Name (Pennant Number): NAZIM (ex-*Tughril*, ex-*Henderson*), (D 156, ex-D 167, ex-DD 785).

KEY RECOGNITION FEATURES

- Blunt bow, low freeboard.
- Continuous maindeck from stem to stern.
- 5 in twin gun mounting ('A' position). (OTO MELARA 3in (76 mm) in Taiwan conversions).
- Twin funnels sloping aft with distinctive black tapered tops.
- Large lattice mainmast astride forward funnel, smaller tapering mast aft of after funnel.

Note: The general recognition features above apply to all of the class. There are too many variants to be covered in this publication. Further details can be obtained from *Jane's Fighting Ships* yearbook.

Note 2: Remaining Pakistan unit now with Maritime Safety Agency, with hull painted white with a distinctive diagonal blue and red band, together with the letters: 'MSA.'

Gearing

TAIWAN – Name (Pennant Number): Wu Chin III – CHIEN YANG (ex-*James E Kyes*) (912 ex-DD 787), LIAO YANG (ex-*Hanson*) (921, ex-DD 832), SHAO YANG (ex-*Hollister*) (929 ex-DD 788), TE YANG (ex-*Sarsfield*) (925, ex-DD 837)), CHEN YANG (ex-*Johnston*) (928 ex-DD 821), SHEN YANG (ex-*Power*) (923 ex-DD 839), YUN YANG (ex-*Hamner*) (927 ex-DD 718).

SPECIFICATION

Displacement, full load, tons: 3,540, (South Korea, Taiwan) 3,500, (Pakistan), 3,690 (Mexico).

Length, feet (metres): 390.5 (119). 390.2 (118.7), Mexican.

Beam, feet (metres): 41.2 (12.6), 41.9 (12.7) (Mexican).

Draught, feet (metres): 19 (5.8), 15 (4.6) (Mexican).

Speed, knots: 30 (South Korea), 15 (Mexico), 32 (Pakistan), 32.5 (Taiwan).

Range, miles: 5,800 at 15 kts. 6 080 at 15 kts (Taiwan)

ARMAMENT

Missiles: SSM McDonnell Douglas Harpoon (South Korean, 2 quad); 4 Hsiung Feng (quad) (Taiwan) SAM – General Dynamics Standard SM1-MR (2 triple; 2 twin), (Taiwan). A/S - Honeywell ASROC Mk 112 octuple launcher; payload Mk 46 torpedoes, (South Korea DD 925, Taiwan)

Note: No missiles fitted to Mexican ships and removed from Pakistani hull.

Guns: 4 - USN 5 in (127 mm)/38 (2 twin) Mk 38. (South Korea, Mexico). 2 - USN 5 in (127 mm)/38 Mk 38 (Pakistan). 1 - OTO MELARA 3 in (76 mm)/62. (Taiwan). 1 - GE/GD 20 mm Vulcan Phalanx Block 1, 6-barrel Mk 15, (South Korea, Pakistan, Taiwan) 2 - Bofors 40 mm/70. (Taiwan). USN/Bofors 40mm/56 (twin) (South Korea.) 1 - 57 mm/70 Mk 2 (Mexico). 4 or 6 - 12.7 mm machine-guns. (Taiwan).

Torpedoes: 6 - 324 mm US Mk 32 (2 triple) tubes. Honeywell Mk 46. (Not Mexican ships).

Depth charges: 1 - Mk IX rack. (South Korean only)

Decoys: 2 - Plessey Shield 6-barrel fixed chaff launchers (Pakistan). 4 - Kung Fen 6 - 16-tubed chaff launchers. Mk T-6 Fanfare torpedo decoy. (Taiwanese ships).

RADARS

Air search – SPS-40 (South Korean, Mexican ships). Signaal DA08, (Taiwan with DA05 aerial) Westinghouse SPS-29 (Mexico).

Surface search - Raytheon SPS-10/SPS-58. Kelvin Hughes 17/9 (Mexican).

Navigation – Marconi LN66 (Mexican). KH 1007, (Pakistan).

Fire control – Western Electric Mk 12/12 (Mexican ships), Western Electric Mk 25 (South Korean, Pakistani ships), Signaal STIR (Standard and 76mm) (Taiwan). Westinghouse W-160, (Bofors guns) (Taiwan).

Sonars: Sangamo SQS-23, hull-mounted, (South Korea); Raytheon SQS-23H; hull-mounted. (Taiwan). No sonar in Mexican and Pakistani ships.

AIR SUPPORT

Helicopters: Aerospatiale SA 316B Alouette III (marine support) or Westland Super Lynx Mk 99/100, (ASW/ASV) for DD 925. MBB BO 105CB (Mexico). McDonnell Douglas MD 500 (ASW) (Taiwan).

Fletcher

CUITLAHUAC

Country: MEXICO

Country of origin: USA

Ship type: DESTROYERS (DD)

Class: FLETCHER

Active: 1

Name (Pennant Number): CUITLAHUAC (ex-*John Rodgers*) (E 01, ex-E 02, ex-F 2, ex-DD 574).

SPECIFICATION

Displacement, tons: 2,100 standard, 3,050 full load.

Length, feet (metres): 376.5 (114.8).

Beam, feet (metres): 39.4 (12).

Draught, feet (metres): 18 (5.5).

Speed, knots: 12.

ARMAMENT

Guns: 5 - USN 5 in (127 mm)/38 Mk 30. 10 - Bofors 40 mm/60 (5 twin) Mk 2.

Torpedoes: 5 - 21 in (533 mm) (quin) tubes.

RADARS

Surface search – Kelvin Hughes 17/9

Navigation – Kelvin Hughes 14/9

Fire control – Western Electric Mk 25.

KEY RECOGNITION FEATURES

- High bow, sweeping maindeck from stem to stern .
- 5 in single gun mountings in 'A', 'B', 'X' and 'Y' positions with additional mounting, abaft aft funnel.
- Squat, square bridge superstructure with fire control aerial atop.
- Thin pole mast just aft of superstructure.
- Two black-topped funnels, forward and aft of midships.
- Torpedo tubes between funnels

De Zeven Provincien

DE RUYTER

Royal Netherlands Navy

Country: NETHERLANDS
Country of origin: NETHERLANDS
Ship Type: DESTROYERS
Class: DE ZEVEN PROVINCIEN (DDG)
Active: 1
Building: 3
Name (Pennant Number): DE ZEVEN PROVINCIEN
(F 801), DE RUYTER (F 802), TROMP (F 803),
EVERTSEN (F 804).

SPECIFICATION

Displacement, full load, tons: 6,048.
Length, feet (metres): 473.1 (144.2) oa.
Beam, feet (metres): 61.7 (18.8).
Draught, feet (metres): 17.1 (5.2).
Speed, knots: 28.
Range: 5,000 at 18 kts.

ARMAMENT

Missiles: SSM – 8 Harpoon in VL tubes behind
mainmast. SAM – Mk 41 VLS Standard SM2-MR
Block IIIA, Evolved Sea Sparrow.
Guns: 1 – OTOBreda 5 in (127 mm)/54. 2 Signaal
Goalkeeper 30mm. 2 – Oerlikon 20 mm.
Torpedoes: 4 - 323 mm (2 twin) tubes, Mk 32
Mod 9 fixed launchers with Mk 46 Mod 6
torpedoes.
Decoys: 4 -SRBOC Mk 36 chaff launchers. Nixie
towed torpedo decoy.

RADARS:

Air search –Signaal SMART L
Air/surface search –Signaal APAR
Surface search – Signaal Scout.
Sonars: STN Atlas DSQS-24C bow-mounted,
active search/attack.

AIR SUPPORT

Helicopters: 1 NFH 90/Lynx (ASW)

KEY RECOGNITION FEATURES

- Continuous sweeping maindeck line from
  stem to stern with open quarterdeck below.
- 5 in gun mounting in 'A' position
- Rounded, smooth slab-sided bridge
  structure
- Squat, stumpy pyramid mast atop bridge
  with air/surface search and fire control
  radars.
- SATCOMS on wings off mainmast.
- Very low 'V' shaped twin funnels
- Slab sided helicopter hanger aft with
  landing deck above open quarterdeck.
- CIWS atop bridge, forward of mainmast,
  and on aft hanger, just above doors.
- Air search radar atop pylon above hanger.

Ferré (Daring)

FERRÉ

Country:	PERU
Country of origin:	UK
Ship Type:	DESTROYERS
Class:	DARING (DDG)
Active:	1

Name (Pennant Number): FERRÉ (ex-*Decoy*),
(DM 74).

SPECIFICATION

Displacement, tons: 2,800 standard, 3,600 full
load.
Length, feet (metres): 390 (118.9).
Beam, feet (metres): 43 (13.1).
Draught, feet (metres): 18 (5.5).
Speed, knots: 32.
Range, miles: 3,000 at 20 kts.

ARMAMENT

Missiles: SSM – 8 Aerospatiale MM 38 Exocet.
Guns: 6 - (3 twin) Vickers 4.5 in (114 mm)/45 Mk
5. 4 - Breda 40mm/70 (2 twin).

RADARS

Air/surface search – Plessey AWS 1.
Surface search – Racal Decca TM 1226.
Fire control – Selenia RTN 10X.

AIR SUPPORT

Helicopters: Platform only.

KEY RECOGNITION FEATURES

- Main deck break aft of bridge
  superstructure.
- 4.5 in guns at 'A', 'B' and 'Y' positions.
- Slim pyramid mast behind bridge with
  air/surface search radar, with pole mast
  atop.
- Single slim funnel well aft of midships.
- Exocet SSM launchers aft of funnel.
- Raised helicopter landing platform at stern.

MARASESTI   *H & L van Ginderen Collection*

Country: ROMANIA	
Country of origin: ROMANIA	
Ship Type: DESTROYERS	
Class: MARASESTI (FFG)	
Active: 1	
Name (Pennant Number): MARASESTI (ex-*Muntenia*) (111)	

SPECIFICATION

Displacement, full load, tons: 5,790.
Length, feet (metres): 474.4 (144.6).
Beam, feet (metres): 48.6 (14.8).
Draught, feet (metres): 23 (7).
Speed, knots: 27.

ARMAMENT

Missiles: SSM – 8 SS-N-2C Styx.
Guns: 4 - USSR 3 in (76 mm)/60, (2 twin).
4 - 30mm/65 6-barrelled.
Torpedoes: 6 - 21 in (533 mm) (2 triple) tubes. Russian 53-65.
A/S mortars: 2 - RBU 6000 12-tubed trainable launchers.
Decoys: 2 - PK 16 chaff launchers.

RADARS

Air/surface search – Strut Curve.
Surface search – Plank Shave.

Navigation – Nayada (MR 212).
Fire control – 2 Drum Tilt. Hawk Screech.
Sonars: Hull-mounted, active search/attack.

AIR SUPPORT

Helicopters: 2 IAR-316B Alouette III (ASW)

KEY RECOGNITION FEATURES

- Continuous sweeping maindeck line from stem to stern with open quarterdeck below. Small break at forward SSM position.
- 3 in gun mountings in 'A' and 'B' positions with Styx SS-N-2C SSM in box-like angled launchers alongside 'B' position and facing astern at aft end of superstructure.
- Tall, box-like bridge superstructure topped by short lattice mast and, immediately above bridge, Hawk Screech fire control radar on raised platform.
- Second lattice mast, aft, on raised platform, forward of square, tapering funnel.

Note: Reclassified a frigate in April, 2001 to conform with NATO classifications.

SMETLIVY

Country: RUSSIA, INDIA, POLAND
Country of origin: RUSSIA
Ship type: DESTROYERS (DDG)
Class: KASHIN (TYPE 61) KASHIN II (RAJPUT, TYPE 61ME), MODIFIED KASHIN (TYPE 61M/61MP), (DDG).
Active: 1 Russia (Kashin Type 61/Modified Kashin Type 61M).
5 India (Kashin II/Rajput class).
1 Poland (Modified Kashin Type 61MP).
RUSSIA – Name (pennant Number): – SMETLIVY, (810).
INDIA – Name (Pennant Number): RAJPUT (ex-*Nadiozny*) (D 51), RANA (ex-*Gubitielny*), (D 52) RANJIT (ex-*Lovky*), (D 53), RANVIR (ex-*Twiordy*), (D 54), RANVIJAY (ex-*Tolkovy*), (D 55).
POLAND – Name (Pennant Number): WARSZAWA (ex-*Smely*), (271).

SPECIFICATION

Displacement, tons: 4,010 standard, 4,750 full load (Kashin); 4,974 (mod. Kashin/Kashin II).
Length, feet (metres): 472.4 (144), 480.5 (146.5) Indian.
Beam, feet (metres): 57.8 (15.8).
Draught, feet (metres): 15.4 (4.7).

KEY RECOGNITION FEATURES

- Russian and Polish units -
- High bow sloping down to stern.
- 3 in gun in 'A' position and SA-N-1 Goa SAM in 'B' position.
- Owl Screech fire control dish immediately forward of bridge
- Two isolated, massive lattice masts, with 'Head Net C' air/surface radar aerial atop forward mast.
- Two slab-sided squat funnels, aft well back from midships.
- Gun mounting in 'Y' position, SA-N-1 SAM in 'X' position.
- Low helicopter landing platform on quarterdeck.
- Angled, tubular Styx tubular launchers, facing astern, port and starboard, alongside aft funnel.

Note: Indian units, as Russian except for – Helicopter hangar replaces 'Y' position gun mounting. SS-N-2D Mod 2 Styx tubular launchers forward of bridge. Aft Owl Screech fire control director omitted.

Kashin

Speed, knots: 32. (35, Indian).
Range, miles: 4,000 at 18 kts. (4,500 at 18 kts., Indian).

ARMAMENT

Missiles: SSM - 4 SS-N-2C Styx (Russian unit *Sderzhanny* and Polish); 8 Zvezda SS-N-25 (Kh 35 Uran) (2 quad) in Russian hull, *Smetlivy*.4 SS-N-2D Mod 2 Styx (Indian). SAM - 2 SA-N-1 Goa twin launchers.

Guns: 2 or 4 - 3 in (76 mm)/60 (1 or 2 twin, Russian hulls) AK 762 (1 twin only in Indian ships); 4 - 30 mm/65 AK 630 6-barrel, in *Sderzhanny* and *Warszawa* (8 with 4 twin AK 230, in Indian ships, *Raijput, Rana* and *Ranjit,* and 4 – 30 mm/65 ADG 630 in *Ranvir* and *Ranvijay*).

Torpedoes: 5 - 21 in (533 mm) (quin tubes).

A/S mortars: 2 - RBU 6000 12-tubed trainable, (RBU 1000 6-tubed in *Smetlivy*).

Decoys: 4 - PK 16 chaff launchers. 2 towed torpedo decoys in Russian and Polish hulls.

RADARS

Air / surface search – 'Head Net C', Big Net. ('Big Net A' in Indian ships for air search).

Navigation – 2 Don 2/Don Kay/Palm Frond, (Russian); 2 SRN 7453 and 1 SRN 207 (Polish); 2 Don Kay (Indian).

Fire control – 2 Peel Group (SA-N-1); Owl Screech (guns); 2 Bass Tilt (30 mm guns, in Indian D 54-55). (Drum Tilt in Indian D 51-53).

Sonar: Bull Nose (MGK 336) or Wolf Paw, hull-mounted, active search/attack. Mare Tail VDS or Vega in *Smetlivy* and Indian hulls. Vcheda MG 311 (Indian ships)

AIR SUPPORT

Helicopters: Platform only (Russian and Polish) 1 Kamov Ka-27/28 Helix (ASW), (Indian).

Sovremenny

BESPOKOINY

Country: RUSSIA, CHINA
Country of origin: RUSSIA
Ship type: DESTROYERS
Class: SOVREMENNY (SARYCH) (TYPE 956/956A) (DDG)

Active:	4 Russia
	2 China
Building:	2 China
Planned:	2 China.

RUSSIA – Name (Pennant Number): BURNY (778), BESPOKOINY (620), NASTOYCHIVY (ex-*Moskowski Komsomolets*) (610), BESSTRASHNY (434).

CHINA – Name (Pennant Number): HANGZHOU (ex-*Vazhny*, ex-*Yekaterinburg*),(136, ex-698), FUZHOU (ex-*Alexander Nevsky*), (137).

SPECIFICATION

Displacement, tons: 6,600 standard, 7,940 full load.
Length, feet (metres): 511.8 (156).
Beam, feet (metres): 56.8 (17.3).
Draught, feet (metres): 21.3 (6.5).
Speed, knots: 32.
Range, miles: 4,000 at 18 kts

ARMAMENT

Missiles: SSM - Raduga SS-N-22 Sunburn (Moskit 3M-80E) (2 quad) launchers. (From *Bespokoiny* onwards, the launchers are longer and fire a modified missile). SAM - 2 - SA-N-7 Gadfly 3K 90 (Uragan). (From *Bespokoiny* onwards, the same launcher is used for the SA-N-17 Grizzly/SA-N-12 Yezh.
Guns: 4 - 130 mm/70 AK 130 (2 twin). 4 - 30 mm/65 6-barrel AK 630.
Torpedoes: 4 - 21 in (533 mm) (2 twin) tubes.
A/S mortars: 2 - RBU 1000 6-barrelled.
Mines: Rails for up to 40.

Decoys: 8 - PK 10 and 2 - PK 2 chaff launchers.

RADARS

Air search - Top Plate 3D.
Surface search - 3 Palm Frond.
Fire control - 6 Front Dome. (SA-N-7/17); Kite Screech, (130 mm guns); 2 Bass Tilt, (30 mm guns)
Sonars: Bull Horn (MGK-335 Platina) and Whale Tongue ; hull-mounted active search/attack.

AIR SUPPORT

Helicopters: 1 Kamov Ka-27PL Helix. (ASW). 2 Harbin Zhi-9A Haitun (Dauphin 2) or Kamov KA-28 Helix, (ASW/ASV) (Chinese units)

KEY RECOGNITION FEATURES

- High bow. Sweeping maindeck aft to break at bridge where tubular quad SSM launchers are fitted, port and starboard.
- 130 mm/70 gun mounting ('A' position).
- SA-N-7 Gadfly SAM launcher ('B' mounting position).
- Prominent Band Stand weapons control dome atop bridge.
- High forward superstructure with large enclosed mainmast at its after end. Large distinctive Top Plate air search radar aerial atop.
- Single, large, square funnel just aft of midships.
- Lattice aftermast immediately aft of funnel with telescopic helicopter hangar below.
- Small raised flight deck forward of aft SA-N-7 SAM launcher.
- 130 mm/70 gun mounting ('Y' position).

Udaloy

ADMIRAL LEVCHENKO

Country: RUSSIA
Country of origin: RUSSIA
Ship type: DESTROYERS
Class: UDALOY (FREGAT) (TYPE 1155) (DDG)
Active: 7
Name (Pennant Number):ADMIRAL TRIBUTS
(564), MARSHAL SHAPOSHNIKOV (543),
SEVEROMORSK (ex-*Simferopol*, ex-*Marshal
Budienny*) (619), ADMIRAL LEVCHENKO, (ex-
Kharbarovsk) (605), ADMIRAL VINOGRADOV (572),
ADMIRAL KHARLAMOV (678), ADMIRAL
PANTELEYEV(648).

Note: *Kulakov* in refit since 1990 but may return
to service in 2002/3.

SPECIFICATION

Displacement tons: 6,700 standard, 8,500 full
load.
Length, feet (metres): 536.4 (163.5).
Beam, feet (metres): 63.3 (19.3).
Draught, feet (metres): 24.6 (7.5).
Speed, knots: 29.
Range, miles: 7,700 at 18 kts.

ARMAMENT

Missiles: SAM - 8 SA-N-9 Gauntlet (Klinok)
vertical launchers. A/S – 2 Raduga SS-N-14
Silex (Rastrub) quad launchers; payload
nuclear or Type E53-72 torpedo.
Guns: 2 - 3.9 in (100 mm)/59. 4 - 30 mm/65 AK
630 6-barrelled.
Torpedoes: 8 - 21 in (533 mm) (2 quad) tubes.
A/S mortars: 2 - RBU 6000 12-tubed, trainable.
Mines: Rails for 26 mines.
Decoys: 2- PK 2 and 8 -PK 10 chaff launchers. US
Prairie Masker type noise reduction.

RADARS

Air search - Strut Pair, Top Plate 3D.
Surface search - 3 Palm Frond.
Fire Control - 2 Eye Bowl, (SS-N-14); 2 Cross
Sword, (SA-N-9); Kite Screech, (100 mm guns);
2 Bass Tilt, (30 mm guns).
Sonars: Horse Jaw (Polinom) hull-mounted, active
search/attack. Mouse Tail VDS, active search.

AIR SUPPORT

Helicopters: 2 Kamov Ka-27 Helix A (ASW).

KEY RECOGNITION FEATURES

- High bow with sweeping maindeck aft to
  break at after funnel.
- 3.9 in gun mountings ('A' and 'B' positions).
- SA-N-9 Gauntlet SAM VLS launcher set
  into the ship's structure on the forecastle
  and forward of helicopter hangers.
- 2 SS-N-14 Silex A/S missile square, tubular
  quad launchers on maindeck level, tucked
  beneath bridge, port and starboard.
- Two square section, twin funnels side by
  side with tapered RAD-HAZ screens at after
  end.
- Two lattice masts forward and aft of
  funnels. After mainmast is larger with Top
  Plate air search radar aerial atop.
- Smaller pyramid mast on bridge roof
  supports Kite Screech fire control radar.
- Large crane derrick aft of after funnels.
- Two hangars set side by side with inclined
  elevating ramps to the flight deck.
Note: UDALOY II class (1 unit).

Udaloy II

ADMIRAL CHABANENKO

Country: RUSSIA
Country of origin: RUSSIA
Ship type: DESTROYERS
Class: UDALOY II (FREGAT) (TYPE 1155.1) (DDG)
Active: 1
Name (Pennant Number): ADMIRAL
CHABANENKO (650, ex-437).

SPECIFICATION

Displacement, tons: 7,700 standard,
  8,900 full load.
Length, feet (metres): 536.4 (163.5).
Beam, feet (metres): 63.3 (19.3).
Draught, feet (metres): 24.6 (7.5).
Speed, knots: 28.
Range, miles: 4,000 at 18 kts.

ARMAMENT

Missiles: SSM – Raduga SS-N-22 Sunburn (3M-
  82 Moskit) (2 quad launchers). SAM - SA-N-9
  Gauntlet (Klinok) VLS. SAM/guns – 2 CADS-N-1
  (Kashtan) each with 30 mm 6-barrel gun,
  combined with SA-N-11 (Grisson) SAMs and
  Hot Flash/Hot Spot fire control radar/optronic
  director. A/S – Novator SS-N-15 Starfish, Type
  40 torpedo.
Guns: 2 - 130 mm/70 (twin) AK 130.
Torpedoes: 8 - 21 in (533 mm) (2 quad tubes).
A/S mortars: 2 - RBU 6000, 12-tubed trainable.
Decoys: 8 - PK 10 and 2 - PK 2 chaff launchers.

RADAR

Air search – Strut Pair II; Top Plate 3D.
Surface search – 3 Palm Frond.
Fire control – 2 Cross Swords (SA-N-9); Kite
  Screech (100 mm gun).
Sonars: Horse Jaw (Polinom) hull-mounted, active
  search/attack; Horse Tail VDS, active search.

AIR SUPPORT

Helicopters: 2 Kamov KA-27 Helix A (ASW).

KEY RECOGNITION FEATURES

- As UDALOY I class, except –
- 130 mm gun only in 'A' position.
- PK 2 chaff launchers in place of gun
  mounting in 'B' position.
- Full length of SS-N-22 Sunburn SSM
  tubular quad launchers exposed, port and
  starboard, below bridge.
- Torpedo tubes protected by hinged flap in
  hull above chine aft of second funnel.
- Crane deck forward of deck break, which is
  further aft than Udaloy I.

Type 42 (Batch 1 and 2)

Country: UNITED KINGDOM, ARGENTINA
Country of origin: UK
Ship type: DESTROYERS
Class: UK - TYPE 42 (BATCH 1 and 2)
ARGENTINA - HERCULES (DDG)
Active: 7 UK, 1 Argentina + 1 Reserve.
UK - Batch 1; Name (Pennant Number):
NEWCASTLE (D 87), GLASGOW (D 88),
CARDIFF (D 108)
Batch 2; Name (Pennant Number): EXETER (D
89), SOUTHAMPTON (D 90), NOTTINGHAM (D 91),
LIVERPOOL (D 92)
ARGENTINA - Name (Pennant Number):
HERCULES (D 1, ex-28), SANTISIMA TRINIDAD* (D 2).
*In reserve.

SPECIFICATION
Displacement, full load, tons: 4,100.
Length, feet (metres): 412 (125) oa.
Beam, feet (metres): 47 (14.3).
Draught, feet (metres): 19 (5.8) (screws).
Speed, knots: 29.
Range, miles: 4,000 at 18 kts.

ARMAMENT
Missiles: SSM - 4 Aerospatiale MM 38 Exocet
(Argentine ships only). SAM - British Aerospace
Sea Dart twin launcher. (Mk 30, Argentine
ships, non-operational).
Guns: Vickers 4.5 in (114 mm)/55 Mk 8. 2 or 4 -
Oerlikon/BMARC 20 mm GAM-BO1. (2 Oerlikon
20 mm only in Argentine ships). 2 - Oerlikon
20 mm Mk 7A (in those British ships with only
2 GAM BO1). 2 GE/GD 20 mm Vulcan Phalanx
Mk 15 (British ships only).
Torpedoes: 6 - 324 mm Plessey STWS Mk 3 (2
triple) tubes. 6 - 324 mm ILAS 3 (2 triple tubes)
in Argentine ships.
Decoys: 4 - Marconi Sea Gnat 130/102 mm 6-
barrel launchers or Barricade IR decoy
launchers and Corvus (Argentine ships.)
Graseby Type 182 or SLQ-25A towed torpedo
decoy. Graseby GI 738 towed torpedo decoy in
Argentine ships.

RADARS
Air search - Marconi/Signaal Type 1022. (Marconi
Type 965P, Argentine ships)
Air/surface search - Plessey Type 996.

CARDIFF

Surface search - Marconi Type 992Q (Argentine
ships).
Navigation - Kelvin Hughes Type 1007 and Racal
Decca Type 1008.
Fire control - 2 Marconi Type 909 (Argentine) or
9091.
Sonars: Ferranti Type 2050 or Plessey Type 2016;
hull-mounted. Graseby Type 184M hull-
mounted, active search/attack (Argentine).
Kelvin Hughes Type 162M.

AIR SUPPORT
Helicopters: 1 Westland Lynx HMA 3/8.
(ASV/ASW). 1 Aerospatiale SA 319B Alouette III
or 1 Sea King. (ASW/ASV) Argentine ships.

KEY RECOGNITION FEATURES

- Continuous maindeck line from stem to stern, high freeboard.
- 4.5 in gun mounting half way between bows and bridge.
- Sea Dart SAM twin launcher immediately forward of bridge.
- High forward superstructure with large Type 909/9091 fire control radar dome atop.
- Large single, black-capped funnel with sloping after end, just aft of midships.
- Large lattice Type 1022 air search radar aerial at after end of forward superstructure.
- Tall, black-topped pole foremast forward of funnel.
- Tall, enclosed, black-topped mainmast aft of funnel, supporting surface search radar aerial.
- Hangar superstructure at forward end of flight deck with large fire Type 909 control radar dome at forward end.
- Open quarterdeck below after end of flight deck.
- Argentine ships –
- Most obvious differences are Type 965P air search bedstead radar aerial atop forward superstructure, large black exhausts on side of funnel.
- Exocet SSM launchers outboard of funnels.
- Aft fire control radome missing.

Note: See Type 42 Batch 3 in UK service.

EDINBURGH

Country: UNITED KINGDOM
Country of origin: UK
Ship type: DESTROYERS
Class: TYPE 42 (BATCH 3) (DDG)
Active: 4
Name (Pennant Number): MANCHESTER (D 95),
GLOUCESTER (D 96), EDINBURGH (D 97),
YORK (D 98)

SPECIFICATION

Displacement, full load, tons: 4,675.
Length, feet (metres): 462.8 (141.1) oa.
Beam, feet (metres): 49 (14.9).
Draught, feet (metres): 19 (5.8) (screws).
Speed, knots: 30+.
Range, miles: 4,000 at 18 kts.

ARMAMENT

Missiles: SAM - British Aerospace Sea Dart twin
launcher.
Guns: Vickers 4.5 in (114 mm)/55 Mk 8. 2 or 4 -
Oerlikon/BMARC 20 mm GAM-BO1. 2 -Oerlikon
20 mm Mk 7A (in those with only 2 GAM-BO1)
2 - GE/GD 20 mm Vulcan Phalanx Mk 15.
Torpedoes: 6 - 324 mm STWS Mk 2 (2 triple)
tubes. Marconi Stingray.
Decoys: 4 - Sea Gnat 130/102 mm 6-barrel
launchers. Graseby Type 182 or SLQ-25A towed
torpedo decoys.

RADARS

Air search - Marconi/Signaal Type 1022.
Air/surface search - Plessey Type 996.
Navigation - Kelvin Hughes Type 1007 and Racal
Decca Type 1008.
Fire control - 2 Marconi Type 909 Mod 1.
Sonars: Ferranti/Thomson Type 2050 or Plessey
Type 2016; hull-mounted.

AIR SUPPORT

Helicopters: 1 Westland Lynx HMA 3/8.
(ASV/ASW).

KEY RECOGNITION FEATURES

Note: See also Type 42 Batch 1 and 2 in
Argentine and UK service.
• Extremely long forecastle, some 50 ft more
than UK Type 42 Batches 1 and 2.
Otherwise very similar to Batch 1 and 2 of
the class.
• Stretched Batch 3s are fitted with a
strengthening beam on each side which
increases width by 2 feet.
• Break in superstructure forward of funnel.

Daring

DARING (Computer graphic)

Country: UNITED KINGDOM
Country of origin: UK
Ship type: DESTROYERS
Class: DARING (DDG)
Building: 6
Planned: 6
Name (Pennant Number): DARING (D 32),
DAUNTLESS (D 33), DIAMOND (D 34), DRAGON (D
35), DEFENDER (D 36), DUNCAN (D 37).

SPECIFICATION

Displacement, full load, tons: 7,350.
Length, feet (metres): 500.1 oa (152.4).
Beam, feet (metres): 69.6 (21.2).
Draught, feet (metres): 17.4 (5.3) (screws).
Speed, knots: 29.
Range, miles: 7,000 at 18 kts.

ARMAMENT

Missiles: SSM – Space for Harpoon (2 quad). SAM
  – DCN Sylver A 50 VLS, Aster 15 and Aster 30..
Guns: Vickers 4.5 in (114 mm)/55 Mk 8 Mod 1. 2
  - 20 mm Vulcan Phalanx CIWS . 2 -30 mm.
Decoys: 4 chaff/IR launchers. SSTD torpedo
  defence.

RADARS

Air/surface search –Signaal/Marconi S1850M
Surveillance/Fire control – BAE Systems Sampson.
Sonars: Ultra MFS-7000.

AIR SUPPORT

Helicopters: 1 Westland Lynx HMA 3/8 or EH
  Industries' EH 101 Merlin HM 1. (ASV/ASW).

KEY RECOGNITION FEATURES

- Extremely long forecastle with 4.5 in gun
  'A' position, with, further aft, raised area
  housing Sylver VLS SAM.
- Space in 'B' position for Harpoon SSM
  launchers.
- Slab-sided superstructure forward of
  funnel, with very prominent and tall
  enclosed pyramidal mast with Sampson
  surveillance and fire control radome atop
  with SATCOM domes on sponsons to port
  and starboard.
- Small tapering funnel.
- Break in superstructure with CIWS
  mounting.
- After of funnel, slender enclosed tapering
  mast, topped by thin pole mast.
- Prominent air/surface search radar on aft
  superstructure.

Note: Some details speculative.
Note 2: Later units may be fitted with 155
  mm gun.

Arleigh Burke

Country: UNITED STATES OF AMERICA
Country of origin: USA
Ship type: DESTROYERS
Class: ARLEIGH BURKE (FLIGHTS I,II, IIA) - (AEGIS) (DDG).
Active: 28 (Flights I and II). 8 (Flight IIA)
Building: 15 (Flight IIA).
Planned: 13 (Flight IIA).

Flights I and II – Name (Pennant Number):
ARLEIGH BURKE (DDG 51), BARRY (ex-*John Barry*)(DDG 52), JOHN PAUL JONES (DDG 53), CURTIS WILBUR (DDG 54), STOUT (DDG 55), JOHN S McCAIN (DDG 56), MITSCHER (DDG 57), LABOON (DDG 58), RUSSELL (DDG 59), PAUL HAMILTON (DDG 60), RAMAGE (DDG 61), FITZGERALD (DDG 62), STETHEM (DDG 63), CARNEY (DDG 64), BENFOLD (DDG 65), GONZALEZ (DDG 66), COLE (DDG 67), THE SULLIVANS (DDG 68), MILIUS (DDG 69), HOPPER (DDG 70), ROSS (DDG 71), MAHAN (DDG 72), DECATUR (DDG 73), McFAUL (DDG 74), DONALD COOK (DDG 75), HIGGINS (DDG 76), O'KANE (DDG 77), PORTER (DDG 78).

Flight IIA – Name (pennant Number):
OSCAR AUSTIN (DDG 79), ROOSEVELT (DDG 80), WINSTON CHURCHILL (DDG 81), LASSEN (DDG 82), HOWARD (DDG 83), BULKELEY (DDG 84), McCAMPBELL (DDG 85), SHOUP (DDG 86), MASON (DDG 87), PREBLE (DDG 88), MUSTIN (DDG 89), CHAFFEE (DDG 90), PINCKNEY (DDG 91), MOMSEN (DDG 92), CHUNG-HOON (DDG 93), NITZE (DDG 94), JAMES E WILLIAMS (DDG 95), ____ (DDG 96), ____ (DDG 97), ____ (DDG 98), ____ (DDG 99), ____ (DDG 100), ____ (DDG 101).

STOUT

SPECIFICATION

Displacement, full load, tons: 8,422, (9,003 from DDG 72 and 9,238, Flight IIA).
Length, feet (metres): 504.5 (153.8) oa. (509.5, (155.3) oa, Flight IIA).
Beam, feet (metres): 66.9 (20.4).
Draught, feet (metres): 20.7 (6.3). (32.7 (9.9) sonar).
Speed, knots: 32.
Range, miles: 4,400 at 20 kts.

ARMAMENT

Missiles: SLCM - 56 GDC/Hughes Tomahawk.
SSM - 8 McDonnell Douglas Harpoon (2 quad).
SAM - GDC Standard SM-2MR Block 4. (SM-2ER in DDG 72 onwards and in Flight IIA). A/S – Loral ASROC VLA; payload Mk 46 Mod 5 Neartip torpedoes. 2 Lockheed Martin Mk 41 Vertical Launch Systems (VLS) for Tomahawk, Standard and ASROC.
Guns: 1- United Defense 5 in (127 mm)/54 Mk 45 Mod 1 (Mod 2 in DDG 79-80). 5 in (127 mm)/62 in DDG 81 onwards) 2 - GE/GD 20 mm Vulcan Phalanx 6-barrel Mk 15 in Flights I and II; 2 - Hughes 20 mm Vulcan Phalanx Mk 15 in Flight IIA.
Torpedoes: 6 - 324 mm Mk 32 Mod 14 (2 triple) tubes. Alliant Mod 46 Mod 5.
Decoys: 2 - Loral Hycor SRBOC 6-barrel fixed Mk 36, Mod 12. SLQ-25 Nixie torpedo decoy. NATO Sea Gnat SLQ-95 AEB, SLQ-39 chaff buoy.

RADARS

Air search/fire control - RCA SPY-1D, 3D.
Surface search - Norden DRS SPS-67(V)3.
Navigation - Raytheon SPS-64(V)9.
Fire control - 3 Raytheon/RCA SPG-62.

Sonars: Gould/Raytheon/GE SQQ-89(V)6; combines SQS-53C, bow-mounted active search/attack with SQR-19B passive towed array. (SQQ-89(V)10 in DDG 79 onwards).

AIR SUPPORT

Helicopters: Platform facilities to refuel/re-arm Sikorsky SH-60F (LAMPS III) (ASW). Hangar facilities for 2 SH-60B/F (LAMPS III) in DDG 79 onwards.

KEY RECOGNITION FEATURES

- High bow with sweeping maindeck aft to break down to flight deck.
- Only obvious armament on forecastle is 5 in gun mounting mid-way between bow and bridge.
- Missile VLS tubes situated between forward gun mounting and bridge and just forward of flight deck.
- High main superstructure with aft-sloping pole mainmast atop.
- Large twin funnels of unusual square section with black exhausts protruding at top. Funnels sited either side of midships.
- CIWS mountings on raised platform immediately forward of bridge and forward of Harpoon SSM launcher.
- Flight deck right aft.

Note: Helicopter hangars incorporated in Flight IIA version with extended transom to increase size of flight deck.

Note 2: Japan operates an improved Arleigh Burke class named 'Kongou' class. See Japanese entry.

Spruance

Country: UNITED STATES OF AMERICA
Country of origin: USA
Ship type: DESTROYERS
Class: SPRUANCE (DD/DDG)
Active: 21
Name (Pennant Number): SPRUANCE (DD 963),
PAUL F FOSTER (DD 964), KINKAID (DD 865),
ELLIOTT (DD 967), ARTHUR W RADFORD (DD 968),
PETERSON (DD 969), CARON (DD 970), DAVID R
RAY (DD 971), OLDENDORF (DD 972), JOHN
YOUNG (DD 973), O'BRIEN (DD 975), BRISCOE (DD
977), STUMP (DD 978), NICHOLSON (DD 982),
CUSHING (DD 985), O'BANNON (DD 987), THORN
(DD 988), DEYO (DD 989), FIFE (DD 991),
FLETCHER (DD 992), HAYLER (DD 997)

SPECIFICATION
Displacement, full load, tons: 8,040.
Length, feet (metres): 563.2 (171.7).
Beam, feet (metres): 55.1 (16.8).
Draught, feet (metres): 19 (5.8).
Speed, knots: 33.
Range, miles: 6,000 at 20 kts.

ARMAMENT
Missiles: SLCM/SSM - GDC Tomahawk. 8
    McDonnell Douglas Harpoon (2 quad).
    SAM - Raytheon GMLS Mk 29 octuple launcher,
    Sea Sparrow. GDC RAM quadruple launcher
    (being fitted to 12 hulls). A/S - Honeywell
    ASROC VLS can be fitted; payload Mk 46 Mod 5
    Neartip torpedoes.
Guns: 2 - FMC 5 in (127 mm)/54 Mk 45 Mod 0/1.
    2 - GE/GD 20 mm/76 6-barrel Mk 15 Vulcan
    Phalanx. 4 - 12.7 mm machine-guns.
Torpedoes: 6 - 324 mm Mk 32 (2 triple) tubes.
    Honeywell Mk 46.
Decoys: 4 - Loral Hycor SRBOC 6-barrel fixed Mk
    36. SLQ-39 chaff buoy. SLQ-25 Nixie torpedo
    decoy. Prairie Masker hull/blade rate noise
    suppression system.

RADARS
Air search - Lockheed SPS-40B/C/D (not in DD
    997). Raytheon SPS-49V (DD 997).
    Hughes Mk 23 TAS.
Surface search - ISC Cardion SPS-55.
Navigation – Raytheon SPS-64(V)9.
Fire control - Lockheed SPG-60. Lockheed SPQ-
    9A. Raytheon Mk 95.

CARON

Sonars: SQQ-89(V)6 including GE/Hughes SQS-
    53B/C; bow-mounted; Gould SQR-19 (TACTAS);
    passive towed array.

AIR SUPPORT
Helicopters: 2 Sikorsky SH-60B LAMPS III or 1
    Kaman SH-2G Seasprite.

KEY RECOGNITION FEATURES

- High bow, high freeboard, sweeping maindeck aft to break at flight deck.
- 5 in gun mounting on forecastle forward of A/S missile launcher and SSM or VLS tubes (on some).
- Unusually high and long main superstructure giving a slab-sided impression.
- Large, square section twin funnels just proud of superstructure, each with several exhausts protruding at the top. After funnel offset to starboard.
- Complex lattice foremast supporting various aerials immediately atop bridge roof.
- Large central, lattice mainmast between funnels supporting air search radar aerial.
- Raised flight deck immediately aft of superstructure.
- Sea Sparrow SAM box launcher just aft of flight deck with 5 in gun mounting ('Y' position). GDC RAM SAM launcher, starboard side, right aft, being fitted.
- 5 in mounting on quarterdeck.

Note: Modular construction makes these ships very similar to *Kidd* class.

Note 2: DD 968 fitted with 88 ft high Advanced Enclosed Mast Sensor System (AEMSS) in 1997, designed for greater stealth properties and to provide better environment for enclosed sensors.

FRIGATES

Koni

Country: ALGERIA, BULGARIA, LIBYA, YUGOSLAVIA
Country of origin: RUSSIA
Ship type: FRIGATES
Class: KONI I//II/III (TYPE 1159) (FF)
Active: 1 Bulgaria. 2 Libya (FFG)
BULGARIA – Name (Pennant Number): SMELI (ex-*Delfin*) (11).
LIBYA – Name (Pennant Number): AL HANI (F 212), AL QIRDABIYAH (F 213).
ALGERIA – Class: MOURAD RAIS (KONI II) (TYPE 1159.2) (FF)
Active: 3
Name (Pennant Number): MOURAD RAIS (901), RAIS KELLICH (902), RAIS KORFOU (903)
YUGOSLAVIA – Class: KONI (SPLIT AND KOTOR) CLASSES (FFG)

Active: 1 (Split/Koni). 2 (Kotor)
Name (Pennant Number): BEOGRAD (ex-*Split*) (31), KOTOR (33), NOVI SAD (ex-*Pula*) (34).

SPECIFICATION

Displacement, full load, tons: 1,900. (1,870 Yugoslavia).
Length, feet (metres): 316.3 (96.4). (317.3 (12.8), (Yugoslavia).
Beam, feet (metres): 41.3 (12.6). (42 (12.8), Yugoslavia).
Draught, feet (metres): 11.5 (3.5). (13.7 (4.2) Yugoslavia).
Speed, knots: 27.
Range, miles: 1,800 at 14 kts.

RADARS:
Air/surface search - Strut Curve. (Algeria, 901 and 902; Pozitiv–ME1.2 in 903).
Surface search - Plank Shave (Libya only).
Navigation - Don 2.
Fire control - Hawk screech.(Owl Screech in Yugoslav ships) Drum Tilt. Pop Group.
Sonars: Herkules (MG 322), or Bull Nose (Yugoslav 33 and 34). Hull-mounted.

RAIS KELLICH

ARMAMENT

Missiles: SSM - 4 SS-N-2C Styx. (Libyan (2 twin) and Yugoslav ships). (Not Algerian or Bulgarian units). SAM - SA-N-4 Gecko twin launcher.
Guns: 4 - 3 in (76 mm)/60 (2 twin). (1 mounting in Yugoslav 33 and 34). 4 - 30 mm/65 (2 twin).
Torpedoes: 4 - 533 mm (2 twin tubes, Algeria only) 4 – 406 mm, USET-95, Libya only.
A/S mortars: 2 - RBU 6000, 12-barrel, trainable. (1 RBU 6000, Libya only).
Depth charges: 2 racks. (Not Yugoslav ships).
Mines: Rails. Capacity 22. (20, Libya)
Decoys: 2 – PK 16 chaff launchers. (Algerian, Bulgarian, Cuban and Libyan units). 2 - Wallop Barricade double layer chaff launchers, (Yugoslav ships).

KEY RECOGNITION FEATURES
- High bow, sweeping maindeck line through to stern.
- 3 in gun twin mounting ('A' position).
- RBU 6000 A/S mortar in 'B' mounting position.
- Stepped main superstructure with enclosed mast at after end supporting Strut Curve air/surface or air search radar aerials.
- Single, squat funnel just aft of midships.
- Short enclosed pyramid mast just forward of funnel supporting Drum Tilt fire control radar aerial.
- SA-N-4 Gecko SAM launcher in 'X' position.
- 3 in gun twin mounting ('Y' position).
- Pop Group fire control director just forward of SAM launcher at aft end of superstructure.

Note: The above features apply to Algerian, Bulgarian and Cuban ships which could easily be confused. Obvious differences in Libyan ships are - forward end of superstructure removed to fit SS-N-2C SSM launcher and lattice mast fitted forward of Pop Group fire control director. Camouflage paint applied to Libyan ships in 1991. Algerian, Cuban and Libyan ships have extended deck housing aft of funnel.

Note 2: Last two Yugoslav units have SS-N-2C Styx in four launchers, two port and two starboard, facing forward alongside bridge superstructure and 'B' position. First has them aft of the funnel, facing astern. In the last pair, the funnel is considerably longer and the mainmast is of the lattice type.

D'Estienne d'Orves

COMMANDANT BLAISON

Country: ARGENTINA, FRANCE, TURKEY

Country of origin: FRANCE

Ship type: FRIGATES

Class: D'ESTIENNE D'ORVES (TYPE A69)/
DRUMMOND/BURAK (FFG)

Active: 3 Argentina (Drummond), 9 France,
6 Turkey

ARGENTINA – Name (pennant Number):
DRUMMOND (ex-*Good Hope*, ex-*Lieutenant de
Vaisseau le Hénaff*) (31, ex-F 789), GUERRICO (ex-
Transvaal, ex-*Commandant l'Herminier*) (32, ex-F
791), GRANVILLE (33).

FRANCE – Name (Pennant Number): LIEUTENANT
DE VAISSEAU LE HÉNAFF (F 789), LIEUTENANT DE
VAISSEAU LAVALLÉE (F 790), COMMANDANT
L'HERMINIER (F 791), PREMIER MAÎTRE L'HER (F
792), COMMANDANT BLAISON (F 793), ENSEIGNE
DE VAISSEAU JACOUBET (F 794), COMMANDANT
DUCUING (F 795), COMMANDANT BIROT (F 796),
COMMANDANT BOUAN (F 797)

TURKEY – Name (Pennant Number): BOZCAADA (ex-
Commandant de Pimodan) (F 500, ex-F 787),
BODRUM (ex-*Drogou*) (F 501, ex-F 783), BANDIRMA
(ex-*Quartier Maître Anquetil*) (F 502, ex-F 786),
BEYKOZ (ex-*d'Estienne d'Orves*) (F 503, ex-F 781),
BARTIN (ex-*Amyot d'Inville*) (F 504, ex-F 782), BAFRA
(ex-*Second Maître Le Bihan*) (F 505, ex-F 788).

Note: The French government has offered to lease
a ship of this class to the Philippines Navy.

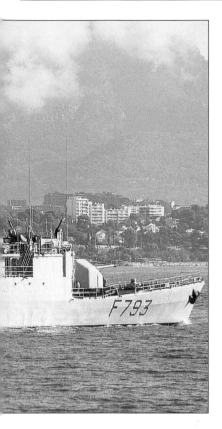

Syracuse SATCOM, (French and Turkish ships).

Guns: 1 - DCN/Cruesot-Loire 3.9 in (100 mm)/55 Mod 68 CADAM automatic. (Creusot-Loire 3.9 in (100mm)/55 Mod 1953 *Drummond* class.)2 Giat 20 mm. (2 Oerlikon 20 mm, 2 - Breda 40 mm/70 (twin) Argentine ships and 2 -12.7 machine-guns.).(4 - 12.7 mm machine-guns, French and Turkish ships).

Torpedoes: 4 - fixed tubes. ECAN L5. (French and Turkish ships). 6 - 324 mm Mk 32 (2 triple tubes), Whitehead A 244, Argentine ships.

A/S mortars: 1 - Creusot-Loire 375 mm Mk 54 6-tubed launcher. (French and Turkish ships only, removed from F 792-794, 796.)

Decoys: 2 - CSEE Dagaie 10-barrel trainable chaff/IR launchers. Nixie SLQ-25 torpedo decoy. (French and Turkish ships). CSEE Dagaie double mounting, chaff, decoys. Corvus sextuple chaff launchers, (Argentine ships).

RADARS

Air/surface search - Thomson-CSF DRBV 51A.
Navigation Racal Decca 1226.
Fire control - Thomson-CSF DRBC 32E.
Sonars: Thomson-Sintra DUBA 25; hull-mounted, active search/attack.

KEY RECOGNITION FEATURES
- Low profile forecastle with 3.9 in gun mounting ('A' position).
- Substantial forward superstructure.
- Single funnel just aft of midships with vertical forward and sloping after end.
- Mast and funnel combined with lattice mainmast atop.
- Break in deck level aft of funnel, with low deckhouse continuing in Argentine ships.
- Exocet SSM launchers, port and starboard, just aft of funnel.
- Ship's boat stowed in davits aft of SSM launchers.
- 375mm A/S mortar launcher atop after superstructure.40 mm/70 turret vice A/S mortar launcher on after superstructure in Argentine ships and Syracuse SATCOM dome in some French ships.
- Torpedo tubes in 'Y' position in *Drummond* class.

SPECIFICATION
Displacement, full load, tons: 1,170 (Argentina) 1,250, (French and Turkish hulls, 1,330 on later ships).
Length, feet (metres): 262.5 (80) (Argentina) 264.1 (80.5) (French and Turkish ships).
Beam, feet (metres): 33.8 (10.3).
Draught, feet (metres): 18 (5.5) (sonar).
Speed, knots: 23.
Range, miles: 4,500 at 15 kts.

ARMAMENT
Missiles: SSM - 4 Aerospatiale MM 40 (or 2 MM 38) Exocet. (4 MM 38, twin launchers, in Argentine and Turkish ships). SAM – Matra Simbad twin launcher for Mistral fitted aft of A/S mortar or

Espora

Without telescopic hangar

PARKER

Country: ARGENTINA
Country of origin: GERMANY
Ship type: FRIGATES
Class: ESPORA (MEKO 140) (FFG)
Active: 5
Building: 1
Name (Pennant Number): ESPORA (41), ROSALES
(42), SPIRO (43), PARKER (44), ROBINSON (45),
GOMEZ ROCA (46)

SPECIFICATION

Displacement, full load, tons: 1,790.
Length, feet (metres): 299.1 (91.2).
Beam, feet (metres): 36.4 (11.1).
Draught, feet (metres): 11.2 (3.4).
Speed, knots: 27.
Range, miles: 4,000 at 18 kts.

ARMAMENT

Missiles: SSM - 4 Aerospatiale MM 38 Exocet.
Guns: 1 - OTO MELARA 3 in (76 mm)/62 Compact.
    4 - Breda 40 mm/70 (2 twin). 2 - 12.7 mm
    machine-guns.
Torpedoes: 6 - 324 mm ILAS 3 (2 triple) tubes.
    Whitehead A 244/S.
Decoys: CSEE Dagaie double mounting.

RADARS

Air/surface search - Signaal DA045.

Navigation - Decca TM 1226.
Fire Control - Signaal WM28.
Sonars: Atlas Elektronik ASO-4; hull-mounted,
    active search/attack.

AIR SUPPORT

Helicopters: 1 Aerospatiale SA 319B Alouette III
    or Aerospatiale AS 555 Fennec (ASW) in 44-46.

KEY RECOGNITION FEATURES

- Blunt bow. Maindeck level raised for the
  length of the superstructure.
- 3 in gun mounting ('A' position).
- 40 mm/70 gun twin mountings ('B' and 'Y'
  positions).
- Exocet SSM ribbed launchers forward of
  40 mm/70 gun mounting on quarterdeck.
- Low integral funnel at after end of upper
  superstructure. Black exhaust protrudes
  from centre of main funnel.
- Tripod style mainmast atop after end of
  bridge structure supporting fire control
  radome.
- Raised flight deck.
- *Parker* and later ships fitted with a
  telescopic hangar.
Note: Scaled down Meko 360s.

ANZAC

Country: AUSTRALIA, GREECE, NEW ZEALAND, PORTUGAL, TURKEY

Country of origin: GERMANY

Ship type: FRIGATES

Class: ANZAC, HYDRA (MEKO 200HN) VASCO DA GAMA, YAVUZ, BARBAROS (MODIFIED MEKO 200) (FF/FFG)

Active: 4 Australia (ANZAC), 4 Greece (Hydra), 2 New Zealand (ANZAC), 3 Portugal (Vasco da Gama), 4 Turkey (Barbaros class), 4 Turkey (Yavuz class)

Building: 4 (Australia)

AUSTRALIA – Name (Pennant Number): ANZAC (150), ARUNTA (ex-*Arrernte*) (151) WARRAMUNGA (ex-*Warumungu*) (152), STUART (153), PARRAMATTA (154), BALLARAT (155), TOOWOOMBA (155), PERTH (157).

GREECE – Name (Pennant Number): HYDRA (F 452), SPETSAI (F 453), PSARA (F 454), SALAMIS (F 455).

NEW ZEALAND – Name (Pennant Number): TE KAHA (F 77), TE MANA (F 111).

PORTUGAL – Name (Pennant Number): VASCO DA GAMA (F 330), ALVARES CABRAL (F 331), CORTE REAL (F 332).

TURKEY (Barbaros class) – **Name (Pennant Number):** BARBAROS (F 244), ORUCREIS (F 245), SALIHREIS (F 246), KEMALREIS (F 247).

TURKEY (Yavuz class) – **Name (Pennant Number):** YAVUZ (F 240), TURGUTREIS (ex-*Turgut*) (F 241), FATIH (F 242), YILDIRIM (F 243).

SPECIFICATION

Displacement, full load, tons: 3,600 (Australia/NZ), 3,350 (Greece), 3,300 (Portugal). 3,380 (Turkish Barbaros class). 2,919 (Turkish Yavuz class)

Length, feet (metres): 380.3 (115.9), (Portugal). 382.9 (116.7), (Turkey). 383.9 (117), (Greece). 387.1 (118), (Australia/NZ/Turkish Barbaros classes). 378.9 (115.5), (Turkish Yavuz class).

Beam, feet (metres): 48.6 (14.8) (Greece, Turkey, Australia/NZ). 48.7 (14.8), (Portugal). 46.6 (14.2), (Turkish Yavuz class).

Draught, feet (metres): 13.5 (4.1), (Greece, Turkish Yavuz class). 14.1 (14.8), (Turkey). 14.3 (4.4), (Australia/NZ). 20 (6.1), (Portugal)

Speed, knots: 27 (Australia/NZ, Turkish Yavuz class) 31 (Greece). 32 (Portugal/Turkish Barbaros classes).

Range, miles: 4 100 at 16 kts (Greece). 4 100 at 18 kts. (Turkey). 6 000 at 18 kts. (Australia/NZ).

Meko 200

ARMAMENT

Missiles: SSM - 8 McDonnell Douglas Harpoon Block 1C (2 quad launchers) (Greece, Portugal, Turkey). (None in Australian/NZ units although this will be included in Phase 3 modernisation of Australian hulls). SAM - Raytheon NATO Sea Sparrow Mk 48 vertical launcher. (Greece). Mk 29 Mod 1 octuple launcher (Portugal). (Aspide; Turkish hulls, apart from F 246-247). Sea Sparrow RIM-7NP Mk 41 Mod 5 octuple VLS. (Australia/NZ), (Turkey F 246 and F 247, with Aspide missiles).

Guns: 1- FMC Mk 45 Mods 2/2A/4 5 in (127 mm)/54. (Australia/NZ, Greece, Turkey. Mod 1 in Turkish Yavuz class). Creusot-Loire 3.9 in (100 mm)/55 Mod 68 CADAM (Portugal). 2 - GD/GE Vulcan Phalanx 20 mm Mk 15 Mod 12. (Greece, 1 only in Australian and NZ| ships). 3 - Oerlikon-Contraves 25 mm Sea Zenith CIWS 4-barrels. (Turkish ships). 2 - 12.7 mm machine-guns, Australian hulls.

Torpedoes: 6 - 324 mm Mk 32 Mod 5 (2 triple) tubes. Honeywell Mk 46 Mod 5 Neartip.

Decoys: SRBOC 6-barrelled Mk 36 Mod 1/2 (Also, Nulka quad expendable decoy launchers, Australian/NZ ships only). SLQ-25 Nixie torpedo decoy. 2 Loral Hycor 6-tubed fixed Mk 36, (Portugal, Turkish hulls).

RADARS

Air search – Raytheon SPS-49(V)8 (Australia/NZ). Signaal MW08, 3D. (Greek, Portuguese ships). Siemens/Plessey AWS 9 (Turkish Barbaros class). Signaal DA08 (Turkish Yavuz class)

Air/surface search – CelsiusTech 9LV 453 TIR (Australia/NZ). Signaal/Magnavox; DA08. (Greek, Portuguese ships). Siemens/Plessey AWS 6 Dolphin (Turkish ships).

Navigation - Atlas Electronik 9600 ARPA (Australia/NZ).Racal Decca 2690 BT, (Greek, Turkish Barbaros class). Kelvin Hughes Type 1007 (Portuguese ships). Racal Decca TM 1226, (Turkish Yavuz class).

Fire control - CelsiusTech 9LV 453 (Australia/NZ). 2 Signaal STIR. (Greek, Portuguese and Turkish ships). Seaguard (for 25 mm), (Turkish ships). Signaal WM25 (Turkish Yavuz class).

Sonars: Thomson-Sintra Spherion B Mod 5 (Australia/NZ).Raytheon SQS-56/DE 1160; hull-mounted and VDS. (Greek, Turkish ships). CDC SQS-510(V), (Portuguese ships).

AIR SUPPORT

Helicopters: 1 Sikorsky S-70B6 Seahawk (Greek). 2 Westland Super Sea Lynx Mk 95 (Portugal). Agusta AB 212 or S-70B Seahawk (ASW), (Turkey). 1 Kaman SH-2G Seasprite (Australia/NZ).

Note: Chile has confirmed a contract to build a stealth version of the MEKO 200 frigate design. Keel of first unit has a planned in-service date of 2006.

Oliver Hazard Perry

SABHA

Country: AUSTRALIA, BAHRAIN, EGYPT, POLAND, SPAIN, TAIWAN, TURKEY, UNITED STATES OF AMERICA

Country of origin: USA

Ship type: FRIGATES

Class: OLIVER HAZARD PERRY/ADELAIDE /SANTA MARÍA/CHENG KUNG/GAZIANTEP (FFGs)

Active: 6 Australia, 1 Bahrain, 4 Egypt, 2 Poland, 6 Spain (Santa María class), 7 Taiwan (Cheng Kung class), 6 Turkey, 33 USA

Building: 1 Taiwan, 1 Turkey.

AUSTRALIA – Name (Pennant Number): ADELAIDE (01), CANBERRA (02), SYDNEY (03), DARWIN (04), MELBOURNE (05), NEWCASTLE (06).

BAHRAIN – Name (Pennant Number): SABHA (ex-*Jack Williams*) (90, ex-FFG 24).

EGYPT – Name (Pennant Number): MUBARAK (ex-*Copeland*) (F 911, ex-FFG 25), TABA (ex-*Gallery*) (F 916, ex-FFG 26), SHARM EL SHEIKH (ex-*Fahrion*) (F 901, ex-FFG 22), TOUSHKA, (ex-*Lewis B Puller*), (F 906, ex-FFG 23).

POLAND – Name (Pennant Number): GENERAL KAZIMIERZ PULASKI (ex-*Clark*) (272, ex- FFG 11), GENERAL T KOSCIUSZKO (ex-*Sides*) (272, ex-FFG 14).

SPAIN – Name (Pennant Number): SANTA MARÍA (F 81), VICTORIA (F 82), NUMANCIA (F 83), REINA SOFÍA (ex-*América*) (F 84), NAVARRA (F 85), CANARIAS (F 86).

TAIWAN – Name (Pennant Number): CHENG KUNG (1101), CHENG HO (1103), CHI KUANG (1105), YUEH FEI (1106), TZU-I (1107), PAN CHAO (1108), CHANG CHIEN (1109). TIEN TAN (1110)*

* Building.

TURKEY – Name (Pennant Number): GAZIANTEP (ex-*Clifton Sprague*) (F 490, ex-FFG 16), GIRESUN (ex-*Antrim*) (F 491, ex-FFG 20), GEMLIK (ex-*Flatley*) (F 492, ex-FFG 21), GELIBOLU (ex-*Reid*) (F 493, ex-FFG 30), GÖKÇEADA (ex-*Mahlon S Tisdale*) (F 494, ex-FFG 27), GEDIZ (ex-*John A Moore*) (F 495, ex-FFG 19).

USA – Name (Pennant Number): McINERNEY (FFG 8), GEORGE PHILIP (FFG 12), SIDES (FFG 14), ESTOCIN (FFG 15), BOONE (FFG 28), STEPHEN W GROVES (FFG 29), JOHN L HALL (FFG 32), JARRETT (FFG 33), UNDERWOOD (FFG 36), CROMMELIN (FFG 37), CURTS (FFG 38), DOYLE (FFG 39), HALYBURTON (FFG 40), McCLUSKY (FFG 41), KLAKRING (FFG 42), THACH (FFG 43), De WERT (FFG 45), RENTZ (FFG 46), NICHOLAS (FFG 47), VANDEGRIFT (FFG 48), ROBERT G BRADLEY (FFG 49), TAYLOR (FFG 50), GARY (FFG 51), CARR (FFG 52), HAWES (FFG 53), FORD (FFG 54), ELROD (FFG 55), SIMPSON (FFG 56), REUBEN JAMES (FFG 57), SAMUEL B ROBERTS (FFG 58), KAUFFMAN (FFG 59), RODNEY M DAVIS (FFG 60), INGRAHAM (FFG 61)

Note: The USA has offered to lease a ship of this class to the Philippines Navy.

Oliver Hazard Perry

SPECIFICATION

Displacement, full load, tons: 4,100, (4,105, Taiwan). 3,638, (Bahrain, Egypt, Poland, Turkey, US FFG 9, 11-13, 19, 30-31, 33.) 4,177, (Spain).

Length, feet (metres): 453 (138.1). 445 (135.6), (Bahrain, Egypt, Poland, Turkey, US FFG 9, 11-13, 19, 30-31, 33). 451.2 (137.7), (Spain). 453 (138.1) Taiwan, US FFG 8,15,28,29,32,36-61.)

Beam, feet (metres): 45 (13.7). 46.9 (14.3), (Spain).

Draught, feet (metres): 14.8 (4.5).

Speed, knots: 29. ~~/~~ ~~v5/~~

Range, miles: 4,500 at 20 kts.

ARMAMENT

Missiles: SSM - McDonnell Douglas Harpoon. SAM - GDC Pomona Standard SM-1MR. Mk 13 Mod 4 launcher for both SAM and SSM systems. (Hsiung Feng II (2 quad) SSM in Taiwanese ships).

Guns: 1 - OTO MELARA 3 in (76 mm)/62 Mk 75 Compact.1 - GE/GD 20 mm/76 Mk 15 Vulcan Phalanx. Up to 4 - 12.7 mm machine-guns, (not Taiwan). (1 Bazán 20 mm/120 12-barrel Meroka Mod 2A or 2B CIWS, Spain). (2 additional Bofors 40mm/70; and 3 - 20 mm Type 75 on hangar roof, when fitted, Taiwan only). (2 - McDonnell Douglas 25 mm Mk 38 can be fitted amidships in US ships).

Torpedoes: 6 - 324 mm Mk 32 (2 triple) tubes. Honeywell Mk 46 Mod 5.

Decoys: 2 - Loral Hycor SRBOC 6-barrel Mk 36. SLQ-25 Nixie towed torpedo decoy. (Prairie Masker hull noise/blade rate suppression in Spanish ships). (4 Kung Fen 6 chaff launchers, Taiwan only).

RADARS

Air search - Raytheon SPS-49(V)4 or 5.

Surface search/navigation - ISC Cardion SPS-55. (Raytheon SPS-55 in Spanish ships).

Navigation – Furuno. (Raytheon 1650/9 or SPS-67 in Spanish ships).

Fire control - Lockheed STIR (modified SPG-60). Sperry Mk 92 (Signaal WM 28). (RCA Mk 92 Mod 2/6, Signaal STING, Selenia RAN 30L/X (RAN 12L + RAN 30X) in Spanish ships). (USN UD 417 STIR, Unisys Mk 92 Mod 6 in Taiwanese ships).

Sonars: Raytheon SQS-53B, hull-mounted, active search/attack. Gould SQR-18A passive towed array.Raytheon SQS-56 hull-mounted, (Australia/Bahrain/Egypt). Raytheon SQS-56 (DE 1160) hull-mounted and Gould SQR-19(V)2 tactical towed array, (Spanish ships). Raytheon SQS-56/DE 1160P and SQR-18A(V)2 passive towed array or BAe/Thomson-Sintra ATAS towed array, Taiwan). Raytheon SQQ-89(V)2; hull-mounted, active search/attack, (US ships).

AIR SUPPORT

Helicopters: 2 Sikorsky S-70B-2 Seahawks, or 1 Seahawk and 1 Aerospatiale AS 350B Squirrel, (Australia). 2 (normally only 1 embarked), Sikorsky SH-70L Seahawk (LAMPS III, (Spain). 2 Sikorsky S-70C(M) Thunderhawks (only 1 embarked), (Taiwan). 2 Kaman SH-2G Seasprite (LAMPS 1) (Egypt/Poland/US) or 2 Sikorsky SH-60B LAMPS III. (ASW/ASV/OTHT). (US ships).

ALI HAIDER

Country:	BANGLADESH

Country: BANGLADESH
Country of origin: UK
Ship type: FRIGATES
Class: LEOPARD (TYPE 41) (FF)
Active: 2
Name (Pennant Number): ABU BAKR (ex-*Lynx*) (F 15), ALI HAIDER (ex-*Jaguar*) (F 17)

SPECIFICATION

Displacement, full load, tons: 2,520.
Length, feet (metres): 339.8 (103.6).
Beam, feet (metres): 40 (12.2).
Draught, feet (metres): 15.5 (4.7) (screws).
Speed, knots: 24.
Range, miles: 7,500 at 16 kts.

ARMAMENT

Guns: 4 - Vickers 4.5 in (115 mm)/45 (2 twin) Mk 6. 1 - Bofors 40 mm/60 Mk 9.
Decoys: Corvus chaff launchers.

RADARS

Air search - Marconi Type 965 with single AKE 1 array.
Air/surface search - Plessey Type 993.
Navigation - Decca Type 978; Kelvin Hughes Type 1007.
Fire control - Type 275.

KEY RECOGNITION FEATURES

- Raised forecastle with break down to 4.5 in gun mounting.
- Prominent Type 275 fire control director atop after end of bridge roof.
- Two masts, lattice foremast immediately aft of fire control director, enclosed mainmast supporting distinctive single bedstead Type 965 air search radar aerial.
- Engine exhausts from short funnel inside lattice mainmast and at top aft end of aftermast.
- 4.5 in gun mounting in 'Y' position.
- Break in maindeck, sloping down to very short quarterdeck.

Salisbury

UMAR FAROOQ

Country: BANGLADESH	
Country of origin: UK	
Ship type: FRIGATES	
Class: SALISBURY (TYPE 61) (FF)	
Active: 1	
Name (Pennant Number): UMAR FAROOQ (ex-*Llandaff*) (F 16)	

SPECIFICATION

Displacement, full load, tons: 2,408.
Length, feet (metres): 339.8 (103.6).
Beam, feet (metres): 40 (12.2).
Draught, feet (metres): 15.5 (4.7).
Speed, knots: 24.
Range, miles: 7,500 at 16 kts.

ARMAMENT

Guns: 2 - Vickers 4.5 in (115 mm)/45 (twin) Mk 6.
2 - Bofors 40 mm/60 Mk 9.
A/S mortars: 1 triple-barrelled Squid Mk 4.
Decoys: Corvus chaff launchers.

RADARS

Air search - Marconi Type 965 with double AKE 2 array.
Air/surface search - Plessey Type 993.

Heightfinder - Type 278M.
Navigation - Decca Type 978.
Fire control - Type 275.
Sonars: Type 174; hull-mounted, active search/attack. Graseby Type 170B; hull-mounted, active attack.

KEY RECOGNITION FEATURES

- Raised forecastle with break down to 4.5 in gun mounting in 'A' position.
- Low superstructure with Type 275 fire control director at aft end of bridge.
- Two large, black-topped mast and funnel combined structures, aftermast supporting double bedstead Type 965 air search radar aerial.
- Engine exhausts at top after end of masts.
- Short lattice mast supporting Type 278M height finder radar aerial between forward mast and fire control director.
- Prominent Type 982 radar aerial on short pylon aft. (Non-operational).
- 40 mm/60 gun mounting in 'Y' position.
- Break down to short quarterdeck.

Wielingen

WANDELAAR

Country:	BELGIUM
Country of origin:	BELGIUM
Ship type:	FRIGATES
Class:	WIELINGEN (E-71)
Active:	3

Name (Pennant Number): WIELINGEN (F 910), WESTDIEP (F 911), WANDELAAR (F 912)

SPECIFICATION

Displacement, full load, tons: 2,430.
Length, feet (metres): 349 (106.4).
Beam, feet (metres): 40.3 (12.3).
Draught, feet (metres): 18.4 (5.6).
Speed, knots: 26.
Range, miles: 6,000 at 15 kts.

ARMAMENT

Missiles: SSM - 4 Aerospatiale MM 38 Exocet (2 twin) launchers. SAM - Raytheon Sea Sparrow Mk 29 octuple launcher.
Guns: 1 - Creusot-Loire 3.9 in (100 mm)/55 Mod 68.
Torpedoes: 2 - 21 in (533 mm) launchers. ECAN L5 Mod 4.
A/S Mortars: Creusot-Loire 375 mm 6-barrel, trainable.
Decoys: 2 - Tracor MBA SRBOC 6-barrel Mk 36. Nixie SLQ-25 towed anti-torpedo decoy.

RADARS

Air/surface search - Signaal DA05
Surface search/fire control - Signaal WM25.
Navigation - Raytheon TM 1645/9X or Signaal Scout.
Sonars: Computing Devices Canada SQS-510, hull-mounted active search/attack.

KEY RECOGNITION FEATURES

- High freeboard with continuous maindeck from bow aft to break for very short quarterdeck.
- 3.9 in gun mounting ('A' position).
- Creusot-Loire 375 mm A/S mortar launcher ('B' mounting position).
- Enclosed mainmast atop superstructure supporting Signaal WM25 search/fire control radar dome.
- Large distinctive funnel amidships with large central exhaust and smaller exhausts protruding at top.
- Short enclosed aftermast supporting DA05 air/surface search radar aerial.
- Two Exocet SSM launchers ('X' mounting position).
- Sea Sparrow SAM box launcher forward of quarterdeck.

Broadsword (Batch 1 and 2)

Country:	BRAZIL, UNITED KINGDOM
Country of origin:	United Kingdom
Ship type:	FRIGATES
Class:	BROADSWORD (TYPE 22) (BATCH 1 and 2) (FFG)
Active:	4 Brazil, 1 United Kingdom

Batch 1
BRAZIL – Name (Pennant Number):
GREENHALGH (ex-*Broadsword*) (F 48, ex-F 88),
DODSWORTH (ex-*Brilliant*) (F 47, ex-F 90),
BOSISIO (ex-*Brazen*) (F 48, ex-F 91), RADEMAKER
(ex-*Battleaxe*) (F 49, ex-F 89).

Batch 2
UNITED KINGDOM – Name (Pennant Number):
(SHEFFIELD (F 96).

SPECIFICATION

Displacement, full load, tons: 4,400. (Batch 1),
4,800 (Batch 2).
Length, feet (metres): 430 (131.2) oa (Batch 1),
480.5 (146.5) oa., (F 96).
Beam, feet (metres): 48.5 (14.8).
Draught, feet (metres): 19.9 (6) (Batch 1), 21
(6.4) (Batch 2) (screws).
Speed, knots: 30.
Range, miles: 4,500 at 18 kts.

ARMAMENT

Missiles: SSM - MM 40 Block II Exocet (Brazilian
ships). SAM - 2 British Aerospace 6-barrel
Seawolf GWS 25 Mod 4 (Brazilian hulls).2
British Aerospace Seawolf GWS 25 Mod 3 (F
96).
Guns: 4 - Oerlikon/BMARC GCM-A03 30 mm/75
(2 twin). 2 - Oerlikon/BMARC 20 mm GAM-B01,
(UK ship). 2 - Bofors 40 mm/70, 2 -
Oerlikon/BMARC 20 mm GAM-B01, (Brazilian
ships).
Torpedoes: 6 - 324 mm Plessey STWS Mk 2 (2
triple) tubes. Marconi Stingray.
Decoys: 4 - Marconi Sea Gnat 130 mm/102 mm
6-barrel fixed launchers. Graseby Type 182
towed torpedo decoy.

RADARS

Air/surface search - Marconi Type 967/968
Navigation - Kelvin Hughes Type 1006 or Type
1008.
Fire control - 2 Marconi Type 911 or Type 910.
Sonars: Plessey Type 2016 or Ferranti/Thomson-

DODSWORTH (Royal Navy Colours)

Sintra Type 2050; hull-mounted. Dowty Type
2031Z (Batch 2 only) towed array.

AIR SUPPORT

Helicopters: 2 Westland Lynx HMA 3/8 (in all); or
1 Westland Sea King HAS 5. (ASW/ASV). (UK
ship).

KEY RECOGNITION FEATURES

- Blunt bow with short forecastle.(Sharper bow in Batch 2).
- Exocet SSM box launcher ('A' mounting position) in Brazilian hulls.
- Seawolf SAM six-barrel launcher ('B' mounting position).
- Raised central maindeck section giving high freeboard.
- High enclosed mainmast at after end of forward superstructure.
- Large funnel, aft of midships, with sloping top and black exhausts just protruding at top.
- SATCOM dome atop superstructure just forward of funnel, (UK ship only).
- Large enclosed black-topped aftermast aft of funnel. This mast is only slightly shorter, and similar in size, to the mainmast.
- After superstructure has Type 910/11 fire control radar aerial atop raised forward section and Seawolf SAM 6-barrel launcher atop hangar.
- Flight deck aft with open quarterdeck below.

Note: Batch 2 14 m longer than Batch 1 and has high sweeping bow profile.
Note 2: Batch 2 has enlarged flight decks to take Sea King or EH 101 Merlin helicopters.
Note 3: One of the paid-off Batch 2 hulls may be sold to Romania.

Niteroi

Country: BRAZIL
Country of origin: UK
Ship type: FRIGATES
Class: NITEROI
Active: 6
Name (Pennant Number): NITEROI (F 40), DEFENSORA (F 41), CONSTITUIÇÃO (F 42*), LIBERAL (F 43*), INDEPENDÊNCIA (F 44), UNIÃO (F 45)
*General Purpose design. Remainder are anti-submarine configuration.

SPECIFICATION

Displacement, full load, tons: 3,707.
Length, feet (metres): 424 (129.2).
Beam, feet (metres): 44.2 (13.5).
Draught, feet (metres): 18.2 (5.5) (sonar).
Speed, knots: 30.
Range, miles: 5,300 at 17 kts.

ARMAMENT

Missiles: SSM - Aerospatiale MM 40 Exocet (2 twin) launchers. SAM - 2 Short Bros Seacat triple launchers. Being replaced by Albatros octuple launcher for Aspide. A/S - 1 Ikara

DEFENSORA

launcher (Branik standard) (A/S version); payload Mk 46 torpedoes.

Guns: 1 or 2 - Vickers 4.5 in (115 mm)/55 Mk 8 (GP version). A/S version only has 1 mounting. 2 - Bofors 40 mm/70. Being replaced by Bofors SAK 40mm/70 Mk 3.

Torpedoes: 6 - 324 mm Plessey STWS-1 (2 triple) tubes. Honeywell Mk 46 Mod 5 Neartip.

A/S mortars: 1 - Bofors 375 mm rocket launcher (twin-tube).

Depth charges: 1 rail; 5 charges (GP version).

Decoys: 2 - Plessey Shield chaff launchers.

RADARS

Air/surface search - Plessey AWS 3, being replaced by AESN RAN 20 S (3L).

Surface search - Signaal ZW06, being replaced by Decca TM 1226.

Navigation: Terma Scanter.

Fire control - 2 Selenia Orion RTN 10X, being replaced by 2 AESN RTN 30X

Sonars: EDO 610E Mod 1; hull-mounted active search/attack. EDO 700E VDS (F 40 and 41).

AIR SUPPORT

Helicopters: 1 Westland Super Lynx SAH-11. (ASW).

Pará

PARANÁ

Mario R.V. Carneiro

Country: BRAZIL
Country of origin: USA
Ship type: FRIGATES
Class: PARÁ (ex-US GARCIA) (FF)
Active: 4
Name (Pennant Number): PARÁ (ex-*Albert David*) (D 27, ex-FF 1050), PARAÍBA (ex-*Davidson*) (D 28, ex-FF 1045), PARANÁ (ex-*Sample*) (D 29, ex-FF 1048), PERNAMBUCO (ex-*Bradley*) (D 30, ex-FF 1041)

SPECIFICATION

Displacement, full load, tons: 3,560.
Length, feet (metres): 414.5 (126.3).
Beam, feet (metres): 44.2 (13.5).
Draught, feet (metres): 14.5 (4.4) keel.
Speed, knots: 27.5.
Range, miles: 4,000 at 20 kts.

ARMAMENT

Missiles: A/S - Honeywell ASROC Mk 112 octuple launcher.
Guns: 2 - USN 5 in (127 mm)/38 Mk 30.
Torpedoes: 6 - 324 mm Mk 32 (2 triple) tubes. 14 Honeywell Mk 46 Mod 5 Neartip.
Decoys: 2 - Loral Hycor Mk 33 RBOC 6-tubed launchers. Mk T-6 Fanfare; torpedo decoy system. Prairie/Masker; hull/blade rate noise suppression.

RADARS

Air search - Lockheed SPS-40B.
Surface search - Raytheon SPS-10C.
Navigation - Marconi LN 66.
Fire control - General Electric Mk 35.
Sonars: EDO/General Electric SQS-26 AXR (D 29 and 30) or SQS-26B; bow-mounted.

AIR SUPPORT

Helicopters: Westland Super Lynx AH-11.

KEY RECOGNITION FEATURES

- Very long forecastle with continuous maindeck line from stem to stern.
- 5 in gun mounting on forecastle approximately mid-point between bow and bridge.
- ASROC A/S missile box launcher between forward mounting and bridge.
- Single black-capped funnel amidships.
- Mast and funnel combined with pole mast atop after end. Large air search radar aerial at forward end of funnel.
- 5 in gun mounting atop after superstructure forward of hangar.
- Flight deck right aft.

CALGARY

Country: CANADA
Country of origin: Canada
Ship type: FRIGATES
Class: HALIFAX (FFH/FFG)
Active: 12
Name (Pennant Number): HALIFAX (330), VANCOUVER (331), VILLE DE QUÉBEC (332), TORONTO (333), REGINA (334), CALGARY (335), MONTREAL (336), FREDERICTON (337), WINNIPEG (338), CHARLOTTETOWN (339), ST JOHN'S (340), OTTAWA (341)

SPECIFICATION

Displacement, full load, tons: 4,770.
Length, feet (metres): 441.9 (134.7) oa.
Beam, feet (metres): 53.8 (16.4).
Draught, feet (metres): 16.4 (5).
Speed, knots: 29.
Range, miles: 9,500 at 13 kts.

ARMAMENT

Missiles: SSM - 8 McDonnell Douglas Harpoon Block 1C (2 quad) launchers. SAM - 2 Raytheon Sea Sparrow RIM-7P Mk 48 octuple vertical launchers.
Guns: 1 - Bofors 57 mm/70 Mk 2. 1 - GE/GD 20 mm Vulcan Phalanx Mk 15 Mod 1. 8 - 12.7 mm machine-guns.
Torpedoes: 4 - 324 mm Mk 32 Mod 9 (2 twin) tubes. Honeywell Mk 46 Mod 5 Neartip.
Decoys: 4 - Plessey Shield Mk 2 decoy launchers. Nixie SLQ-25 towed acoustic decoy.

RADARS

Air search - Raytheon SPS-49(V)5.
Air/surface search - Ericsson Sea Giraffe 150HC.
Navigation - Sperry Mk 340, being replaced by Kelvin Hughes 1007.
Fire control - 2 Signaal SPG-503 STIR 1.8.
Sonars: Westinghouse SQS-505(V)6; hull-mounted. CDC SQR-501 CANTASS towed array.

AIR SUPPORT

Helicopters: 1 Sikorsky CH-124A ASW or 1 CH-124B Heltas Sea King.

KEY RECOGNITION FEATURES

- Squat 57 mm/70 gun mounting mid-forecastle.
- Short and squat lattice mast supporting large SPS-49(V)5 air search radar aerial mid-forward superstructure.
- Tall lattice mainmast after end of forward superstructure.
- Unusually large, square section funnel amidships, offset to port with grilled intakes top, forward.
- Break in superstructure aft of funnel with Harpoon launchers.
- High after superstructure with CIWS mounting at after end.
- Flight deck aft of hangar with small break down to short, shallow quarterdeck.

Leander

Country: CHILE, ECUADOR, INDIA, NEW ZEALAND, PAKISTAN

Country of origin: UK

Ship Type: FRIGATES

Class: LEANDER/LEANDER BROAD-BEAMED /NILGIRI (FF/FFG)

Active: 3 Chile (Leander/FFG), 2 Ecuador (Leander/FFG), 5 India (Nilgiri/FF), 1 New Zealand (Broad-beamed Leander/FF), 2 Pakistan (Broad-beamed Leander/FF)

CHILE – Name (Pennant Number): CONDELL (06), LYNCH (07), MINISTRO ZENTENO (ex-*Achilles*) (08, ex-F 12).

ECUADOR – Name (Pennant Number): PRESIDENTE ELOY ALFARO (ex-*Penelope*) (FM 01, ex-F 127), MORAN VALVERDE (ex-*Danae*) (FM 02, ex-F 47).

INDIA – Name (Pennant Number): HIMGIRI (F 34), UDAYGIRI (F 35), DUNAGIRI (F 36), TARAGIRI (F 41), VINDHYAGIRI (F 42).

NEW ZEALAND – Name (Pennant Number): CANTERBURY (F 421).* *Wellington* used for alongside training.

PAKISTAN – Name (Pennant Number): ZULFIQUAR (ex-*Apollo*) (F 262), SHAMSHER (ex-*Diomede*) (F 263).

SPECIFICATION

Displacement, full load, tons: 3,200. 2,945 (Broad-beamed); 2,962, (Chilean, Pakistan and Indian ships).

Length, feet (metres): 372 (113.4) oa.

Beam, feet (metres): 41 (12.5). 43 (13.1), (Broad-beamed).

Draught, feet (metres): 18 (5.6) (screws).

Speed (knots): 28 (29, Chile).

Range, miles: 5,500 at 15 kts. (NZ). 4,000 at 15 kts (Ecuador, Pakistan).

ARMAMENT

Missiles: SSM - MM 38/40 Exocet (Chile). MM 38 Exocet (Ecuador). SAM – Short Bros Seacat GWS 22 quad launchers in Chilean units. 3 twin Matra Simbad launchers for Mistral, Ecuadorian units only. No missiles fitted in Indian, NZ and Pakistan ships.

Guns: Vickers 4.5 in (114 mm)/45 Mk 6 (twin) semi-automatic. (Not Ecuador). 2 - Bofors 40 mm/60 Mk 9 (Ecuador); 1 - GE/GD 20 mm Vulcan Phalanx CIWS Mk 15, Mod 11, (NZ). 4 -

LYNCH

30 mm/65 (2 twin) AK 630, (India). 6 - 25 mm/60 (3 twin), (Pakistan). 2 - Oerlikon/BMARC 20 mm GAM-B01 (Ecuador). 4 - Oerlikon 20 mm Mk 9 (2 twin), (Chile). 2 - Oerlikon 20 mm/70, (India). 4 or 6 - 12.7 mm machine-guns, (NZ).

A/S mortars: UK MoD Mortar Mk 10, 3-barrel. (Pakistan). 1 Limbo Mk 10 triple-tubed launcher (India –except *Taragiri* and *Vindhyagiri* which have Bofors 375 mm twin-tubed launcher). (No mortars in other units).

Torpedoes: 6 - 324 mm Mk 32 (2 triple) Honeywell Mk 46, Mod 2, (Chile and NZ only). 6 – 324 mm ILAS-3 (2 triple) tubes, Whitehead A 244, Ecuador and India, (*Taragiri* and *Vindhyagiri* only).

Decoys: 2 - Loral Hycor SRBOC Mk 36 6-barrel launchers. (NZ). Graseby Type 182 towed torpedo decoy, (Ecuador, NZ and Pakistan). Graseby Type 738 towed torpedo decoy, (India). 2 Vickers Corvus 8-barrel chaff launchers. (Chile, Ecuador, Pakistan). Wallop Barricade double layer chaff launchers, (Chile).

RADARS

Air Search – Marconi Type 965/966 (Chile, Ecuador, Pakistan). Signaal LW08 (India, NZ).

Surface search - Marconi Type 992 Q or Plessey Type 994 (F 08), (Chile). Plessey Type 994, (Ecuador, Pakistan). Plessey Type 993 (NZ).

Signaal ZW06, (India).

Navigation – 1 Kelvin Hughes Type 1006 (Chile, Ecuador, NZ, Pakistan). Decca 1226, Signaal M 45, (India).

Fire control – RCA TR 76 (NZ). Plessey Type 903/904, (Chile, Ecuador, Pakistan).

Sonars: Graseby Type 184M/P, hull-mounted, active search/attack; Graseby Type 170 B, hull-mounted, active; Kelvin Hughes Type 162M hull-mounted, sideways-looking, (Chile, Pakistan). Graseby Type 184P/Kelvin Hughes Type 162M, (Ecuador, Pakistan). Westinghouse SQS-505/Graseby 750 (India). Westinghouse VDS in first three Indian ships. Graseby Type 750/Kelvin Hughes Type 162M (N7)

AIR SUPPORT

Helicopters: 1 Bell 206B JetRanger (ASW) or Nurtanio NAS 332C Cougar (ASV/ASW) (Chile, F 08). Bell 412EP Sentinel (Ecuador). 1 HAL SA 319B Chetak (Alouette III) (ASW) in Indian ships; 1 Sea King Mk 42A (ASW) in *Taragiri* and *Vindhyagiri*. 1 Kaman SH-2G Seasprite, (NZ). 1 Aerospatiale SA 319B Alouette III (ASW), (Pakistan).

KEY RECOGNITION FEATURES

- High forecastle, break at after end of bridge with continuous maindeck to stern
- 4.5 in gun twin mounting at 'A' position. (MM 38 Exocet SSM launchers on forecastle in Ecuadorian ships).
- Substantial midships superstructure with tall enclosed mainmast aft of bridge.
- Twin Matra Simbad SAM launchers atop bridge and at aft of superstructure in Ecuadorian units.
- Single funnel just aft of bridge. (Extensions fitted to funnel uptakes on *Canterbury*).
- After superstructure has large enclosed aftermast atop. (Chilean ships have MM 40 Exocet launchers adjacent to after superstructure (F 06, 07) and alongside funnel (F 08).
- Larger hangars for Chetak or Sea King helicopters in Indian ships *Taragiri* and *Vindhyagiri*.
- Limbo A/S mortar on quarterdeck of Pakistani units.

Note: India acquired Broad-beamed Leander frigate *Andromeda* in 1995 from UK and converted her into the training ship *Krishna*, (F 46, ex-F-57). Armament reduced.

Note 2: The six *Ahmad Yani* (Van Speijk) class FFGs of the Indonesia Navy based on Leander design) and acquired 1986-90 from the Netherlands.

Jianghu I/II

Country: CHINA, BANGLADESH, EGYPT
Country of origin: CHINA
Ship type: FRIGATES
Class: JIANGHU I/II (TYPE 053) (FFG)
Active: 1 Bangladesh (Osman Jianghu I/Type 053 H1), 27 China (Jianghu I), 1 China (Jianghu II), 2 Egypt (Jianghu I)
BANGLADESH – Name (Pennant Number): OSMAN (ex-*Xiangtan*) (F 18 ex-556).
CHINA – Name (Pennant Number): (Jianghu I): CHANG DE (509), SHAOXING (510), NANTONG (511), WUXI (512), HUAYIN (513), ZHENJIANG (514), XIAMEN (515), JIUJIANG (516), NANPING (517), JIAN (518), CHANGZHI (519), NINGPO (533), JINHUA (534), DANDONG (543), LINFEN (545), MAOMING (551), YIBIN (552), SHAOGUAN (553), ANSHUN (554), ZHAOTONG (555), JISHOU (557), ZIGONG (558), KANGDING (559), DONGGUAN (560), SHANTOU (561), JIANGMEN (562), ZHAOQING (563). (Jianghu II): SIPING (544).
EGYPT – (Name (Pennant Number): NAJIM AL ZAFFER (951), EL NASSER (956).

SPECIFICATION

Displacement, full load, tons: 1,702, 1,865 (Jianghu II).
Length, feet (metres): 338.5 (103.2).
Beam, feet (metres): 35.4 (10.8).
Draught, feet (metres): 10.2 (3.1).
Speed, knots: 26.
Range, miles: 4,000 at 15 kts.

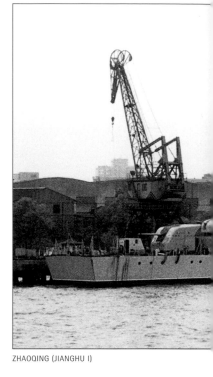

ZHAOQING (JIANGHU I)

ARMAMENT

Missiles: SSM - 4 HY-2 (C-201) (2 twin) launchers (CSSC-3 Seersucker). (2 twin in Jianghu II).
Guns: 2 or 4 - China 3.9 in (100 mm)/56 (2 twin). 1 - Creusot-Loire 3.9 in (100 mm)/55 (Jianghu II). 4 - China 57mm/70 (2 twin) in Egyptian ships. 12 - China 37 mm/63 (6 twin) (8 (4 twin) in some Chinese units).
Torpedoes: 6 - 324 mm ILAS (2 triple) tubes (Jianghu II).Yu-2 (Mk 46 Mod 1). (None in Jianghu I or Bangladesh or Egyptian ships).
A/S mortars: 2 - RBU 1200 5-tubed fixed launchers (4 in some).
Depth charges: 2 - BMB-2 projectors; 2 racks.
Mines: Up to 60 can be carried by Bangladesh and Egyptian units.
Decoys: 2 - SRBOC 6-barrel Mk 33 chaff launchers or 2 China 26-barrel launchers. 2 Loral Hycor SRBOC Mk 36 6-barrel chaff launchers (Bangladesh ship)

RADARS

Air/surface search - MX 902 Eye Shield (Type 354). Type 765 (Egyptian ships). Rice Screen/Shield in Chinese units, *Zigong* onwards.
Surface search/fire control - Square Tie (254/352).
Navigation - Don 2 or Fin Curve or Racal Decca. (Decca RM 1290A in Egyptian ships).
Fire control - Wok Won or Rice Lamp. Sun Visor, with Wasp Head (some Jianghu I). Fog Lamp. (Egyptian ships).
Sonars: Echo Type 5; hull-mounted, active search/attack.

AIR SUPPORT

Helicopters: Harbin Zhi-9A Haitun (Dauphin 2) (ASV, in Jianghu II).

KEY RECOGNITION FEATURES

- Long slim hull with a high bow, low in water.
- 3.9 in gun single or twin mounting in 'A' position. (Creusot-Loire 3.9 in gun in Jianghu II; Egyptian ships have 57mm/70 twin mounting).
- Squat rounded funnel aft of midships.
- Box-like HY-2 SSM launchers forward and aft of funnel. (Only one in Jianghu II, forward of funnel)
- Tall lattice mainmast aft of forward superstructure.
- 2 37 mm/63 gun mountings forward of bridge, two outboard of mainmast (in some) and two atop after superstructure in 'X' position (in some.) (*Dongguan* has 37mm/63 turrets in 'B' and 'X' positions. In Jianghu II, 'X' position mounting omitted in lieu of helicopter hangar; 37mm/63 gun mountings just aft of funnel).
- 3.9 in twin gun mounting in 'Y' position. (Omitted in Jianghu II, in lieu of flight deck). (Egyptian ships have 57mm/70 twin gun mountings in 'Y' position).

Note: here are several variants of the Jianghu I class, but the basic outline is similar.

Note 2: Jianghu II are similar to Jianghu I except that aft of the funnel, is a through deck with hangar forward of flight deck.

Jianghu III/IV

HUANGSHI (TYPE III)

Ships of The World

Country: CHINA
Country of origin: CHINA,
Ship type: FRIGATES
Class: JIANGHU III/IV (TYPE 053 HT) (FFG)
Active: 3
Name (Pennant Number): (Jianghu III):
HUANGSHI (535), WUHU (536). (Jianghu IV):
ZHOUSHAN (537).

SPECIFICATION

Displacement, full load, tons: 1,924.
Length, feet (metres): 338.5 (103.2).
Beam, feet (metres): 35.4 (10.8).
Draught, feet (metres): 10.2 (3.1).
Speed, knots: 28.
Range, miles: 4,000 at 15 kts.

ARMAMENT

Missiles: SSM - 8 YJ-1 (Eagle Strike) (C-801)
   (CSS-N-4 Sardine). Jianghu IV fitted for
   improved C-802 (CSS-N-8 Saccade).
Guns: 4 - China 3.9 in (100 mm)/56 (2 twin). 8 -
   China 37 mm/63 (4 twin).
A/S mortars: 2 - RBU 1200 5-tubed launchers.
Depth charges: 2 - BMB-2 projectors; 2 racks.
Mines: Can carry up to 60.
Decoys: 2 - China 26-barrel chaff launchers.

RADARS

Air/surface search - MX 902 Eye Shield.
Surface search/fire control - Square Tie.
Navigation - Fin Curve.

Fire Control - Rice Lamp, Sun Visor B (with Wasp
   Head).
Sonars: Echo Type 5; hull-mounted active
   search/attack.

KEY RECOGNITION FEATURES

- High bow, with 3.9 in gun twin mounting
  in 'A' position.
- Maindeck higher in the midships section.
- Forward superstructure with enclosed
  mainmast at after end, enclosed lower
  section lattice top.
- Large, low funnel aft of midships with
  ship's boats in davits outboard.
- Two 37 mm/63 gun mountings forward of
  bridge and two at after end of maindeck
  level, port and starboard, outboard of short
  mast with Rice Lamp fire control radar
  atop.
- Distinctive 'X' shape communications aerial
  aft of funnel on short lattice mast.
- YJ-1 SSM launchers in pairs, trained
  outboard, port and starboard, forward and
  aft of funnel.
- 3.9 in gun twin mounting in 'Y' position.
Note: See modified Jianghu III, *Chao Phraya*
   class of Thailand.
Note 2: CIWS PL 8H (combined gun/SAM)
   may be mounted vice some of the 37 mm
   guns.

Jiangwei I/II

Country: CHINA	
Country of origin: CHINA	
Ship type: FRIGATES	
Class: JIANGWEI I/II (Type 053/053 H2G) (FFG)	
Active: 4 (Jiangwei I), 7 (Jiangwei II)	
Building: 1 (Jiangwei II)	

Name (Pennant Number): (Jiangwei I): ANQING (539), HUAINAN (540) (548 out of area), HUAIBEI (541), TONGLING (542). **(Jiangwei II):** JIAXIN (521, ex-597), LIANYUNGANG (522), SANMING (523), PUTIAN (524), YICHANG (564), YULIN (565), YUXI (566), ——— (567).

SPECIFICATION

Displacement, full load, tons: 2,250.
Length, feet (metres): 366.5 (111.7).
Beam, feet (metres): 39.7 (12.1).
Draught, feet (metres): 15.7 (4.8).
Speed, knots: 25.
Range, miles: 4,000 at 18 kts.

ARMAMENT

Missiles: SSM - 6 YJ-1 (Eagle Strike) (C-801) (CSSN-4 Sardine) or C-802 (2 triple) launchers. SAM - 1 HQ-61 sextuple launcher, (Jiangwei I), HQ-7 octuple launcher (Jiangwei II).
Guns: 2 - China 3.9 in (100 mm)/56 (twin). 8 - China 37 mm/63 Type 76A (4 twin).
A/S mortars: 2 - RBU 1200; 5-tubed fixed launchers.
Decoys: 2 - SRBOC Mk 33 6-barrel chaff launchers. 2 - China 26-barrel launchers.

RADARS

Air/surface search –Knife Rest. (Jiangwei I) Type 360, (Jiangwei II)
Fire Control - Sun Visor (with Wasp Head), (Jiangwei I). Type 347G, (Jiangwei II).Rice Lamp. Fog Lamp.
Navigation - Racal Decca 1290 and China Type 360.

HUAIBEI (JIANGWEI I)   *Ships of The World*

Sonars: Echo Type 5; hull-mounted, active search/attack.

AIR SUPPORT

Helicopters: 1 Harbin Zhi-9A Haitun (Dauphin 2). (ASV).

Type FS 1500

Colombia

ALMIRANTE PAOILLA

Country:	COLOMBIA, MALAYSIA
Country of origin:	GERMANY
Ship type:	FRIGATES
Class:	ALMIRANTE PADILLA (TYPE FS 1500) (FL) KASTURI (FSG)
Active:	4 Columbia, 2 Malaysia*

* Rated as corvettes.

COLUMBIA – Name (Pennant Number):
ALMIRANTE PADILLA (FL 51), CALDAS (FL 52),
ANTIOQUIA (FL 53), INDEPENDIENTE (FL 54).

MALAYSIA – Name (Pennant Number): KASTURI
(25), LEKIR (26).

SPECIFICATION

Displacement, full load, tons: 2,100, (Colombian).
1,850 (Malaysian).
Length, feet (metres): 325.1 (99.1). (Colombian).
319.1 (97.3), (Malaysian).
Beam, feet (metres): 37.1 (11.3).
Draught, feet (metres): 12.1 (3.7), (Colombian).
11.5 (3.5, (Malaysian)
Speed, knots: 27. 28, (Malaysian).
Range, miles: 7,000 at 14 kts. 5,000 at 14 kts.,
(Malaysian).

ARMAMENT

Missiles: SSM - 8 Aerospatiale MM 40 Exocet.
(Colombian). 4 MM 38 Exocet, (Malaysian).
Guns: 1 - OTO MELARA 3 in (76 mm)/62 Compact,
(Colombian). 1 - Creusot-Loire 3.9 in (100
mm)/55 Mk 2 Compact, (Malaysian). 2 - Breda
40 mm/70 (twin); 4 - Oerlikon 30 mm/75 Mk
74 (2 twin), (Colombian).1 - Bofors 57 mm/70
and 4 - Emerson Electric 30 mm (2 twin),
(Malaysian).
Torpedoes: 6 - 324 mm Mk 32 (2 triple) tubes.
(None in Malaysian ships).

A/S mortars: 1 - Bofors 375 mm twin trainable
launcher. (Malaysian ships only).
Decoys: 1 - CSEE Dagaie double mounting. (2 in
Malaysian ships).

RADARS

Air/Surface search – Thomson-CSF Sea Tiger.
(Colombian ships). Signaal DA08. (Malaysian
ships).
Navigation – Decca TM 1226C (Malaysian).
Furono, (Colombian).
Fire control - Castor II B, (Colombian). Signaal
WM22, (Malaysian).
Sonars: Atlas Elektronik ASO-4-2; hull-mounted,
(Colombian). Atlas Elektronik DSQS-21C, hull-
mounted, (Malaysian).

AIR SUPPORT

Helicopters: 1 MBB BO 105CB, (ASW).
(Colombian). Platform for Westland Wasp HAS
1 (Malaysian).

KEY RECOGNITION FEATURES

- Low forecastle with break up to high
  midships maindeck and down to short
  quarterdeck.
- 3 in gun mounting (Colombian ships), 3.9
  in gun mounting, (Malaysian ships) in 'A'
  position,.
- Bofors twin 375 mm A/S/ mortar in 'B'
  position in Malaysian ships with prominent
  angled screen.
- Tall flat fronted bridge structure with large
  enclosed mainmast at after end. Pole mast
  atop after end of mainmast. WM22 radome
  atop mainmast in Malaysian ships.
- Large, tapered funnel with wedge shaped
  smoke deflector atop.
- Exocet SSM launchers between funnel and
  forward superstructure.
- Flight deck aft of after superstructure at
  maindeck level.
- 40 mm/70 gun mounting ('Y' position)
  (Colombian ships). 57 mm/70 mounting in
  Malaysian ships.
- DA08 air/surface search radar aerial on
  raised platform atop after superstructure in
  Malaysian ships.

Niels Juel

OLFERT FISCHER

Country: DENMARK
Country of origin: DENMARK
Ship type: FRIGATES
Class: NIELS JUEL (FFG)
Active: 3
Name (Pennant Number): NIELS JUEL (F 354),
OLFERT FISCHER (F 355), PETER TORDENSKIOLD (F
356)

SPECIFICATION

Displacement, full load, tons: 1,320.
Length, feet (metres): 275.5 (84).
Beam, feet (metres): 33.8 (10.3).
Draught, feet (metres): 10.2 (3.1).
Speed, knots: 28.
Range, miles: 2,500 at 18 kts.

ARMAMENT

Missiles: SSM - 8 McDonnell Douglas Harpoon (2
quad) launchers. SAM - Raytheon NATO Sea
Sparrow Mk 29 octuple launcher or MK 48 VLS
modular launchers. 4 Stinger mountings (2
twin.)
Guns: 1 - OTO MELARA 3 in (76 mm)/62 Compact.
4 - Oerlikon 20 mm (1 each side of the funnel
and 2 abaft the mast), can be fitted, to be
replaced by 2 - 12.7 mm machine-guns.
Depth charges: 1 rack.
Decoys: 2 - DL-12T Sea Gnat 12-barrel chaff
launchers.

RADARS

Air search – DASA TRS-3D.
Surface search – Philips 9GR 600.
Navigation - Burmeister & Wain Elektronik
    Scanter Mil 009.
Fire control - 2 Mk 95,(SAM). Philips 9LV 200 Mk
    1 Rakel 203C. (guns, SSM).
Sonars: Plessey PMS 26; hull-mounted, active
    search/attack.

KEY RECOGNITION FEATURES

- Unusual profile and easily identified frigate.
- Low forecastle with 3 in gun mounting ('A'
  position).
- High midships maindeck section, slab-sided.
- Unusually robust enclosed mainmast
  amidships, supporting 9GR 600 surface
  search radar aerial, on forward gantry, and
  AWS 5 or DASA TRS-3D air search radar atop.
- Large, black-capped funnel with sloping
  top sited well aft of midships.
- Harpoon SSM angled launchers, port and
  starboard, aft of funnel.
- 2 fire control directors mounted on sturdy
  pedestals aft of bridge and forward of
  quarterdeck.
- Sea Sparrow SAM octuple or VLS modular
  launcher on quarterdeck.

Thetis

HVIDBJØRNEN

Country: DENMARK	
Country of origin: DENMARK	
Ship type: FRIGATES	
Class: THETIS (FF)	
Active: 4	

Name (Pennant Number): THETIS (F 357), TRITON (F 358), VAEDDEREN (F 359), HVIDBJØRNEN (F 360)

SPECIFICATION

Displacement, full load, tons: 3,500.
Length, feet (metres): 369.1 (112.5) oa.
Beam, feet (metres): 47.2 (14.4).
Draught, feet (metres): 19.7 (6).
Speed, knots: 20.
Range, miles: 8,500 at 15.5 kts.

ARMAMENT

Guns: 1 - OTO MELARA 3 in (76 mm)/62 Super Rapid. 1 or 2 - Oerlikon 20 mm.
Depth charges: 2 rails (door in stern).
Decoys: 2 - DL-12T Sea Gnat 12-barrel chaff/IR flares.

RADARS

Air/surface search - Plessey AWS 6.
Surface search - Terma Scanter Mil.

Navigation - Furuno FR 1505DA.
Fire control – CelsuisTech 9LV Mk 3.
Sonars: Thomson-Sintra TSM 2640 Salmon; hull-mounted and VDS.

AIR SUPPORT

Helicopters: 1 Westland Lynx Mk 91, (Surface search).

KEY RECOGNITION FEATURES

- Short forecastle with 3 in gun mounting ('A' position).
- High, slab-sided midships section.
- Large enclosed mainmast at after end of forward superstructure with distinctive AWS 6 air/surface search radome atop.
- Large, very squat, black-capped funnel amidships.
- Ship's boats in davits outboard of funnel, port and starboard.
- Long flight deck with domed SATCOM aerial on pedestal atop hangar roof.

Note: *Thetis* has a modified stern for seismological equipment.

Descubierta

Country: EGYPT, MOROCCO, SPAIN

Country of origin: SPAIN

Ship type: FRIGATES

Class: DESCUBIERTA/
MODIFIED DESCUBIERTA (FFG)

Active: 2 Egypt, 1 Morocco,
(Modified Descubierta), 6
Spain

EGYPT – Name (Pennant
Number): ABU QIR (ex-
Serviola) (F 946), EL SUEZ (ex-
Centinela) (F 941).

MOROCCO – Name (Pennant
Number):
LIEUTENANT COLONEL
ERRAHAMANI (501).

DESCUBIERTA

SPAIN – Name (Pennant Number): DESCUBIERTA
(P 75, ex-F 31), DIANA (M 11, ex-F 32), INFANTA
ELENA (F 33), INFANTA CRISTINA (F 34),
CAZADORA (F 35), VENCEDORA (F 36)

SPECIFICATION

Displacement, full load, tons: 1,666. (Spain).
1,479, (Egypt, Morocco).
Length, feet (metres): 291.3 (88.8).
Beam, feet (metres): 34 (10.4).
Draught, feet (metres): 12.5 (3.8).
Speed, knots: 25.
Range, miles: 4,000 at 18 kts.

ARMAMENT

Missiles: SSM - 8 McDonnell Douglas Harpoon (2
quad) launchers. Normally 2 pairs are
embarked. (MM38 Exocet, Morocco). SAM -
Selenia Albatros octuple launcher, Aspide.
Guns: 1 - OTO MELARA 3 in (76 mm)/62 Compact.
1 or 2 - Bofors 40 mm/70, (Spain). 2 - Bofors
400 mm/70, (Egypt). 2 - Breda Bofors 40
mm/70, (Morocco). 2 – Oerlikon 20 mm
(Spanish hulls P 75 and M 11).
Torpedoes: 6 - 324 mm US Mk 32 (2 triple) tubes.
Honeywell Mk 46 Mod 5 Neartip, (Spain). (Mod
1 (Morocco). Marconi Stingray, (Egypt).
A/S mortars: 1 - Bofors 375 mm twin-barrel,
trainable launcher.
Decoys: 2 - Loral Hycor SRBOC 6-barrel Mk 36.
US Prairie Masker; blade rate suppression,
(Spain and Egypt). 2 CSEE Dagaie double
trainable launcher, (Morocco).

RADARS

Air/surface search - Signaal DA05/2.
Surface search - Signaal ZW06.
Navigation – 2 Furuno (Spanish hulls).
Fire control - Signaal WM 22/41 or WM 25/41
system.
Sonars: Raytheon DE 1160B; hull-mounted.

KEY RECOGNITION FEATURES

- Short forecastle with 3 in gun mounting
  ('A' position).
- Distinctive Bofors 375 mm A/S mortar
  mounting forward of bridge ('B' mounting
  position).
- Short forward superstructure with pyramid
  mainmast at after end. WM22/41 or
  WM25/41 fire control radome atop; surface
  search ZW06 radar on forward gantry.
- Harpoon SSM angled launchers between
  mainmast and funnels, (Spain and Egypt;
  MM38 Exocet in Moroccan ship.).
- Unusual, black-capped 'V' formation funnels
  amidships with a large aerial atop each one.
- Short aftermast aft of funnels supporting
  DA05 air/surface search radar aerial.
- Two 40 mm/70 gun mountings, on two
  levels, aft of aftermast. (Breda/Bofors
  turrets, Morocco).
- Aspide SAM Albatros octuple box launcher
  on afterdeck ('Y' position).

Knox

Country: EGYPT, GREECE, MEXICO, SPAIN, TAIWAN, THAILAND, TURKEY

Country of origin: USA/SPAIN

Ship type: FRIGATES

Class: KNOX/EPIRUS/BALEARES (F 70)/TEPE CLASS (FF/FFG)

Active: 2 Egypt, 2 Greece (Epirus class), 4 Mexico (FF), 5 Spain (Baleares class), 8 Taiwan, 2 Thailand, 6 Turkey (Tepe class).

EGYPT – Name (Pennant Number): DAMYAT (ex-*Jesse L Brown*) (961, ex-FF 1089), RASHEED (ex-*Moinester*) (966, ex-FF 1097).

GREECE – Name (Pennant Number): EPIRUS (ex-*Connole*) (F 456, ex-FF 1056), –– (ex- WHIPPLE).

MEXICO – Name (Pennant Number): IGNACIO ALLENDE (ex-*Stein*) (E 50, ex-FF 1065), MARIANO ABASOLO (ex-*Marvin Shields*) (E 51, ex-FF 1066), GUADALOUPE VICTORIA (ex-*Pharris*) (E 52, ex-FF 1094).

SPAIN – Name (Pennant Number): BALEARES (F 71), ANDALUCÍA (F 72), CATALUÑA (F 73), ASTURIAS (F 74), EXTREMADURA (F 75)

TAIWAN – Name (Pennant Number): CHIN YANG (ex-*Robert E Peary*) (932, ex-FF 1073), FONG YANG (ex-*Brewton*) (933, ex-FF 1086), FENG YANG (ex-*Kirk*) (934, ex-FF 1087), LAN YANG (ex-*Joseph Hewes*) (935, ex-FF 1078), HAE YANG (ex-*Cook*) (936, ex-FF 1083), HWAI YANG (ex-*Barbey*) (937 ex-FF 1088), NING YANG (ex-*Downes*) (938, ex-FF 1070), YI YANG (ex-*Aylwin*) (939, ex-FF 1081).

THAILAND – Name (Pennant Number): PHUTTHA YOTFA CHULALOK (ex-*Truett*) (461, ex-FF 1095),

PHUTTHA LOETLA NAPHALAI (ex-*Ouellet*) (462, ex-FF 1077).

TURKEY – Name (Pennant Number): MUAVENET (ex-*Capodanno*) (F 250, ex-FF 1093), KOCATEPE (ex-*Reasoner*) (F 252, ex-FF 1063), ZAFER (ex-*Thomas C Hart*) (F 253, ex-FF 1092) TRAKYA (ex-*McCandless*) (F 254, ex-FF 1084), KARADENIZ (ex-*Donald B Beary*) (F 255, ex-FF1085), EGE (ex-*Ainsworth*) (F 256, ex-FF 1090).

SPECIFICATION

Displacement, full load, tons: 4,177 ('Baleares' class). 4,260 ('Knox' class).

Length, feet (metres): 438 (133.6), ('Baleares' class) 439.6 (134), ('Knox' class).

Beam, feet (metres): 46.9 (14.3), ('Baleares' class). 46.8 (14.3), ('Knox' class).

Draught, feet (metres): 15.4 (4.7), ('Baleares' class) 15 (4.6), ('Knox' class).

Speed, knots: 28, ('Baleares' class). 27, ('Knox' class).

Range, miles: 4,000 at 22 kts

KEY RECOGNITION FEATURES

- Long forecastle with 5 in gun mounting well forward of ASROC A/S box missile launcher.
- Very unusual and prominent large cylindrical mast and funnel combined amidships; air search radar aerial at forward end and short lattice mast atop after end supporting large surface search radar aerial.
- 'Baleares' class has prominent square air search radar atop mast.
- 'Baleares' class also has Harpoon launchers atop aft low superstructure, immediately aft of short lattice mast omitted from other 'Knox' class units.
- CIWS in 'Y' position on 'Knox' class ships. Standard SAM launch in 'X' position at aft end of superstructure in 'Baleares' class.
- Flight deck aft, except 'Baleares' class.

Note: 'Baleares' class built in Spain after very close co-operation between Spain and the USA. 'Knox' class units transferred from the US Navy.

Note 2: In Mexican hulls, SAM launcher only in *Ignacio Allende* in 'Y' position.

PHUTTHA LOETLA NAPHALAI

ARMAMENT

Missiles: SSM - 8 McDonnell Douglas Harpoon (4 normally carried). (Not carried in Mexican hulls).   SAM - 16 GDC Pomona Standard SM-1MR; Mk 22 Mod 0 launcher. ('Baleares' class, but see Note 2).A/S - Honeywell ASROC Mk 112 octuple launcher; payload Mk 46 torpedoes, ('Baleares' class). A/S - ASROC Mk 16 octuple launcher (with 2 cells modified to fire Harpoon), ('Knox' class). Greek ships have Stinger or Redeye SAM posts fitted.

Guns: 1 - FMC 5 in (127 mm)/54 Mk 42 Mod 9, (all ships). 2 - Bazán 20 mm/120 12-barrel Meroka, ('Baleares' class). 1 - GE/GD 20 mm/76 Vulcan Phalanx Mk 15, ('Knox' class, not Mexican.). 2 - Rheinmetall 20 mm; 4 - 12.7 mm machine-guns, (Greek ships). 2 - 12.7 mm machine-guns, ('Baleares' class)   4 - Type 75 20 mm (Taiwanese ships).

Torpedoes: 4 - 324 mm US Mk 32 (2 twin) tubes. Honeywell Mk 46 Mod 5. (all ships). 2   484 mm US Mk 25 stern tubes. Westinghouse Mk 37; no longer used. ('Baleares' class).

Mines: Rail for 8 mines can be fitted in Greek ships.

Decoys: 4 - Loral Hycor SRBOC 6-barrelled Mk 36, (all ships). T Mk-6 Fanfare/SLQ-25 Nixie torpedo decoy. Prairie Masker hull and blade rate noise suppression, ('Knox' class).

RADARS

Air search - Hughes SPS-52B, 3D. ('Baleares' class) Lockheed SPS-40B/D ('Knox' class).

Surface search - Raytheon SPS-10 ('Baleares' class). SPS-10 or Norden SPS-67. ('Knox' class).

Navigation - Raytheon Marine Pathfinder, ('Baleares' class). Marconi LN66 ('Knox' class).

Fire control - Western Electric SPG-53B. Raytheon SPG-51C. Selenia RAN 12L. 2 Sperry VPS 2, ('Baleares' class). SPG-53A/D/F ('Knox' class).

Sonars: Raytheon SQS-56 (DE 1160); hull-mounted. EDO SQS-35V; VDS, ('Baleares' class). EDO/GE SQS-26CX ('Knox' class).

AIR SUPPORT

Helicopters: 1 Kaman SH-2G Seasprite, (Egyptian ships). 1 Agusta AB 212 (ASW), (Greek ships). 1 MBB BO 105CB (Patrol), (Mexico). 1 Hughes MD 500, (short-range ASW), (Taiwan). 1 Bell 212 or SH-2G Seasprite in due course, (Thai ships). 1 Agusta AB 212 (ASW) (Turkish ships).

ADMIRAL PITKA

Harald Caestens

Country: ESTONIA
Country of origin: DENMARK
Ship type: FRIGATES
Class: MODIFIED HVIDBJØRNEN (FF)
Active: 1
Name (Pennant Number): ADMIRAL PITKA (ex-*Beskytteren*).

SPECIFICATION

Displacement, full load, tons: 1,970.
Length, feet (metres): 245 (74.7).
Beam, feet (metres): 40 (12.2).
Draught, feet (metres): 17.4 (5.3) keel.
Speed, knots: 18.
Range, miles: 6,000 at 13 kts.

ARMAMENT

Guns: 1 - USN 3 in (76 mm)/50 Mk 22.
Decoys: 2 - THORN EMI Sea Gnat 6-barrell chaff..
Radars: Litton Marine.

AIR SUPPORT

Helicopters: 1 Westland Lynx type.

Note: Transferred by gift from Denmark, July, 2000. Strengthened for ice operations.

KEY RECOGNITION FEATURES

- Short forecastle with maindeck line dipping to superstructure.
- 3 in gun mounting on forecastle approximately mid-point between bow and bridge.
- Single black-capped tapering funnel amidships.
- Mast atop bridge superstructure topped by prominent bulbous radome.
- Short pylon mast on after superstructure.
- Flight deck right aft above open quarterdeck.

Florèal

GERMINAL

Country: FRANCE, MOROCCO
Country of origin: FRANCE
Ship type: FRIGATES
Class: FLORÉAL (FFG)
Active: 6 France, 1 Morocco
Building: 1 Morocco
FRANCE – Name (Pennant Number): FLORÉAL (F 730), PRAIRIAL (F 731), NIVÔSE (F 732), VENTÔSE (F 733), VENDÉMAIRE (F 734), GERMINAL (F 735)
MOROCCO – Name (Pennant Number): MOHAMMED V (502), HASSAN II (503).

SPECIFICATION

Displacement, full load, tons: 2,950.
Length, feet (metres): 306.8 (93.5).
Beam, feet (metres): 45.9 (14.4).
Draught, feet (metres): 14.1 (4.3).
Speed, knots: 20.
Range, miles: 10,000 at 15 kts.

ARMAMENT

Missiles: SSM - 2 Aerospatiale MM 38 Exocet. SAM – 2 Matra Simbad twin launchers can replace 20 mm guns or Dagaie launcher.
Guns: 1 - DCN 3.9 in (100 mm)/55 Mod 68 CADAM. (Probably 1 OTOBreda 76mm/62 in Moroccan hulls). 2 - Giat 20 F2 20 mm.
Decoys: 2 - CSEE Dagaie Mk II; 10-barrel trainable chaff/IR launchers.

RADARS

Air/surface search - Thomson-CSF Mars DRBV 21A.
Navigation - 2 Racal Decca 1229 (DRBN 34A)

AIR SUPPORT

Helicopters: 1 Aerospatiale AS 565MA Panther or platform for 1 AS 332F Super Puma.

KEY RECOGNITION FEATURES

- Low forecastle with 3.9 in gun mounting raised above ('B' position). (Probably 76 mm in Moroccan hulls).
- High central superstructure with complex enclosed mainmast at after end of bridge.
- Unusual, twin, rectangular side-by-side funnels with exhausts protruding at top.
- Exocet SSM angled launchers sited between funnel and mainmast.
- Syracuse II SATCOM atop slab-sided platform adjacent funnels. (Missing in Moroccan hulls)
- 20 mm gun mounting on hangar roof.
- Long flight deck with break down to small quarterdeck.
- Ship's boat in starboard side davits adjacent to SSM launcher.

La Fayette

Country: FRANCE, SAUDI ARABIA, SINGAPORE, TAIWAN

Country of origin: FRANCE

Ship type: FRIGATES

Class: LA FAYETTE/TYPE F-3000S/ARRIVAD (MODIFIED LA FAYETTE)/KANG DING (KWANG HUA PROJECT II) (FFG)

Active: 5 France, 6 Taiwan (Kang Ding).

Building: 3 Saudi Arabia (Type F-3000S)

Ordered: 6 Singapore

FRANCE – Name (Pennant Number): LA FAYETTE (F 710), SURCOUF (F 711), COURBET (F 712), ACONITE (ex-*Jauréguiberry*) (F 713), GUÉPRATTE (F 714).

SAUDI ARABIA – Name (Pennant Number): AL RYADH (812), MAKKAH (814), AL DAMMAM (816).

SINGAPORE – Name (Pennant Number): none allocated.

TAIWAN – Name (Pennant Number): KANG DING (1202), SI NING (1203), KUN MING (1205), DI HUA (1206), WU CHANG (1207), CHEN TE (1208).

SPECIFICATION

Displacement, full load, tons: 3,700, (French), 3,800 (Taiwanese), 4,650 (Saudi).

Length, feet (metres): 407.5 (124.2) oa, (French and Taiwanese) 442.9 (135), (Saudi).

Beam, feet (metres): 50.5 (15.4), (French and Taiwanese). 56.4 (17.2), (Saudi).

Draught, feet (metres): 19.4 (5.9) (French), 18 (5.5) (Taiwanese), 13.5 (4.1), (Saudi).

Speed, knots: 25.

Range, miles: 9,000 at 12 kts.

ARMAMENT

Missiles: SSM - 8 Aerospatiale MM 40 Block II Exocet. (French and Saudi). Hsiung Feng II (2 quad) (Taiwanese). SAM - Thomson-CSF Crotale Naval CN 2 octuple launcher, (French). Eurosam SAAM octuple VLS for Aster 15. (Saudi). Sea Chaparral quad launcher, (Taiwanese).

Guns: 1 - DCN 3.9 in (100 mm)/55 Mod 68 CADAM. (French) 1 - Giat 3.9 in (100 mm)/55 Compact Mk 2 (Saudi). 1 - OTO MELARA 76 mm/62 Mk 75 (Taiwanese). 2 - Giat 20F2 20 mm, 2 - 12.7 mm machine-guns, (French and Saudi ships). 1 Hughes 20 mm/76 Vulcan Phalanx Mk 15 Mod 2; 2 - Bofors 40mm/70; 2 - CS 20 mm Type 75, (Taiwanese ships).

Torpedoes: 4 - 21 in (533 mm) tubes, ECAN F17P. (Saudi ships). 6 - 324 mm Mk 32 (2 triple) tubes, Alliant Mk 36 Mod 5. (Taiwanese)

Decoys: 2 - CSEE Dagaie Mk 2 10-barrel launchers, (all ships). SLAT anti-wake homing torpedoes system. (French and Saudi ships).

RADARS

Air/surface search - Thomson-CSF Sea Tiger (DRBV 15C).(French ships). DRBV 26D Jupiter II (Saudi and Taiwanese ships).

Surface search – Thomson-CSF Triton G (Taiwanese ships)

Surveillance/Fire control – Thomson-CSF Arabel 3D (Saudi ships)

Navigation – 2 Racal Decca 1226, (DRBN 34A). 2 Racal Decca 20V90 (Taiwanese).

Fire control - Thomson-CSF Castor 2J.

Sonars: Thomson Marconi CAPTAS 20. (Saudi ships). BAe/Thomson-Sintra ATAS(V)2 active towed array; Thomson-Sintra Spherion B, bow-mounted active search. (Taiwanese)

AIR SUPPORT

Helicopters: 1 Aerospatiale AS565 MA Panther or platform for 1 Super Frelon. (France). 1 Aerospatiale SA 365 Dauphin 2 (Saudi).1 Sikorsky S-70C(M)1 (ASW) (Taiwanese).

SURCOUF

KEY RECOGNITION FEATURES

- 3.9 in gun mounting ('A' position). (OTO MELARA 76mm/62 in Taiwanese ships). (Giat 3.9 in/55 in Saudi ships).
- High, flush central superstructure with pyramid mainmast amidships. (Short mainmast in Taiwanese ships).
- Unusual forward-sloping mast and funnel combined, supporting ESM aerial. (SATCOM on forward gantry in French ships).
- Saudi ships have additional two pylon masts on superstructure. First, atop forward superstructure, is squat, and supports air search radar. Second, tall, cylindrical, aft of midships, with Thomson-CSF Arabel 3D surveillance/fire control radome atop.
- Taiwanese hulls have shorter mast funnel, supporting distinctive air/surface radar. Second, squat mast aft with pole mast atop, with surface search and fire control radars on very chunky gantries facing aft.
- Crotale Naval CN 2 SAM launcher at after end of main superstructure in French ships. CIWS in Taiwanese hulls.
- Long flight deck right aft.

Note: All superstructure inclines at 10° to the vertical to reduce radar echo area.

Note 2: External equipment such as capstans and bollards are either hidden or installed as low as possible.

Note 3: Unusual smooth uncluttered profile for a warship.

Note 4: Singapore hulls expected to be different from other builds. Reported that ships will displace around 3,000 tons and 360 ft (110 m) long with helicopter deck.   First to be delivered in 2005.

Note 5: *La Fayette* will have short cylindrical mast, top by a bulbous fire control radome after mid-life modernisation

Note 6: Planned to move CIWS to bridge roof and fit 2 RAM launchers on the hangar in Taiwanese hulls.

Brandenburg

BAYERN

Country: GERMANY
Country of origin: GERMANY
Ship type: FRIGATES
Class: BRANDENBURG (TYPE 123) (FFG)
Active: 4
Name (Pennant Number): BRANDENBURG (F 215), SCHLESWIG-HOLSTEIN (F 216), BAYERN (F 217), MECKLENBURG-VORPOMMERN (F 218).

SPECIFICATION

Displacement, full load, tons: 4,900.
Length, feet (metres): 455.7 (138.9) oa.
Beam, feet (metres): 54.8 (16.7).
Draught, feet (metres): 22.3 (6.8).
Speed, knots: 29.
Range, miles: 4,000 at 18 kts.

ARMAMENT

Missiles: SSM - 4 Aerospatiale MM 38 Exocet, (2 twin). SAM - Martin Marietta VLS Mk 41 Mod 3, for NATO Sea Sparrow. 2 RAM 21 cell Mk 49 launchers.
Guns: 1 - OTO MELARA 76 mm/62 Mk 75. 2 - Rheinmetall 20 mm Rh 202 (to be replaced by Mauser 27 mm).
Torpedoes: 4 - 324 mm Mk 32 Mod 9 (2 twin) tubes. Honeywell 46 Mod 2.
Decoys: 2 - Breda SCLAR.

RADARS

Air search - Signaal LW08.
Air/surface search - Signaal SMART, 3D.
Navigation - 2 Raytheon Raypath.

Fire control - 2 Signaal STIR 180 trackers.
Sonars: Atlas Elektronik DSQS-23BZ; hull-mounted, active search/attack.

AIR SUPPORT

Helicopters: 2 Westland Sea Lynx Mk 88 or 88A. (ASW/ASV).

KEY RECOGNITION FEATURES

- High freeboard, continuous maindeck from bow to break down to flight deck.
- 76 mm/62 gun mounting ('A' position).
- RAM SAM box launcher ('B' position).
- High central superstructure with bridge well aft from bows.
- NATO Sea Sparrow SAM (VLS) tubes immediately forward of bridge.
- Large, sturdy, enclosed mainmast forward of midships.
- Large twin angled funnels between forward and after superstructures.
- After superstructure with aftermast atop, supporting large Signaal LW08 air search radar aerial.
- Exocet SSM twin launchers between funnel and mainmast.
- RAM SAM box launcher atop hangar.
- Flight deck right aft with open quarterdeck below.

Note: Germany's new 'Sachsen' class based on Type 123 hull.

BLOYS VAN TRESLONG   W.Sartori

Country: GERMANY, GREECE, NETHERLANDS,
UNITED ARAB EMIRATES (UAE).

Country of origin: NETHERLANDS

Ship type: FRIGATES

Class: KORTENAER/BREMEN (MODIFIED
KORTENAER TYPE 122)/ELLI (FFG)

Active: 8 Germany (Bremen/Modified
Kortenaer/Type 122), 7 Greece (Elli),
1 Netherlands (Kortenaer), 2 UAE (Kortenaer)

GERMANY – Name (Pennant Number): BREMEN
(F 207), NIEDERSACHSEN (F 208), RHEINLAND-
PFALZ (F 209), EMDEN (F 210), KÖLN (F 211),
KARLSRUHE (F 212), AUGSBURG (F 213), LÜBECK
(F 214).

GREECE – Name (Pennant Number): ELLI (ex-*Pieter
Florisz*) (F 450, ex-F 812), LIMNOS (ex-*Witte de
With*) (F 451, ex-F 813), AEGEON (ex-*Banckert*) (F
460, ex-F 810), ADRIAS (ex-*Callenburgh*), (F 459, ex-
F 808), NAVARINON (ex-*Van Kinsbergen*) (F 461, ex-
F 809), KOUNTOURIOTIS (ex-*Kortenaer*), (F 462, ex-F
807), BOUBOULINA (ex-*Pieter Floris*, ex-*Willem van
der Zaan*), (F43, ex- F826).

NETHERLANDS – Name (Pennant Number):
BLOYS VAN TRESLONG (F 824).

KEY RECOGNITION FEATURES

- Similar hull and basic profile to the *Jacob
  Van Heemskerck* class.
- Easily identifiable differences are: 3 in gun
  mounting ('A' position), WM25 fire control
  radar dome atop mainmast, Pomona
  Standard SAM launcher not fitted, low
  hangar, flight deck with open quarterdeck
  below.
- Sea Sparrow SAM box launcher in 'B'
  position.
- Harpoon SSM launchers, angled port and
  starboard, in break in superstructure.
- LW08 air search radar atop short open
  pylon, forward edge of hangar, aft of
  funnel.
- Greek ships have 3 in gun mounting atop
  hangar.
- *Bremen* class has tall lattice mast
  immediately forward of funnel and main
  deck not continuous. Taller hangar aft.

Kortenaer

UNITED ARAB EMIRATES – Name (Pennant Number): ABU DHABI (ex-*Abraham Crijnssen*) (F 01,ex-F 816), AL EMIRAT (ex-*Piet Heyn*) (F 02, ex-F 811).

SPECIFICATION

Displacement, full load, tons: 3,630 (3,680, German ships).

Length, feet (metres): 428 (130.5) (426.4 (130), German ships).

Beam, feet (metres): 47.9 (14.6). (47.6 (14.5) German ships).

Draught, feet (metres): 20.3 (6.2), (screws). (21.3 (6.5) German ships).

Speed, knots: 30.

Range, miles: 4,700 at 16 kts.

ARMAMENT

Missiles: SSM - McDonnell Douglas Harpoon (2 quad) launchers. SAM - Raytheon Sea Sparrow Mk 29 octuple launcher. 2 GDC RAM (German ships only).

Guns: 1 - OTO MELARA 3 in (76 mm)/62 Mk 75 Compact. (2 in some Greek ships) Signaal SGE-30 Goalkeeper with General Electric 30 mm. (Dutch and UAE ships). 1 or 2 - GE/GD Vulcan Phalanx 20 mm Mk 15. (Greek ships). 2 - Oerlikon 20 mm, (Dutch and UAE ships only). 2 - Rheinmetall 20 mm Rh 202, to be replaced by Mauser 27 mm, (German ships only).

Torpedoes: 4 - 324 mm US Mk 32 (2 twin) tubes. Honeywell Mk 46 Mod 5 Neartip. (Mod 2 in German ships, to be replaced by Mu 90; Mod1/2 in Greek ships).

Decoys: 2 - Loral Hycor SRBOC 6-barrel Mk 36 chaff launchers. (4 in German ships). SLQ-25 Nixie towed torpedo decoy; Prairie Bubble noise reduction, (German ships).

RADARS

Air search - Signaal LW08. (Dutch, Greek and UAE units).

Air/surface search DASA TRS-3D/32. German ships only.

Surface search - Signaal ZW06, (Dutch, Greek units). Signaal Scout (UAE ships).

Navigation – SMA 3 RM 20, (German ships only).

Fire control - Signaal STIR. Signaal WM25.

Sonars: Westinghouse SQS-509, bow-mounted active search/attack, (Dutch ships). SQS-505, hull-mounted, (Greek and UAE ships). Atlas Elektronik DSQS-21BZ (BO), (German ships).

AIR SUPPORT

Helicopters: 2 Westland Sea Lynx Mk 88 or 88A. (ASW/ASV), (German ships). 2 Agusta AB 212 (ASW), (Greek). 2 Westland SH-14B Lynx (ASW), (Dutch). 2 Eurocopter AS 545 Panther, (ASW), (UAE).

Sachsen

SACHSEN (FIRST DOCKING OUT)   *Michael Nimtz*

Country: GERMANY
Country of origin: GERMANY
Ship type: FRIGATES
Class: SACHSEN (TYPE 124) (FFG)
Active: 0
Building: 3
Name (Pennant Number): SACHSEN (F 219),
HAMBURG (F 220), HESSEN (F 221)

SPECIFICATION

Displacement, full load, tons: 5,600.
Length, feet (metres): 469.2 (143) oa.
Beam, feet (metres): 57.1 (17.4).
Draught, feet (metres): 14.4 (4.4).
Speed, knots: 29.
Range, miles: 4,000 at 18 kts.

ARMAMENT

Missiles: SSM –8 Harpoon, (2 quad). SAM - VLS
   Mk 41, for NATO Evolved Sea Sparrow.   2 RAM
   21 cell Mk 49 launchers.
Guns: 1 - OTOBreda 76 mm/62 IRDF . 2 - Mauser
   27 mm.
Torpedoes: 6 - 324 mm Mk 32 Mod 9 (2 triple)
   tubes. Eurotorp Mu 90 Impact.
Decoys: 6 - SRBOC 130 mm chaff launchers.

RADARS

Air search – Signaal SMART L
Air/surface search - Signaal APAR, phased array.
Surface search: Triton G
Navigation – 2 sets.
Sonars: Atlas DSQS-21B; bow-mounted, active
   search/attack. Active towed array.

AIR SUPPORT

Helicopters: 2 NFH 90 or Westland Sea Lynx Mk
   88A. (ASW/ASV).

KEY RECOGNITION FEATURES

- High freeboard, continuous maindeck from
  bow to break down to short flight deck.
- 76 mm/62 gun mounting ('A' position).
- RAM SAM box launcher ('B' position).
- High central superstructure with bridge
  well aft from bows.
- Mk 41 (VLS) SAM tubes immediately
  forward of bridge.
- Massive sturdy, enclosed mainmast forward
  of midships with black circular APAR
  phased arrays at top; above thin, short pole
  mast.
- Thin pyramid enclosed mast forward of
  funnels.
- Large twin angled funnels aft of midships,
  atop superstructure..
- After superstructure with aftermast atop,
  supporting large rectangular SMART air
  search radar aerial.
- Harpoon twin launchers between funnel
  and mainmast.
- RAM SAM box launcher atop hangar.
- Flight deck right aft.
Note: Based on German Type 123
  'Brandenburg' hull with improved stealth
  features.

Godavari/Improved Godavari

GOMATI

Country: INDIA
Country of origin: India
Ship type: FRIGATES
Class: GODAVARI/MODIFIED GODAVARI (PROJECT 16A) (FFG)
Active: 5
Building: 1
Name (Pennant Number): GODAVARI (F 20), GOMATI (F 21), GANGA (F 22), BRAHMAPUTRA (F 31), BEAS (F 32), BETWA (F 33)

SPECIFICATION

Displacement, full load, tons: 3,850. 4,450, (Modified Godavari)
Length, feet (metres): 414.9 (126.5).
Beam, feet (metres): 47.6 (14.5).
Draught, feet (metres): 14.8 (4.5).
Speed, knots: 27.
Range, miles: 4,500 at 12 kts.

ARMAMENT

Missiles: SSM - 4 SS-N-2D Styx. (F 20 –22) SS-N-25 (4 quad). SS-N-25 Sapless (Kh 35 Uran) (F 31-33). SAM - SA-N-4 Gecko twin launcher, (F20-22). Trishful launcher to be fitted in F 31-33.
Guns: 2 - 57 mm/70 (twin). (Replaced by OTO MELARA 76 mm/62 gun in Mod.Godavari). 8 - 30 mm/65 (4 twin) AK 230. (Replaced by 4 – 30 mm/65 AK 630 in Mod. Godavari).
Torpedoes: 6 - 324 mm ILAS 3 (2 triple) tubes. Whitehead A244S.
Decoys: 2 chaff launchers. Graseby G738 towed torpedo decoy.

RADARS

Air search - Signaal LW 08. (LW 08/Bharat RAWL PLN 517, Mod. Godavari).
Air/surface search – 'Head Net C', 3D. (Bharat RAWS 03 PFN 513, Mod. Godavari).
Navigation/helo control - 2 Signaal ZW 06; or Don Kay.
Fire control – 2 Drum Tilt. (30 mm), Muff Cob (57 mm), Pop Group (SA-N-4), (F 20-22). Contraves Seaguard (30 mm and SSM), Bharat Aparna, (SAM), (F 31-33).
Sonars: Bharat APSOH. Thomson-Sintra DSBV 62 (Ganga) passive towed array. Fathoms Oceanic VDS. Type 162M.

AIR SUPPORT

Helicopters: 2 Sea King and 1 HAL SA 319B Chetak, (Alouette III). (ASW)

Talwar

TALWAR

Country:	INDIA
Country of origin:	India
Ship type:	FRIGATES
Class:	TALWAR (Type 1135.6/PROJECT 17) (FFG)
Active:	1
Building:	3
Planned:	2

Name (Pennant Number): TALWAR (F40),
TRISHUL (F43), TABAR (F44), –– (-).

SPECIFICATION

Displacement, full load, tons: 3,250.
Length, feet (metres): 408.5 (124.5).
Beam, feet (metres): 49.9 (15.2).
Draught, feet (metres): 13.8 (4.2).
Speed, knots: 32.
Range, miles: 4,500 at 18 kts.

ARMAMENT

Missiles: SSM – 8 – SS-N-27 Novator Alfa Klub
(EM-5-54E1) in VLS silo. SAM – SA-N-7 Gadfly
(Kashmir/Uragan). SAM/guns – 2 CADS-N-1
(Kortik) with twin 30 mm Gatling combined
with SA-N-11 'Grisson' and Hot Flash/Hot Spot
radar/optronic director.
Guns: 1 - 100 mm/59 A 190.
Torpedoes: 4 – PTA-53 533 mm (2 twin) tubes..
Decoys: 2 - PK 2 chaff launchers.

RADARS

Air/surface search – 'Top Plate', 3D.
Surface search – Palm Frond.
Fire control – 2 Front Dome (SA-N-7) Kite Screech
B (SSM/100 mm gun).

Sonars: Bharat APSOH. VDS active search.

AIR SUPPORT

Helicopters: 1 Kamov Ka-28/Ka-31 Helix (ASW) or
HAL Advanced Light Helicopter (ASV/ASW).

KEY RECOGNITION FEATURES

- Unusually long forecastle.
- Five weapons systems forward of the
  bridge; from the bow aft, 100 mm/59 gun
  mounting; SA-N-7 Gadfly SAM launcher;
  SS-N-27 Klub SSM in raised VLS silo; RBU
  6000 A/S Mortar on raised platform
  immediately forward of bridge.
- Midships superstructure with pyramid
  mainmast at after end and enclosed
  pyramid pylon immediately above bridge.
- Sloping tapered lattice mast at aft end of
  bridge superstructure.
- Low funnel well aft of midships with pylon
  immediately forward supporting Front
  Dome fire control radar.
- Slab-sided after superstructure (hangars)
  with dome at aft end, and GADS-N-1
  SAM/guns system adjacent, port and
  starboard.
- Flight deck with break down to very short
  quarterdeck.
- Note: First three dramatic modification of
  original 'Krivak III class design. Later ships
  will incorporate stealth features.

Van Speijk

AHMAD YANI

Country: INDONESIA
Country of origin: NETHERLANDS
Ship type: FRIGATES
Class: VAN SPEIJK/AHMAD YANI (FFG)
Active: 6
Name (Pennant Number): AHMAD YANI (ex-*Tjerk Hiddes*) (351), SLAMET RIYADI (ex-*Van Speijk*) (352), YOS SUDARSO (ex-*Van Galen*) (353), OSWALD SIAHAAN (ex-*Van Nes*) (354), ABDUL HALIM PERDANAKUSUMA (ex-*Evertsen*) (355), KAREL SATSUITUBUN (ex-*Isaac Sweers*) (356)

SPECIFICATION

Displacement, full load, tons: 2,835.
Length, feet (metres): 372 (113.4).
Beam, feet (metres): 41 (12.5).
Draught, feet (metres): 13.8 (4.2).
Speed, knots: 28.5.
Range, miles: 4,500 at 12 kts.

ARMAMENT

Missiles: SSM - 8 McDonnell Douglas Harpoon.
SAM - 2 Short Bros Seacat quad launchers. (Being replaced by 2 Matra Simbad twin launchers for Mistral).
Guns: 1 - OTO MELARA 3 in (76 mm)/62 Compact. 2 - 12.7 mm machine-guns.
Torpedoes: 6 - 324 mm Mk 32 (2 triple) tubes. Honeywell Mk 46.
Decoys: 2 - Knebworth Corvus 8-tubed trainable launchers.

RADARS

Air search - Signaal LW03.
Air/surface search - Signaal DA05.
Navigation - Racal Decca 1229.
Fire control - Signaal M 45. (76 mm and SSM) 2 Signaal M 44 (for Seacat SAM, being removed).
Sonars: Signaal CWE 610; hull-mounted; VDS.

AIR SUPPORT

Helicopters: 1 Westland Wasp HAS Mk 1 (ASW).

KEY RECOGNITION FEATURES

- Similar to British *Leander* class.
- Long, raised forecastle with OTO MELARA 3 in (76 mm)/62 Compact gun mounting ('A' position).
- Midships superstructure with pyramid mainmast atop, just aft of bridge.
- Single, 'capped' funnel just aft of midships.
- Short aftermast supporting large LW03 air search radar aerial.
- Mistral SAM Simbad launchers on hangar roof, (replacing Seacat quad launchers).
- Torpedo tubes, port and starboard, on maindeck at forward end of long flight deck.

Fatahillah

FATAHILLAH

Country: INDONESIA
Country of origin: NETHERLANDS
Ship type: FRIGATES
Class: FATAHILLAH (FFG)
Active: 3
Name (Pennant Number): FATAHILLAH (361),
MALAHAYATI (362), NALA (363)

SPECIFICATION

Displacement, full load, tons: 1,450.
Length, feet (metres): 276 (84).
Beam, feet (metres): 36.4 (11.1).
Draught, feet (metres): 10.7 (3.3).
Speed, knots: 30.
Range, miles: 4,250 at 16 kts.

ARMAMENT

Missiles: SSM - 4 Aerospatiale MM 38 Exocet.
Guns: 1 - Bofors 4.7 in (120 mm)/46. 1 or 2 -
Bofors 40 mm/70 (2 in Nala). 2 - Rheinmetall
20 mm.
Torpedoes: 6 - 324 Mk 32 or ILAS 3 (2 triple)
tubes (none in Nala). 12 Mk 46 (or A244S)
torpedoes.
A/S mortars: 1 - Bofors 375 mm twin-barrelled.
Decoys: 2 - Knebworth Corvus 8-tubed trainable
launchers. 1 T-Mk 6 torpedo decoy.

RADARS

Air/surface search - Signaal DA05.
Surface search - Racal Decca AC 1229.

Fire control - Signaal WM28.
Sonars: Signaal PHS-32; hull-mounted active
search/attack.

AIR SUPPORT

Helicopters: 1 Westland Wasp HAS (Mk 1). (ASW).
(Nala only).

KEY RECOGNITION FEATURES

- 4.7 in gun mounting ('A' position) with
Bofors 375 mm A/S mortar launcher ('B'
mounting position).
- Low, slab-sided superstructure centred
forward of midships.
- Very substantial pyramid mainmast with
pole mast atop its after end.
- WM28 fire control radome atop short
pyramid mainmast above bridge.
- Large, square-shaped, low profile funnel
well aft of midships.
- Exocet SSM launchers between funnel and
after superstructure.
- Large DA05 air/surface search radar aerial
on pedestal atop small after superstructure.
- 40 mm/70 gun mounting aft of maindeck
at break down to small quarterdeck.
Note: Nala has no after mounting and the
maindeck is extended to provide a hangar
and short flight deck.

Ki Hajar Dewentara

KI HAJAR DEWANTARA

Country: INDONESIA
Country of origin: YUGOSLAVIA
Ship type: FRIGATES
Class: KI HAJAR DEWANTARA (FFG)
Active: 1
Name (Pennant Number): KI HAJAR DEWANTARA (364).

SPECIFICATION
Displacement, full load, tons: 2,050.
Length, feet (metres): 317.3 (96.7).
Beam, feet (metres): 36.7 (11.2).
Draught, feet (metres): 15.7 (4.8).
Speed, knots: 26.
Range, miles: 4,000 at 18 kts.

ARMAMENT
Missiles: SSM - 4 Aerospatiale MM 38 Exocet.
Guns: 1 - Bofors 57mm/70. 2 - Rheinmetall 20 mm.
Torpedoes: 2 – 21 in (533 mm) tubes. AEG SUT dual purpose torpedoes.
A/S mortars: 1 projector
Decoys: 2 -128 mm twin-tubed flare launchers.

RADARS
Surface search - Racal Decca AC 1229.
Fire control - Signaal WM28.

Sonars: Signaal PHS-32; hull-mounted active search/attack.

AIR SUPPORT
Helicopters: Platform for Nurtanio NBO 105C (Support)

KEY RECOGNITION FEATURES

- 4.7 in gun mounting ('A' position) with 20 mm cannon in 'B' mounting position on raised platform..
- Long, slab-sided superstructure centred forward of midships.
- Very substantial lattice mainmast with fire control radome at top at aft end of bridge superstructure with pole mast atop its after end.
- Large, rounded and tapered funnel well aft of midships.
- Ships boats on davits just aft of funnel.
- Exocet SSM launchers aft of funnel and after superstructure.
- Flight deck above open quarterdeck.

Claud Jones

Country:	INDONESIA, TURKEY
Country of origin:	USA
Ship type:	FRIGATES
Class:	CLAUD JONES/SAMADIKUN/BERK (MODIFIED CLAUD JONES) (FFG/FF)
Active:	4 Indonesia ('Samadikun' class), 1 Turkey ('Berk' class)

INDONESIA – Name (Pennant Number): SAMADIKUN (ex-*John R Perry*) (341, ex-DE 1034), MARTADINATA (ex-*Charles Berry*) (342, ex-DE 1035), MONGINSIDI (ex-*Claud Jones*) (343, ex-DE 1033), NGURAHRAI (ex-*McMorris*) (344, ex-DE 1036).

MARTADINATA

TURKEY – Name (Pennant Number): PEYK (D 359)

SPECIFICATION

Displacement, full load, tons: 1,968, Indonesian ships. 1,950, Turkish hull.
Length, feet (metres): 310. (95, Indonesian. 311.7 (95.3), Turkish.
Beam, feet (metres): 38.7 (11.8).
Draught, feet (metres): 18 (5.5).
Speed, knots: 22.
Range, miles: 3,000 at 18 kts.

ARMAMENT

Guns: 1 or 2 - USN 3 in (76mm)/50 Mk 34. (Indonesian) 4 - USN 3 in (76mm)/50 (2 twin), (Turkish). 2 - USSR 37 mm/63 (twin) (Indonesian only).
Torpedoes: 6 – 364 mm Mk 32 (2 triple tubes). Honeywell Mk 46.
A/S mortars: 2 - Mk 11 Hedgehog rocket launchers. (Turkish ship only)
Depth charges: 1 rack, (Turkish ship). 2 throwers, (Indonesian).

RADARS

Air search – Westinghouse SPS SPS-6E, (Indonesia.) Lockheed SPS-40 (Turkish ship).
Surface search - Raytheon SPS-5D or Raytheon SPS-4 (*Nagurahrai* only). Raytheon SPS-10 (Turkish ship).
Navigation – Racal Decca 1226.
Fire control – Lockheed SPG-52, (Indonesia). 2 Western Electric Mk 34, (Turkish ship).

Sonars: EDO (*Samadikun*) SQS-45V (remainder of Indonesian hulls)) hull-mounted active search/attack. Sangamo SQS-29/31, hull-mounted active search and attack, (Turkish ship).

AIR SUPPORT

Helicopters: Platform for AB 212 (ASW) (Turkish hull).

KEY RECOGNITION FEATURES

- 3 in gun mounting on raised platform forward of bridge.
- Tall, slab-sided superstructure centred forward of midships. Bridge has circular structure above.
- Tall thin cylindrical mainmast with triangular support aft. Short pole mast atop its after end.
- Large, rounded and tapered funnel aft of midships. (Turkish ship).
- Two shorter funnel in Indonesian units, one above each other.
- Ships boats on davits just aft of funnel.
- Deck break aft of superstructure to long quarterdeck. (Turkish unit has 3 in gun on quarterdeck; some Indonesians have a 37 mm twin mounting here).
- Tall pole mast aft of funnel (Indonesian units only)
- **Note:** Some Indonesian hulls have a 76 mm gun vice the 37 mm.

Parchim

Country: INDONESIA, RUSSIA

Country of origin: EAST GERMANY

Ship type: FRIGATES

Class: PARCHIM I (TYPE 1331) (KAPITAN PATIMURA) (FS)*

*Officially rated as corvettes.

Active: 16 (Indonesia)

Name (Pennant Number): KAPITAN PATIMURA (ex-*Prenzlau*), (371, ex-231), UNTUNG SUROPATI (ex-*Ribnitz*) (372, ex-233), NUKU (ex-*Waren*) (373, ex-224), LAMBUNG MANGKURAT (ex-*Angermünde*) (374, ex-214), CUT NYAK DIEN (ex-*Lübz*) (375, ex-P 6169, ex-221), SULTAN THAHA SYAIFUDDIN (ex-*Bad Doberan*) (376, ex-222), SUTANTO (ex-*Wismar*) (377, ex-P 6170, ex-241), SUTEDI SENOPUTRA (ex-*Parchim*) (378, ex-242), WIRATNO (ex-*Perleberg*) (379, ex-243), MEMET SASTRAWIRIA (ex-*Bützow*) (380, ex-244), TJIPTADI (ex-*Bergen*), (381, ex-213), HASAN BASRI (ex-*Güstrow*) (382, ex-223), IMAN BONJOL (ex-*Teterow*) (383, ex-P 6168, ex-234), PATI UNUS (ex-*Ludwiglust*) (384, ex-232), TEUKU UMAR (ex-*Grevesmühlen*) (385, ex-212), SILAS PAPARE (ex-*Gadebusch*) (386, ex-P 6167, ex-211).

Class: PARCHIM II (TYPE 1331) (FFL)

Active: 8 (Russia)

Name (Pennant Number): MPK 67 (242), MPK 105 (245), KAZANIETS MPK 205 (244), MPK 213 (222), MPK 216 (258), MPK 224 (243), MPK 227 (243), KALMYKIA MPK 229 (232).

UNTUNG SUROPATI   M. Declerck

SPECIFICATION

Displacement, full load, tons: 960. (769, Parchim I).

Length, feet (metres): 246.7 (75.2).

Beam, feet (metres): 32.2 (9.8).

Draught, feet (metres): 14.4 (4.4). (11.5 (3.5), Parchim I).

Speed, knots: 26. (24, Parchim I).

ARMAMENT

Missiles: SAM - 2 - SA-N-5 Grail quad launchers. (Also in some Parchim I units).

Guns: 1 - 3 in (76 mm)/66 AK 176. 1 - 30 mm/65 AK 630 6 barrels. (Parchim II). 1 - USSR 57 mm/80 (twin) automatic, 2 - 30 mm (twin), (Parchim I).

Torpedoes: 4 - 21 in (533 mm) (2 twin) tubes. 4 - 400 mm tubes, (Parchim I).

A/S mortars: 2 - RBU 6000 12-tubed, trainable.

Depth charges: 2 racks.

Mines: Rails fitted.

Decoys: 2 - PK 16 chaff launchers.

RADARS

Air/surface search - Cross Dome. (Strut Curve in Indonesian ships).

Navigation - TSR 333 or Nayala or Kivach III.

Fire control - Bass Tilt. (Muff Cob in Indonesian ships).

Sonars: Bull Horn, (MGT 332T) hull-mounted. Lamb Tail, helicopter type VDS. (Elk Tail VDS on starboard side in some Indonesian hulls).

KEY RECOGNITION FEATURES

- High bow, short forecastle.
- Low main superstructure with high central superstructure atop.
- 30mm/65 AK 630 CIWS mounting at forward end of main superstructure.
- RBU 6000 A/S mortar mounting forward of bridge.
- Substantial lattice mainmast atop central superstructure. Small 'Y' shaped (in profile) lattice mast protruding aft.
- Large Cross Dome air/surface search radome atop mainmast. (Strut Curve array in Indonesian units).
- SA-N-5 Grail quad SAM launcher at after end of forward superstructure (Russian units)
- Large, enclosed aftermast supporting distinctive drum-shaped Bass Tilt fire control radar aerial.
- 3 in gun mounting ('Y' position).

Note: Most obvious differences between Parchim I and II are conventional air/surface search radar aerial atop mainmast in Indonesian units and much smaller, shorter enclosed aftermast supporting Muff Cob fire control radar aerial.

Note 2: SA-N-5/8 SAM launchers fitted in some Indonesian ships – these may be replaced by twin Simbad SAM launchers

Note 3: Indonesian ships all ex-East German units, transferred in January 1993 after refit.

Note 4: Russian units operate in Baltic. One more, *MPK 228*, damaged by fire in 1999 and unlikely to become operational.

Alvand

ALVAND   *Guy Toremons*

Country: IRAN
Country of origin: UK
Ship type: FRIGATES
Class: ALVAND (VOSPER MARK 5) (FFG)
Active: 3
Name (Pennant Number): ALVAND (ex-*Saam*)
(71), ALBORZ (ex-*Zaal*) (72), SABALAN (ex-
Rostam) (73).

SPECIFICATION

Displacement, full load, tons: 1,350.
Length, feet (metres): 310 (94.5).
Beam, feet (metres): 36.4 (11.1).
Draught, feet (metres): 14.1 (4.3).
Speed, knots: 29.
Range, miles: 3,650 at 18 kts.

ARMAMENT

Missiles: SSM - 4 China YJ-2 (C-802, CSS-N-8
Saccade) (2 twin) (*Alborz* and *Sabalan*). 1 Sistel
Sea Killer II quin launcher, (*Alvand*). (Top row of
cassettes removed to incorporate BM-21
multiple rocket launcher.)
Guns: 1 - Vickers 4.5 in (114 mm)/55 Mk 8. 2 -
Oerlikon 35mm/90 (twin). 3 - Oerlikon GAM-
BO1 20 mm. 2 - 12.7 mm machineg-guns.
A/S mortars: 1 - 3-tubed Limbo Mk 10.
Decoys: 2 - UK Mk 5 rocket flare launchers.

RADARS

Air/surface search - Plessey AWS 1.
Surface search - Racal Decca 1226.
Navigation - Decca 629.
Fire control - 2 Contraves Sea Hunter.
Sonars: Graseby 174; hull-mounted, active search.
  Graseby 170; hull-mounted, active attack.

KEY RECOGNITION FEATURES

- Similar hull and superstructure profile to
  Pakistani British 'Type 21' frigates.
- Long forecastle with 4.5 in gun mounting
  ('A' position).
- Short pyramid mainmast just forward of
  midships.
- Low profile, sloping funnel, well aft with
  distinctive gas turbine air intakes forward
  of funnel, port and starboard.
- AWS 1 air/surface radar aerial immediately
  forward of funnel.
- Sited on afterdeck, from forward to aft, YJ-
  2 or Sea Killer II SSM launcher; Limbo A/S
  mortar and 35 mm/90 twin gun turret
  mounting.

Lupo

PERSEO

Country: ITALY, PERU, VENEZUELA

Country of origin: ITALY

Ship type: FRIGATES

Class: LUPO, ARTIGLIERE, CARVAJAL, MODIFIED LUPO (FFG)

Active: 4 Italy (Lupo), 4 Italy (Artigliere)*, 4 Peru (Carvajal), 6 Venezuela (Modified Lupo)
* Originally built for Iraq.

ITALY – Name (Pennant Number): LUPO (F 564), SAGITTARIO (F 565), PERSEO (F 566), ORSA (F 567)

Name (Pennant Number): ARTIGLIERE (ex-*Hittin*) (F 582, ex-F 14), AVIERE (ex-*Thi Qar*) (F 583 ex-F 15), BERSAGLIERE (ex-*Al Yarmouk*), (F 584 ex-F 17), GRANATIERE (ex-*Al Qadisiya*) (F 585 ex-F 16)

PERU – Name (Pennant Number): CARVAJAL (FM 51), VILLAVICENCIO (FM 52), MONTERO (FM 53), MARIATEGUI (FM 54).

VENEZUELA – Name (Pennant Number): MARISCAL SUCRE (F 21), ALMIRANTE BRIÓN (F 22), GENERAL URDANETA (F 23), GENERAL SOUBLETTE (F 24), GENERAL SALOM (F 25), ALMIRANTE GARCIA (ex-*José Felix Ribas*) (F 26).

SPECIFICATION

Displacement, full load, tons: 2 525, (Italian *Lupo/Artigliere*). 2 500, (Peru), 2 520, (Venezuela).

Length, feet (metres): 371.3 (113.2).

Beam, feet (metres): 37.1 (11.3).

Draught, feet (metres): 12.1 (3.7).

Speed, knots: 35.

Range: 3,450 at 20.5 kts.

ARMAMENT

Missiles: SSM - 8 OTO MELARA Teseo Mk 2 (TG 2). (Italian and Venezuelan ships; 16 in *Lupo* class). 8 OTO MELARA/Matra Otomat Mk 2 (TG 1), (Peruvian ships). SAM - Raytheon NATO Sea Sparrow Mk 29 octuple launcher, (Italian *Lupo* class). Albatros/Aspide octuple launcher (*Artigliere* class, Peruvian and Venezuelan ships).

Guns: 1 - OTO MELARA 5 in (127 mm)/54. 4 - Breda 40 mm/70 (2 twin) Compact. 2 -Oerlikon 20 mm can be fitted in Italian ships of both classes.

Lupo

Torpedoes: 6 - 324 mm US Mk 32 tubes.
Honeywell Mk 46. (Italian *Lupo* class; no
torpedoes fitted in *Artigliere* class.) 6 - 324 mm
ILAS (2 triple) tubes; Whitehead A244,
(Peruvian and Venezuelan units).

Decoys: 2 - Breda 105 mm SCLAR 20-tubed. (All
ships). SLQ-25 Nixie towed torpedo decoy,
(Italian *Lupo* class only).

RADARS

Air search - Selenia SPS-774 (RAN 10S).

Surface search/target indication - SMA SPS-702,
(Italian *Lupo* class).

Surface search - SMA SPQ-2 F, (Italian *Lupo* class).
SPQ-712 (RAN 12L/X), (*Artigliere*), Selenia RAN
11LX, (Peru andVenezuela).

Navigation - SMA SPN-748. (Italian *Lupo* class).
SMA SPN-703 (*Artigliere*). SMA 3RM 20R.
(Peruvian and Venezuelan).

Fire control - Selenia SPG-70 (RTN 10X). 2 Selenia
SPG-74 (RTN 20X). (All ships but also 2 Orion
RTN 10XP in Venezuelan ships). US Mk 95 Mod
1, (Italian *Lupo* class only, for SAM).

Sonars: Raytheon DE 1160B; hull-mounted,
(Italian *Lupo* class.) EDO SQS-29 Mod 610E in
Peruvian and Venezuelan ships. None fitted in
Artigliere class.

AIR SUPPORT

Helicopters: 1 Agusta AB 212 (ASW.)

Maestrale

ALISEO

Country: ITALY
Country of origin: ITALY
Ship type: FRIGATES
Class: MAESTRALE (FFG)
Active: 8
Name (Pennant Number): MAESTRALE (F 570), GRECALE (F 571), LIBECCIO (F 572), SCIROCCO (F 573), ALISEO (F 574), EURO (F 575), ESPERO (F 576), ZEFFIRO (F 577)

SPECIFICATION

Displacement, full load, tons: 3,200.
Length, feet (metres): 405 (122.7).
Beam, feet (metres): 42.5 (12.9).
Draught, feet (metres): 15.1 (4.6).
Speed, knots: 32.
Range, miles: 6,000 at 16 kts.

ARMAMENT

Missiles: SSM - 4 OTO MELARA Teseo Mk 2 (TG 2). SAM - Selenia Albatros octuple launcher; Aspide.
Guns: 1 - OTO MELARA 5 in (127 mm)/54 automatic. 4 - Breda 40 mm/70 (2 twin) Compact. 2 - Oerlikon 20 mm. (2 - Breda Oerlikon 20 mm fitted for Gulf deployments in 1990-91).
Torpedoes: 6 - 324 mm US Mk 32 (2 triple) tubes. Honeywell Mk 46. 2 - 21 in (533 mm) B516 tubes in transom. Whitehead A184.
Decoys: 2 - Breda 105 mm SCLAR 20-tubed rocket launchers. SLQ-25 towed torpedo decoy. Prairie Masker; noise suppression system.

RADARS

Air/surface search - Selenia SPS-74 (RAN 10S).
Surface search - SMA SPS-702.
Navigation - SMA SPN-703.
Fire control - Selenia SPG-75 (RTN 30X). 2 Selenia SPG 74 (RTN 20X).
Sonars: Raytheon DE 1164; hull-mounted; VDS.

AIR SUPPORT

Helicopters: 2 Agusta AB 212 (ASW).

KEY RECOGNITION FEATURES

- Bridge well aft from bows.
- 5 in gun mounting ('A' position).
- Albatros/Aspide SAM launcher ('B' mounting position).
- High forward superstructure with pointed pyramid mainmast atop.
- Single, rectangular funnel with wedge shaped, black smoke diffuser at top.
- Teseo SSM launchers, two port, two starboard, angled outboard sited immediately aft of funnel.
- Small, white, domed SATCOM aerial atop hangar roof.
- Flight deck right aft with open quarterdeck below.

Abukuma

OOYODO   *Hachiro Nakai*

Country: JAPAN
Country of origin: JAPAN
Ship type: FRIGATES
Class: ABUKUMA (FFG/DE)
Active: 6
Name (Pennant Number): ABUKUMA (DE 229),
JINTSU (DE 230), OOYODO (DE 231), SENDAI (DE
232), CHIKUMA (DE 233), TONE (DE 234)

SPECIFICATION

Displacement, full load, tons: 2,550.
Length, feet (metres): 357.6 (109).
Beam, feet (metres): 44 (13.4).
Draught, feet (metres): 12.5 (3.8).
Speed, knots: 27.

ARMAMENT

Missiles: SSM - 8 McDonnell Douglas Harpoon (2
  quad) launchers. A/S - Honeywell ASROC Mk
  112 octuple launcher; payload Mk 46 Mod 5
  Neartip torpedoes.
Guns: 1 - OTO MELARA 3 in (76 mm)/62 Compact.
  1 GE/GD 20 mm Phalanx CIWS Mk 15.
Torpedoes: 6 - 324 mm Type 68 (2 triple) tubes.
  Honeywell Mk 46 Mod 5 Neartip.
Decoys: 2 - Loral Hycor SRBOC 6-barrel Mk 36.

RADARS

Air search - Melco OPS-14C.

Surface search - JRC OPS-28C/D.
Fire control - Type 2-21.
Sonars: Hitachi OQS-8; hull-mounted.

KEY RECOGNITION FEATURES

- Long, sweeping, uncluttered forecastle with
  3 in gun mounting midway between bow
  and vertical bridge front.
- High forward superstructure with large
  lattice mainmast at after end, top half
  offset.
- Distinctive curved, OPS-14C lattice air
  search radar aerial on platform at forward
  end of mast.
- Two rectangular shaped black-capped
  funnels, forward one slightly taller.
- ASROC A/S missile box launcher sited
  between funnels.
- Gas turbine air intakes aft of after funnel,
  port and starboard.
- Short lattice aftermast atop after
  superstructure.
- Harpoon SSM angled launchers on raised
  structure immediately aft of aftermast.
- CIWS mounting on afterdeck.
Note - Non-vertical and rounded surfaces are
  employed for stealth reasons.

Chikugo

CHIKUGO CLASS   Hachiro Nakai

Country:	JAPAN
Country of origin:	JAPAN
Ship type:	FRIGATES
Class:	CHIKUGO (FF/DE)
Active:	1
Name (Pennant Number):	NOSHIRO (DE 225)

SPECIFICATION

Displacement, standard, tons: 1,500.
Length, feet (metres): 305 (93).
Beam, feet (metres): 35.5 (10.8).
Draught, feet (metres): 11.5 (3.5).
Speed, knots: 24.
Range, miles: 10,900 at 12 kts.

ARMAMENT

Missiles: A/S - Honeywell ASROC Mk 112 octuple
    launcher; payload Mk 46 Mod 5 Neartip
    torpedoes.
Guns: 2 - USN 3in (76 mm)/50 Mk 33 (twin). 2 -
    Bofors 40 mm/60 Mk 1 (twin).
Torpedoes: 6 -324 mm Type 68 (2 triple) tubes.
    Honeywell Mk 46 Mod 5 Neartip.

RADARS

Air search - Melco OPS-14/14B
Surface search - JRC OPS-16C/D/18-3.
Fire control - Type 1B.
Sonars: Hitachi OQS-3A; hull-mounted, active
    search and attack. EDO SPS (35(J); VDS.

KEY RECOGNITION FEATURES

- High bow with continuous sweeping
  maindeck through to stern.
- 3 in gun mounting within high breakwater
  ('A' position).
- High forward superstructure with large
  lattice mainmast at after end.
- Mainmast supports air search and
  air/surface search radar aerials.
- Single, sloping, black-capped funnel
  amidships.
- Small lattice aftermast.
- ASROC A/S missile box launcher sited
  between funnel and aftermast.
- 40 mm/60 gun mounting on sponson on
  afterdeck.

YUUBARI

Country: JAPAN
Country of origin: JAPAN
Ship type: FRIGATES
Class: ISHIKARI/YUUBARI CLASSES (FFG/DE)
Active: 3
Name (Pennant Number): ISHIKARI (DE 226),
YUUBARI (DE 227), YUUBETSU (DE 228).

SPECIFICATION

Displacement, full load, tons: 1,690, (1,450, DE
226).
Length, feet (metres): 298.5 (91). (278.8, (85), DE
226).
Beam, feet (metres): 35.4 (10.8).
Draught, feet (metres): 11.8 (3.6).
Speed, knots: 25.

ARMAMENT

Missiles: SSM – Harpoon (2 quad).
Guns: 1 - OTO MELARA 3in (76 mm)/62 Compact.
1 - GE/GD 20 mm Phalanx CIWS Mk 15.
Torpedoes: 6 - 324 mm Type 68 (2 triple) tubes.
Honeywell Mk 46 Mod 5 Neartip.
A/S mortars: 1 – 375 mm Bofors Type 41, 4-6-
barrel.
Decoys: 2 - Loral Hycor SRBOC 6-barrel Mk 36
chaff.

RADARS

Surface search - JRC OPS-28B/28-1.
Navigation – Fujitsu OPS-19B
Fire control - Type 2-21.
Sonars:NEC SQS-36J ; hull-mounted,
active/passive.

KEY RECOGNITION FEATURES

- Long forecastle with 3 in rounded gun
  turret in 'A' Position and prominent A/S
  mortar at 'B' position.
- Low forward supstructure with squat
  enclosed pylon supporting fire control
  radar.
- Lattice mast at aft end of bridge
  superstructure with complex pole mast
  atop.
- Squat tapered funnel with square exhaust
  on top well fat of midships.
- Break down to long quarterdeck with two
  Harpoon quad launchers port and
  starboard at stern.

Note: *Yuubari* slightly longer version of
Ishikari.

Soho

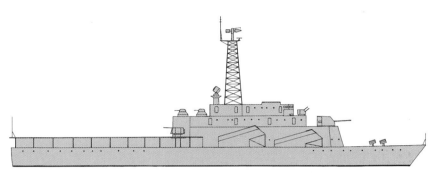

SOHO CLASS

Country: KOREA, NORTH	
Country of origin: KOREA, NORTH	
Ship type: FRIGATES	
Class: SOHO CLASS (FFG)	
Active: 1	
Name (Pennant Number): ––– (823).	

SPECIFICATION

Displacement, full load, tons: 1,640
Length, feet (metres): 242.1 (73.8).
Beam, feet (metres): 50.9 (15.5).
Draught, feet (metres): 12.5 (3.8).
Speed, knots: 23.

ARMAMENT

Missiles: SSM – 4 CSS-N-2.
Guns: 1 – 3.9in (100 mm)/56. 4 – 37mm/63 (2
twin). 4 – 30 mm/66 (2 twin). 4 – 25 mm/60 (2
twin).
A/S mortars: 2 RBU 1200 5-tube fixed launchers.

RADARS

Surface search –Square Tie.
Fire control – Drum Tilt.
Sonars: Stag Horn, hull-mounted active
search/attack.

AIR SUPPORT

Helicopters: Platform for medium helicopter.

KEY RECOGNITION FEATURES

- Twin hull design.
- Low freeboard, continuous maindeck from stem to stern.
- Wide beam.
- Clear forecastle with two A/S mortars only.
- Slab-sided superstructure with 2 box launchers, port and starboard, on either side of superstructure.
- Prominent 3.9 in gun turret on forward edge of superstructure, with two twin 25 mm mountings immediately above and just forward of bridge.
- Very high lattice mast on superstructure just forward of midships.
- Long platform aft for medium helicopter.

Najin

NAJIN 531

Country:	KOREA, NORTH
Country of origin:	KOREA, NORTH
Ship type:	FRIGATES
Class:	NAJIN CLASS (FFG)
Active:	2
Name (Pennant Number):	(531), (631).

SPECIFICATION

Displacement, full load, tons: 1,500
Length, feet (metres): 334.6 (102).
Beam, feet (metres): 32.8 (10).
Draught, feet (metres): 8.9 (2.7).
Speed, knots: 24.
Range, miles: 4,000 at 13 kts.

ARMAMENT

Missiles: SSM – 2 CSS-N-1.
Guns: 2 – 3.9in (100 mm)/56. 4 – 57mm/80 (2 twin). 12 or 4 – 30 mm/66 (6 or 2 twin). 16 or 14 - 14.5mm machine-guns (4 quad).
A/S mortars: 2 RBU 1200 5-tube fixed launchers.
Depth charges: 2 projectors, 2 racks.
Mines: 30.
Decoys: 6 chaff launchers.

RADARS

Air search – Square Tie.
Surface search – Pot Head
Navigation – Pot Drum
Fire control – Drum Tilt.

Sonars: Stag Horn, hull-mounted active search/attack.

KEY RECOGNITION FEATURES

- High bows with sweeping, continuous maindeck from stem to stern.
- Long forecastle with an array of weapons systems. From stem to bridge superstructure – 2 RBU A/S mortars; 3.9 in single gun turret; 1 twin 57 mm gun in open mounting, 2 quad 14.5 mm machine-gun mountings.
- Tall bridge structure with box-like optical director atop with Square Tie air search radar just aft.
- High lattice mast, aft of bridge superstructure, just forward of midships.
- Two funnels, one just aft of bridge, with 30 mm mounting aft; the other funnel well aft of midships.
- SSM launchers between funnels.
- Low lattice aft mast just forward of aft funnel.
- 3.9 in gun turret in 'Y' position, 57 mm opening mounting in 'X' position.

Note: Some resemblance to the ex-Soviet 'Kola' class, now deleted.

Ulsan

BUSAN

Country:	KOREA, SOUTH
Country of origin:	KOREA, SOUTH
Ship type:	FRIGATES
Class:	ULSAN (FFG)
Active:	9

Name (Pennant Number): ULSAN (FF 951), SEOUL (FF 952), CHUNG NAM (FF 953), MASAN (FF 955), KYONG BUK (FF 956), CHON NAM (FF 957), CHE JU (FF 958), BUSAN (FF 959), CHUNG JU (FF 961)

SPECIFICATION

Displacement, full load, tons: 2,180 (2,300 for FF 957 onwards).
Length, feet (metres): 334.6 (102).
Beam, feet (metres): 37.7 (11.5).
Draught, feet (metres): 11.5 (3.5).
Speed, knots: 34.
Range, miles: 4,000 at 15 kts.

ARMAMENT

Missiles: SSM - 8 McDonnell Douglas Harpoon (4 twin) launchers.
Guns: 2 - 3 in OTO MELARA (76 mm)/62 Compact. 8 Emerson Electric 30 mm (4 twin) (FF 951-955). 6 Breda 40 mm/70 (3 twin) (FF 956-961).
Torpedoes: 6 - 324 mm Mk 32 (2 triple) tubes. Honeywell Mk 46 Mod 1.
Depth charges: 12.
Decoys: 4 - Loral Hycor SRBOC 6-barrel Mk 36. SLQ-25 Nixie towed torpedo decoy.

RADARS

Air/surface search - Signaal DA05.
Surface search - Signaal ZW06 (FF 951-956).
Marconi S 1810 (FF 957-961).
Fire control - Signaal WM28 (FF 951-956).
Marconi ST 1802 (FF 957-961).
Navigation - Raytheon SPS-10C (FF 957-961).
Sonars: Signaal PHS-32; hull-mounted active search and attack.

Lekiu

LEKIU

Sattler & Steele

Country: MALAYSIA
Country of origin: UK
Ship type: FRIGATES
Class: LEKIU (FFG)
Active: 2
Name (Pennant Number): LEKIU (30), JEBAT (29)

SPECIFICATION

Displacement, full load, tons: 2,390.
Length, feet (metres): 346 (105.5) oa.
Beam, feet (metres): 42 (12.8).
Draught, feet (metres): 11.8 (3.6).
Speed, knots: 28.
Range, miles: 5,000 at 14 kts.

ARMAMENT

Missiles: SSM - 8 Aerospatiale MM 40 Exocet,
    Block 2. SAM - British Aerospace VLS Seawolf.
Guns: 1 - Bofors 57 mm/70 SAK Mk 2. 2 - MSI
    Defense Systems 30 mm/75 DS 30B.
Torpedoes: 6 - Whitehead B 515 324 mm (2
    triple) tubes. Marconi Stingray.
Decoys: 2 - Super Barricade 12-barrel launchers.
    Graseby Sea Siren torpedo decoy.

RADARS

Air search - Signaal DA08.
Surface search - Ericsson Sea Giraffe 150HC.

Navigation - Racal Decca.
Fire control - 2 Marconi 1802.
Sonars: Thomson-Sintra Spherion; hull-mounted,
    active search/attack.

AIR SUPPORT

Helicopters: 1 Westland Super Lynx ASW

KEY RECOGNITION FEATURES

- High bow with straight leading edge
  sloping down towards bridge.
- 57 mm gun mounting ('A' position).
- Seawolf VLS SAM launchers immediately
  forward of bridge ('B' position).
- Raised angular bridge structure with all-
  round windows.
- Large enclosed mainmast amidships with
  sloping forward edge and vertical after
  edge.
- Distinctive DA08 air search radar aerial
  atop aftermast.
- Very large square section funnel with
  shallow sloping after edge abaft aftermast.
- Steeply sloping hangar doors down to
  large, low profile flight deck.

Bronstein

NICOLAS BRAVO (old pennant number)   *Mexican Navy*

Country: MEXICO
Country of origin: USA
Ship type: FRIGATES
Class: BRONSTEIN (FF)
Active: 2
Name (Pennant Number): HERMENGILDO
GALEANA (ex-*Bronstein*) (F202, ex-E 42, ex-FF
1037), NICOLAS BRAVO (ex-*McCloy*) (F201, ex-E
40, ex-FF 1038).

SPECIFICATION

Displacement, full load, tons: 2,650.
Length, feet (metres): 371.5 (113.2).
Beam, feet (metres): 40.5 (12.3).
Draught, feet (metres): 13.5 (4.1).
Speed, knots: 24.
Range, miles: 3,925 at 15 kts.

ARMAMENT

Missiles: A/S – Honeywell ASROC Mk 112 octuple
launcher. (Non-operational).
Guns: 1 – USN 3 in (76mm)50 (twin), or 1 –
Bofors 57 mm/70 Mk2 SAK.
Torpedoes: 6 – 324 mm US Mk 32 Mod 7 (2
triple) tubes.
Decoys: 2 – Loral Hycor 6-barrel launchers.
Chaff/IR flares.

RADARS

Air search –Lokcheed SPS-40D.
Surface search –Raytheon SPS-10F.

Navigation – Marconi LN66.
Fire control – General Electric Mk 35.
Sonars: EDO/General Electric SQS-26 AXR bow-
mounted, active search/attack.

AIR SUPPORT

Helicopters: Platform only.

KEY RECOGNITION FEATURES

- Sweeping continuous maindeck to break
  down to low freeboard quarterdeck.
- Stem anchor and portside anchor (just
  forward of 3 in gun mounting)
  necessitated by large bow sonar dome.
- Long forecastle with 3 in gun mounting on
  raised plaftform.
- ASROC box launcher immediately aft with
  wide break before bridge superstructure.
- Tall bridge structure with box above all-
  round windows.
- Large enclosed mainmast/ funnel combined
  amidships with V-shaped exhausts and
  complex array of radar aerials.
- Torpedo tubes alongside supersurcture just
  aft of midships.
- Ship's boats on prominent davits at aft end
  of supersstructure.
- Short helicopter platform but no hangar
  facilities.

Jacob van Heemskerck

WITTE DE WITH

Country: NETHERLANDS

Country of origin: NETHERLANDS

Ship type: FRIGATES

Class: JACOB VAN HEEMSKERCK (FFG)

Active: 2

Name (Pennant Number): JACOB VAN
HEEMSKERCK (F 812), WITTE DE WITH (F 813)

SPECIFICATION

Displacement, full load, tons: 3,750.
Length, feet (metres): 428 (130.5).
Beam, feet (metres): 47.9 (14.6).
Draught, feet (metres): 14.1 (4.3)
Speed, knots: 30.
Range, miles: 4,700 at 16 kts.

ARMAMENT

Missiles: SSM - 8 McDonnell Douglas Harpoon (2
quad) launchers. SAM - 40 GDC Pomona
Standard SM-1MR; Mk 13 Mod 1 launcher.
Raytheon Sea Sparrow Mk 29 octuple launcher.

Guns: 1 - Signaal SGE-30 Goalkeeper CIWS with
General Electric 30 mm. 2 - Oerlikon 20 mm.

Torpedoes: 4 - 324 mm US Mk 32 (2 twin) tubes.
Honeywell Mk 46 Mod 5 Neartip.

Decoys: 2 - Loral Hycor SRBOC 6-barrel Mk 36
(quad) launchers.

RADARS

Air search - Signaal LW08.
Air/surface search –Signaal SMART, 3D.
Surface search - Signaal Scout.

Fire control – 2 Signaal STIR 240. Signaal STIR
180.

Sonars: Westinghouse SQS-509 hull-mounted,
active search/attack.

KEY RECOGNITION FEATURES

- Continuous maindeck from stem to stern.
- No weapons on forecastle.
- Sea Sparrow SAM octuple launcher ('B'
  mounting position).
- Forward superstructure has large pyramid
  enclosed mast at after end supporting
  Signaal SMART 3D air/surface search radar
  aerial.
- Pole mast immediately aft of mainmast.
- Harpoon angled quad SSM launchers
  immediately aft of mainmast.
- Prominent spherical SATCOM domes at port
  and startboard on raised platforms aft of
  mainmast.
- Large funnel with sloping top just aft of
  midships.
- After superstructure with raised forward
  section supporting large LW08 air search
  radar aerial at forward end and STIR 240
  fire control radar aft.
- Standard SM-1MR SAM launcher aft of
  raised superstructure.
- Goalkeeper CIWS mounting on
  quarterdeck.

Karel Doorman

VAN AMSTEL

Country: NETHERLANDS
Country of origin: NETHERLANDS
Ship type: FRIGATES
Class: KAREL DOORMAN (FFG)
Active: 8
Name (Pennant Number): KAREL DOORMAN (F 827), WILLEM VAN DER ZAAN (F 829), TJERK HIDDES (F 830), VAN AMSTEL (F 831), ABRAHAM VAN DER HULST (F 832), VAN NES (F 833), VAN GALEN (F 834), VAN SPEIJK (F 828)

SPECIFICATION

Displacement, full load, tons: 3,320.
Length, feet (metres): 401.2 (122.3) oa.
Beam, feet (metres): 47.2 (14.4).
Draught, feet (metres): 14.1 (4.3).
Speed, knots: 30.
Range, miles: 5,000 at 18 kts.

ARMAMENT

Missiles: SSM - McDonnell Douglas Harpoon Block 1C (2 quad) launchers. SAM - Raytheon Sea Sparrow Mk 48 vertical launchers.
Guns: 1 - OTO MELARA 3 in (76 mm)/62 Compact Mk 100. 1 - Signaal SGE-30 Goalkeeper with General Electric 30 mm. 2 - Oerlikon 20 mm.
Torpedoes: 4 - 324 mm US Mk 32 (2 twin) tubes (mounted inside the after superstructure). Honeywell Mk 46 Mod 5 Neartip.
Decoys: 2 - Loral Hycor SRBOC 6-barrel Mk 36 (quad) fixed launchers. SLQ-25 Nixie towed torpedo decoy.

RADARS

Air/surface search - Signaal SMART, 3D.
Air search - Signaal LW08.
Surface search - Signaal Scout.
Navigation - Racal Decca 1226.
Fire control - 2 Signaal STIR.
Sonars: Signaal PHS-36; hull-mounted active search/attack. Thomson-Sintra Anaconda DSBV 61; towed array.

AIR SUPPORT

Helicopters: 1 Westland SH-14D Lynx.

KEY RECOGNITION FEATURES

- Continuous maindeck from stem to stern.
- 3 in gun mounting ('A' position).
- High forward superstructure topped by tall enclosed mainmast at after end supporting SMART air/surface search radar aerial.
- Squat, square shaped funnel with sloping after end, just aft of midships.
- After superstructure has distinctive pedestal mounted LW08 air search radar aerial at forward end. Small, white SATCOM dome immediately forward.
- Large hangar with Goalkeeper CIWS mounting atop at after end.
- Long flight deck with open quarterdeck below.

Oslo

BERGEN

Country: NORWAY	
Country of origin: NORWAY	
Ship type: FRIGATES	
Class: OSLO (FFG)	
Active: 3	

Name (Pennant Number): BERGEN (F 301),
TRONDHEIM (F 302), NARVIK (F 304)

SPECIFICATION

Displacement, full load, tons: 1,950.
Length, feet (metres): 317 (96.6).
Beam, feet (metres): 36.8 (11.2).
Draught, feet (metres): 18 (5.5) (screws).
Speed, knots: 25+.
Range, miles: 4,500 at 15 kts.

ARMAMENT

Missiles: SSM – 4 Kongsberg Penguin Mk 1. SAM
– Raytheon RIM-7M Sea Sparrow Mk 29
octuple launcher.
Guns: 2 – US 3 in (76 mm)/50 Mk 33 (twin). 1 –
Bofors 40 mm/70. 2 – Rheinmetall 20 mm/20
(not in all).
Torpedoes: 6 – 324 mm US Mk 32 (2 triple)
tubes. Marconi Stingray.
A/S mortars: Kongsberg Terne III 6-tubed.
Mines: mine-laying capability.
Decoys: 2 – chaff launchers.

RADARS

Air search – Siemens/Plessey AWS-9.

Surface search - Racal Decca TM 1226.
Navigation - Decca.
Fire control - NobelTech 9LV 218 Mk 2. Raytheon
Mk 95, (Sea Sparrow).
Sonars: Thomson-Sintra/Simrad TSM 2633;
combined hull and VDS, Simrad Terne III.

KEY RECOGNITION FEATURES

- High bow with continuous sweeping
  maindeck from stem to stern.
- Long forecastle with 3 in gun twin
  mounting forward of Kongsburg Terne III
  6-tube A/S mortar launchers.
- High superstructure with large pedestal-
  mounted AWS-9 air search radar aerial
  atop.
- Unusual tripod/pole mainmast
  configuration at after end of forward
  superstructure sloping at an angle aft.
- Low, slim, black-capped angled funnel
  below angled mainmast.
- After superstructure has tall slim pedestal-
  mounted Mk 95 fire control radar aerial
  atop.
- Sea Sparrow SAM box launcher at after
  end of after superstructure.
- 40 mm/70 gun mounting ('Y' position).
- Penguin SSM launcher right aft on
  quarterdeck.

Fridtjof Nansen

FRIDTJOF NANSEN (Computer graphic)

2000 Baran

Country: NORWAY
Country of origin: SPAIN
Ship type: FRIGATES
Class: FRIDTJOF NANSEN (PROJECT SMP 6088) (FFG)
Building: 5
Name (Pennant Number): FRIDTJOF NANSEN (F 310), ROALD AMUNDSEN (F 311), OTTO SVERDRUP (F 312), HELGE INGSTAD (F 313), THOR HEYERDAHL (F 314).

SPECIFICATION

Displacement, full load, tons: 5,121.
Length, feet (metres): 433.1 (132).
Beam, feet (metres): 55.1 (16.8).
Draught, feet (metres): 16.1 (4.9).
Speed, knots: 27.

ARMAMENT

Missiles: SSM - 8 Kongsberg NSM. SAM – Mk 41 with 8 cells for 32 Evolved Sea Sparrow.
Guns: 1 - 3 in (76 mm)/62 Super Rapid. 2 – 12.7 mm machinge-guns.
Torpedoes: 6 - 324 mm (2 double) tubes. Marconi Stingray.
Decoys: Terma SKWS chaff, IR/acoustic.

RADARS

Air search –Lopckheed Martin SPY-1F phased array.
Surface search -Litton.
Navigation – 2 Litton.

Fire control - 2 Mk 82
Sonars: Thomson- Marconi Spherion MRS 2000 and Captas Mk 2 VDS.

AIR SUPPORT

Helicopters: 1 NH 90.

Amazon

Country: PAKISTAN

Country of origin: UK

Ship type: FRIGATES

Class: AMAZON (TARIQ) (TYPE 21)
(DDG/DD/FFG/FF)

Active: 6

Name (Pennant Number): TARIQ (ex-*Ambuscade*)
(D 181 (ex-F 172), BABUR (ex-*Amazon*) (D 182,
ex-F 169), KHAIBAR (ex-*Arrow*) (D 183, ex-F 173),
BADR (ex-*Alacrity*) (D 184, ex-F 185), TIPPU
SULTAN (ex-*Avenger*) (D 185, ex-F 185),
SHAHJAHAN (ex-*Active*) (D 186, ex-F 171).

SPECIFICATION

Displacement, full load, tons: 3,700.
Length, feet (metres): 384 (117) oa.
Beam, feet (metres): 41.7 (12.7).
Draught, feet (metres): 19.5 (5.9) screws.
Speed, knots: 30.
Range, miles: 4,000 at 17 kts.

KEY RECOGNITION FEATURES

- Long forecastle with raised bows.
- 4.5 in gun mounting in 'A' position.
- China LY 60N sextuple SAM box launchers
  on raised platform immediately forward of
  bridge in D 181, D 183 and D 185. Harpoon
  SSM launchers in D 186, D 184 and D 182.
- Low superstructure with tall enclosed mast
  aft of bridge, topped by Type 992R
  air/surface search radar in D 186; being
  replaced by Signaal DA08 larger array in D
  185, D 181 and D 183.
- Low, squat funnel with sloping top from
  forward to aft.
- Slim black-painted aftermast immediately
  forward of funnel.
- Vulcan Phalanx CIWS aft end of hanger. D
  186 has Selenia Type 912 (RTN-10X) fire
  control radar atop hanger roof, forward of
  CIWS mounting and torpedo tubes at break
  down to flight deck (latter, also D 184).
- Short helicopter flight deck, with break
  down to very short quarterdeck.

ARMAMENT

Missiles: SSM – 4 - Harpoon 1C in D 182, 184
  and 186. SAM – China LY 60N sextuple
  launcher in D 181, 183 and 185.
Guns: 1 - Vickers 4.5 in (114 mm)/55 Mk 8. 4 -
  25 mm/60 (2 twin). 1 - 20 mm Vulcan Phalanx
  Mk 15 replacing Seacat in D 182, 184 and 186.
  2 or 4 - Oerlikon 20 mm Mk 7A or 1 -MSI DS
  30B 30 mm/75 and 2 - GAM-B01 20 mm.
Torpedoes: 6 - 324 mm Plessey STWS Mk 2 (2
  triple) tubes in D 184 and 186. All being fitted

BADR

with Bofors Type 43X2 single or quad launchers.

Decoys: 2 - Vickers Corvus 8-tubed trainable launchers. SRBOC Mk 36 launchers in D 181, D 182-183 and D 185. Graseby Type 182 towed torpedo decoy.

RADAR

Air/surface search – Marconi Type 992R; replaced by Signaal DA08 in D 181,183, 185.

Surface search – Kelvin Hughes Type 1006 in D 184, 186. (Type 1007 in D 182).

Fire control – 2 Selenia Type 912 (RTN 10X). 1 China LL-1 in D 181, 183 and 185 (for LY 60N).

Sonars: Graseby Type 184P hull-mounted, active search/attack. Kelvin Hughes Type 162M, hull-mounted. Thomson-Marconi ATAS, active.

AIR SUPPORT

Helicopters: 1 Westland Lynx HAS 3 (ASW/ASV).

Cannon

RAJAH HUMABON

Country: PHILIPPINES, THAILAND
Country of origin: USA
Ship type: FRIGATES
Class: CANNON (FF)
PHILIPPINES – Active: 1
Name (Pennant Number): RAJAH HUMABON (ex-*Hatsuhi*, ex-*Atherton*) (PF 11, ex-PF 78, ex-DE 263, ex-DE 169).

THAILAND – Active: 1
Name (Pennant Number): PIN KLAO (ex-*Hemminger*) (413, ex-3, ex-1, ex-DE 746).

SPECIFICATION

Displacement, full load, tons: 1,930, (Thailand), 1,750, (Philippines).
Length, feet (metres): 306 (93.3).
Beam, feet (metres): 36.6 (11.2).
Draught, feet (metres): 14 (4.3).
Speed, knots: 18.
Range, miles: 6,700 at 19 kts.

ARMAMENT

Guns: 3 – USN 3 in (76mm)/50 Mk 22. 6 – Bofors 40mm/56 (3 twin).
Torpedoes: 6 – 324 mm US Mk 32 .
A/S mortars: 1 Hedgehog Mk 10
Depth charges: 8 projectors; 2 racks. (Thai unit). 8 – K-gun Mk 6 projectors, 1 rack, (Philippines ship).

RADARS

Air/surface search – Raytheon SPS-5 (Thai unit only)
Surface search Raytheon SPS-5 (Philippines).
Navigation – Raytheon SPS-21, (Thailand). RCA/GE Mk 26, (Philippines).
Fire control – Western Electric Mk 34. General Electric Mk 26, (Thai unit).
Sonars: SQS-11 hull-mounted active attack, (Thai ship). SQS-17B, hull mounted active search and attack, (Philippines).

HONORIO BARRETO

Country: PORTUGAL

Country of origin: SPAIN

Ship type: FRIGATES

Class: BAPTISTA DE ANDRADE/
JOÃO COUTINHO (FS)*

*Classified as corvettes.

Active: 4 (Baptista de Andrade), 6 (João Coutinho)

Baptista de Andrade' – Name (Pennant
Number): BAPTISTA DE ANDRADE (F 486), JOÃO
ROBY (F 487), AFONSO CERQUEIRA (F 488),
OLIVEIRA E CARMO (F 489).

'João Coutinho' – Name (Pennant Number):
ANTONIO ENES (F 471), JOÃO COUTINHO (F 475),
JACINTO CANDIDO (F 476), GENERAL PEREIRA
D'ECA (F 477), AUGUSTO DE CASTILHO (F 484),
HONORIO BARRETO (F 485).

SPECIFICATION

Displacement, full load, tons: 1,380.

Length, feet (metres): 277.5 (84.6).

Beam, feet (metres): 33.8 (10.3).

Draught, feet (metres): 10.2 (3.1), (10.8 (3.3) in
João Coutinho class).

Speed, knots: 22.

Range, miles: 5,900 at 18 kts.

Guns: 1 - Creusot-Loire 3.9 in (100 mm)/55 Mod
1968. 2 - US 3 in (76mm)/50 (twin) Mk 33 in
João Coutinho class. 2 - Bofors 40 mm/70. (2 -
Bofors 40 mm/60 (twin) in João Coutinho
class).

RADARS

Air/surface search - Plessey AWS 2. (Kelvin
Hughes in João Coutinho class).

Navigation - Decca RM 316P. (Racal Decca RM
1226C in João Coutinho class).

Fire control - Thomson-CSF Pollux. (Western
Electric SPG-34 in João Coutinho class).

AIR SUPPORT

Helicopters: Platform only for 1 Westland Super
Lynx Mk 95.

KEY RECOGNITION FEATURES

- Stepped forecastle with 3.9 in gun
  mounting ('A' position). (3 in twin
  mounting in João Coutinho class).
- Tall lattice mainmast just forward of
  midships with large distinctive Plessey ASW
  2 air/surface search radar aerial atop.(AWS
  2 absent from João Coutinho class,
  replaced by smaller Kelvin Hughes.).
- Large, single, black-capped funnel with
  sloping after end.
- 40 mm/70 mounting atop superstructure
  aft of funnel. (Substituted with 40 mm/60
  twin mountings in João Coutinho class).
- Note: All ASW equipment removed in
  1999/2000.

COMMANDANTE HERMENGIDO CAPELO

J.Mortimer

Country: PORTUGAL, URUGUAY

Country of origin: FRANCE

Ship type: FRIGATES

Class: COMANDANTE JOÃO BELO (FF), COMMANDANT RIVIÈRE (FFG)

Active: 3 Portugal (João Belo), 3 Uruguay (Commandant Rivière)

PORTUGAL – Name (Pennant Number): COMMANDANTE JOÃO BELO (F 480), COMMANDANTE HERMENEGILDO CAPELO (F 481), COMMANDANTE SACADURA CABRAL (F 483)

URUGUAY – Name (Pennant Number): URUGUAY (ex-*Commandant Bourdais*) (1), GENERAL ARTIGAS (ex-*Victor Schoelcher*) (2), MONTEVIDEO (ex-*Admiral Charner*) (3, ex-4).

SPECIFICATION

Displacement, full load, tons: 2,250.

Length, feet (metres): 336.9 (102.7).

Beam, feet (metres): 38.4 (11.7).

Draught, feet (metres): 14.4 (4.4), (Portugal). 14.1 (4.3), (Uruguay).

Speed, knots: 25.

Range, miles: 7,500 at 15 kts.

ARMAMENT

Guns: 2 - Creusot-Loire or DCN 3.9 in (100 mm)/55 Mod 1953. 2 - Bofors 40 mm/60/70.

Torpedoes: 6 - 324 mm Mk 32 Mod 5 (2 triple tubes). Honeywell Mk 46 Mod 5 Neartip, (Portugal). 6 - 21.7 mm (550 mm) (2 triple) tubes; ECAN L3. (Uruguay).

A/S mortars: 1 Mortier 305 mm 4-barrel launcher. (Uruguay ships only, to be removed).

Decoys: 2 - Loral Hycor SRBOC 6-barrel Mk 36 SBROC chaff launchers. SLQ-25 Nixie towed torpedo decoy. (Portuguese ships only).

RADARS

Air search - Thomson-CSF DRBV 22A.

Surface search - Thomson-CSF DRBV 50 (Portugal only)

Navigation - Kelvin Hughes KH 1007 (Portugal). Racal Decca 1226 (Uruguay).

Fire control - Thomson-CSF DRBC 31D (Portugal). Thomson-CSF DRBC 32C (Uruguay).

Sonars: CDC SQS-510 hull-mounted active search/attack (Portugal). EDOm SQS-17, hull-mounted, (Uruguay). Thomson-Sintra DUBA 3A; hull-mounted (both classes).

KEY RECOGNITION FEATURES

- Long forecastle with high forward superstructure and high freeboard.
- 3.9 in gun turret ('A' position).
- Mortier 305 mm 4 barrel A/S launcher on Uruguay ships ('B' position).(To be removed).
- Large lattice mainmast at after end of forward superstructure.
- Single large, black-capped funnel well aft of midships.
- DRBC 31D fire control director atop after superstructure.
- 3.9 in gun mountings aft ('X' positions). (Also in 'Y' position in some Portuguese ships).

Note: SSM launchers removed from Uruguay units in 1999/2000 refits.

Tetal/Improved Tetal

ADMIRAL PETRE BARBLINEAU

Country: ROMANIA	
Country of origin: ROMANIA	
Ship type: FRIGATES (FF)	
Class: TETAL/IMPROVED TETAL*	
* Rated as corvettes	

Active: 4 (Tetal), 2 (Improved Tetal)

'Tetal' class – Name (Pennant Number):
ADMIRAL PETRE BARBUNEANU (260), VICE
ADMIRAL VASILE SCODREA (261), VICE ADMIRAL
VASILE URSEANU (262), VICE ADMIRAL EUGENIU
ROSCA (263).

Improved Tetal' class – Name (Pennant
Number): CONTRE ADMIRAL EUSTATIU SEBASTIAN
(264), ADMIRAL HORIA MACELARIU (265)

SPECIFICATION

Displacement, full load, tons: 1,440. 1,500
(Improved Tetal).
Length, feet (metres): 303.1 (95.4).
Beam, feet (metres): 38.4 (11.7).
Draught, feet (metres): 9.8 (3). 10 (3.1) (Improved
Tetal).
Speed, knots: 24.

ARMAMENT

Guns: 4 - USSR 3 in (76 mm)/60 (2 twin), (Tetal).
1 - USSR 3 in (76 mm)/60, (Improved Tetal). 4 -
USSR 30 mm/65 (2 twin), (Tetal). 4 - 30 mm/65
AK 630, (Improved Tetal). 2 - 14.5 mm
machine-guns, (Tetal).
Torpedoes: 4 - 21 in (533 mm) (twin) tubes.
Russian Type 53-65.
A/S mortars: 2 - RBU 2500 16-tubed, (Tetal). 2 -
RBU 6000 (Improved Tetal).
Decoys: 2 - PK 16 chaff launchers

RADARS

Air/surface search - Strut Curve.
Navigation – Nayada.

Fire control - Drum Tilt. Hawk Screech. (Drum Tilt
only in Improved Tetal).
Sonars: Hercules (MG 322) hull-mounted, active
search/attack.

AIR SUPPORT

Helicopters: 1 IAR 316B Alouette III (ASW).
(Improved Tetal only).

KEY RECOGNITION FEATURES

- Regular profile hull with continuous
  maindeck from stem to stern.
- Very long forecastle with 3 in gun
  mounting ('A' position).
- A/S mortar mounting ('B' mounting
  position).
- Long superstructure centred well aft of
  midships.
- Large mainmast amidships, with enclosed
  bottom half and lattice top. (Lattice
  throughout in Improved Tetal).
- Hawk Screech fire control radar aerial atop
  after end of bridge structure in Tetal class.
  Drum Tilt in Improved Tetal.
- Drum Tilt fire control radar aerial mounted
  atop tall pedestal towards after end of
  superstructure, (Tetal class only).
- Short, squat black-capped funnel aft of
  mainmast and aft of superstructure in
  Improved Tetal.
- 30 mm/65 gun mountings at after end of
  after superstructure, one port one
  starboard.
- 3 in gun mounting ('Y' position) in Tetal
  class. Missing from Improved Tetal – long
  helicopter deck substituted.

Note: Heavily modified Soviet 'Koni' design.

Grisha I/II/III

Country: RUSSIA, LITHUANIA, POLAND, UKRAINE
Country of origin: RUSSIA
Ship type: FRIGATES
Class: GRISHA I (TYPE 1124) (ALBATROS) (FFL)
Active: 1 Russia
Class: GRISHA II (TYPE 1124P) (ALBATROS) (FFL)
Active: 2 Ukraine
Class: GRISHA III (TYPE 1124M) (ALBATROS) (FFL)
Active: 2 Lithuania, 3 Russia, one designated
'Grisha IV'.
Class: GRISHA V (TYPE 1124EM/P) (ALBATROS)
(FFL)
Active: 20 Russia, 1 Ukraine
Class: KASZUB (TYPE 620) (FSG)
Active: 1 Poland.
LITHUANIA – Name (Pennant Number): ZEMAITIS
(F 11 ex-MPK 108), AUKSTAITIS (F 12 ex-MPK 44).
UKRAINE – Name (Pennant Number: Grisha II –
VINNITSA (ex-*Dnepr*) (U 206). Grisha V – LUTSK (U
200, ex-400).
POLAND – Name (Pennant Number): KASZUB
(240).

RUSSIAN GRISHA III

SPECIFICATION

Displacement, full load, tons: 1,200. (1,150,
  Ukraine). (1,183, *Kaszub*).
Length, feet (metres): 233.6 (71.2). (270 (82.3)
  Kaszub).
Beam, feet (metres): 32.2 (9.8). (32.8 (10)
  Kaszub).
Draught, feet (metres): 12.1 (3.7). (10.2 (3.1)
  Kaszub).
Speed, knots: 30. (27, *Kaszub*).
Range, miles: 2 500 at 14 kts. (3 500 at 14 kts.,
  Kaszub).

ARMAMENT

Missiles: SAM - SA-N-4 Gecko twin launcher
  (Grisha I, III and V classes). 2 - SA-N-5 quad
  launchers, (*Kaszub*).
Guns: 2 - 57 mm/80 (twin) (2 twin in Grisha II
  class). 1 - 3 in (76 mm)/60 (Grisha V). 1 - 30
  mm/65 (Grisha III and V classes). 1 - USSR 3 in
  (76 mm)/66 AK 176 and 6 - ZU-23-2M Wrobel
  23 mm/87 (3 twin), (*Kaszub*).
Torpedoes: 4 - 21 in (533 mm) (2 twin) tubes.
  (Tubes removed from Lithuanian ships F 12 and
  F 11).
A/S mortars: 2 - RBU 6000 12-tubed. (Only 1 in
  Grisha Vs.)

Depth charges: 2 racks/rails.
Decoys: 2 - PK 16 chaff launchers or 4 PK 10. (1 –
  10-barrel 122 mm Jashrzab chaff launcher in
  Polish unit fitted in 1999).

RADARS

Air/surface search - Strut Curve (Strut Pair in
  early Grisha Vs). Half Plate Bravo (in the later
  Grisha Vs).
Surface search – Nogat SRN 7453 (*Kaszub* only).
  (Racal Decca RM 1290, Lithuania).
Navigation - Don 2. (SRN 441XT, *Kaszub* only).
  Terma Scanter (Lithuania).
Fire control - Pop Group (Grisha I, III and V).
  Muff Cob (except in Grisha III and V). Bass Tilt (Grisha III and V).
Sonars: Bull Nose (MGK 335MS) hull-mounted.
  Elk Tail, VDS. (Grisha). (MG 322T bow-mounted,
  MG 329M stern-mounted dipping type,
  Kaszub).

KEY RECOGNITION FEATURES

- High bow with sweeping lines to stern.
- SA-N-4 Gecko SAM launcher ('A' mounting position). (57mm/80 gun twin mounting in this position in Grisha II).
- Two A/S mortar launchers, port and starboard ('B' mounting position).
- Pyramid mainmast at after end of forward superstructure.
- Small 'Y' shaped (in profile) lattice mast at top after end of mainmast. (Enclosed in Grisha II).
- Pop Group fire control radar aerial atop forward superstructure, forward of mainmast. (except Grisha II).
- Single, low profile, square shaped funnel just aft of midships.
- Small after superstructure with slender lattice mast at forward end, and Muff Cob fire control radar aerial atop after end. (Bass Tilt in Grisha III/V with 30mm/65 mountings).
- 57 mm/80 gun mounting ('Y' position).

Note: Most obvious identification of Grisha II is 57 mm/80 gun mounting ('A' position). Grisha III same as Grisha I except for raised after superstructure with Bass Tilt fire control radar aerial atop. Grisha V is the only type with 3 in gun mounting in 'Y' position. Grisha IV is a Grisha III modified as trials unit for SA-N-9/Cross Swords SAM system, in service in Black Sea.

Note 2: *Kaszub*, based on Grisha design, has 3 in gun mounting in 'A' position, long low superstructure aft of mainmast and no obvious funnel. ZU-23-2M Wrobel 23 mm/87 twin gun mountings fitted on aft superstructure in 'X' position and aft of mainmast.

Note 3: Ukrainian units have diagonal blue and yellow stripes painted on hull midships.

Note 4: The Russian Border Guard also operates some 'Grisha III' units. These hulls have diagonal white/blue/red stripes in all units except those based in the Black Sea.

Note 5: Indonesian 'Parchim'class similar but with higher freeboard and different armament.

Note 6: Only Russian 'Grisha I' is operational with Northern Fleet, where there are 11 'Grisha Vs'.

Krivak I/II/III

Country: RUSSIA, UKRAINE

Country of origin: RUSSIA

Ship type: FRIGATES

Class: KRIVAK I/II/III (TYPE 1135/1135M/1135MP) (FFG/FF/FFH)

Active: 15 Russia, 2 Ukraine

RUSSIA

Type I/Type I Mod – Name (Pennant Number): DRUZHNY (754), LEGKY (ex-*Leningradsky Komsomolets*) (930), LETUCHY (661), PYLKY (702), ZADORNY (955), LADNY (801).

Type II – Name (Pennant Number): NEUKROTIMY (731), PYTLIVY (808).

Type III – Name (Pennant Number): MENZHINSKY (113), DZERZHINSKY (057), OREL (ex-*Imeni XXVII Sezda KPSS*) (156), PSKOV (ex-*Imeni LXX Letiya VCHK-KGB*)(104), ANADYR (ex-*Imeni LXX Letiya Pogramvoysk*) (060), KEDROV (103), VOROVSKY (052).

UKRAINE

Type I – Name (Pennant Number): MIKOLAIV (ex-Bezukoriznenny) (U 133).

Type II – Name (Pennant Number): HETMAN SAGAIDACHNY (U 130, ex-201).

SPECIFICATION

Displacement, full load, tons: 3,650.

Length, feet (metres): 405.2 (123.5).

Beam, feet (metres): 46.9 (14.3).

Draught, feet (metres): 16.4 (5).

Speed, knots: 32.

Range, miles: 4,600 at 20 kts.

ARMAMENT

Missiles: SSM – Zvezda SS-N-25 Sapless (Kh 35 Uran) (2 quad); (Krivak I after modernisation not Ukraine unit). SAM - 2 SA-N-4 Gecko twin launchers (1 in Krivak III). A/S – Raduga SS-N-14 Silex quad launcher (not in Krivak III); payload nuclear or Type E53-72 torpedo.

Guns: 4 – 3 in (76 mm)/60 (2 twin) (Krivak I). 2 - 3.9 in (100 mm)/59 (Krivak II) (1 in Krivak III). 2 - 30 mm/65 (Krivak III).

Torpedoes: 8 - 21 in (533 mm) (2 quad) tubes.

Mines: Capacity for 20.

A/S mortars: 2 – RBU 6000 12-tubed; (not modernised Krivak I).

Decoys: 4 - PK 16 or 10 - PK 10 chaff launchers. Towed torpedo decoy.

RADARS

Air search - Head Net C, 3D, or Top Plate (Krivak mod I and Krivak III).

Surface search - Don Kay or Palm Frond or Don 2 or Spin Trough and Peel Cone (Krivak III).

Navigation – Kivach (Krivak III)

Fire control - 2 Eye Bowl (not in Krivak III). 2 Pop Group (1 in Krivak III). Owl Screech (Krivak I). Kite Screech (Krivak II and III). Bass Tilt (Krivak III).

Sonars: Bull Nose (MGK 335MS); hull-mounted, active search/attack. Mare Tail or Steer Hide (some Krivak Is after modernisation); VDS.

AIR SUPPORT

Helicopters: 1 Kamov Ka-27 Helix (ASW). (Krivak III).

NEUKROTIMY, RUSSIAN KRIVAK II

KEY RECOGNITION FEATURES

Krivak I

- Long forecastle with, from forward, Raduga SS-N-14 Silex A/S curved missile launcher, SA-N-4 Gecko SAM launcher and SS-N-25 SSM launcher (latter not Ukraine).
- Forward superstructure with, at after end, complex of three lattice masts forming the mainmast structure with large air search radar aerial atop.
- Single, low profile funnel well aft of midships.
- Pop Group and Owl Screech fire control radar aerials mounted on complex structure between mainmast and funnel.
- 3 in gun mountings ('Y' and 'X' positions).

Note: Most obvious identification of Krivak II/III is RBU 6000 A/S mortar mounting in place of SSM launcher on forecastle. Krivak III has a 3.9 gun mounting ('A' position) and a flight deck over open quarterdeck, replacing gun mountings in 'X' and 'Y' positions.

Note 2: See entry for Indian 'Talwar' class – dramatic development of improved Krivak III.

Note 3: The Russian Border Guard also operates some 'Krivak III' units. These hulls have diagonal white/blue/red stripes in all units except those based in the Black Sea.

Neustrashimy

NEUSTRASHIMY

Country: RUSSIA
Country of origin: RUSSIA
Ship type: FRIGATES
Class: NEUSTRASHIMY (JASTREB) (TYPE 1154) (FFG)
Active: 1
Name (Pennant Number): NEUSTRASHIMY (712)

SPECIFICATION

Displacement full load, tons: 4,250.
Length, feet (metres): 430.4 (131.2) oa.
Beam, feet (metres): 50.9 (15.5).
Draught, feet (metres): 15.7 (4.8).
Speed, knots: 30.
Range, miles: 4,500 at 16 kts.

ARMAMENT

Missiles: SSM - Fitted for, but not with 8 SS-N-25
Sapless (Kh 35 Uran). SAM - 4 SA-N-9 Gauntlet
(Klinok) sextuple vertical launchers. SAM/Guns 2
CADS-N-1 (Kortik/Kashtan); each has a twin 30
mm Gatling combined with 8-SAN-11 Grisson
and Hot Flash/Hot Spot fire control radar/optronic
director. A/S - SS-N-15/16. Type 40 torpedo or
nuclear warhead, fired from torpedo tubes.
Guns: 1 - 3.9 in (100 mm)/59.
Torpedoes: 6 - 21 in (533 mm) tubes combined
with A/S launcher. Can fire SS-N-15/16 missiles
or anti-submarine torpedoes.
A/S mortars: 1- RBU 12000; 10-tubed, trainable.
Mines: 2 rails.
Decoys: 8 - PK 10 and 2 - PK 16 chaff launchers.

RADARS

Air/surface search - Top Plate, 3D.
Navigation - 2 Palm Frond.
Fire control – Cross Sword. (SAM) Kite Screech
Bravo (SSM/guns).

Sonars: Ox Yoke and Whale Tongue; hull-
mounted. Ox Tail VDS or towed sonar array.

AIR SUPPORT

Helicopters: 1 Kamov Ka-27PL Helix (ASW).

KEY RECOGNITION FEATURES

- Elegant profile with front of long
  forecastle slightly depressed.
- 3.9 in gun mounting ('A' position).
- SA-N-9 Gauntlet (Klinok) SAM VLS tubes
  just aft of forward mounting.
- RBU 12000 A/S mortar mounting ('B'
  mounting position).
- Forward superstructure has short forward
  mast at its after end supporting Cross
  Sword fire control radar aerial.
- Twin funnels. Forward one aft of forward
  superstructure, after one aft of mainmast.
- Large, pyramid mainmast well aft of
  midships with distinctive Top Plate
  air/surface radar aerial atop.
- 2 horizontal launchers at main deck level,
  alongside aft funnel, port and starboard,
  angled at 18° from forward that double for
  A/S missiles and torpedoes.
- CADS-N-1 SAM/Guns mounting at after
  end of after superstructure, just forward of
  flight deck.
- VDS towing array right aft.

Note: Class slightly larger than *Krivak*.
Helicopter deck extends across the full
width of the ship.

Note 2 - After funnel is unusually flush
decked, therefore not obvious in profile.

Madina

ABHA

Country: SAUDI ARABIA
Country of origin: FRANCE
Ship type: FRIGATES
Class: MADINA (TYPE F 2000S) (FFG)
Active: 4
Name (Pennant Number): MADINA (702),
HOFOUF (704), ABHA (706), TAIF (708)

SPECIFICATION

Displacement, full load, tons: 2,870.
Length, feet (metres): 377.3 (115).
Beam, feet (metres): 41 (12.5).
Draught, feet (metres): 16 (4.9) (sonar).
Speed, knots: 30.
Range, miles: 8,000 at 15 kts; 6,500 at 18 kts.

ARMAMENT

Missiles: SSM - 8 OTO MELARA/Matra Otomat Mk
2 (2 quad). SAM - Thomson-CSF Crotale Naval
octuple launcher.
Guns: 1 - Creusot-Loire 3.9 in (100 mm)/55
compact Mk 2. 4 - Breda 40 mm/70 (2 twin).
Torpedoes: 4 - 21 in (533 mm) tubes. ECAN
F17P.
Decoys: CSEE Dagaie double trainable mounting.

RADARS

Air/surface search/IFF - Thomson-CSF Sea Tiger
(DRBV 15).

Navigation - Racal Decca TM 1226.
Fire control - Thomson-CSF Castor IIB/C.
Thomson-CSF DRBC 32.
Sonars: Thomson-Sintra Diodon TSM 2630; hull-
mounted, integrated Sorel VDS.

AIR SUPPORT

Helicopters: 1 Aerospatiale SA 365F Dauphin 2.
(SSM targeting).

KEY RECOGNITION FEATURES

- Long forecastle. Continuous maindeck
  profile with break down to quarterdeck.
- 3.9 in gun mounting ('A' position).
- Forward superstructure has slim tripod
  mainmast at after end.
- Unusually large funnel with large black,
  wedge shaped smoke deflector at after
  end, sited just aft of midships.
- Otomat SSM launchers in break between
  funnel and forward superstructure.
- Crotale SAM launcher atop after
  superstructure.
- Small flight deck.
- Short quarterdeck with VDS operating gear.

Meko A-200

MEKO A-200 (computer image)

Country: SOUTH AFRICA	
Country of origin: GERMANY	
Ship type: FRIGATES	
Class: MEKO A-200 (FSG)	
Planned: 4	

Name (Pennant Number): ––– (––), ––– (––), –
–– (––), ––– (––).

SPECIFICATION

Displacement, full load, tons: 3,590.
Length, feet (metres): 397 (12.1.
Beam, feet (metres): 53.8 (16.4).
Draught, feet (metres): 20.3 (6.2).
Speed, knots: 28.
Range, miles: 7,700 at 15 kts.

ARMAMENT

Missiles: SSM - 8 Exocet MM 40 Block 2 (2
    quad). SAM – Umkhonto 16 cell VLS.
Guns: 1 – OTOBreda 76mm/62 Compact. 2 – LIW
    DPG 35 mm (twin). 2 - Oerlikon 20 mm.
Torpedoes: 4 - 324 mm (2 twin tubes).
Decoys: 2 Super Barricade chaff launchers.

RADARS

Air/surface search - Thomson-CSF 3D
Navigation – 2 sets.
Fire control - 2 sets.

Sonars: Thomson Marconi Kingklip, hull-mounted,
    active search.

AIR SUPPORT

Helicopters: 1 Westland Super Lynx.

KEY RECOGNITION FEATURES

- Long forecastle, angled main
  superstructure profile with break down to
  flight deck.
- 3 in gun mounting ('A' position).
- Tall forward superstructure has large
  enclosed mainmast topped with air/surface
  search radar and thin pole mast at after
  end.
- Break in superstrructure with Exocet SSM
  angled launchers pointing port, starboard.
- Squat funnel raised above aft
  superstructure, sited just aft of midships
  and topped by thin, tall pyramid mast at
  forward edge.
- "Window" in superstructure revealing
  ship's boat.
- 35 mm twin cannon aft end of hanger.
- Small flight deck.

Alvaro de Bazán

ALVARO DE BAZÁN

Camil Busquets i Vilanova

Country: SPAIN

Country of origin: SPAIN

Ship type: FRIGATES

Class: ALVARO DE BAZÁN (FFG)

Building: 4

Name (Pennant Number): ALVARO DE BAZÁN
(F 101), ALMIRANTE DON JUAN DE BORBÓN (F
102), BLAS DE LEZO (F 103), MENDEZ NUÑEZ (F
104).

SPECIFICATION

Displacement, full load, tons: 5,853.

Length, feet (metres): 481.3 (141.7) oa.

Beam, feet (metres): 61 (18.6).

Draught, feet (metres): 16.1 (4.9).

Speed, knots: 28.

Range, miles: 4,500 at 18 kts.

ARMAMENT

Missiles: SSM - 8 Harpoon Block II (2 quad). SAM
–Mk 41 VLS for Evolved Sea Sparrow and
Standard SM-2MR Block IIIA..

Guns: 1 – FMC 5 in (127mm)/54 Mk 45 Mod 2.1–
Bazán 20 mm/120 Meroka 2B. 2 - Oerlikon 20
mm.

Torpedoes: 4 - 324 mm (2 twin tubes). Mk 46
Mod 5 Neartip.

A/S mortars: 2 - ABCAS/SSTDS lauchers.

Decoys: 4 - SRBOC Mk 36 Mod 2 chaff launchers.
SLQ-25A Nixie torpedo decoy.

RADARS

Air/surface search – Aegis SPY-1D

Surface search – DRS SPS-67 (RAN-12S)

Fire control - 2 Mk 99 (for SAM).

Sonars:Raytheon DE 1160 F, hull-mounted, active
search/attack.

AIR SUPPORT

Helicopters: 1 SH-60B Seahawk LAMPS III.

Note: Main gun, for gunfire support for land
force, taken from US 'Tarawa' class.

KEY RECOGNITION FEATURES

- Long forecastle, with curving break down
to slab-side bridge superstructure.
- 5 in gun mounting ('A' position).
- VLS SAM in forecastle at curving break in
deckline
- Tall massive forward superstructure has
Aegis SPY-1D panels above bridge.
- Thin pyramid mainmast, sloping aft with
forward gantries.
- Two funnels, forward integrated into
bridge superstructure, aft very low and
squat and angled.
- Break in superstructure with Harpoon SSM
angled launchers pointing port, starboard.
Cranes alongside aft funnel.
- Fire control radar on large pyramid
structure on hanger roof.
- 20 mm cannon raised turret aft end of
hanger.
- Flight deck dropping down to very short
quarterdeck.
- Rounded surfaces for stealth

Chao Phraya

CHAO PHRAYA

Country: THAILAND
Country of origin: CHINA
Ship type: FRIGATES
Class: CHAO PHRAYA (TYPES 053 HT and 053 HT(H)) (Modified Jianghu III) (FFG)
Active: 4
Name (Pennant Number): CHAO PHRAYA (455), BANGPAKONG (456), KRABURI (457), SAIBURI (458)

SPECIFICATION

Displacement, full load, tons: 1,924.
Length, feet (metres): 338.5 (103.2).
Beam, feet (metres): 37.1 (11.3).
Draught, feet (metres): 10.2 (3.1).
Speed, knots: 30.
Range, miles: 3,500 at 18 kts.

ARMAMENT

Missiles: SSM - 8 - YJ-1(C-801). SAM – HQ-61 launcher for PL-9 or Matra Sadral/Mistral to be fitted.
Guns: 2 - (457 and 458) or 4 China 100 mm/56 (1 or 2 twin). 8 - China 37 mm/76 (4 twin) H/PJ 76A.
A/S mortars: 2 - RBU 1200 (China Type 86) 5-tubed launchers.
Depth charges: 2 - BMB racks.
Decoys: 2 - China Type 945 GPJ 26-barrel chaff launchers.

RADARS

Air/surface search - China Type 354 Eye Shield.
Surface search/fire control - China Type 352C Square Tie.
Navigation - Racal Decca 1290 A/D ARPA and Anritsu RA 71CA.
Fire control - China Type 343 Sun Visor. China Type 341 Rice Lamp.
Sonars: China Type SJD-5A; hull-mounted, active search/attack.

AIR SUPPORT

Helicopters: Platform for Bell 212 (Commando assault/support). (457 and 458).

KEY RECOGNITION FEATURES

- RBU 1200 A/S mortar mounting forward of 100 mm/56 gun twin mounting in 'A' position.
- 37 mm/76 gun twin mounting in 'B' position.
- High forward superstructure with distinctive domed Sun Visor fire control director atop.
- Pyramid mainmast at after end of forward superstructure with slim lattice mast atop its after end.
- YJ-1 SSM angled, ribbed launchers forward and aft of funnel.
- Single, angular low profile funnel well aft of midships.
- Ship's boat on davits between funnel and mainmast.
- Short lattice mast aft of after SSM launchers with Rice Lamp fire control. 37 mm/76 gun mounting immediately astern.
- 100 mm/76 gun mounting ('Y' position) in 455 and 456. The other two have a raised flight deck over open quarterdeck.

Naresuan

TAKSIN

Hachiro Nakai

Country: THAILAND
Country of origin: CHINA
Ship type: FRIGATES
Class: NARESUAN (TYPE 25T) (FFG)
Active: 2
Name (Pennant Number): NARESUAN (421, ex-621), TAKSIN (422, ex-622)

SPECIFICATION

Displacement, full load, tons: 2,980.
Length, feet (metres): 393.7 (120).
Beam, feet (metres): 42.7 (13).
Draught, feet (metres): 12.5 (3.8).
Speed, knots: 32.
Range, miles: 4,000 at 18 kts.

ARMAMENT

Missiles: SSM - 8 McDonnell Douglas Harpoon (2 quad) launchers.
    SAM - Mk 41 LCHR 8 cell VLS launcher, Sea Sparrow.
Guns: 1 - FMC 5 in (127 mm)/54 Mk 45 Mod 2. 4 - China 37 mm/76 (2 twin) H/PJ 76A.
Torpedoes: 6 - 324 mm Mk 32 Mod 5 (2 triple) tubes. Honeywell Mk 46.
Decoys: 4 - China Type 945 GP J 26-barrel chaff launchers.

RADARS

Air search - Signaal LW08.
Surface search - China Type 360.
Navigation – 2 Raytheon SPS-64(V)5.
Fire control – 2 Signaal STIR, (SSM and 5 in gun).
    China 374 G, (37 mm gun)

Sonars: China SJD-7; hull-mounted, active search/attack.

AIR SUPPORT

Helicopters: 1 Kaman SH-2G Seasprite (in due course).

KEY RECOGNITION FEATURES

- High bow, 5 in gun mounting in 'A' position.
- Sea Sparrow SAM VLS launchers below maindeck level between forward mounting and bridge.
- High, slab-sided forward superstructure with lattice mainmast atop at after end of bridge.
- Harpoon SSM launchers aft of forward superstructure.
- Large platform amidships supporting Signaal LW08 air search radar aerial.
- Square section funnel with wedge shaped smoke deflector atop.
- After superstructure has Signaal STIR fire control radar at forward end, China 374 G fire control director on low enclosed pylon, and JM-83H optical fire control director aft.
- 37 mm/76 gun mountings, port and starboard, outboard of STIR fire control radar and one deck level down.
- Flight deck aft with open quarterdeck below.

Tapi/Bayandor

TAPI

Country: THAILAND, IRAN
Country of origin: USA
Ship type: FRIGATES
Class: PF 103 (TAPI) (FF) (BAYANDOR) (FS)
THAILAND – Active: 2
Name (Pennant Number): TAPI (431, ex-5),
KHIRIRAT (432, ex-6)
IRAN – Active: 2
Name (Pennant Number): BAYANDOR (ex-US *PF 103*) (81), NAGHDI (ex-US *PF 104*) (82).*
*Officially rated as corvettes.

SPECIFICATION

Displacement, full load, tons: 1,135, (Iran). 1,172 (Thailand).
Length, feet (metres): 275.6 (84.0), (Iran). 275 (83.8), (Thailand).
Beam, feet (metres): 33.1 (10.1), (Iran). (33 (10), Thailand).
Draught, feet (metres): 10.2 (3.1), (Iran). (10 (3), Thailand).
Speed, knots: 20.
Range, miles: 4,800 at 12 kts.

ARMAMENT

Guns: 2 - US 3 in (76 mm)/50 Mk 3/4. 2 - Bofors 40 mm/60 (twin). 2 - Oerlikon GAM-BO1 20 mm. 2 - 12.7 mm machine-guns, (Iran). 1 - OTO MELARA 3 in (76 mm)/62 Compact. 1 - Bofors 40 mm/70. 2 - Oerlikon 20 mm. 2 - 12.7 machine-guns, (Thailand).
Torpedoes: 6 - 324 mm UK Mk 32 (2 triple) tubes. Honeywell Mk 46. (Thai ships only).

RADARS

Air/surface search - Westinghouse SPS-6C.
(Signaal LW04, Thailand).
Surface search - Racal Decca. (Raytheon SPS-53E, Thailand).
Navigation - Raytheon 1650, (Iran).
Fire control - Western Electric Mk 36, (Iran). Signaal WM22-61, (Thailand).
Sonars: EDO SQS-17A; hull-mounted, (Iran). Atlas Elektronik DSQS-21C, hull-mounted, active search/attack, (Thailand).

KEY RECOGNITION FEATURES

- Unusual curved bow.
- Long, sloping forecastle with open 3 in gun mounting ('A' position). (Not present in Thai units).
- 20 mm gun mounting ('B' position) in Iranian units. (OTO MELARA 3 in, on bigger raised platform, Thai ships).
- High, complex midships superstructure with sloping pole mainmast atop.
- Large SPS-6C (LW04, Thailand) air/surface search radar aerial on forward platform halfway up mainmast.
- Tall, sloping, black-capped funnel with curved after profile. (Straight after end to funnel profile in Thai ships).
- 3 in gun mounting ('Y' position) and 40 mm/60 mounting ('X' position), (Iranian ships). 40mm/70 gun mounting in 'Y' position in Thai ships.
- 20 mm mounting after end of quarterdeck in Iranian ships. (Torpedo tubes on quarterdeck in Thai ships).

MAKUT RAJAKUMARIN

Country: THAILAND

Country of origin: UK

Ship type: FRIGATES

Class: YARROW TYPE (FF/AX)

Active: 1

Name (Pennant Number): MAKUT RAJAKUMARIN
(43, ex-7)

SPECIFICATION

Displacement, full load, tons: 1,900.
Length, feet (metres): 320 (97.6).
Beam, feet (metres): 36 (11).
Draught, feet (metres): 18.1 (5.5).
Speed, knots: 26.
Range, miles: 5,000 at 18 kts.

ARMAMENT

Guns: 2 – Vickers 4.5 in (114 mm)/55 Mk 8. 2 –
Bofors 40 mm/70 (twin). 2 – Oerlikon 20mm.
Torpedoes: 6 - Plessey PMW 49A tubes.
Honeywell Mk 46.
A/S mortars: 1 Limbo 3-tube Mk 10.
Depth charges: 1 rack.
Decoys: 2 - Loral Mk 135 chaff launchers.

RADARS

Air/surface search - Signaal DA08.
Surface search –Signaal ZW06.

Navigation –Racal Decca.
Fire control – Signaal WM22/61.
Sonars: Atlas Elektronik DSQS-21C; hull-mounted,
active search/attack.

Note: Lost flagship role, now a training ship.

KEY RECOGNITION FEATURES

- High bow, with continuous sweeping
  maindeck to very sharp break down to
  short quarterdeck.
- 4.5 in gun turret just forward of bridge
  superstructure.
- Low superstructure with enclosed
  mainmast forward of midships, with
  forward gantry and spherical fire control
  radar atop.
- Low, angled funnel well aft of midships.
- Short pedestal mast supporting prominent
  air/surface search radar aerial forward of
  funnel.
- Ship's boat on davits just aft of funnel.
- Twin 40mm/70 gun turret aft end of
  superstructure.
- 4.5 in gun turret in 'Y' position.

Broadsword (Batch 3)

CORNWALL

Country: UNITED KINGDOM
Country of origin: UK
Ship type: FRIGATES
Class: BROADSWORD (TYPE 22) (BATCH 3) (FFG)
Active: 4
Name (Pennant Number): CORNWALL (F 99),
CUMBERLAND (F 85), CAMPBELTOWN (F 86),
CHATHAM (F 87)

SPECIFICATION

Displacement, full load, tons: 4,900.
Length, feet (metres): 485.9 (148.1).
Beam, feet (metres): 48.5 (14.8).
Draught, feet (metres): 21 (6.4).
Speed, knots: 30.
Range, miles: 4,500 at 18 kts.

ARMAMENT

Missiles: SSM – 8 - McDonnell Douglas Harpoon
Block 1C (2 quad) launchers. SAM – 2 - British
Aerospace Seawolf GWS 25 Mod 3.
Guns: 1 - Vickers 4.5 in (114 mm)/55 Mk 8. 1 -
Signaal/General Electric 30 mm 7-barrel
Goalkeeper. 2 - DES/MSI DS 30B 30 mm/75
and/or 2 – Oerlikon 20 mm.
Torpedoes: 6 - 324 mm Plessey STWS Mk 2 (2
triple) tubes. Marconi Stingray.

Decoys: 4 - Marconi Sea Gnat 6-barrel 130
mm/102 mm fixed launchers. Graseby Type 182
towed torpedo decoy.

RADARS

Air/surface search - Marconi Type 967/968.
Surface search – Racal Decca Type 2008.
Navigation - Kelvin Hughes Type 1007.
Fire control - Two Marconi Type 911.
Sonars: Ferranti/Thomson-Sintra Type 2050; hull-
mounted, active search/attack. Dowty Type
2031 towed array.

AIR SUPPORT

Helicopters: 2 Westland Lynx HMA 3/8; or 1
Westland Sea King HAS 5 (ASW/ASV).

KEY RECOGNITION FEATURES

- Similar in profile to Broadsword class Type
  22 Batch 2. Major identification differences
  are as follows:
- Steeper angle stern profile.
- 4.5 gun mounting ('A' position).
- Harpoon SSM angled launchers forward of
  mainmast.
- Signaal/GE Goalkeeper CIWS immediately
  forward of mainmast.

Duke

IRON DUKE

Country:	UNITED KINGDOM
Country of origin:	UK
Ship type:	FRIGATES
Class:	DUKE (TYPE 23) (FFG)
Active:	16

Name (Pennant Number): NORFOLK (F 230), ARGYLL (F 231), LANCASTER (F 229, ex-F 232), MARLBOROUGH (F 233), IRON DUKE (F 234), MONMOUTH (F 235), MONTROSE (F 236), WESTMINSTER (F 237), NORTHUMBERLAND (F 238), RICHMOND (F 239), SOMERSET (F 82), GRAFTON (F 80), SUTHERLAND (F 81), KENT (F 78), PORTLAND (F 79), ST ALBANS (F 83).

SPECIFICATION

Displacement, full load, tons: 4,200.
Length, feet (metres): 436.2 (133).
Beam, feet (metres): 52.8 (16.1).
Draught, feet (metres): 18 (5.5) (screws).
Speed, knots: 28.
Range, miles: 7,800 at 15 kts.

ARMAMENT

Missiles: SSM - McDonnell Douglas Harpoon (2 quad) launchers.
SAM - British Aerospace Seawolf GWS 26 Mod 1 VLS.
Guns: 1 - Vickers 4.5 in (114 mm)/55 Mk 8. 2 - DES/MSI 30B 30 mm/75.
Torpedoes: 4 - Cray Marine 324 mm (2 twin) tubes. Marconi Stingray.
Decoys: 4 - Marconi Sea Gnat 6-barrel 130 mm/102 mm launchers. Type 2070 (SLQ-25A) towed torpedo decoy.

RADARS

Air/surface search - Plessey Type 996(1), 3D.
Surface search – Racal Decca Type 1008.
Navigation - Kelvin Hughes Type 1007.
Fire control - 2 Marconi Type 911.
Sonars: Ferranti/Thomson-Sintra Type 2050; bow-mounted, active search/attack. Dowty Type 2031Z; towed array. (F 229-239). To be replaced by Type 2007 from 2005.

AIR SUPPORT

Helicopters: 1 Westland Lynx HMA 3/8 or EH Industries' EH 101 Merlin HM 1. (ASV/ASW).

KEY RECOGNITION FEATURES

- High bow with continuous maindeck through to stern.
- Three major weapons sited on forecastle from the bow aft, 4.5 in gun mounting, Seawolf SAM VLS launchers, Harpoon SSM angled launchers.
- Forward superstructure has large enclosed mainmast at after end with distinctive SATCOM domes, port and starboard, on wing platforms at its base.
- Unusual square section funnel amidships with two large black exhausts protruding from the top forward edge.
- Square profile after superstructure with short pyramid mast at forward edge.
- Flight deck aft above open quarterdeck.

Note: All vertical surfaces have a 7^0 slope and rounded edges to reduce IR emissions.

CORVETTES

EL CHIHAB (without main armament),   *Diego Quevedo*

Country: ALGERIA
Country of origin: ALGERIA
Ship type: CORVETTES
Class: DJEBEL CHINOISE (C 58) (TYPE 802) (FS)
Active: 2
Building: 1
Name (Pennant Number): DJEBEL CHINOISE (351), EL CHIHAB (352), ——- (353).

SPECIFICATION

Displacement, full load, tons: 540.
Length, feet (metres): 191.6 (58.4).
Beam, feet (metres): 27.9 (8.5).
Draught, feet (metres): 8.5 (2.6).
Speed, knots: 31.

ARMAMENT

Missiles: SSM – 4 China C802 (2 twin).

Guns: 1 - Russian 3 in (76 mm)/60. 2 - Breda 40 mm/70 (twin). 4 – USSR 23 mm (2 twin).

RADARS

Surface search – Racal Decca 1226.

KEY RECOGNITION FEATURES

- Continuous main deck from high, sharp bow, to low freeboard at stern.
- 3 in gun mounting on forecastle immediately forward of bridge superstructure.
- Steep fronted, high forward superstructure with all round bridge windows.
- Tall pole mainmast at after end of forward superstructure.
- "Step down" in superstructure after of mainmast.
- Very low after superstructure.
- 2 - 40 mm/70 gun open mountings at after end of superstructure, port and starboard.
- Long low quarterdeck.

Note: Hull size suggests association with Bazán 'Cormoran' class.

Note 2: First two ships fitted with 55m and 76mm guns as main armament.

Nanuchka

Nanchhka II

Country: ALGERIA, INDIA, LIBYA, RUSSIA

Country of origin: RUSSIA

Ship type: CORVETTES

Class: NANUCHKA (BURYA/VETER/NAKAT/DURG) (TYPE 1234) (FSG)

Active: 3 Algeria (Nanuchka II/Burya), 1 India (Nanuchka II /'Durg' class), 3 Libya (Nanuchka II/Burya), Russia - 11 Nanuchka III (Veter) (Type 1234.1); 1 Nanuchka IV (Nakat) (Type 1234.2)

ALGERIA – Name (Pennant Number): RAIS HAMIDOU (801), SALAH RAIS (802), RAIS ALI (803).

INDIA – Name (Pennant Number): SINDHUDURG (K 72).

LIBYA – Name (Pennant Number): TARIQ IBN ZIYAD (ex-*Ean Mara*) (416), EAN AL GAZALA (417), EAN ZARA (418).

RUSSIA – Name (Pennant Number): PRILIV (562), PASSAT (570), SMERCH (423), RAZLIV (450), ZYB (560), LIVEN (551), BURUN (566), GEJZER (555), RASSVET (520), MIRAZH (617), MOROZ (409), INEJ (432). Nanuchka IV – NAKAT (526).

SPECIFICATION

Displacement, full load, tons: 660.

Length, feet (metres): 194.5 (59.3).

Beam, feet (metres): 38.7 (11.8).

Draught, feet (metres): 8.5 (2.6).

Speed, knots: 33.

Range, miles: 2,500 at 12 kts.

ARMAMENT

Missiles: SSM – 4 SS-N-2C Styx (Durg/Nanuchka II). 6 Chelomey SS-N-9 Siren (Malakhit) (2 triple) launchers. (Russian ships). Zvezda SS-N-25 in Algerian hull 802. SAM - SA-N-4 Gecko twin launcher.

Guns: 2 - 57 mm/80 twin automatic (Nanuchka I/II). 1 - 3 in (76 mm)/60 (Nanuchka III and IV). 1 - 30 mm/65 (Nanuchka III - IV and Algerian hull 802.).

Decoys: 2 - PK 16 (Nanuchka I/II) or 4 - PK 10 (Nanuchka III) chaff launchers.

RADAR

Air/surface search –Peel Pair. (Plank Shave in later Nanuchka IIIs).

Surface search - Square Tie (Nanuchka II, Algerian hulls 801, 803).

Navigation – Nayada (Russian units). Don 2

SALAH RAIS

(Burya/Durg class).

Fire control – Pop Group, (SA-N-4). Muff Cob (Nanuchka I/II). Bass Tilt (Nanuchka III).

Al Manama/Victory/Muray Jib

Country: BAHRAIN, SINGAPORE, UNITED ARAB
EMIRATES (UAE)

Country of origin: GERMANY

Ship type: CORVETTES

Class: AL MANAMA/VICTORY/MURAY JIB
(LÜRSSEN MGB 62) (FSG)

Active: 2 Bahrain (Al Manama class), 6 Singapore
(Victory class), 2 UAE (Muray Jib class)

BAHRAIN – Name (Pennant Number): AL
MANAMA (50), AL MUHARRAQ (51).

SINGAPORE – Name (Pennant Number): VICTORY
(P 88), VALOUR (P 89), VIGILANCE (P 90), VALIANT
(P 91), VIGOUR (P 92), VENGEANCE (P 93).

UAE – Name (Pennant Number): MURAY JIB (CM
01, ex-P 6501), DAS (CM 02, ex-P 6502).

SPECIFICATION

Displacement, full load, tons: 632, (Bahrain). 630,
(UAE). 595, (Singapore).

Length, feet (metres): 206.7 (63), (Bahrain and
UAE). 204.7 (62.4) oa, (Singapore).

Beam, feet (metres): 30.5 (9.3), (Bahrain and
UAE). 27.9 (8.5), (Singapore).

Draught, feet (metres): 9.5 (2.9), (Bahrain). 8.2
(2.5), (UAE). 10.2 (3.1), (Singapore).

Speed, knots: 32, (Bahrain and UAE). 35,
(Singapore).

Range, miles: 4,000 at 16 kts., (Bahrain and UAE).
4,000 at 18 kts., (Singapore).

ARMAMENT

Missiles: SSM – 4 - Aerospatiale MM 40 Exocet
Block II (2 twin) launchers, (Bahrain and UAE).
8 -McDonnell Douglas Harpoon, (Singapore
only). SAM – Thomson-CSF modified Crotale
Navale octuple launcher, (UAE). IAI/Rafael
Barak 1, 2 octuple launchers, (Singapore).

Guns: 1 - OTO MELARA 3 in (76 mm)/62 Compact.
(Super Rapid, Singapore). 2 - Breda 40 mm/70
(twin). 2 - Oerlikon GAM-BO1 120 mm/93,
(Bahrain). 1 - Signaal Goalkeeper CIWS 30 mm,
(UAE). 4 - CIS 50 12.7 mm machine-guns,
(Singapore). 1 – 7.62 mm machine-gun,
(Bahrain).

Torpedoes: 6 - 324 mm Whitehead B 515 (2 triple
tubes), Whitehead A 244S. (Singapore ships
only).

Decoys: CSEE Dagaie. (Bahrain and UAE). 2 Plessey
Shield chaff launchers and 4 Rafael long-range
launchers, (2 twin), (Singapore).

MURAY JIB

RADARS

Air/surface search – Ericsson Sea Giraffe
50/150HC.

Navigation – Racal Decca 1226. (Bahrain, UAE).
Kelvin Hughes 1007, (Singapore).

Fire control – CelsiusTech 9LV 331, (gun and SSM),
(Bahrain). Bofors Electronic 9LV 223, (UAE).
Thomson-CSF DRBV 51C (Crotale, UAE ships). 2
Elta EL/M-2221(X), (Singapore).

Sonars: Thomson-Sintra TSM 2064; VDS.
(Singapore only).

AIR SUPPORT

Helicopters: 1 Eurocopter BO 105, (Bahrain). 1
Aerospatiale SA 316 Alouette, (UAE).

KEY RECOGNITION FEATURES

- Continuous maindeck from stem to stern.
- Low freeboard.
- Forward superstructure has enclosed mainmast centrally sited atop. Singapore ships' mainmast more massive and taller with angled pole-mast atop. Upper portion of UAE ships' taller mast latticed.
- 3 in gun mounting ('A' position).
- Flat-topped after superstructure with helicopter platform atop, (Bahrain and UAE units).
- No deck house with helicopter platform on Singapore ships. SATCOM dome atop short pole-mast aft of Harpoon SSM angled launchers with torpedo tubes outboard in these units.
- 40 mm/70 mountings ('Y' position), (Bahrain ships).
- Goalkeeper CIWS immediately aft of mainmast in UAE ships.
- Exocet SSM launchers between main superstructure and helicopter platform in Bahrain/UAE ships.
- Crotale SAM launcher right aft in UAE ships.
- Barak SAM launchers fitted either side of VDS in Singapore hulls.

Barroso

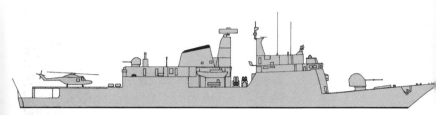

BARROSO

Country: BRAZIL	
Country of origin: BRAZIL	
Ship type: CORVETTES	
Class: BARROSO (FSG)	
Building: 1	
Planned: 1	
Name (Pennant Number): BARROSO (V 34)	

SPECIFICATION

Displacement, full load, tons: 2,350.
Length, feet (metres): 328 (100).
Beam, feet (metres): 37.4 (11.4).
Draught, feet (metres): 12.1 (5.3).
Speed, knots: 29.
Range, miles: 4,000 at 15 kts.

ARMAMENT

Missiles: SSM - 4 Aerospatiale MM 40 Exocet.
Guns: 1 - Vickers 4.5 in (115 mm) Mk 8. 1 Bofors
SAK Sea Trinity CIWS 40 mm/70 Mk 3. 2 - 12.7
machine-guns.
Torpedoes: 6 - 324 mm Mk 32 (2 triple) tubes.
Honeywell Mk 46 Mod 5 Neartip.
Decoys: 2 - IPqM chaff launchers.

RADAR

Surface search – AESN RAN-20S
Navigation – Racal Decca TM 1226C or Terma
Scanter.
Fire control – AESN RTN-30-X

Sonars: EDO 997(F); hull-mounted, active.

AIR SUPPORT
Helicopters: 1 Westland Super Lynx AH-11A
(ASW/ASV).

KEY RECOGNITION FEATURES

- Very sharp bow with forecastle sloping
  steeply down to slab-sided forward
  superstructure. 4.5 in gun mounting two-
  thirds from stem to bridge.
- Steep fronted, high forward superstructure.
- Short mast at after end of forward
  superstructure topped by pole mast.
  Forward edge sloping aft.
- Break between forward and aft
  superstructures with angled Exocet
  launchers pointing port and starboard.
- Large enclosed mainmast at forward edge
  of aft superstructure topped by surface
  search radar.
- Squat, tapered, black-capped funnel aft of
  midships, atop after superstructure.
- 40mm/70 CIWS turret at after end of
  hanger.
- Flight deck on main deck level forward of
  break down to open quarterdeck.

196

Inhaúma

INHAÚMA

Country: BRAZIL
Country of origin: BRAZIL
Ship type: CORVETTES
Class: INHAÚMA (FSG)
Active: 4
Name (Pennant Number): INHAÚMA (V 30),
JACEGUAY (V 31), JULIO DE NORONHA (V 32),
FRONTIN (V 33)

SPECIFICATION

Displacement, full load, tons: 1,970.
Length, feet (metres): 314.2 (95.8).
Beam, feet (metres): 37.4 (11.4).
Draught, feet (metres): 12.1 (5.3).
Speed, knots: 27.
Range, miles: 4,000 at 15 kts.

ARMAMENT

Missiles: SSM - 4 - Aerospatiale MM 40 Exocet.
Guns: 1 - Vickers 4.5 in (115 mm) Mk 8. 2 -
Bofors 40 mm/70.
Torpedoes: 6 - 324 mm Mk 32 (2 triple) tubes.
Honeywell Mk 46 Mod 5 Neartip.
Decoys: 2 - Plessey Shield chaff launchers.

RADAR

Surface search - Plessey ASW 4.
Navigation - Kelvin Hughes Type 1007.

Fire control - Selenia Orion RTN 10X.
Sonars: Atlas Elektronik DSQS-21C; hull-mounted,
active.

AIR SUPPORT

Helicopters: 1 Westland Super Lynx AH-11
(ASW/ASV) or Aerospatiale UH-12/13 Esquilo
(support).

KEY RECOGNITION FEATURES

- Apart from forecastle and quarterdeck,
  unusually high freeboard superstructure,
  flush with ship's side.
- 4.5 in gun mounting ('A' position).
- Steep fronted, high forward superstructure.
- Large enclosed mainmast at after end of
  forward superstructure topped by slender
  lattice mast.
- Lattice aftermast atop forward end of after
  superstructure.
- Squat, tapered, black-capped funnel aft of
  midships atop after superstructure.
- 40 mm/70 gun mountings at after end of
  superstructure, port and starboard.
- Flight deck on maindeck level forward of
  break down to quarterdeck.

Brunei

NAKHODA RAGHAM (at launch)

Country: BRUNEI
Country of origin: UK
Ship type: CORVETTES
Class: BRUNEI (FSG)
Active: 1
Name (Pennant Number): NAKHODA RAGHAM
(28), BENDAHARA SAKAM (29), JERAMBAK (30).

SPECIFICATION
Displacement, full load, tons: 1,940.
Length, feet (metres): 311.7 (95) oa.
Beam, feet (metres): 42 (12.8).
Draught, feet (metres): 11.8 (3.6).
Speed, knots: 30.
Range, miles: 5,000 at 12 kts.

ARMAMENT
Missiles: SSM - 8 - Aerospatiale MM 40 Exocet
Block II, SAM - BAe 16 cell VLS Seawolf
Guns: 1 - OTOBreda 3 in (76 mm) Super Rapid. 2
- GAM-BO1 20 mm.
Torpedoes: 6 - 324 mm Marconi (2 triple) tubes.
Decoys: 2 Super Barricade chaff launchers.

RADAR
Air/Surface search - Plessey ASW 9.
Navigation - Kelvin Hughes Type 1007.

Fire control - 2 Marconi 1802.
Sonars: Thomson Marconi or FMS 21/3.

AIR SUPPORT
Helicopters: Platform for 1 medium.

KEY RECOGNITION FEATURES

- Scaled down version of Malaysian 'Leiku'
  class frigates.
- Continuous main deck sweeping from high
  sharply raked bows to low freeboard stern,
  over open quarterdeck.
- 3 in gun turret mounting on raised
  platform immediately forward of VLS SAM
  and bridge.
- Low superstructure with large enclosed
  angled mainmast at after end, topped by
  slender pole mast.
- Clear break in superstructure with Exocet
  angled quad launchers, pointing port and
  starboard.
- Squat, tapered, and very long black-capped
  funnel aft of midships.
- Long flight deck on main deck level –
  platform only.

MULNIYA

Country: BULGARIA, INDIA, POLAND, ROMANIA, RUSSIA, UKRAINE, VIETNAM, YEMEN

Country of origin: Russia

Ship type: CORVETTES

Class: TARANTUL I (TYPE 1241.1) (ZBORUL, GORNIK, VEER, TYPE 1241 RE). TARANTUL II (TYPE 1241.1M), (VEFR, TYPF 1241RF) TARANTUL III (TYPE 1241.1MP). (MOLNYA) (FSG)

Active: 1 Bulgaria (Tarantul II), 12 India (Tarantul I/'Veer' class), 4 Poland (Tarantul I/'Gornik' class), 3 Romania (Tarantul I/'Zborul' class), Russia – 2 Tarantul II; 21 III , 2 Ukraine (Tarantul I) (May not be operational). 4 Vietnam (Tarantul I), 1 Yemen. (Tarantul I).

Building: 1 India

Planned: 3 India.

BULGARIA – Name (Pennant Number): MULNIYA (101).

INDIA – Name (Pennant Number): VEER (K 40), NIRBHIK (K 41), NIPAT (K 42), NISHANK (K 43), NIRGHAT (K 44), VIBHUTI (K 45), VIPUL (K 46), VINASH (K 47), VIDYUT (K 48), NASHAK (K 83), PRAHAR (K 98) PRABAL (K 99), PRALAYA (–).

POLAND – Name (Pennant Number): GORNIK (434), HUTNIK (435), METALOWIEC (436), ROLNIK (437).

ROMANIA – Name (Pennant Number): ZBORUL (188), PESCARUSUL (189), LASTUNUL (190).

Tarantul I/II/III

RUSSIA 'Tarantul I' – Name (Pennant Number): (860), (847).
'Tarantul II' – Name (Pennant Number): (832), (833).
'Tarantul III' – Name (Pennant Number): (819), (825), (855), (860), (874), (921), (924), (953), (937), (940), (944), (946), (954), (955), (870), (964), (971), (978), (991), (994), (995), (952)).
UKRAINE – Name (Pennant Number): NICOPOL (U 155), KREMENCHUK (U 156)*
* Not operational. May be scrapped.
VIETNAM – Name (Pennant Number): HQ 371, HQ 372, HQ 373, HQ 374.
YEMEN – Name (Pennant Number): 124 (ex-971)

SPECIFICATION

Displacement, full load, tons: 455. (450, Vietnam, 580, Yemen ships)
Length, feet (metres): 184.1 (56.1).
Beam, feet (metres): 37.7 (11.5).
Draught, feet (metres): 8.2 (2.5).
Speed, knots: 36.
Range, miles: 1,650 at 14 kts.

ARMAMENT

Missiles: SSM – 4 - Raduga SS-N-2C/D Mod 1 Styx launchers. SS-N-22 Sunburn (3M-82 Moskit) (2 twin) launchers (Tarantul III). SAM – SA-N-5 Grail quad launcher. SAM/Guns - CADS-N-1 (Kashtan) 30 mm Gatling/SA-N-11 mounting (Russian Tarantul II 962 only).
Guns: 1 - 3 in (76 mm)/60. 2 - 30 mm/65 AK 630.
Decoys: 2 - PK 16 or 4 - PK 10 (Tarantul III) chaff launchers. PK 16 chaff launchers (Indian and Polish hulls).

RADAR

Air/surface search - Plank Shave (Tarantul I), Band Stand (with Plank Shave) (Tarantul II and III).
Navigation - Spin Trough or Kivach II. (Mius, Indian ships). Perchora 436, 437 (Vietnam). Racal Decca Bridgemaster, (Poland).
Fire control - Bass Tilt.
Sonars: Foal Tail, VDS, active. (Poland, Russia, Vietnam).

Pauk I/II

BODRI

Country: BULGARIA, CUBA, INDIA, RUSSIA, UKRAINE, VIETNAM

Country of origin: Russia

Ship type: CORVETTES

Class: PAUK I (TYPE 1241P) (RESHITELNI), PAUK II (TYPE 1241PE), (ABHAY), IMPROVED PAUK ('HO-A') (FS/FSG/PCF)

Active: 2 Bulgaria (Pauk I 'Reshitelni' class FS/PCF), 1 Cuba (Pauk II FS), 4 India (Pauk II, 'Abhay' class FS), 18 Russia (Pauk I), 1 Ukraine (Pauk I), (plus 3, Border Guard). 1 Improved Pauk, Vietnam.

Planned: 1 Vietnam.

BULGARIA – Name (Pennant Number): RESHITELNI (13), BODRI (14).

CUBA – Name (Pennant Number): 321.

INDIA – Name (Pennant Number): ABHAY (P 33), AJAY (P 34), AKSHAY (P 35), AGRAY (P 36).

RUSSIA – Name (Pennant Number): PSKR 800-805, PSKR 806-812, PSKR 814-818.

UKRAINE – Name (Pennant Number): KHMELNITSKY (U 208). *Border Guard* – GRIGORY KUROPIATNIKOV (BG 50, ex-PSKR 817), POLTAVA (BG 51, ex-PSKR 813), GRIGORY GNATENKO (BG 52, ex-PSKR 815).

VIETNAM – Name (Pennant Number): HQ 381

SPECIFICATION

Displacement, full load, tons: 440. (485, Indian units).

Length, feet (metres): 195.2 (59.5), (Bulgaria). (189 (57.5), Cuba, India, Russia).

Beam, feet (metres): 33.5 (10.2)

Draught, feet (metres): 10.8 (3.3).(11.2 (3.4), Cuba).

Speed, knots: 32.

Range, miles: 2,200 at 18 kts.

ARMAMENT

Missiles: SAM - SA-N-5 Grail quad launcher. (No SAM launchers in Ukrainian Border Guard ships).

Guns: 1 – 3 in (76 mm)/60. 1 - 30 mm/65 AK 630. (4 – 25 mm (2 twin) fitted on stern of Cuban ship).

Torpedoes: 4 - 16 in (406 mm) tubes. Type 40, (Pauk I, not Cuban ship) or 4 - 21 in (533 mm) (Pauk II). SET-65E , (India).

A/S mortars: 2 - RBU 1200 5-tubed.

Depth charges: 2 racks, (not Cuban or Indian ships).

Decoys: 2 - PK 16 or PK 10 chaff launchers.

RADAR

Air/surface search - Peel Cone (Pauk I), Positive E (Pauk II). Cross Dome, (Indian hulls).

Surface search - Kivach. (Russia), Spin Trough, (Bulgaria).

Navigation - Pechora, (Cuba, India).

Fire control - Bass Tilt.

Sonars: Rat Tail; VDS (mounted on transom), (Cuba, India,). Foal Tail VDS (Bulgaria, Russia).

Pauk I/II

KEY RECOGNITION FEATURES

- High angled bow with long forecastle.
- 3 in gun mounting ('A' position).
- Large, central, stepped superstructure extending from forecastle to afterdeck.
- Prominent raised pedestal supporting fire control radar aerial sited amidships atop superstructure.
- Tall lattice mainmast well aft of midships with small lattice mast atop at after end.
- Torpedo tubes mounted on maindeck, two port two starboard. One pair adjacent bridge, second pair adjacent mainmast. (Not Cuban ship).
- A/S mortars on maindeck, either side of forward superstructure.
- 30 mm/65 AK 630 gun mounting right aft ('X' position).

Note: This appears to be an ASW version of the Tarantul class.

Note 2: First three of Russian Pauk I have a lower bridge than successors.

Note 3: Indian Pauk IIs have longer superstructure than Pauk I.

Note 4: All remaining Russian hulls operated by Border Guard with white, blue and red diagonal stripes painted on hulls.

Note 5: Ukrainian Border Guard hulls are black painted with blue and yellow diagonal stripes. Upper works are painted white.

Note 6: Vietnam's Improved Pauk has full load displacement of 517 tons, length of 203.4 (62 metres), and a beam of 36 (11 metres). These ships are armed with 8 Zvezda SS-N-25 (KH-35 Uran) SSMs, the SA-N-10 SAM, 1 - 3 in(76mm)/60 gun and 1 - 30 mm/65 AK 630, together with 2 - 12.7 mm machine-guns. The superstructure is set back well aft, with a lattice mast supporting a Cross Dome radome, aft of midships with SSM angled launchers outboard.

AJAY (India)

Kralj

KRALJ PETAR KRESIMIR

Country: CROATIA
Country of origin: CROATIA
Ship type: CORVETTES
Class: KRALJ (TYPE R-03) (FSG)
Active: 2
Name (Pennant Number): KRALJ PETAR KRESIMIR IV (ex-*Sergej Masera*) (RTOP 11), KRALJ DMITAR ZVONIMIR (RTOP 12).

SPECIFICATION

Displacement, full load, tons: 385.
Length, feet (metres): 175.9 (53.6).
Beam, feet (metres): 27.9 (8.5).
Draught, feet (metres): 7.5 (2.3).
Speed, knots: 36.
Range, miles: 1,800 at 18 kts.

ARMAMENT

Missiles: SSM - 4 or 8 - Saab RBS 15B (2 or 4 twin).
Guns: 1 - Bofors 57 mm/70. (Launchers for illuminants on side of mounting.) 1 - 30 mm/65 AK 630.
Mines: 4 – AIM-70 magnetic or 6 SAG-1 acoustic in lieu of SSMs.
Decoys: 2 Wallop Barricade chaff/IR launcher.

RADAR

Surface search - Racal BT 502.
Navigation - Racal 1290A.
Fire control - BEAB 9LV 249 Mk 2.
Sonars: RIZ PP 10M; hull-mounted, active search.

KEY RECOGNITION FEATURES

- Smooth, rounded hull with low forecastle and continuous maindeck from stem to stern.
- 57 mm/70 gun mounting ('A' position).
- Long, central superstructure, raised in bridge area and at aft end.
- Pyramid shaped, lattice mainmast aft of bridge.
- 30 mm/65 AK 630 mounting on raised platform at aft end of superstructure.
- Saab RBS 15 SSM angled box launchers on afterdeck, port and starboard, trained forward.

Note: Derived from the 'Koncar' fast attack (missile) class with a stretched hull and a new superstructure. Mine rails may be removed in favour of increasing SSM capability

Assad

Country: ECUADOR, IRAQ, MALAYSIA
Country of origin: ITALY
Ship type: CORVETTES
Class: ASSAD/ESMERALDAS/LAKSAMANA (FSG)
Active: 6 Ecuador (Esmeraldas class), 2 Iraq (Assad class)*, 4 Malaysia (Laksamana class) * Iraqi ships moored in Italian ports because of UN sanctions. Malaysian ships formerly built for Iraq.
ECUADOR – Name (Pennant Number): ESMERALDAS (CM 11), MANABI (CM 12), LOS RIOS (CM 13), EL ORO (CM 14), LOS GALAPAGOS (CM 15), LOJA (CM 16)
IRAQ – Name (Pennant Number): MUSSA BEN NUSSAIR (F 210), TARIQ IBN ZIAD (F 212).
MALAYSIA – Name (Pennant Number): LAKSAMANA HANG NADIM (ex-*Khalid Ibn Al Walid*) (F 134, ex-F 216), LAKSAMANA TUN ABDUL JAMIL (ex-*Saad Ibn Abi Waccade*) (F 135, ex-F 218), LAKSAMANA MUHAMMAD AMIN (ex-*Abdulla Ben Abi Sarh*) (F 136, ex-F 214), LAKSAMANA TAN PUSHMAH (ex-*Salahi Ad Deen Alayoori*) (F 137, ex-F 220).

SPECIFICATION

Displacement, full load, tons: 685. (Ecuador and Iraq). (705, Malaysian ships).

Length, feet (metres): 204.4 (62.3).

Beam, feet (metres): 30.5 (9.3).

Draught, feet (metres): 8 (2.5).

Speed, knots: 36.

Range, miles: 4,000 at 14 kts., (Ecuador). 2,300 at 18 kts., (Malaysia)

ARMAMENT

Missiles: SSM - 6 - Aerospatiale MM 40 Exocet (2 triple) launchers, (Ecuador). 6 - OTO MELARA/Matra Otomat Teseo Mk 2 (TG 2) (3 twin) (Iraq, Malaysia). SAM - Selenia Elsag Albatros quad launcher, Aspide.

Guns: 1 - OTO MELARA 3 in (76 mm)/62 Compact, (Ecuador, Iraq), Super Rapid, (Malaysia). 2 - Breda 40 mm/70 (twin). (Not Iraqi ships)

Torpedoes: 6 -324 mm ILAS-3 (2 triple) tubes. Whitehead Motofides A244S.

Decoys: 1 or 2 Breda 105 mm SCLAR chaff/illuminants launcher.

ESMERALDAS

RADAR

Air/surface search - Selenia RAN-10S. (Ecuador) RAN 12L/X (Iraq, Malaysia).

Navigation - SMA SPN-703 (3 RM 20), (Ecuador, Iraq). Kelvin Hughes 1007, (Malaysia).

Fire control - 2 Selenia Orion 10X.

Sonars: Thomson Sintra Diodon; hull-mounted. (Ecuador). Atlas Elektronik ASO 84-41, hull-mounted, (Iraq, Malaysia).

AIR SUPPORT

Helicopters: 1 Bell 206B (platform only), (Ecuador). 1 Agusta AB 212, (Iraq).

KEY RECOGNITION FEATURES

- High bow with sweeping continuous main deck aft to stern.
- 3 in gun mounting ('A' position).
- Square profile main superstructure with raised bridge area, (Ecuador only) (Iraqi and Malaysian ships have flatter roofs to bridge with slight slope in line with superstructure).
- Pyramid mainmast atop centre of main superstructure.
- Prominent Aspide SAM Albatros box launcher atop after end of main superstructure.
- 2 Exocet SSM launchers immediately aft of forward superstructure and 40 mm/70 gun turret in 'Y' position, (Ecuador).
- 40 mm/70 gun turret mounting on superstructure, just aft of midships, with angled Otomat Teseo SSM launchers, facing port and starboard, on main deck after of superstructure. (Malaysian ships)
- Raised helicopter landing platform aft of SSM launchers (Ecuador and Iraq, not Malaysian ships). (Telescopic hangar, Iraqi ships).

K 130

K130 (Computer graphic)

Country: GERMANY
Country of origin: GERMANY
Ship type: CORVETTES
Class: K 130 (FSG)
Ordered: 5
Name (Pennant Number): none available.

SPECIFICATION

Displacement, full load, tons: 1,662.
Length, feet (metres): 289.8 (88.3).
Beam, feet (metres): 41.7 (12.7).
Draught, feet (metres): 15.7 (4.8).
Speed, knots: 26.
Range, miles: 2,500 at 15 kts.

ARMAMENT

Missiles: SSM - 4 Saab RBS - 15. SAM – 8
Polyphem VLS; 2 RAM 21 cell Mk 49 launchers.
Guns: 1- OTOBreda 76 mm/62. 2 – Mauser 27
mm.
Decoys: 2 chaff launchers.

RADAR

Air/Surface search – DASA TRS-3D.

AIR SUPPORT

Helicopters: 2 VTOL drones.

KEY RECOGNITION FEATURES

- High forecastle with central superstructure flush with ship's side.
- Long, low freeboard flight deck with Polyphem SAM VLS beneath.
- 76 mm gun on forecastle immediately forward of raised platform with RAM launcher.
- Tall enclosed, chunky pyramidal mast at aft end of bridge superstructure, with air search radar atop.
- Tall slender funnel aft of midships.
- Second RAM launcher aft end of superstructure.

Niki

NIKI

Country: GREECE

Country of origin: GERMANY

Ship type: CORVETTES

Class: NIKI (THETIS) (TYPE 420) (FS/PG)

Active: 5

Name (Pennant Number): NIKI (ex-*Thetis*) (P 62,
ex-P 6052), DOXA (ex-*Najade*) (P 63,ex-P 6054),
ELEFTHERIA (ex-*Triton*) (P 64, ex-P 6055),
CARTERIA (ex-*Hermes*) (P 65, ex-P 6053), AGON
(ex-*Andreia*, ex-*Theseus*) (P 66, ex-P 6056).

SPECIFICATION

Displacement, full load, tons: 732.

Length, feet (metres): 229.7 (70).

Beam, feet (metres): 26.9 (8.2).

Draught, feet (metres): 8.6 (2.7).

Speed, knots: 19.5.

Range, miles: 2,760 at 15 kts.

ARMAMENT

Guns: 4 - Breda 40 mm/70 (2 twin). 2 – 12.7
machine-guns.

Torpedoes: 4 - 324 mm single tubes. 4 Honeywell
Mk 46 Mod 5 Neartip..

Depth charges: 2 rails.

RADAR

Surface search - Thomson-CSF TRS 3001.

Navigation - Kelvin Hughes 14/9.

Sonars: Atlas Elektronik ELAC 1 BV; hull-mounted,
active search/attack.

KEY RECOGNITION FEATURES

- 40 mm/70 gun twin mounting ('A' position).
- High, smooth, forward superstructure with tripod mainmast at after end.
- Black-capped, sloping-topped funnel amidships.
- Torpedo tubes, port and starboard, on maindeck outboard of after superstructure.
- 40 mm/70 gun twin mounting at after end of after superstructure.

Note: *Doxa* has a deckhouse before bridge for sick bay.

Khukri/Kora

KHUKRI

Country: INDIA
Country of origin: INDIA
Ship type: CORVETTES
Class: KHUKRI /KORA (PROJECTS 25 and 25A) (FSG)

'KHUKRI' CLASS
Active: 4
Name (Pennant Number): KHUKRI (P 49), KUTHAR (P 46), KIRPAN (P 44), KHANJAR (P 47).

'KORA' CLASS
Active: 4
Name (Pennant Number): KORA (P 61), KIRCH (P 62), KULISH (P 63), KARMUKH (P 64).

SPECIFICATION

Displacement, full load, tons: 1,350.
Length, feet (metres): 298.6 (91).
Beam, feet (metres): 34.4 (10.5).
Draught, feet (metres): 13.1 (4), Khukri. 14.8 (4.5), Kora.
Speed, knots: 25.
Range, miles: 4,000 at 16 kts.

ARMAMENT

Missiles: SSM - 4 SS-N-2D Styx (2 twin) launchers, (Khukri class). Zvezda SS-N-25 (Kh 35 Uran) Sapless (2 quad), (Kora class). SAM - SA-N-5 Grail.
Guns: 1 - USSR 3 in (76 mm)/60 AK 176. 2 - 30 mm/65 (twin) AK 630.
Decoys: 2 - PK 16 chaff launchers, (Khukri class) 4 - PK 10 (Kora). NPOL (Cochin) towed torpedo decoy.

RADAR

Air search - Cross Dome.
Air/surface search - Plank Shave.
Navigation - Bharat 1245.
Fire control - Bass Tilt.

AIR SUPPORT

Helicopters: Platform only for HAL SA 319B Chetak, (Alouette III).

KEY RECOGNITION FEATURES

- High bow with steep sloping forecastle.
- 3 in gun mounting mid-forecastle.
- SS-N-2D Mod 1 Styx SSM box launchers forward of bridge, port and starboard in Khukri class.
- SS-N-25 Sapless tubular SSM launchers in same position in Kora class.
- Unusual curved sloping front up to bridge windows in Khukri class only.

Both classes share the following recognition features:

- Midships superstructure has large lattice mainmast at after end.
- Distinctive Positive E/Cross Dome air search radome atop mainmast.
- Low funnel, with three pipe exhausts, aft of mainmast.
- 30 mm/65 gun mountings on platforms, port and starboard, immediately aft of funnel.
- Raised flight deck forward of short quarterdeck.

EITHNE

Country: IRELAND
Country of origin: IRELAND
Ship type: CORVETTES
Class: EITHNE (OPV)
Active: 1
Name (Pennant Number): EITHNE (P 31)

SPECIFICATION

Displacement, full load, tons: 1,910.
Length, feet (metres): 265 (80.8).
Beam, feet (metres): 39.4 (12).
Draught, feet (metres): 14.1 (4.3).
Speed, knots: 20+.
Range, miles: 7,000 at 15 kts.

ARMAMENT

Guns: 1- Bofors 57 mm/70 Mk 1. 2 - Rheinmetall
20 mm/20. 2 - Wallop 57 mm launchers for
illuminants.

RADAR

Air/surface search - Signaal DA05 Mk 4.

Navigation - Racal Decca 1629C.
Sonars: Plessey PMS 26; hull-mounted.

AIR SUPPORT

Helicopters: 1 Aerospatiale SA 365F Dauphin 2.

KEY RECOGNITION FEATURES

- High freeboard with high central
  superstructure.
- Short forecastle with 57 mm/70 gun
  mounting ('B' position).
- Large, solid based lattice mainmast atop
  superstructure just aft of bridge.
- Tall tapered funnels at after end of
  superstructure.
- Long flight deck with break down to short
  quarterdeck.
- Distinctive flight deck overhang.
- Ship's boats in davits high up
  superstructure, amidships.

Eilat (Saar 5)

Country: ISRAEL
Country of origin: Israel
Ship type: CORVETTES
Class: EILAT (SAAR 5) (FSG)
Active: 3
Planned: 5.
Name (Pennant Number): EILAT (501), LAHAV (502), HANIT (503)

SPECIFICATION
Displacement, full load, tons: 1,227.
Length, feet (metres): 283.5 (86.4) oa.
Beam, feet (metres): 39 (11.9).
Draught, feet (metres): 10.5 (3.2).
Speed, knots: 33.
Range, miles: 3,500 at 17 kts.

ARMAMENT
Missiles: SSM - McDonnell Douglas Harpoon (2 quad) launchers. SAM - 2 Israeli Industries Barak I (vertical launch).

KEY RECOGNITION FEATURES
- High bow, short sloping forecastle.
- 3 in gun mounting or Vulcan Phalanx CIWS on raised forecastle position.
- Barak I SAM in vertical launch tubes immediately forward of bridge superstructure.
- Pair of decoy launchers, port and starboard, atop bridge.
- High, bulky forward slab-sided superstructure with tall pole mainmast atop.
- Harpoon SSM angled launchers immediately aft of forward superstructure.
- Squat, square black-capped funnel with unusual sloping forward edge.
- Barak I SAM VLS launcher immediately aft of funnel.
- Substantial angular after superstructure with after pole mast atop.
- Large Elta EL/M-2218S air search radar aerial atop after superstructure.
- Flight deck right aft with low freeboard.

Guns: 1 - OTO MELARA 3 in (76 mm)/62 Compact. Interchangeable with a Bofors 57 mm gun or Vulcan Phalanx CIWS. 2 - Sea Vulcan 25 mm CIWS.
Torpedoes: 6 - 324 mm Mk 32 (2 triple) tubes. Honeywell Mk 46.
Decoys: 3 Elbit/Deseaver chaff launchers. Rafael ATC-1 towed torpedo decoy.

EILAT

RADAR
Air search – Elta EL/M-2218S.
Surface search - Cardion SPS-55.
Fire control - 3 Elta EL/M-2221 GM STGR.
Sonars: EDO Type 796 Mod 1; hull-mounted.
  Rafael towed array.

AIR SUPPORT
Helicopters: 1 Aerospatiale SA 366G Dauphin.

Minerva

SFINGE

Country: ITALY	
Country of origin: ITALY	
Ship type: CORVETTES	
Class: MINERVA (FS)	
Active: 8	

Name (Pennant Number): MINERVA (F 551), URANIA (F 552), DANAIDE (F 553), SFINGE (F 554), DRIADE (F 555), CHIMERA (F 556), FENICE (F 557), SIBILLA (F 558)

SPECIFICATION

Displacement, full load, tons: 1,285.
Length, feet (metres): 284.1 (86.6).
Beam, feet (metres): 34.5 (10.5).
Draught, feet (metres): 10.5 (3.2).
Speed, knots: 24.
Range, miles: 3,500 at 18 kts.

ARMAMENT

Missiles: SSM - Fitted for but not with 4 or 6 Teseo Otomat between the masts. SAM - Selenia Elsag Albatros octuple launcher, Aspide.
Guns: 1 - OTO MELARA 3 in (76 mm)/62 Compact.
Torpedoes: 6 - 324 mm Whitehead B 515 (2 triple) tubes. Honeywell Mk 46.
Decoys: 2 - Wallop Barricade double layer launchers. SLQ-25 Nixie towed torpedo decoy.

RADAR

Air/surface search - Selenia SPS-774 (RAN 10S).
Navigation - SMA SPN-728(V)2.
Fire control - Selenia SPG-76 (RTN 30X).
Sonars: Raytheon/Elsag DE 1167; hull-mounted.

KEY RECOGNITION FEATURES

- Continuous maindeck from bow to break down to quarterdeck.
- Long forecastle with 3 in gun mounting at mid-point.
- Isolated forward superstructure with short pole mast at after end.
- Midships enclosed mainmast supporting distinctive SPS-774 air/surface search radar aerial.
- Tapered black-capped funnel atop central after superstructure with unusual forward sloping top and black smoke deflectors.
- Aspide SAM Albatros box launcher at after end of after superstructure.
- Low freeboard quarterdeck.

TRAL 671

Country: KOREA, NORTH
Country of origin: KOREA, NORTH/RUSSIA
Ship type: CORVETTES
Class: SARIWON/TRAL (FS)
'Sariwon' class Active: 3
Name (Pennant Number): 513, 671, 725*
*Some doubt about accuracy of last pennant number.
'Tral' class Active: 2
Name (Pennant Number): 726, 727*
*Some doubt about accuracy of these pennant numbers.

SPECIFICATION

Displacement, full load, tons: 650, (Sariwon), 580, (Tral).
Length, feet (metres): 203.7 (62.1).
Beam, feet (metres): 23.9 (7.3).
Draught, feet (metres): 7.8 (2.4).
Speed, knots: 16.
Range, miles: 2,700 at 16 kts.

ARMAMENT

Guns: 1 – 85 mm/52 tank turret, (Tral). 4 - 57 mm/80 (2 twin) (Sariwon). 2 or 4 - 37 mm/6 (single, Tral, 2 twin, Sariwon). 16 – 14.5 mm machine-guns, 4 quad.
A/S mortars: 2 – RBU 1200 5-tube in Sariwon 513 only.
Depth charges: 2 rails.
Mines: 2 rails.

RADAR

Surface search – Pot Head or Don 2.
Navigation – Model 351.
Sonars: Stag Horn hull-mounted in Sariwon 513 only.

KEY RECOGNITION FEATURES

- Very high forecastle, with sharp break at aft end of superstructure to very low freeboard.
- 'Tral' class has 85mm gun in tank turret, raised, on forecastle.
- Unusual slanting stern.
- Short bridge superstructure topped by pedestal mast with tall pole mast atop.
- Ship's boat on davits in break between superstructure.
- Narrow angled funnel on low superstructure amidships.
- 2 - 37 mm gun open mountings on long quarterdeck. (Tral).
- Minelaying rails visible along whole of upper deck after of bridge superstructure.
- 'Sariwon' design based on original Soviet 'Tral' fleet minelayer design of mid-1930s.
Note: Three 'Sariwon' built in North Korea in mid-1960s. Two 'Tral' transferred by USSR in mid-1950s, paid off in the early 1980s, but returned to service in the early 1990s.

213

Dong Hae

DONG HAE

Country:	KOREA, SOUTH
Country of origin:	KOREA, SOUTH
Ship type:	CORVETTES
Class:	DONG HAE (FS)
Active:	4

Name (Pennant Number): DONG HAE (751), SU WON (752), KANG REUNG (753), AN YANG (755).

SPECIFICATION

Displacement, full load, tons: 1,076.
Length, feet (metres): 256.2 (78.1).
Beam, feet (metres): 31.5 (9.6).
Draught, feet (metres): 8.5 (2.6).
Speed, knots: 31.
Range, miles: 4,000 at 15 kts.

ARMAMENT

Guns: 1 - OTO MELARA 3 in (76 mm)/62 Compact. 4 - Emerson Electric 30 mm (2 twin). 2 – Bofors 40 mm/60 (twin).
Torpedoes: 6 - 324 mm Mk 32 (2 triple) tubes. Honeywell Mk 46.
Depth charges: 12.
Decoys: 4 - MEL Protean fixed launchers.

RADAR

Surface search - Raytheon SPS-64.
Fire control - Signaal WM28.
Sonars: Signaal PHS-32 hull-mounted, active search and attack.

KEY RECOGNITION FEATURES

- Continuous deck level sweeping from high bow to lower freeboard stern.
- 3 in gun mounting ('A' position). Emmerson Electric 30 mm twin gun mounting in 'B' position.
- High forward superstructure with tall lattice mainmast at after end with distinctive WM28 spherical radome atop.
- Large funnel well aft of midships, with torpedo tubes immediately forward.
- Ship's boats outboard in davits at funnel level.
- Twin 30 mm gun mounting on afterdeck.

NAM WON

Country: KOREA, SOUTH
Country of origin: SOUTH KOREA
Ship type: CORVETTES
Class: PO HANG (FS/FSG)
Active: 24
Name (Pennant Number): PO HANG (756), KUN
SAN (757), KYONG JU (758), MOK PO (759), KIM
CHON (761), CHUNG JU (762), JIN JU (763), YO SU
(765), JIN HAE (766), SUN CHON (767), YEE REE
(768), WON JU (769), AN DONG (771), CHON AN
(772), SONG NAM (773), BU CHON (775), JAE
CHON (776), DAE CHON (777), SOK CHO (778),
YONG JU (779), NAM WON (781), KWAN MYONG
(782), SIN HUNG (783), KONG JU (785).

SPECIFICATION

Displacement, full load, tons: 1,220.
Length, feet (metres): 289.7 (88.3).
Beam, feet (metres): 32.8 (10).
Draught, feet (metres): 9.5 (2.9).
Speed, knots: 32.
Range, miles: 4,000 at 15 kts.

ARMAMENT

Missiles: SSM - 2 Aerospatiale MM 38 Exocet
(756-759 only).
Guns: 1 or 2 - OTO MELARA 3 in (76 mm)/62
Compact. 4 - Emerson Electric 30 mm (2 twin)
(756-759). 4 - Breda 40 mm/70 (2 twin), (761
onwards).
Torpedoes: 6 - 324 mm Mk 32 (2 triple) tubes.
Honeywell Mk 46 in 756-759 only.

Depth charges: 12 (761 onwards).
Decoys: 4 - MEL Protean fixed launchers. 2 - Loral
Hycor SRBOC 6-barrel Mk 36 (in some).

RADAR

Surface search - Marconi 1810 and/or Raytheon
SPS-64.
Fire control - Signaal WM28; or Marconi 1802.
Sonars: Signaal PHS-32 hull-mounted active
search and attack

KEY RECOGNITION FEATURES

- 3 in gun mounting ('A' position). Breda 40
  mm/70 twin gun mounting in 'B' position
  761 onwards; Emerson Electric 30 mm twin
  mounting in 'B' position in 756-759.
- High forward superstructure with enclosed
  mainmast at after end.
- WM28 fire control radome atop mainmast.
- Large funnel well aft of midships with gas
  turbine air intakes immediately forward.
- Ship's boats in davits at funnel level
  outboard of air intakes.
- Exocet SSM box launchers at after end of
  after superstructure in 756-759. Replaced
  by 40 mm/70 gun turret mounting 761
  onwards.
- Twin 30 mm or OTO MELARA 3 in gun
  mounting on afterdeck.

Mk 9 Vosper Thornycroft Type

ERINOMI

Country: NIGERIA	
Country of origin: UK	
Ship type: CORVETTES	
Class: Mk 9 VOSPER THORNYCROFT TYPE (FS)	
Active: 1*	

*Second in repair.
Name (Pennant Number): ERINOMI (F 83),
ENYMIRI (F 84).

SPECIFICATION

Displacement, full load, tons: 780.
Length, feet (metres): 226 (69).
Beam, feet (metres): 31.5 (9.8).
Draught, feet (metres): 9.8 (3).
Speed, knots: 27.
Range, miles: 2,200 at 14 kts.

ARMAMENT

Missiles: SAM - Short Brothers Seacat triple
launcher. (Non-operational).
Guns: 1 – OTO Melara 76 mm/62 Mod 6 Compact.
1 – Breda Bofors 40 mm/70 Type 350. 2 –
Oerlikon 20 mm.
A/S mortars: 1 – Bofors 375 mm twin launcher.

RADAR

Air/surface search –Plessey AWS 2.
Navigation –Racal Decca TM 1226.
Fire control – Signaal WM24.
Sonars: Plessey PMS 26 hull-mounted, active
attack.

KEY RECOGNITION FEATURES

- Sharp bow, short forecastle with 3 in gun
  immediately forward of bridge.
- Tall bridge structure with all round
  windows.
- Long central superstructure with short
  lattice mainmast immediately aft of bridge
  with spherical fire control radome atop.
- Very large and prominent angled and
  tapered funnel amidships.
- Break in main deck immediately aft of
  funnel.
- Very short quarterdeck.

Qahir

QAHIR AL AMWAJ

Country: OMAN
Country of origin: UK
Ship type: CORVETTES
Class: QAHIR (FSG)
Active: 2
Name (Pennant Number): QAHIR AL AMWAJ (Q 31), AL MUA'ZZER (Q 32)

SPECIFICATION

Displacement, full load, tons: 1,450.
Length, feet (metres): 274.6 (83.7) oa.
Beam, feet (metres): 37.7 (11.5)
Draught, feet (metres): 11.8 (3.6).
Speed, knots: 28.
Range, miles: 4,000 at 10 kts.

ARMAMENT

Missiles: SSM - 8 Aerospatiale MM 40 Block II Exocet. SAM - Thomson-CSF Crotale NG, octuple launcher.
Guns: 1 - OTO MELARA 3 in (76 mm)/62 Super Rapid. 2 - Oerlikon/Royal Ordnance 20 mm GAM-BO1.
Torpedoes: 6 - 324 mm (2 triple tubes) may be fitted.
Decoys: 2 Barricade 12-barrel chaff launchers.

RADAR

Air/surface search - Signaal MW08.
Navigation – Kelvin Hughes 1007.

Fire control - Signaal STING, Thomson CSF DRBV 51C.
Sonars: Thomson-Sintra/BAeSEMA ATAS towed array.

AIR SUPPORT

Helicopters: Platform for 1 Super Puma type.

KEY RECOGNITION FEATURES

- Sloping straight-edged bow with long, gently sloping forecastle.
- 2 Exocet SSM launchers immediately forward of bridge, after one trained to port, forward one to starboard.
- 3 in gun mounting forward of SSM launchers.
- Large, smooth midships superstructure with angled surfaces for low reflective radar signature.
- Squat black-capped funnel immediately abaft mainmast.
- Crotale NG SAM box launcher at after end of superstructure immediately forward of flight deck.
- Long flight deck.

Orkan (Sassnitz)

Poland

GROM

LG Nilsson

Country: POLAND, GERMANY
Country of origin: EAST GERMANY
Ship type: CORVETTES
Class: ORKAN (SASSNITZ) (TYPE 660, ex-151) FSG
POLAND
Active: 3
Name (Pennant Number): ORKAN (421), PIORUN
(422), GROM (ex-*Huragan*) (423).
GERMANY
Active: 2 (Coast guard)
Name (Pennant Number): NEUSTRELITZ (ex-
Sassnitz) (BG 22, ex-P 6165, ex-591), BAD DÜBEN
(ex-*Binz*) (BG 23, ex-593).

SPECIFICATION

Displacement, full load, tons: 326, Polish hulls.
369 German.
Length, feet (metres): 163.4 (49.8), Poland. (160.4
(48.9) German)
Beam, feet (metres): 28.5 (8.7).
Draught, feet (metres): 7.2 (2.2).
Speed, knots: 38 (Polish ships). 25, German.
Range, miles: 1,600 at 14 kts.

ARMAMENT

Missiles: SSM - Saab RBS 15 Mk 3 (2 twin)
launchers being fitted from 2000. SAM – SA-N-
5 Grail quad launcher. (Polish ships only – no
missiles in German hulls).
Guns: 1 – USSR 3 in 76 mm/66 AK 176. 1 - 30
mm/65 AK 630. (Polish ships only). 2 – 7.62
machine-guns, (German ships' only armament).

Decoys: Jastrzab 81 mm and 1 – 10-barrel
Jastrzab 122 mm chaff launchers. (Polish ships
only).

RADAR

Surface search –UR-27XA (Poland). Racal AC 2690
BT (Germany).
Navigation – SRN 443XTA, (Poland). Racal ARPA,
(Germany).
Fire control – Bass Tilt MR-123. (Polabd only).

KEY RECOGNITION FEATURES

- Continuous main deck lines from stem to
  stern.
- 1 USSR 3 in gun mounting ('A' position).
  (Polish ships only).
- Low bridge structure with prominent
  wings.
- Long central superstructure with, midships,
  large lattice mainmast atop.
- Tall square funnel just aft of midships,
  (German hulls).
- 30 mm/65 AK 630 gun mounting on
  afterdeck, (Polish ships only).
- German coast guard ships have blue hulls,
  yellow, orange and black diagonal stripes,
  and white and light blue upper works.
  "KUSTENWACHE" painted in white letters
  on hull.

Badr

HITTEEN

Country: SAUDI ARABIA
Country of origin: USA
Ship type: CORVETTES
Class: BADR (FSG)
Active: 4
Name (Pennant Number): BADR (612), AL
YARMOOK (614), HITTEEN (616), TABUK (618)

SPECIFICATION

Displacement, full load, tons: 1,038.
Length, feet (metres): 245 (74.7).
Beam, feet (metres): 31.5 (9.6).
Draught, feet (metres): 8.9 (2.7).
Speed, knots: 30.
Range, miles: 4,000 at 20 kts.

ARMAMENT

Missiles: SSM - McDonnell Douglas Harpoon (2
quad) launchers.
Guns: 1- FMC/OTO MELARA 3 in (76 mm)/62 Mk
75 Mod 0. 1 - GE/GD 20 mm 6-barrel Vulcan
Phalanx. 2 - Oerlikon 20 mm/80. 1 - 81 mm
mortar. 2 - 40 mm Mk 19 grenade launchers.
Torpedoes: 6 - 324 mm US Mk 32 (2 triple) tubes.
Honeywell Mk 46.
Decoys: 2 - Loral Hycor SRBOC 6-barrel Mk 36
fixed launchers.

RADAR

Air search - Lockheed SPS-40B.
Surface search - ISC Cardion SPS-55.
Fire control - Sperry Mk 92.
Sonars: Raytheon SQS-56 (DE 1164); hull-
mounted, active search/attack.

KEY RECOGNITION FEATURES

- Long forecastle with 3 in gun mounting
  midpoint between bows and bridge.
- Centrally sited superstructure with fat
  central lattice mainmast with SPS-40Bair
  search radar and tall pole mast above.
- Sperry Mk 92 fire control spherical radome
  atop bridge roof.
- Short, black-capped funnel at after end of
  superstructure.
- Torpedo tubes on maindeck level at after
  end of superstructure.
- Harpoon SSM angled launchers on long
  afterdeck.
- CIWS mounting right aft.

Göteborg

GÄLVE

Country: SWEDEN	
Country of origin: SWEDEN	
Ship type: CORVETTES	
Class: GÖTEBORG (FSG)	
Active: 4	

Name (Pennant Number): GÖTEBORG (K 21), GÄLVE (K 22), KALMAR (K 23), SUNDSVALL (K 24)

SPECIFICATION

Displacement, full load, tons: 399.
Length, feet (metres): 187 (57).
Beam, feet (metres): 26.2 (8).
Draught, feet (metres): 6.6 (2).
Speed, knots: 30.

ARMAMENT

Missiles: SSM - Saab RBS 15 (4 twin) launchers.
Guns: 1 - Bofors 57 mm/70 Mk 2. 1 Bofors 40 mm/70.
Torpedoes: 4 - 15.75 in (400 mm) tubes. Swedish Ordnance Type 43/45 or A244S.
A/S mortars: 4 - Saab Elma LLS-920 9-tubed launchers.
Depth charges: On mine rails.
Decoys: 4 - Philips Philax launchers. (A/S mortars adapted to fire IR/chaff decoys).

RADAR

Air/surface search - Ericsson Sea Giraffe 150HC.
Navigation - Terma PN 612.
Fire control – 2 Bofors Electronics 9GR 400.
Sonars: Thomson-Sintra TSM 2643 Salmon; VDS. Simrad SA 950; hull-mounted, active attack.

KEY RECOGNITION FEATURES

- Continuous maindeck lines from stem to stern.
- 57 mm/70 gun mounting ('A' position).
- Saab Elma A/S mortar launchers ('B' mounting position).
- Long central superstructure with, midships, large pyramid enclosed mainmast atop. Topmast modified in *Sundsvall* with IRST detector fitted aft of mast.
- Torpedo tubes on maindeck outboard of bridge.
- Saab RBS 15 SSM angled twin box launchers, two port, two starboard, on maindeck at after end of superstructure. Aft pair outboard of low enclosed mast with fire control radar atop.
- 40 mm/70 gun mounting on afterdeck. Turret in K 22 stealth adapted, producing angled, sloping profile.
- VDS towing equipment right aft.

MALMÖ

Country:	SWEDEN
Country of origin:	SWEDEN
Ship type:	CORVETTES
Class:	STOCKHOLM (FSG)
Active:	2

Name (Pennant Number): STOCKHOLM (K 11), MALMÖ (K 12)

SPECIFICATION

Displacement, full load, tons: 335.
Length, feet (metres): 164 (50).
Beam, feet (metres): 24.6 (7.5).
Draught, feet (metres): 6.9 (2.1).
Speed, knots: 32.

ARMAMENT

Missiles: SSM - Saab RBS 15 Mk II (4 twin) launchers.
Guns: 1 - Bofors 57 mm/70 Mk 2. 1 Bofors 40 mm/70.
Torpedoes: 2 - 21 in (533 mm) tubes. FFV Type 613. 4 - 15.75 in (400 mm) tubes. Swedish Ordnance Type 43 or Whitehead A 244S Mod 2.
A/S mortars: 4 - Saab Elma LLS-920 9-tubed launchers.
Depth charges: On mine rails.
Decoys: 2 - Philips Philax launchers.

RADAR

Air/surface search - Ericsson Sea Giraffe 50HC.
Navigation - Terma PN 612.
Fire control - Philips 9LV 200 Mk 3.
Sonars: Simrad SA 950; hull-mounted, active attack. Thomson-Sintra TSM 2642 Salmon; VDS.

KEY RECOGNITION FEATURES

- Long forecastle with Saab Elma LLS-920 A/S mortar launcher at forward end and 57mm/70 gun mounting midpoint between bows and bridge.
- Short, high, slab-sided central superstructure with lattice mainmast at after end.
- Fire control radar atop bridge.
- Distinctive RBS 15 SSM angled twin box launchers; two port, two starboard, on maindeck at after end of superstructure.
- Short, slim lattice aftermast isolated, aft of SSM launchers.
- 40 mm/70 gun mounting right aft, forward of VDS.

Note: Developed from 'Spica II' class.

Visby

VISBY (after launch)

Country: SWEDEN	
Country of origin: SWEDEN	
Ship type: CORVETTES	
Class: VISBY (FSG)	
Active: 1	
Building: 4	

Name (Pennant Number): VISBY (K 31), HELSINGBORG (K 32), HÄRNÖSAND (K 33), NYKÖPING (K 34), KARLSTAD (K 35).

SPECIFICATION

Displacement, full load, tons: 620.
Length, feet (metres): 236.2 (72).
Beam, feet (metres): 34.1 (10.4).
Draught, feet (metres): 8.2 (2.5).
Speed, knots: 35.

ARMAMENT

Missiles: SSM - 8 Saab RBS 15 Mk II (Batch 2).
Guns: 1 - Bofors 57 mm/70 SAK Mk. 3.
Torpedoes: 4 - 15.75 in (400 mm) fixed tubes. Swedish Ordnance Type 43/45.
A/S mortars: Saab Alecto 601 127mm launchers.
Decoys: Chaff launchers. (A/S mortars adapted to fire IR/chaff decoys).

RADAR

Air/surface search - Ericsson Sea Giraffe 3D.
Surface search – Celsiustech Pilot.
Fire control – CEROS 200 Mk 3.
Sonars: DC Hydra bow-mounted active, plus passive towed array and VDS.

AIR SUPPORT

Helicopters: 1 Agusta A109M (ASW) or UAV.

KEY RECOGNITION FEATURES

- Continuous maindeck lines from stem to stern with sharp bows.
- Angular 57 mm/70 gun mounting ('A' position).
- Short, central "swept back" slab-sided angled superstructure with high bridge amidships.
- Low pyramid enclosed mast atop bridge.
- Helicopter flight deck aft, occupying 40% of overall length.

Hua hin

HUA HIN (after launch)

Royal Thai Navy

Country: THAILAND
Country of origin: THAILAND
Ship type: CORVETTES
Class: HUA HIN (FS)
Active: 3
Name (Pennant Number): HUA HIN (541),
KLAENG (542), SI RACHA (543).

SPECIFICATION

Displacement, full load, tons: 645.
Length, feet (metres): 203.4 (62).
Beam, feet (metres): 29.2 (8.9).
Draught, feet (metres): 8.9 (2.7).
Speed, knots: 25.
Range, miles: 2,500 at 15 kts.

ARMAMENT

Guns: 1 - OTOBreda 76 mm/62 Compact. 1 -
    Bofors 40 mm/70. 2 - Oerlikon 20 mm GAM-
    BO1. 2 - 12.7 mm machine-guns.

RADAR

Surface search   Sperry Rascar.
Navigation – Sperry APAR.

KEY RECOGNITION FEATURES

- Continuous main deck lines from stem to
  stern with sharp bows.
- 76 mm/62 Compact gun mounting
  immediately forward of slope-sided bridge
  with all-round windows..
- Lattice mast after of bridge on
  superstructure with pole mast aft.
- Long central superstructure with, long
  angled funnel aft of midships.
- 40 mm/70 gun mounting on short
  quarterdeck.

Note: Derived from the 'Khamronsin' design.

Khamronsin

THAYANCHON

Country: THAILAND
Country of origin: UK
Ship type: CORVETTES
Class: KHAMRONSIN (FS)
Active: 3
Name (Pennant Number): KHAMRONSIN (531, ex-1), THAYANCHON (532, ex-2), LONGLOM (533, ex-3)

SPECIFICATION

Displacement, full load (tons): 630.
Length, feet (metres): 203.4 (62) oa.
Beam, feet (metres): 26.9 (8.2).
Draught, feet (metres): 8.2 (2.5).
Speed, knots: 25.
Range, miles: 2,500 at 15 kts.

ARMAMENT

Guns: 1 - OTO MELARA 76 mm/62 Mod 7. 2 - Breda 30 mm/70 (twin). 2 - 12.7 mm machine-guns.
Torpedoes: 6 - Plessey PMW 49A (2 triple) launchers. Marconi Stingray.

RADAR

Air/surface search - Plessey AWS 4.
Navigation – Racal Decca 1226.
Sonars: Atlas Elektronik DSQS-21C; hull-mounted, active search/attack.

KEY RECOGNITION FEATURES

- Short forecastle with 76 mm/62 gun mounting ('A' position).
- High freeboard, slab sided superstructure running from forecastle to afterdeck.
- Lattice mainmast amidships, atop central superstructure.
- Squat, black-capped funnel with sloping top aft of mainmast.
- 30 mm/70 gun mounting ('X' position).
- Break down from maindeck to short quarterdeck.

Note: Based on a Vosper Thornycroft *Province* class 56 m design, stretched by increasing the frame spacing along the whole length of the hull.
Note 2: Fourth of class, lightly armed with different superstructure, active with marine police.

Rattanakosin

RATTANAKOSIN

Country: THAILAND

Country of origin: USA

Ship type: CORVETTES

Class: RATTANAKOSIN (FSG)

Active: 2

Name (Pennant Number): RATTANAKOSIN (441, ex-1), SUKHOTHAI (442, ex-2)

SPECIFICATION

Displacement, full load, tons: 960.
Length, feet (metres): 252 (76.8).
Beam, feet (metres): 31.5 (9.6).
Draught, feet (metres): 8 (2.4).
Speed, knots: 26.
Range, miles: 3,000 at 16 kts.

ARMAMENT

Missiles: SSM - McDonnell Douglas Harpoon (2 quad) launchers. SAM - Selenia Elsag Albatros octuple launcher, Aspide.

Guns: 1 - OTO MELARA 3 in (76 mm)/62 Compact. 2 - Breda 40 mm/70 (twin). 2 Rheinmetall 20 mm.

Torpedoes: 6 - 324 mm US Mk 32 (2 triple) tubes. Marconi Stingray.

Decoys: CSEE Dagaie 6 or 10-tubed trainable launchers.

RADAR

Air/surface search - Signaal DA05.

Surface search - Signaal ZW06.

Navigation - Decca 1226.

Fire control - Signaal WM 25/41.

Sonars: Atlas Elektronik DSQS-21C; hull-mounted, active search/attack.

KEY RECOGNITION FEATURES

- High bow, short forecastle.
- 3 in gun mounting ('A' position).
- 40 mm/70 gun twin mounting ('B' position).
- Slab-sided high superstructure running from forecastle to afterdeck.
- Large, solid pyramid mainmast atop forward superstructure supporting spherical WM25/41 fire control radome.
- Low, tapered funnel well aft of midships with curved after profile and twin exhaust protruding from top.
- Short, enclosed aftermast, immediately aft of funnel, supporting DA05 air/surface search radar aerial.
- Harpoon SSM angled launchers atop after end of superstructure.
- Aspide SAM Albatros launcher right aft on quarterdeck.

PATROL
FORCES

OSA

Country: ALGERIA, AZERBAIJAN, BULGARIA, CROATIA, CUBA, EGYPT, ERITREA, FINLAND, INDIA, IRAQ, NORTH KOREA, LATVIA, LIBYA, POLAND, ROMANIA, SYRIA, VIETNAM, YEMEN, YUGOSLAVIA.

Country of origin: RUSSIA

Ship Type: PATROL FORCES

Class: OSA I (TYPE 205) (PUCK), OSA II (TYPE 205M) (PCFG)

Active: 9 Osa II, Algeria. 1 Osa II, Azerbaijan. 3 Osa II, 2 Osa I, Bulgaria. 1 Modified Osa I, Croatia (PCF/ML)*. 6 Osa II, Cuba. 4 Osa I, Egypt. 1 OSA Iraq. 3 Osa II Bulgaria. 1 Osa II, Eritrea. 4 Modified Osa II, Finland ('Tuima' class, MLI). 2 Osa II, India. 8 Osa I, North Korea. 2 Osa I, Latvia (PCF). 5 Osa II, Libya. 5 Osa I, Poland ('Puck' class). 3 Osa I, Romania. 8 Osa II, Syria. 8 Osa II, Vietnam. 2 Osa II, Yemen. 5 Osa I, Yugoslavia.*

* Captured from the Yugoslav Navy.

ALGERIA - Name (Pennant Number): 644-652.

AZERBAIJAN - Name (Pennant Number): None available.

BULGARIA - Name (Pennant Number): Osa I – BURYA (103), SMERCH (113). Osa II – TYPHOON (112), URAGON (102), SVETKAVITSA (111).

CROATIA - Name (Pennant Number): DUBROVNIK (ex-*Mitar Acev*) (OBM 41, ex-310).

CUBA - Name (Pennant Number): 261, 262, 267, 268, 271, 274.

EGYPT - Name (Pennant Number): 631, 633, 641, 643.

ERITREA - Name (Pennant Number): FMB 161.

FINLAND - Name (Pennant Number): TUIMA (11), TUISKU (12), TUULI (14), TYRSKY (15).

INDIA - Name (Pennant Number): CHAMAK (K 95), CHATAK (K 96).

IRAQ - Name (Pennant Number): HAZIRANI (R15)

NORTH KOREA - Name (Pennant Number): (Not available).

LATVIA - Name (Pennant Number): ZIBENS (ex-*Joseph Schares*) (P 01, ex-753), HEINDRICH DOR (ex-*Fritz Gast*) (P 02, ex-714).

LIBYA - Name (Pennant Number): AL ZUARA (513), AL RUHA (515), AL FIKAH (523), AL MATHUR (525), AL BITAR (531).

POLAND - Name (Pennant Number): PUCK (427), DARLOWO (430), SWINOUJSCIE (431), DZIWNÓW (432), WLADYSLAWOWO (433).

ROMANIA - Name (Pennant Number): VULTURUL (195), ERETELE (198), ALBATROSUL (199).

SYRIA - Name (Pennant Number): 33-40.

VIETNAM - Name (Pennant Number): HQ 354, +7.

KEY RECOGNITION FEATURES:

- 30 mm/65 gun mounting ('A' position).
- Low profile rounded superstructure running from the forecastle almost to the stern.
- Pole mainmast just forward of midships with surface search radar aerial atop.
- Prominent raised pedestal aft supporting fire control radar aerial.
- 4 large distinctive Styx SSM launchers, two outboard of mainmast (1 port one starboard) and 2 outboard of fire control director (aft), (1 port, 1 starboard). Launchers tilted up at forward end and lying forward and aft. (Not Azerbaijan, Croatian, Cuban, Finnish and Latvian units.)
- 30 mm/65 mounting right aft.

Note: Similar 'Huangfen' class also operated by China (30), Bangladesh ('Durdharsha' class) (5), North Korea (4), Pakistan (3) and Yemen, (3).

Note 2: Croatian unit converted to a minelayer in 1995. Finnish boats had similar conversion, 1993-96. Distinctive low ribbed superstructure extended aft in Crotian, Finnish and Latvian units.

Note 3: 'Matka' class hydrofoil PHGs, with similar hulls to 'Osa' operated by Russia, (3) Georgia (1) and Ukraine, (2, as 'Vekhr' class).

Note 4: Cuban units have had missiles disembarked for use in shore batteries. One was sunk as a tourist attraction in 1998.

Note 5: Some Libyan hulls painted with camouflage stripes in 1991 and some painted blue in 1993.

Note 6: Pennant numbers carried on sideboards on the bridge in Polish units.

Note 7: Romanian 'Naluca' class (12) based on 'Osa' class with torpedo tubes in lieu of SSMs.

DUBROVNIK (CROATIA) Modified OSA I without Styx Missile

YEMEN - Name (Pennant Number): 122, 124.
YUGOSLAVIA - Name (Pennant Number):
STEVAN FILIPOVIĆ STEVA (304), ZIKICA
JOVANOVIĆ ŠPANAC (305), NIKOLA MARTINOVIĆ
(306), ZOSIP MAŽAR SOSA (307), KRALO ROJC
(308).

SPECIFICATION

Displacement full load, tons: 210 (Osa I), 245
(Osa II).
Length, feet (metres): 126.6 (38.6).
Beam, feet (metres): 24.9 (7.6).
Draught, feet (metres): 8.8 (2.7).
Speed, knots: 35 (Osa I), 37 (Osa II).
Range, miles: 400 at 34 kts (Osa I), 500 at 35 kts
(Osa II).

ARMAMENT

Missiles: SSM - 4 SS-N-2A/B Styx (Osa I), 4 SS-N-
2B/C Styx (Osa II). (Not Croatian, Cuban, Finnish
or Latvian units). SAM - SA-N-5 Grail (Egyptian
Osa I). SA-N-5 Grail quad launcher, (Poland).
Guns: 4 - 30 mm/65 (2 twin). (Additional 2 - 12.7
mm machine-guns, Egypt.) 2 - Wrobel 23 mm
Zu-23-2M (twin); 2 - 30 mm/65 AK 230, (twin),
(Latvia).
Mines: 14-30, (Croatia). 30 (Finland).

RADARS

Air/surface search – Kelvin Hughes, (Egypt only).
Surface search – Raytheon ARPA, (Finnish units).
Surface search/fire control - Square Tie.
Navigation – Racal Decca 916 (Egypt). SRN 207M,
(Poland).
Fire control - Drum Tilt.

TRIDENT

Country: ALGERIA, BARBADOS

Country of origin: UNITED KINGDOM

Ship type: PATROL FORCES

Class: KEBIR (PC)

Active: 11 Algeria, 1 Barbados

ALGERIA - Name (Pennant Number): EL YADEKH (341), EL MOURAKEB (342), EL KECHEF (343), EL MOUTARID (344), EL RASSED (345), EL DJARI (346), EL SAHER (347), EL MOUKADEM (348), —— - (349), ——- (350), EL MAYHER (354).

BARBADOS - Name (Pennant Number): TRIDENT (PO 1).

SPECIFICATION

Displacement, full load, tons: 200, Algeria, 190, Barbados.

Length, feet (metres): 123 (37.5).

Beam, feet (metres): 22.6 (6.9).

Draught, feet (metres): 5.6 (1.7).

Speed, knots: 27.

Range, miles: 3 300 at 15 kts.

ARMAMENT

Guns: 1 – OTO MELARA 76 mm/62 Compact (in some Algerian units.) 4 – USSR 25 mm/60; (2 twin) (remainder, Algerian hulls). 2 – USSR 14.5 (twin) in first five Algerian units. 4 - 12.7 mm machine-guns in Barbados hull.

RADARS

Surface search – Racal Decca 1226. (Algeria). Racal Decca Bridgemaster (Barbados).

KEY RECOGNITION FEATURES

- Continuous maindeck from stem to stern.
- 76mm/62 Compact gun mounting ('A' position) in some Algerian hulls. Others have 25mm gun. Machine-gun mounting in Barbados unit.
- Stepped, central superstructure.
- Open bridge atop enclosed bridge with all round windows.
- Large whip aerial either side of forward end of superstructure.
- Lattice mainmast amidships with small pole structure.
- Small ship's boat stowed at after end of superstructure with small crane.

TNC 45

AL TAWEELAH

Country: ARGENTINA, BAHRAIN, ECUADOR, GHANA, KUWAIT, MALAYSIA, SINGAPORE, THAILAND, UNITED ARAB EMIRATES (UAE).

Country of origin: GERMANY

Ship type: PATROL FORCES

Class: INTREPIDA, AHMAD EL FATEH, QUITO, JERONG, SEA WOLF, PRABPARAPAK, BAN YAS (TNC 45) (PCF/PCFG),

Active: 2 Argentina ('Intrepida' class). 4 Bahrain ('Ahmad el Fateh' class). 3 Ecuador ('Quito' class). 2 Ghana. 1 Kuwait. 6 Malaysia ('Jerong' class). 6 Singapore ('Sea Wolf' class). 3 Thailand ('Prabparapak' class). 6 UAE ('Ban Yas' class)

ARGENTINA - Name (Pennant Number): INTREPIDA (P 85), INDOMITA (P 86)

BAHRAIN - Name (Pennant Number): AHMAD EL FATEH (20), AL JABIRI (21), ABDUL RAHMAN AL FADEL (22), AL TAWEELAH (23)

ECUADOR - Name (Pennant Number): QUITO (LM 21), GUAYAQUIL (LM 23), CUENCA (LM 24).

GHANA - Name (Pennant Number): DZATA (P 26), SEBO (P 27).

KUWAIT - Name (Pennant Number): AL SANBOUK (P 4505)*

*Survivor of a class of 6. Rest casualties in 1991 Gulf War.

MALAYSIA - Name (Pennant Number): JERONG (3505), TODAK (3506), PAUS (3507), YU (3508), BAUNG (3509), PARI (3510).

SINGAPORE - Name (Pennant Number): SEA WOLF (P 76), SEA LION (P 77), SEA DRAGON (P 78), SEA TIGER (P 79), SEA HAWK (P 80), SEA SCORPION (P 81).

THAILAND - Name (Pennant Number): PRABPARAPAK (311, ex-1), HANHAK SATTRU (312, ex-2), SUPHAIRIN (313, ex-3).

UAE - Name (Pennant Number): BAN YAS (P 4501), MARBAN (P 4502), RODQM (P 4503), SHAHEEN (P 4504), SAGAR (P 4505), TARIF (P 4506).

SPECIFICATION

Displacement, full load, tons: 259, (Bahrain). 268, (Argentina, Thailand). 269, (Ghana). 255, (Ecuador, Kuwait). 244, (Malaysia). 254, (Singapore). 260, (UAE).

Length, feet (metres): 147.3 (44.9). 147.6 (45), (Ecuador). (149 (45.4), Thailand).

Beam, feet (metres): 22.9 (7). 24.3 (7.4), (Argentina, Thailand). 23 (7), (Ecuador, Ghana, Kuwait, Malaysia, Singapore, UAE).

Draught, feet (metres): 8.2 (2.5). (7.5 (2.3), Kuwait, Thailand). (8.9 (2.7), Ghana).

Speed, knots: 38. (32, Malaysia, 35 Singapore, 27 Ghana).

Range, miles: 1 800 at 16 kts.

ARMAMENT

Missiles: SSM - 4 Aerospatiale MM 40 Exocet (2 twin) launchers. (MM 38 in Argentine *Intrepida*

231

only and Ecuador ships) (No missiles in Ghana, Malaysia ships). McDonnell Douglas Harpoon (2 twin) (Singapore). IAI Gabriel (1 triple, 2 single), (Thailand). SAM – Matra Simbad twin launcher, Mistral, (Singapore only).

Guns: 1 - OTO MELARA 3 in (76 mm)/62 Compact, (all, except Ghana, Malaysia, Singapore and Thailand.); 2 - Bofors 40 mm/70, (Ghana); 1 - Bofors 57 mm/70, (Malaysia, Singapore, Thailand). 1- Bofors 40 mm/70, (Malaysia, Thailand); 1 or 2- Bofors 40 mm/70 in (Argentina); 2 -Oerlikon 35 mm/90 (twin), (Ecuador); 2 - Breda 40 mm /70, (Bahrain, Kuwait, UAE). 3 - 7.62 mm machine-guns, (Bahrain); 2 - 7.62 mm machine-guns, (UAE).

Decoys: CSEE Dagaie launcher. (Bahrain, Kuwait, UAE). 2 - Hycor Mk 137 sextuple RBOC chaff launchers; 4 - Rafael (2 twin) long-range chaff launchers, (Singapore).

Torpedoes: 2 - 21 in (533 mm) tubes. AEG SST-4. (Argentine ships only).

RADARS

Air/surface search – Ericsson Sea Giraffe 150 HC (Bahrain, Kuwait, UAE). Decca 626 (Argentina) Thomson-CSF Triton (Ecuador). Racal Decca 1226 (Malaysia, Singapore).

Surface search – Kelvin Hughes Type 17. (Thailand). Decca TM 1226C, (Ghana, Kuwait).

Navigation - Racal Decca 1226, (Bahrain, Ecuador,Malaysia). Signaal Scout, (UAE).

Fire control - CelsiusTech 9LV 226/231 (Bahrain). CelsiusTech 9LV 200 MK 2/3, (Kuwait, UAE). Signaal WM22 (guns/missiles); Signaal Mk 11 (torpedo guidance), (Argentina). Thomson-CSF Pollux, (Ecuador). Signaal WM28/5, (Singapore, Thailand).

Dabur

BARADERO

Country: ARGENTINA, CHILE, FIJI, ISRAEL, NICARAGUA

Country of origin: ISRAEL

Ship type: PATROL FORCES

Class: DABUR (BARADERO), (GRUMETE DIAZ), (VAI), (PC)

Active: 4 Argentina ('Baradero' class), 10 Chile ('Grumete Diaz' class), 4 Fiji ('Vai' class), 15 Israel, 3 Nicaragua

ARGENTINA - Name (Pennant Number): BARADERO (P 61), BARRANQUERAS (P 62), CLORINDA (P 63), CONCEPCIÓN DEL URUGUAY (P 64).

CHILE - Name (Pennant Number): DIAZ (1814), BOLADOS (1815), SALINAS (1816), TELLEZ (1817), BRAVO (1818), CAMPOS (1819), MACHADO (1820), JOHNSON (1821), TRONCOSO (1822), HUDSON (1823).

FIJI - Name (Pennant Number): VAI (301), OGO (302), SAKU (303), SAQA (304).

ISRAEL - Name (Pennant Number): 860-920 series.

NICARAGUA - Name (Pennant Number): G.C. (201), G.C. (203), G.C. (205).

SPECIFICATION

Displacement, full load, tons: 39.
Length, feet (metres): 64.9 (19.8).
Beam, feet (metres): 18 (5.5).
Draught, feet (metres): 5.8 (1.8).
Speed, knots: 19.
Range, miles: 450 at 13 kts.

ARMAMENT

Guns: 2 - Oerlikon 20 mm; 2 - 12.7 mm machine-guns; Carl Gustav 84 mm portable rocket launchers, (Israel). 2 - Oerlikon 20 mm, (Chile). 2 - Oerlikon 20 mm; 2 - 12.7 mm machine-guns, (Argentina). 2 -Oerlikon 20 mm; 2 - 7.62 mm machine-guns, (Fiji). 2 - Oerlikon 25 mm (twin), 2 - 12.7 mm machine-guns, (Nicaragua).

Torpedoes: 2 - 324 mm tubes, Honeywell Mk 46, (Israel only).

RADARS

Surface search – Decca 101, (Argentina, Nicaragua). Racal Decca Super 101 Mk 3, (Chile, Fiji, Israel).

Sonars: Active search/attack, (Israel only).

KEY RECOGNITION FEATURES

- Low sleek hull
- Low compact superstructure with open bridge and slim enclosed mast aft of bridge.
- Guns forward and aft of superstructure

Note: Similar in profile to 'Dvora/Super Dvora' classes, which are derived from 'Dabur' class. 'Dabur' class has shorter deck aft of superstructure.

GAWLER

Country: AUSTRALIA
Country of origin: UK
Ship type: PATROL FORCES
Class: FREMANTLE (PC)
Active: 15
Name (Pennant Number): FREMANTLE (203), WARRNAMBOOL (204), TOWNSVILLE (205), WOLLONGONG (206), LAUNCESTON (207), WHYALLA (208), IPSWICH (209), CESSNOCK (210), BENDIGO (211), GAWLER (212), GERALDTON (213), DUBBO (214), GEELONG (215), GLADSTONE (216), BUNBURY (217)

SPECIFICATION

Displacement, full load, tons: 245.
Length, feet (metres): 137.1 (41.8).
Beam, feet (metres): 23.3 (7.1).
Draught, feet (metres): 5.9 (1.8).
Speed, knots: 30.
Range, miles: 1 450 at 30 kts.

ARMAMENT

Guns: 1 - Bofors AN 4-40 mm/60; 1 - 81 mm
mortar; 3 - 12.7 mm machine-guns.

RADARS

Navigation - Kelvin Hughes Type 1006.

KEY RECOGNITION FEATURES

- Continuous maindeck from stem to stern.
- 40 mm/60 open gun mounting ('A' position).
- Stepped, central superstructure.
- Sloping top to forward end of superstructure with bridge set back.
- Open bridge atop after end of enclosed bridge.
- Large whip aerial either side of forward end of superstructure.
- Pole mainmast amidships with small lattice structure supporting navigation radar just forward.
- Small ship's boat stowed at after end of superstructure.

Stenka

STENKA

Country: AZERBAIJAN, CUBA, GEORGIA, RUSSIA, UKRAINE

Country of origin: RUSSIA

Ship type: PATROL FORCES

Class: STENKA (TYPE 205P) (PCF)

Active: 2 Azerbaijan, 3 Cuba (Border Guard), Georgia 14 Russia, 10 Ukraine (Border Guard)

AZERBAIJAN - Name (Pennant Number): (None available).

CUBA - Name (Pennant Number): (None available).

GEORGIA - Name (Pennant Number): BATUMI (ex-PSKR638) (301, ex-648)

RUSSIA - Name (Pennant Number): (None available).

UKRAINE - Name (Pennant Number): Border Guard – KRIM (BG 01),* VOLIN (ex-020), MIKOLAIV (BG 57,ex-028), ZAKARPATTIYA (ex-031), PAVEL DERZHAVIN (ex-037), ZHANOROZHSKAYA SEC (ex-032), ODESSA (ex-033), BUKOVINA (ex-034), DONBASS (BG 32, ex-035), PODILLIYA (ex-036).
* Used as presidential yacht, based at Yalta.

SPECIFICATION

Displacement, full load, tons: 253.
Length, feet (metres): 129.3 (39.4).
Beam, feet (metres): 25.9 (7.9).
Draught, feet (metres): 8.2 (2.5).
Speed, knots: 37. (34, Cuban ships).
Range, miles: 800 at 24 kts.

ARMAMENT

Guns: 2 - 30 mm/65 AK 230 (2 twin).

Torpedoes: 4 - 16 in (406 mm) tubes.
(Not Cuban ships)
Depth charges: 2 racks. (12). (Not Cuban ships).

RADARS

Surface search - Pot Drum or Peel Cone.
Navigation – Palm Frond.
Fire control - Drum Tilt. (Muff Cobb, Cuba).
Sonars: Stag Ear or Foal Tail VDS. (Not Cuba).

KEY RECOGNITION FEATURES

- Short high freeboard forecastle with 30 mm/65 or 23 mm/87 gun mounting ('A' position).
- Large superstructure, higher at forward end, extending to quarterdeck. Superstructure has vertical ribbed appearance.
- Complex tripod mainmast atop after end of bridge supporting surface search radar aerial.
- Distinctive Drum Tilt fire control radar aerial on pedestal at after end of superstructure.
- 30 mm/65 gun mounting on quarterdeck ('X' position).

Note: 'Turya' class has similar 'ribbed' sides to superstructure.

Note 2: Ukraine Border Guard vessels are dark grey with a thick yellow/thin blue diagonal line painted on the hull. Upperworks are white.

Al Riffa

AL RIFFA

Country: BAHRAIN
Country of origin: GERMANY
Ship type: PATROL FORCES
Class: AL RIFFA (FPB 38) (PCF)
Active: 2
Name (Pennant Number): Al RIFFA (10), HAWAR (11).

SPECIFICATION

Displacement, full load, tons: 205.
Length, feet (metres): 126.3 (38.5).
Beam, feet (metres): 22.9 (7).
Draught, feet (metres): 7.2 (2.2).
Speed, knots: 32.
Range, miles: 1 100 at 16 kts.

ARMAMENT

Guns: 2 - Breda 40 mm/70. 1 – 57 mm Starshell rocket launcher.
Decoys: 1 – Wallop Barricade chaff launcher.

RADARS

Surface search – Philips 9GR 600
Navigation – Racal Decca 1226.

KEY RECOGNITION FEATURES

- Smooth, uncluttered lines from bow to stern.
- Small, central superstructure with sloping face to enclosed bridge, topped by open bridge with prominent wings.
- 40 mm/70 gun twin mounting at 'A' position.
- Low, lattice mainmast aft of open bridge.

Madhumati / Sea Dragon

MADHUMATI

Country: BANGLADESH, KOREA, SOUTH
Country of origin: SOUTH KOREA
Ship type: PATROL FORCES
Class: MADHUMATI/SEA DRAGON (PC/OPV)
Active: 1 Bangladesh ('Madhumati' class), 6 South
Korea (operated by Maritime Police)
BANGLADESH - Name (Pennant Number):
MADHUMATI (P 911).
SOUTH KOREA - Name (Pennant Number): PC
501, 502, 503, 505, 506, 507.

SPECIFICATION

Displacement, full load, tons: 640, South Korea,
635, Bangladesh.
Length, feet (metres): 199.5 (60.8).
Beam, feet (metres): 26.2 (8).
Draught, feet (metres): 8.9 (2.7).
Speed, knots: 24.
Range, miles: 6 000 at 15 kts.

ARMAMENT

Guns: 1 - Bofors 57 mm/70 Mk 1. 1 – Bofors 40
mm/70; 2 - Oerlikon 20 mm, Bangladesh. 1 –
Bofors 40 mm/60; 2 - Oerlikon 20 mm; 2 –
Browning 12.7 mm machine guns, South Korea.

RADARS

Surface search – Kelvin Hughes KH 1007.
(Bangladesh).
Navigation – GEM Electronics SPN-753B.
(Bangladesh).

KEY RECOGNITION FEATURES

- Sweeping main deck from high sharp bow,
  with low break just forward of bridge, then
  smooth, uncluttered lines to low stern.
- Tall I, flat fronted, central superstructure
  with prominent bridge wings.
- 57 mm/70 gun mounting at 'A' position,
  Bangladesh unit.
- 47mm/70 gun open mounting at 'A'
  position, South Korean hulls.
- Tall, lattice mainmast aft end of central
  superstructure, South Korean hulls. Thin
  enclosed mast in Bangladesh ship.
- Distinctive black-topped rounded funnel
  aft of superstructure
- Ship's boat outboard of funnel on davits.
- 40 mm/70 open mounting on quarterdeck,
  Bangladesh unit.

GURUPÁ

Country: BANGLADESH, BRAZIL
Country of origin: UK
Ship type: PATROL FORCES
Class: MEGNA/GRAJAÚ (PG)
Active: 2 Bangladesh ('Meghna' class), 12 Brazil ('Grajau' class)
BANGLADESH - Name (Pennant Number): MEGHNA (P 211), JAMUNA (P 212).
BRAZIL - Name (Pennant Number): GRAJAÚ (P 40), GUAIBA (P 41), GRAÚNA (P 42), GOIANA (P 43), GUAJARÁ (P 44), GUAPORÉ (P 45), GURUPÁ (P 46), GURUPI (P 47), GUANABARA (P48), GUARUJA (P 49), GUARATUBA (P 50), GRAVATAÍ (P 51).

SPECIFICATION

Displacement, full load, tons: 263, (Brazil), 410, Bangladesh.
Length, feet (metres): 152.6 (46.5).
Beam, feet (metres): 24.6 (7.5).
Draught, feet (metres): 7.5 (2.3).
Speed, knots: 22.
Range, miles: 2 000 at 12 kts.

ARMAMENT

Guns: 1- Bofors 40 mm/70. 2 - Oerlikon 20 mm, (P 40-43, Brazil). 2 - Oerlikon/BMARC 20 mm GAM-B01 (P 44-51, Brazil). Bangladesh: 1 - Bofors 57 mm/70 Mk 1; 1 - Bofors 40 mm/70; 2- 7.62 mm machine-guns.

RADARS

Surface search - Racal Decca 1290A. (Brazil). Decca 1229, Bangladesh.

KEY RECOGNITION FEATURES

- Smooth, uncluttered lines from bow to stern.
- Small, flat fronted, central superstructure stepped down at after end.
- 40 mm/70 gun mounting at 'A' position, P 40-43, Brazilian units.
- 57mm/70 gun mounting at 'A' position, Bangladesh hulls.
- Tall, lattice mainmast atop central superstructure.
- "Step down" at aft end of superstructure.
- 20 mm gun mounting on afterdeck (Brazil) or 40mm/70 open mounting, Bangladesh.

Hainan

HAINAN 643 - CHINA

Country: BANGLADESH, BURMA, CHINA, EGYPT, NORTH KOREA

Country of origin: CHINA

Ship type: PATROL FORCES

Class: HAINAN (DURJOY) (TYPE 037) (PC)

Active: 1 Bangladesh ('Durjoy' class), 10 Burma, 95 China, 8 Egypt, 6 North Korea

BANGLADESH - Name (Pennant Number): NIRBHOY (P 812).

BURMA - Name (Pennant Number): YAN SIT AUNG (441), YAN MYAT AUNG (442), YAN NYEIN AUNG (443), YAN KHWIN AUNG (444), YAN MIN AUNG (445), YAN YF AIING (446), YAN PAING AUNG (447), YAN WIN AUNG (448), YAN AYE AUNG (449), YAN ZWE AUNG (450).

CHINA - Name (Pennant Number): (275-285), (290), (302), (305), (609), (610), (618-622), (626-629), (636-643), (646-681), (683-687), (689-692) (695-699) (701), (707), (723-733), (740-742).

EGYPT - Name (Pennant Number): AL NOUR (430), AL HADY (433), AL HAKIM (436), AL WAKIL (439), AL QATAR (442), AL SADDAM (445), AL SALAM (448), AL RAFIA (451).

NORTH KOREA - Name (Pennant Number): (201-204), (292-293).

SPECIFICATION

Displacement, full load, tons: 392.

Length, feet (metres): 192.8 (58.8).

Beam, feet (metres): 23.6 (7.2).

Draught, feet (metres): 7.2 (2.2).

Speed, knots: 30.5.

Range, miles: 1 300 at 15 kts.

ARMAMENT

Missiles: Chinese units can be fitted with 4 YJ-1 (C-801) SSM launchers in lieu of after 57 mm gun.

Guns: 4 - China 57 mm/70 (2 twin). 4 - USSR 25 mm /60 (2 twin). (23 mm (2 twin) in Egyptian ships).

Torpedoes: 6 - (322 mm) (2 triple) tubes in 2 of

Egyptian class. Mk 44 or Marconi Stingray.

A/S mortars: 4 - RBU 1200.

Depth charges: 2 - BMB-2 projectors; 2 racks.

Mines: Rails fitted for 12.

Decoys: 2 - PK 16 chaff launchers, (North Korea).

RADARS

Surface search - Pot Head or Skin Head.

Navigation – Raytheon Pathfinder (Burma). Decca, (Egypt).

Sonars: Stag Ear; hull-mounted. (Thomson-Sintra SS 12 VDS on at least two of Chinese units). Tamir II, hull-mounted, (Bangladesh ships).

KEY RECOGNITION FEATURES

- High bow, long sloping forecastle, low freeboard.
- RBU 1200 A/S mortars towards forward end of forecastle.
- 57 mm/70 gun twin mounting ('A' position).
- 25 mm/60 gun twin mounting ('B' position).
- Tall, angular midships superstructure.
- Small lattice mainmast atop after end of bridge.
- 57 mm/70 gun twin mounting ('Y' position).
- 25 mm/60 gun twin mounting ('X' position on raised platform).

Note: A larger Chinese-built version of Soviet SO 1. North Korea also operates 19 of this class.

Note 2: Missile launchers can be fitted in lieu of the after 57 mm mounting. Later Chinese ships have a tripod foremast and a short stub mainmast. First six Burmese hulls are of this type.

Note 3: 'Houxin' (Type 037/1G) class is a missile-armed version of the 'Hainan' class. See separate entry.

615 (EGYPT)

A. Sheldon Duplaix

Country: BANGLADESH, CHINA, EGYPT, PAKISTAN

Country of origin: CHINA

Ship type: PATROL FORCES

Class: HEGU/HOUKU (TYPE 024) (DURBAR) (PCFG)

Active: 5 Bangladesh ('Durbar' class), 25 China, 4 Egypt, 4 Pakistan

BANGLADESH - Name (Pennant Number): DURBAR (P 8111), DURANTA (P 8112), DURVEDYA (P 8113), DURDAM (P 8114), UTTAL (P 8141).

CHINA - Name (Pennant Number): (1100) and (3100) series

EGYPT - Name (Pennant Number): (609), (611), (613), (615).

PAKISTAN - Name (Pennant Number): HAIBUT (P1021), JALALAT (P1022), JURAT (P1023), SHUJAAT (P1024).

SPECIFICATION

Displacement, full load, tons: 79.2.

Length, feet (metres): 88.6 (27).

Beam, feet (metres): 20.7 (6.3).

Draught, feet (metres): 4.3 (1.3).

Speed, knots: 37.5.

Range, miles: 400 at 30 kts.

ARMAMENT

Missiles: SSM - 2 - SY-1, (CSS-N-1 Scrubbrush).

Guns: 2 - USSR 25 mm/60 (twin).

(2 - 23mm (twin), Egyptian units).

(2 - Norinco 25mm/80 (twin) Pakistan units).

RADARS

Air/surface search - Square Tie.

KEY RECOGNITION FEATURES

- Low freeboard.
- 23 mm/60 or 25 mm/60 gun twin mounting ('A' position).
- Very small and low central superstructure.
- Stout, pole mainmast atop central superstructure.
- Square Tie air/surface search radar aerial atop mainmast.
- Two large, distinctive SSM launchers on quarterdeck, both raised at forward end and angled slightly outboard.

Note: Chinese variant of the Russian 'Komar' class.

Note 2: Chinese hydrofoil variant, 'Hema' class, has a semi-submerged foil forward and extra 6 feet in length, allowing the mounting of a second twin 25 mm gun abaft the missile launchers.

Bizerte

BIZERTE

A Companera i Rovira

Country: CAMEROON, SENEGAL, TUNISIA

Country of origin: FRANCE

Ship type: PATROL FORCES

Class: BIZERTE (TYPE PR 48) (PC)

Active: 1 Cameroon, 3 Senegal, 3 Tunisia

CAMEROON - Name (Pennant Number): L'AUDACIEUX (P 103).

SENEGAL - Name (Pennant Number): SAINT LOUIS, POPENGUINE, PODOR.

TUNISIA - Name (Pennant Number): BIZERTE (P 301), HORRIA (ex-*Liberté*) (P 302), MONASTIR (P 304).

SPECIFICATION

Displacement, full load, tons: 250.

Length, feet (metres): 157.5 (48), Tunisia, Cameroon. 156 (47.5), Senegal.

Beam, feet (metres): 23.3 (7.1).

Draught, feet (metres): 7.5 (2.3), Tunisia and Cameroon. 8.1 (2.5), Senegal.

Speed, knots: 20.

Range, miles: 2 000 at 16 kts.

ARMAMENT

Missiles: SSM – 8 Aerospatiale SS 12M, (Tunisia only). (Cameroon fitted for these missiles, but not carried).

Guns: 4 – 37mm/63 (2 twin), Tunisia. 2 – Bofors 40 mm/70; 2 – 7.62 mm machine-guns, Senegal. 2 – Bofors 40 mm/70, Cameroon.

RADARS

Surface search – Thomson-CSF DRBN 31, Tunisia. Racal Decca 1226, Senegal.

KEY RECOGNITION FEATURES

- Continuous deck sweeping down from high bow..
- 37 mm/63 gun twin open mounting ('A' position), Tunisia; vice, 40 mm/70, Senegal and Cameroon.
- Very small and low central superstructure with wide step up to bridge windows, with open bridge atop.
- Lattice mainmast atop central superstructure.
- Rounded aft edge of superstructure, outboard of funnel.
- 37 mm/63 gun twin open mounting on quarterdeck. Tunisia; vice 40 mm/70, Senegal, Cameroon.

La Combattante II/IIA

Country: CHILE, GERMANY, GREECE, IRAN, LIBYA, MALAYSIA

Country of origin: FRANCE

Ship type: PATROL FORCES

Class: LA COMBATTANTE II/IIA (RIQUELME, TIGER, ANNINOS, VOTSIS, KAMAN, PERDANA) (PGF/PCFG)

Active: 4 Chile ('Riquelme' class Type 148), 3 Germany ('Tiger' class, Type 148), 4 Combattante II, ('Anninos') 6 Combattante IIA ('Votsis' class), Greece. 10 Iran ('Kaman' class), 7 + 2 reserve Libya, 4 Malaysia ('Perdana' class)

CHILE - Name (Pennant Number): RIQUELME (ex-*Wolf*) (LM 36, ex-P 6149), ORELLA (ex-*Elster*) (LM 37, ex-P 6154), SERRANO (ex-*Tiger*) (LM 38, ex-P 6141), URIBE (ex-*Luchs*) (LM 39, ex-P 6143).

GERMANY - Name (Pennant Number): FUCHS (P 6146), LÖWE (P 6148).

GREECE - Name (Pennant Number):
'Anninos' class - ANTHIPOPLOIARCHOS ANNINOS (ex-*Navsithoi*) (P 14), IPOPLOIARCHOS ARLIOTIS (ex-*Evniki*) (P 15), IPOPLOIARCHOS KONIDIS (ex-*Kymothoi*) (P 16), IPOPLOIARCHOS BATSIS (ex-*Calypso*) (P 17)

'Votsis' class – IPOPLIARCHOS VOTSIS (ex-*Iltis*) (P 72, ex-P 51), ANTIPLIARCHOS PEZOPOULOS (ex-*Storch*) (P 73, ex-P 30), PLOTARCHIS VLAHAVAS (ex-*Marder*) (P 74), PLOTARCHIS MARIDAKIS (ex-*Häher*) (P 75), IPOPLOIARCHOS TOURNAS (ex-*Leopard*) (P 76), PLOTARCHIS SAKIPIS (ex-*Jaguar*) (P 77).

IRAN - Name (Pennant Number): KAMAN (P 221), ZOUBIN (P 222), KHADANG (P 223), FALAKHON (P 226), SHAMSHIR (P 227), GORZ (P 228), GARDOUNEH (P 229), KHANJAR (P 230), NEYZEH (P 231), TARBARZIN (P 232).

LIBYA - Name (Pennant Number): SHARABA (ex-*Beir Grassa*) (518), WAHAG (ex-*Beir Gzir*) (522), SHEHAB (ex-*Beir Gtifa*) (524) SHOUAIA (ex-*Beir Algandula*) (528), SHOULA (ex-*Beir Ktitat*) (532), SHAFAK (ex-*Beir Alkrarim*) (534), LAHEEB (ex-*Beir Alkuefat*) (542).

MALAYSIA - Name (Pennant Number): PERDANA (3501), SERANG (3502), GANAS (3503), GANYANG (3504).

SPECIFICATION

Displacement, full load, tons: 255, (Greek 'Anninos' class); 311 (Libya), 265 (Chile, Germany, Greek 'Votsis' class and Malaysia), 275, (Iran).

Length, feet (metres): 154.2 (47). (160.7 (49), Libya).

IPOPLOIARCHOS KONIDIS

Beam, feet (metres): 23.3 (7.1). (23.1 (7), Chile, Germany, Greek 'Votsis' class and Malaysia).

Draught, feet (metres): 8.2 (2.5), Greek 'Anninos' class. (6.2, (1.9), Iran). (6.6 (2), Libya). (12.8 (3.9), Malaysia). (8.9 (2.7), Chile, Germany, Greek 'Votsis' class).

Speed, knots: 36.5. (31, Chile).

Range, miles: 850 at 25 kts.

ARMAMENT

Missiles: SSM - 4 Aerospatiale MM 38 Exocet, (Chile, Germany, Greece, 2 only in Malaysian ships). OTO MELARA/Matra Otomat Mk 2 (TG 1), (Libya). 2 or 4 Chinese C-802 (1 or 2 twin) or Harpoon (2 twin), (Iranian ships).

Guns: 4 - Oerlikon 35 mm/90 (2 twin), (Greek 'Anninos'). 1 - OTO MELARA 3 in (76mm)/62 Compact, 1 – Breda/Bofors 40 mm/70 (some have 20 mm or 23 mm gun vice 40 mm) and 2 - 12.7 machine-guns (Iran). 1 - OTO MELARA 3 in (76mm)/62 Compact, 1 - Bofors 40 mm/70 (twin), (Chile, Germany, Greek 'Votsis' class, Libya). 1 - Bofors 57 mm/70; 1 - Bofors 40 mm/70, (Malaysia)

Torpedoes: 2 - 21 in (533 mm) tubes AEG SST-4, (Greek 'Anninos' only).

RADARS

Surface search - Thomson-CSF Triton, (Chile, German. Greek ships. Libyan and Malaysian ships).
Surface search/fire control – Signaal WM28 (Iran).
Navigation – Racal Decca 1226C, (Greek 'Anninos', Iran). Racal Decca 616 (Malaysia). SMA 3 RM 20, (Chile, Germany, Greek 'Votsis' class).
Fire control - Thomson-CSF Pollux, (Greek 'Anninos' and Malaysian ships). Thomson-CSF Castor IIB, (Chile, Germany, Greek 'Votsis' class and Libya).

KEY RECOGNITION FEATURES

- Small bridge superstructure forward of midships.
- 35 mm/90 gun mounting ('A' position), Greek 'Anninos' class. (57 mm/70 gun in Malaysian ships, OTO MELARA 3 in, Chilean, German, Greek 'Votsis' class, Libyan and Iranian ships).
- Tall lattice mainmast at after end of superstructure. (Fire control radome atop in Iranian ships).
- Fire control radar aerial atop bridge roof, (not Iranian ships).
- SSM launchers aft of superstructure. Forward two immediately aft of superstructure trained forward and to starboard, after two trained forward and to port. (2 Exocet launchers only in Malaysian ships. 2 twin Harpoon or 4 C-802 SSM in Iranian ships).
- 35 mm/90 gun mounting aft in 'Y' position, (Greek 'Anninos' class). 40 mm/70 in same position in Malaysian ships and in some Iranian units (some with 20 mm). (Chilean, German, Greek 'Votsis' class and Libyans with 40 mm/70 turret mounting).

Note: See 'Combattante III' entry, in service with Greece, Nigeria, Qatar and Tunisia.

Reshef / Saar 4

Country: CHILE, ISRAEL, SOUTH AFRICA, SRI LANKA
Country of origin: ISRAEL
Ship type: PATROL FORCES
Class: RESHEF (SAAR 4), (CASMA, WARRIOR (EX-MINISTER) (PCFG)
Active: 3 Chile 'Casma' class. 2 Israel 'Reshef' class. 5 South Africa 'Warrior', ex-'Minister' class. 2 Sri Lanka.
CHILE - Name (Pennant Number): CASMA (ex-*Romah*) (LM 30), CHIPANA (ex-*Keshet*) (LM 31), ANGAMOS (ex-*Reshef*) (LM 34).
ISRAEL - Name (Pennant Number): NITZHON, ATSMOUT.
SOUTH AFRICA - Name (Pennant Number): ADAM KOK (ex-*Frederic Creswell*), (P 1563), ISAAC DYOBHA (ex-*Frans Erasmus*) (P 1565), RENÉ SETHREN (ex-*Oswald Pirow*) (P 1566), GALESHEWE (ex-*Hendrik Mentz*) (P 1567), MAKHANDA (ex-*Magnus Malan*) (P 1569).
SRI LANKA - Name (Pennant Number): NANDIMITHRA (ex-*Moledt*) (P 701), SURANIMALA (ex-*Komemiut*) (P 702).

RENÉ SETHREN

SPECIFICATION

Displacement, full load, tons: 450, (Israeli, Sri Lankan and Chilean ships). 430 (South Africa).
Length, feet (metres): 190.6 (58). (204 (62.2), South Africa).
Beam, feet (metres): 25 (7.8).
Draught, feet (metres): 8 (2.4).
Speed, knots: 32.
Range, miles: 4 000 at 17.5 kts.

ARMAMENT

Missiles: SSM - McDonnell Douglas Harpoon (twin or quad) launchers; 4-6 IAI Gabriel II, (Israel). 4 Gabriel I or II, (Chile, Sri Lanka). 8 Skerpioen (licence-built Gabriel II), (South Africa).
Guns: 1 or 2 - OTO MELARA 3 in (76 mm)/62 Compact; 2 - Oerlikon 20 mm; 1 - GE/GD Vulcan Phalanx Mk 15; 2 - 12.7 mm machine-guns, (Israel). 2 - OTO MELARA 3 in(76 mm)/62 Compact, (Chile, South Africa, Sri Lanka). 2 - Oerlikon 20 mm, (Chile, Sri Lanka). 2 - LIW Vektor 35 mm (twin) may replace 1 - 76 mm gun in 1 South African hull for trials, plus 2 - LIW Mk 1 20 mm and 2 - 12.7 mm machine-guns, (South Africa).

Decoys: 1 - 45-tube, 4 or 6 - 24-tube, 4 single tube chaff launchers, (Israel). 4 - Rafael LRCR decoy launchers, (Chile). 4 - ACDS chaff launchers, (South Africa). Not fitted in Sri Lankan units.

RADARS

Air/surface search - Thomson-CSF TH-D 1040 Neptune, (Chile, Israel, Sri Lanka). Elta EL/M 2208, (South Africa).
Navigation – Raytheon 20X (Chile).
Fire control - Selenia Orion RTN 10X or Elta M-2221 in some Chilean ships.
Sonars: EDO 780; VDS; occasionally fitted in some of the Israeli ships.

KEY RECOGNITION FEATURES

- Long sleek hull, bhigh bows, low freeboard.
- CIWS mounting ('A' position) with distinctive domed top, (Israeli ships). 3 in gun mounting forward of bridge in Chilean and South African units.
- Short superstructure well forward of midships.
- Large complex lattice mainmast at after end of superstructure.
- Air/surface search radar aerial atop mainmast.
- Combination of Harpoon and Gabriel SSM launchers aft of superstructure and forward of after mounting, (Israeli ships). Gabriel/Skerpioen SSM launchers in Chilean and South African ships.
- 3 in gun mounting ('Y' position).

Note: Easily confused with the 'Saar 4.5' class. Israeli Nirit upgrade converted some of this class to Saar 4.5. *Yaffo* latest to be completed in July, 1998. Now in Saar 4.5 class.

PANYU 773

Country: CHINA
Country of origin: CHINA
Ship type: PATROL FORCES
Class: HOUJIAN/HUANG (TYPE 037/2) (PGG)
Active: 6
Name (Pennant Number): YANGJIANG(770),
SHUNDE (771), NANHAI (772), PANYU (773), -
(774), - (775).

SPECIFICATION

Displacement, standard, tons: 520.
Length, feet (metres): 214.6 (65.4).
Beam, feet (metres): 27.6 (8.4).
Draught, feet (metres): 7.9 (2.4).
Speed, knots: 32.
Range, miles: 1 800 at 18 kts.

ARMAMENT

Missiles: SSM – 6 - YJ-1 (Eagle Strike) (C-801) (C
  SS-N-4 Sardine) (2 triple).
Guns: 2 -37 mm/63 (twin) Type 76A. 4 - 30
  mm/65 (2 twin) Type 69.

RADARS

Surface search - Square Tie.
Navigation – Type 765
Fire control - Rice Lamp.

KEY RECOGNITION FEATURES

- High bow, sloping forecastle.
- 37 mm/63 gun twin mounting ('A'
  position).
- Main superstructure stepped down at after
  end.
- Tall, lattice mainmast at after end of bridge
  superstructure.
- Distinctive Rice Lamp fire control director
  atop bridge roof.
- Boxlike C-801 SSM launchers aft of
  forward superstructure, port and starboard,
  trained forward and slightly outboard.
- 2 - 30mm/65 gun mountings ('Y' and 'X'
  positions).

Houxin

HOUXIN 56 (CHINA)

Country: CHINA, BURMA, SRI LANKA
Country of origin: CHINA
Ship type: PATROL FORCES
Class: HOUXIN (TYPE 037/1G) (PGG/PCF)
Active: 6 Burma, 16 China, 1 Sri Lanka
Building: 3 China
BURMA - Name (Pennant Number): MAGA (471), SAITTRA (472), DUWA (473), ZEDYA (474), (475 - 476).
CHINA - Name (Pennant Number): (751-760), (764-769).
SRI LANKA - Name (Pennant Number): PARAKRAMABAHU (P 351).

SPECIFICATION

Displacement, full load, tons: 478.
Length, feet (metres): 203.4 (62.8).
Beam, feet (metres): 23.6 (7.2).
Draught, feet (metres): 7.5 (2.4).
Speed, knots: 28.
Range, miles: 1 300 at 15 kts.

ARMAMENT

Missiles: SSM - 4 YJ-1 (Eagle Strike)(C-801) (2 twin). (Not Sri Lanka unit).
Guns: 4 - 37 mm/63 Type 76A (2 twin), 4 - 14.5 mm machine-guns Type 69 (2 twin).
A/S mortars: 2 - Type 87 6-tube launchers, (Sri Lanka only).

RADARS

Surface search - Square Tie, (Burmese and Chinese ships).
Navigation - Anritsu RA 723 (Sri Lanka).
Fire control - Rice Lamp.
Sonars: Stag Ear, hull-mounted active search/attack, (Sri Lankan ship only).

Flyvefisken

RAVNEN   *H.M. Steele*

Country: DENMARK
Country of origin: DENMARK
Ship type: PATROL FORCES
Class: FLYVEFISKEN (PG/MHC/MLC/AGSC)
Active: 14

Name (Pennant Number): FLYVEFISKEN (P 550), HAJEN (P 551), HAVKATTEN (P 552), LAXEN (P 553), MAKRELEN (P 554), STØREN (P 555), SVAERDFISKEN (P 556), GLENTEN (P 557), GRIBBEN (P 558), LOMMEN (P 559), RAVNEN (P 560), SKADEN (P 561), VIBEN (P 562), SØLØVEN (P 563)

SPECIFICATION

Displacement, full load, tons: 480.
Length, feet (metres): 177.2 (54).
Beam, feet (metres): 29.5 (9).
Draught, feet (metres): 8.2 (2.5).
Speed, knots: 30.
Range, miles: 2 400 at 18 kts.

ARMAMENT

Missiles: SSM - 8 McDonnell Douglas Harpoon from 2001. SAM – 3 Mk 48 Mod 3 twin launchers, Sea Sparrow. (Fitted for attack/MCM/minelaying roles).
Guns: 1 - OTO MELARA 3 in (76 mm)/62 Super Rapid. 2 - 12.7 mm machine-guns.
Torpedoes: 2 - 21 in (533 mm) tubes. FFV Type 613.
Mines: 60 (minelaying role only).
Decoys: 2 - Sea Gnat 130 mm DL-6T 6-barrel chaff launcher.

RADARS

Air/surface search - Plessey AWS 6 (P 550-P 556). Telefunken System Technik TRS-3D (P 557-P 563)
Surface search – Terma Scanter Mil.
Navigation - Furuno.
Fire control - CelsiusTech 9LV 200 Mk 3.
Sonars: Thomson-Sintra TSM 2640 Salmon; VDS. CelsiusTech CTS-36/39; hull-mounted.

KEY RECOGNITION FEATURES

- 3 in gun mounting ('A' position).
- High freeboard with break down to afterdeck adjacent to funnel.
- High, angular central superstructure flush with ship's side.
- Tall enclosed mainmast amidships with AWS 6 or TRS-3D (P557-563) air/surface search radar aerial atop.
- Very low profile, black-capped funnel aft of mainmast with sloping after end.
- 2 Harpoon SSM angled launchers, athwartships in crossover configuration, aft of funnel adjacent to break in maindeck.
- 2 torpedo tubes, one port one starboard, outboard of SSM launchers.
- **Note:** The overall design allows ships to change as required to the attack, patrol, MCMV or minelayer roles. Requirement is to be able to change within 48 hours.

Ramadan

EL KADESSAYA

H & L *van Ginderen Collection*

Country: EGYPT

Country of origin: UNITED KINGDOM

Ship type: PATROL FORCES

Class: RAMADAN (PCFG)

Active: 6

Name (Pennant Number): RAMADAN (670), KHYBER (672), EL KADESSAYA (674), EL YARMOUK (676), BADR (678), HETTEIN (680)

SPECIFICATION

Displacement, full load, tons: 307.

Length, feet (metres): 170.6 (52).

Beam, feet (metres): 25 (7.6).

Draught, feet (metres): 7.5 (2.3).

Speed, knots: 40.

Range, miles: 1 600 at 18 kts.

ARMAMENT

Missiles: SSM - 4 - OTO MELARA/Matra Otomat Mk 1. SAM – Portable SA-N-5 sometimes carried.

Guns: 1 - OTO MELARA 3 in (76 mm)/62 Compact; 2 - Breda 40 mm/70 (twin).

Decoys: 4 - Protean fixed chaff launchers.

RADARS

Air/surface search - Marconi S 820

Navigation - Marconi S 810.

Fire control - Two Marconi ST 802.

KEY RECOGNITION FEATURES

- Very short forecastle with 3 in gun mounting ('A' position)
- Main superstructure well forward of midships.
- Large, pyramid mainmast at after end of superstructure with pole mast atop the after end.
- Distinctive Marconi S 820air/surface search radome atop mainmast.
- Small after superstructure supporting short enclosed mast with radome atop.
- Otomat SSM launchers sited between superstructures. Forward 2 trained to port, after 2 starboard. All launchers angled towards the bow.
- 40 mm/70 gun mounting ('Y' position).

Note: US Navy's 'Cyclone' PCFs based on 'Ramadan' design but of markedly different appearance. See separate entry.

Storm

Missiles now deleted from quarterdeck

BULTA

Country: ESTONIA, LATVIA, LITHUANIA
Country of origin: NORWAY
Ship type: PATROL FORCES
Class: STORM (PCF)
Active: 1 Estonia (Border Guard), 3 Latvia, 3 Lithuania
ESTONIA - Name (Pennant Number): TORM (ex-*Arg*) (PVL 105, ex-P 968).
LATVIA - Name (Pennant Number): BULTA (ex-*Traust*) (P 04, ex-P 973), LODE (P02), LINEA (P03).
LITHUANIA - Name (Pennant Number): DZŪKAS (ex-*Glimt*) (P 31, ex-P 962), SELIS (ex-*Skuud*), SKALVIS (ex-Steil) (P33, ex-P969) .

Note: Three further hulls may be transferred from Norway in 2001 to all three countries.

SPECIFICATION

Displacement, full load, tons: 135.
Length, feet (metres): 120 (36.5).
Beam, feet (metres): 20 (6.1).
Draught, feet (metres): 5 (1.5).
Speed, knots: 32.
Range, miles: 800 at 25 kts.

ARMAMENT

Guns: 1 – Bofors 40 mm/60, (Latvia and Lithuania). 1 - 12.7 mm machine-gun, Lithuania. 2 - 25 mm/80 (twin); 2 - 14.5 mm (twin) machine-guns, (Estonia).

RADARS

Surface search - Racal Decca TM 1226.

KEY RECOGNITION FEATURES

- Low profile, compact craft.
- Long clear forecastle on Latvian hull.
- 40 mm open mounting immediately forward of bridge on Lithuanian hull.
- Twin 25 mm/80 on raised platform, immediately forward of bridge, in Estonian boat.
- Low, rounded central superstructure.
- Central tripod mainmast
- Twin 14.5 mm MG on raised platform on quarterdeck, Estonian unit.
- 40 mm fun mounting on quarterdeck, Latvian craft.

Super Dvora / Super Dvora Mk II

SUPER DVORA MK II (ISRAEL)

Country: ERITREA, INDIA, ISRAEL, SLOVENIA, SRI LANKA

Country of origin: ISRAEL

Ship Type: PATROL FORCES

Class: SUPER DVORA/SUPER DVORA MK II (PCF)

Active: 4 Eritrea (Mk II), 1 India (Mk II), 13 Israel (9 Mk I, 4 Mk II), 2 Slovenia (Mk II), 4 (Mk I), 5 (Mk II), Sri Lanka

Planned: 15 (India, some for coast guard).

ERITREA - Name (Pennant Number): (P 101), (P 102), (P 103), (P 104).

INDIA - Name (Pennant Number): T 80, T 81.

ISRAEL - Name (Pennant Number): 811-819, (Mk I), 820-823, (Mk II).

SLOVENIA - Name (Pennant Number): ANKARAN (HPL 21).

SRI LANKA - Name (Pennant Number): Mk I - P 440-443 (ex-P 465-468). Mk II - P 460 (ex-P 441), P 461 (ex-P 496), P 462 (ex-P497), P 464, P 465

SPECIFICATION

Displacement, full load, tons: 54, (60, India, 58, Slovenia and Eritrea. 64, Sri Lanka, Mk II.).

Length, feet (metres): 71 (21.6), (Mk I). 82 (25), (Mk II).

Beam, feet (metres): 18 (5.5), (Mk I). 18.4 (5.6), (Mk II).

Draught, feet (metres): 5.9 (1.8), (Mk I). 3.6 (1.1), (Mk II).

Speed, knots: 36, (Mk I). 46 (Mk II).

Range, miles: 1,200 at 17 kts.

ARMAMENT

Missiles: SSM – Hellfire, (sometimes carried, Israel only).

Guns: 2 - Oerlikon 20mm/80 or Bushmaster 25 mm/87 Mk 96 or 3 - Rafael Typhoon 12.7 mm (triple machine-guns); 2 - 12.7 or 7.62 mm machine-guns; 1 - 84 mm rocket launcher, (Israel). 2 - 23 mm (twin); 2 - 12 mm machine-guns, (Eritrea). 1 - Oerlikon 20 mm; 2 - 12.7 mm machine-guns, (India). 2 - Oerlikon 20 mm; 2 - 12.7 mm machine-guns, (Sri Lanka, Mk I). 1 - Typhoon 20 mm or 22 Royal Ordnance GCM-A03 30 mm (twin); 2 - 12.7 mm machine-guns. 2- 7.62 mm machine-guns, (Sri Lanka, Mk II). 2 - 12.7 mm machine-guns, (Slovenia).

RADARS

Surface search – Raytheon, (Eritrea, Israel). Koden, MD 3220, (India, Slovenia, Sri Lanka, Mk II). Decca 926 (Sri Lanka, Mk I).

KEY RECOGNITION FEATURES

- Low profile, compact craft.
- Slight raised bow with continuous maindeck from stem to stern. Low freeboard.
- Low profile superstructure with slim enclosed mast aft of open bridge.
- Gun mountings forward of bridge and right aft.

Hamina

HAMINA

Country: FINLAND
Country of origin: FINLAND
Ship type: PATROL FORCES
Class: HAMINA (PCFG)
Active: 1
Building: 1
Name (Pennant Number): HAMINA (74) ––– (––).

SPECIFICATION

Displacement, full load, tons: 270.
Length, feet (metres): 164 (50.8).
Beam, feet (metres): 26.2 (8.3).
Draught, feet (metres): 6.2 (2).
Speed, knots: 32.
Range, miles: 500 at 30 kts.

ARMAMENT

Missiles: SSM - 6 Saab RBS 15SF. SAM - Matra
    Sadral sextuple launcher; Mistral.
Guns: Bofors 40 mm/70; (6 - 103 mm rails for
    rocket illuminants). 2 Sako 23 mm/87 (twin)
    can be fitted instead of Sadral. 2 – 12.7 mm
    machine-guns.
A/S mortars: 4 - Saab Elma LLS-920 9-tubed
    launchers.
Depth charges: 1 rail.
Decoys: Philax chaff launcher.

RADARS

Surface search – Signaal Scout.
Navigation – Raytheon ARPA.
Fire control – Bofors Electronic 9LV 225.
Sonars: Simrad Subsea Toadfish sonar; search and
    attack. Finnyards Sonac/PTA towed array.

KEY RECOGNITION FEATURES

- High, sharply raked bow with maindeck
  sweeping down to low stern.
- 40 mm/70 gun turret mounting mid-
  forecastle.
- Central, angular, stepped superstructure,
  with bridge set back.
- Short, robust enclosed mainmast
  amidships.
- RBS 15F SSM angled box launchers aft of
  superstructure on very short quarterdeck.
Note: SAM and 23 mm guns are
  interchangeable within the same barbette.
Note 2: Continuation of the 'Rauma' class
  design.

Helsinki

TURKU

Country: FINLAND
Country of origin: FINLAND
Ship type: PATROL FORCES
Class: HELSINKI (PCFG)
Active: 4
Name (Pennant Number): HELSINKI (60), TURKU (61), OULU (62), KOTKA (63)

SPECIFICATION

Displacement, full load, tons: 300.
Length, feet (metres): 147.6 (45).
Beam, feet (metres): 29.2 (8.9).
Draught, feet (metres): 9.9 (3).
Speed, knots: 30.

ARMAMENT

Missiles: SSM - 8 Saab RBS 15. SAM - 2 sextuple Sadral launchers; Mistral.
Guns: 1 - Bofors 57 mm/70. 4 - Sako 23 mm/87 (2 twin) (in place of Sadral launcher).
Depth charges: 2 rails.
Decoys: Philax chaff launcher.

RADARS

Surface search - 9GA 208.
Navigation - Raytheon ARPA.
Fire control - CelsiusTech 9LV 225.
Sonars: Simrad Marine SS 304. Finnyards Sonac/PTA towed array

KEY RECOGNITION FEATURES

- Short forecastle with 57 mm/70 gun mounting ('A' position).
- High rounded superstructure forward of midships.
- Tall, slender, enclosed mainmast atop superstructure aft of bridge.
- 2 - 23 mm/87 gun mountings on wings at after end of superstructure. (Can be replaced by Sadral/Mistral SAM launcher)
- 4 twin RBS 15 SSM launchers on afterdeck; 2 port, 2 starboard, trained forward and angled outboard.

Note: See also *Rauma* class which was developed from this design.

Rauma

PORVOO

Country: FINLAND	
Country of origin: FINLAND	
Ship type: PATROL FORCES	
Class: RAUMA (PCFG)	
Active: 4	
Name (Pennant Number): RAUMA (70), RAAHE (71), PORVOO (72), NAANTALI (73)	

SPECIFICATION

Displacement, full load, tons: 248.
Length, feet (metres): 157.5 (48).
Beam, feet (metres): 26.2 (8).
Draught, feet (metres): 4.5 (1.5).
Speed, knots: 30.

ARMAMENT

Missiles: SSM - 6 Saab RBS 15SF. SAM - Matra Sadral sextuple launcher; Mistral.
Guns: 1 - Bofors 40 mm/70; (6 - 103 mm rails for rocket illuminants). 2 - Sako 23 mm/87 (twin) can be fitted instead of Sadral.
A/S mortars: 4 - Saab Elma LLS-920 9-tubed launchers.
Depth charges: 1 rail.
Decoys: Philax chaff launcher.

RADARS

Surface search - 9GA 208.
Navigation - Raytheon ARPA
Fire control – CelsiusTech 9LV 225.
Sonars: Simrad Subsea Toadfish sonar. Finnyards Sonac/PTA towed array.

KEY RECOGNITION FEATURES

- High bow with long forecastle.
- 40 mm/70 gun mounting mid-forecastle.
- Saab Elma LLS-920 A/S mortar between mounting and forward superstructure.
- Central, angular, stepped superstructure.
- 9LV 225 fire control radar aerial atop bridge roof.
- Short, robust pole mainmast amidships.
- 9GA 208 surface search radar aerial atop mainmast.
- 2 RBS 15 SSM launchers outboard of after end of superstructure with second two right aft on the port and starboard quarter.

Note: SAM and 23 mm guns are interchangeable within the same barbette.

P 400

LA TAPAGEUSE

Country: FRANCE, GABON, OMAN

Country of origin: FRANCE

Ship type: PATROL FORCES

Class: P 400 (PATRA/AL BUSHRA) (PC/OPV)

Active: 10 France, 2 Gabon ('Patra' class), 3 Oman ('Al Bushra' class OPV)

FRANCE - Name (Pennant Number):
L'AUDACIEUSE (P 682), LA BOUDEUSE (P 683), LA CAPRICIEUSE (P 684), LA FOUGUEUSE (P 685), LA GLORIEUSE (P 686), LA GRACIEUSE (P 687), LA MOQUEUSE (P 688), LA RAILLEUSE (P 689), LA RIEUSE (P 690), LA TAPAGEUSE (P 691)

GABON - Name (Pennant Number): GÉNÉRAL d'ARMÉE BA-OUMAR (P 07), COLONEL DJOUE-DABANY (P 08).

OMAN - Name (Pennant Number): AL BUSHRA (B 1), AL MANSOOR (B 2), AL NAJAH (B 3).

SPECIFICATION

Displacement, full load, tons: 477. (475 Oman, 446 Gabon.).

Length, feet (metres): 178.6 (54.5).

Beam, feet (metres): 26.2 (8).

Draught, feet (metres): 8.5 (2.5) (8.9 (2.7), Oman).

Speed, knots: 24.5

Range, miles: 4 200 at 15 kts.

ARMAMENT

Guns: 1 - Bofors 40 mm/60. 1 - Giat 20F2 20 mm. 2 - 12.7 mm machine-guns, (France.) 1 - Bofors 57 mm/70 SAK 57 Mk 2 (P 07); 2 - Giat 20F2 20 mm (twin) (P 08 which also has an Oerlikon 20 mm), (Gabon). In Omani ships, 40 mm/60 is being replaced by OTO MELARA 76 mm/62 Super Rapid; 2 - Oerlikon/Royal Ordnance 20 mm GAM-B01 20 mm and 2 - 12.7 mm machine-guns also in Omani ships.

RADARS

Surface search - Racal Decca 1226. (French, Gabon ships). Kelvin Hughes 1007 ARPA (Oman).

Albatros

SEEADLER

Country: GERMANY	
Country of origin: GERMANY	
Ship type: PATROL FORCES	
Class: ALBATROS (TYPE 1438B) (PCFG)	
Active: 10	

Name (Pennant Number): ALBATROS (P 6111), FALKE (P 6112), GEIER (P 6113), BUSSARD (P 6114), SPERBER (P 6115), GREIF (P 6116), KONDOR (P 6117), SEEADLER (P 6118), HABICHT (P 6119), KORMORAN (P 6120)

SPECIFICATION

Displacement, full load, tons: 398.
Length, feet (metres): 189 (57.6).
Beam, feet (metres): 25.6 (7.8).
Draught, feet (metres): 8.5 (2.6).
Speed, knots: 40.
Range, miles: 1,300 at 30 kts.

ARMAMENT

Missiles: SSM - Aerospatiale MM 38 Exocet (2 twin) launchers.
Guns: 2 - OTO MELARA 3 in (76 mm)/62 Compact; 2 - 12.7 mm machine-guns may be fitted.
Torpedoes: 2 - 21 in (533 mm) aft tubes. AEG Seeal.
Decoys: Buck-Wegmann Hot Dog/Silver Dog chaff/IR flare dispenser.

RADARS

Surface search/fire control - Signaal WM 27.
Navigation - SMA 3 RM 20.

KEY RECOGNITION FEATURES

- Long forecastle, prominent breakwater forward of 3 in gun mounting ('A' position).
- Narrow, long central superstructure, stepped down aft of bridge.
- Lattice structure aft of bridge supporting distinctive WM27 surface search/fire control radome.
- Tall tripod pole mainmast at after end of superstructure.
- Exocet SSM ribbed launchers aft of superstructure, trained forward and to port and immediately aft, trained forward and to starboard.
- 3 in gun mounting aft of SSM launchers ('Y' position).
- 2 torpedo tubes outboard of after gun mounting, trained aft.

Gepard

DACHS

Country: GERMANY
Country of origin: Germany
Ship type: PATROL FORCES
Class: GEPARD (TYPE 143 A) (PCFG)
Active: 10
Name (Pennant Number): GEPARD (P 6121),
PUMA (P 6122), HERMELIN (P 6123), NERZ (P
6124), ZOBEL (P 6125), FRETTCHEN (P 6126),
DACHS (P 6127), OZELOT (P 6128), WIESEL (P
6129), HYÄNE (P 6130)

SPECIFICATION

Displacement, full load, tons: 391.
Length, feet (metres): 190 (57.6).
Beam, feet (metres): 25.6 (7.8).
Draught, feet (metres): 8.5 (2.6).
Speed, knots: 40.
Range, miles: 2,600 at 16 kts.

ARMAMENT

Missiles: SSM - 4 - Aerospatiale MM 38 Exocet.
SAM - GDC RAM 21 cell point defence system.
Guns: 1 - OTO MELARA 3 in (76 mm)/62
Compact.

Decoys: Buck-Wegmann Hot Dog/Silver Dog
chaff/IR flare dispenser.

RADARS

Surface search/fire control - Signaal WM 27.
Navigation - SMA 3 RM 20.

KEY RECOGNITION FEATURES

- Long forecastle with 3 in gun mounting ('A' position).
- Central superstructure with high forward end, stepped down aft of bridge.
- Distinctive surface WM27 search/fire control radome atop short lattice mast after end of bridge.
- Tall tripod pole mainmast at after end of superstructure.
- 2 Exocet SSM launchers aft of superstructure trained forward and to port and 2 further aft trained forward and to starboard.
- RAM SAM box launcher right aft.

La Combattante III/IIIB/IIIM

Country: GREECE, NIGERIA, QATAR, TUNISIA

Country of origin: FRANCE

Ship type: PATROL FORCES

Class: LA COMBATTANTE III/IIIB/IIIM (LASKOS, DAMSAH) (PCFG)

Active: 9 Greece ('Laskos' class), 3 Nigeria (Combattante IIIB), 3 Qatar ('Damsah' Combattante IIIM class), 3 Tunisia (Combattante IIIM class)

GREECE - Name (Pennant Number): ANTIPLOIARCHOS LASKOS (P 20), PLOTARHIS BLESSAS (P 21), IPOPLOIARCHOS MIKONIOS (P 22), IPOPLOIARCHOS TROUPAKIS (P 23), SIMEOFOROS KAVALOUDIS (P 24), IPOPLOIARCHOS DEGIANNIS (P 26), SIMEOFOROS XENOS (P 27), SIMEOFOROS SIMITZOPOULOS (P 28), SIMEOFOROS STARAKIS (P 29)

NIGERIA - Name (Pennant Number): SIRI (P 181), AYAM (P 182), EKUN (P 183).

QATAR - Name (Pennant Number): DAMSAH (Q 01), AL GHARIYAH (Q 02), RBIGAH (Q 03).

TUNISIA - Name (Pennant Number): LA GALITÉ (501), TUNIS (502), CARTHAGE (503).

PLOTARHIS BLESSAS

SPECIFICATION

Displacement, full load, tons: 425 (Greece, P 20-23, Tunisia); 429 (Greece, P 24-29). 395 (Qatar). 430 (Nigeria).

Length, feet (metres): 184 (56.2), (Greece, Nigeria). 183.7 (56), (Qatar, Tunisia).

Beam, feet (metres): 26.2 (8), (Greece). 26.9 (8.2), (Qatar, Tunisia). 24.9 (7.6), (Nigeria).

Draught, feet (metres): 7 (2.1), (Greece, Nigeria). 7.2 (2.2), (Qatar, Tunisia).

Speed, knots: 36 (Greece, P 20-23); 32.5 (Greece, P 24-29). 38 (Nigeria, Qatar, Tunisia)

Range, miles: 2,700 at 15 kts. (Greece). 2,000 at 15 kts. (Remainder).

ARMAMENT

Missiles: SSM - 4 - Aerospatiale MM 38 Exocet (Greece, P 20-23, Nigeria). MM 40 Exocet (2 quad), (Qatar, Tunisia). 6 - Kongsberg Penguin Mk 2 (Greece, P 24-29).

Guns: 2 - OTO MELARA 3 in (76 mm)/62 Compact; 4 - Emerson Electric 30 mm (2 twin), (Greece). 1 - OTO MELARA 3 in (76 mm)/62; 2 - Breda 40 mm/70 (twin), (Nigeria, Qatar, Tunisia). 4 - Emerson Electric 30 mm (2 twin), (Nigeria). 4 - Oerlikon 30 mm/75 (2 twin), (Qatar, Tunisia).

Torpedoes: 2 - 21 in (533 mm) aft tubes. AEG SST-4. (Greece only).

Decoys: Wegmann launchers, (Greece). CSEE Dagaie single trainable launcher, (Qatar, Tunisia).

RADARS

Air/surface search - Thomson-CSF Triton.

Navigation - Racal Decca 1226C, (Greece, Qatar). Racal Decca TM 1226, (Nigeria).

Fire control - Thomson-CSF Castor II/Thomson-CSF Pollux.

KEY RECOGNITION FEATURES

- Low freeboard craft with 3 in gun mounting ('A' position).
- Long, low profile, rounded superstructure well forward of midships.
- Fire control radar aerial mounted on lattice structure atop bridge roof.
- Tall lattice mainmast atop mid-superstructure.
- Surface search radar aerial atop mainmast.
- 2 - 30 mm gun mountings, one port one starboard, atop after end of superstructure.
- Low profile after superstructure forward of 3 in gun mounting ('Y' position), (Greek ships only. 40 mm/70 twin mounting in Nigerian, Qatar and Tunisian units).
- SSM ribbed launchers between forward and after superstructures. Tube launchers, port and starboard, in Qatar ships.
- 2 single torpedo tubes trained aft and sited outboard either side of after mounting. (Greek ships only).

Note: See entry on Combattante II class in service with Chile, Germany, Greece, Iran, Libya and Malyasia.

Lürssen FPB 57

Country: GHANA, INDONESIA, KUWAIT, NIGERIA, TURKEY

Country of origin: GERMANY

Ship type: PATROL FORCES

Class: LÜRSSEN FPB 57 (SINGA), (KAKAP) (EKPE) (DOGAN) (PC/PCF/PCFG)

Active: 2 Ghana, 4 'Singa' class (PC), 4 'Kakap' class (PC), Indonesia, 1 Kuwait, 2 Nigeria ('Ekpe' class), 8 Turkey ('Dogan' class PCFG)

GHANA - Name (Pennant Number): ACHIMOTA (P 28), YOGAGA (P 29).

INDONESIA - Name (Pennant Number): 'Singa' class - SINGA (651), AJAK (653), PANDRONG (801), SURA (802). 'Kakap' class - KAKAP (811), KERAPU (812), TONGKOL (813), BARAKUDA (ex-*Bervang*) (814).

KUWAIT - Name (Pennant Number): ISTIQLAL (P 5702).

NIGERIA - Name (Pennant Number): EKPE (P 178), AGU (P 180).

TURKEY - Name (Pennant Number): DOGAN (P 340), MARTI (P 341), TAYFUN (P 342), VOLKAN (P 343), RÜZGAR (P 344), POYRAZ (P 345), GURBET (P 346), FIRTINA (P 347)

SPECIFICATION

Displacement, full load, tons: 389 (Ghana). 410, (Kuwait). 423, (Indonesian 'Kakap' class). 428 (Indonesia 'Singa' class). 436. (Turkey). 444, (Nigeria).

Length, feet (metres): 190.6 (58.1)

Beam, feet (metres): 25. (7.6) (24.9 (7.6), Kuwait, Nigeria).

Draught, feet (metres): 8.8 (2.7) Turkey. (8.9 (2.7), Kuwait). (9.2 (2.8), Ghana, Indonesia). (10.2 (3.1), Nigeria).

Speed, knots: 42, Nigeria. (38, Turkey). (30, Ghana). (27, Indonesia).

ARMAMENT

Missiles: SSM - McDonnell Douglas Harpoon (2 quad) launchers, (Turkey). 4 - Exocet MM 40, (Kuwait). (No missiles, Ghana, Indonesia, Nigeria)

Guns: 1 - OTO MELARA 3 in (76 mm)/62 Compact. 2 - Oerlikon 35 mm/90 (twin), (Turkish ships). 1 - OTO MELARA 3 in (76 mm)/62 Compact, 1 - Breda 40 mm/70 (twin), (Ghana, Kuwait, Nigeria). 1 - Bofors SAK 57 mm/70 Mk 2; 1 - Bofors SAK 40 mm/70; 2 - Rheinmetall 20 mm

(Indonesia 'Singa' class). 1 - Bofors 40 mm/60; 2 - 12.7 mm machine-guns, (Indonesian 'Kakap' class).

Torpedoes: 2 - 21 in (533 mm) Toro tubes; AEG SUT. (Some Indonesian 'Singa' units only).

Decoys: 2 multi-barrelled launchers. (Not Ghana or Nigeria). CSEE Dagaie training mounting, (Kuwait). 2- Mk 36 SRBOC chaff launchers, (Turkey).

RADARS

Surface search - Racal Decca 1226, (Turkish, Nigerian ships). Thomson-CSF Canopus A (Ghana). Racal Decca 2459 (Indonesia). Marconi S 810 (Kuwait).

Navigation – Decca TM 1226C (Ghana, Kuwait). Kelvin Hughes 1007, (Indonesian 'Kakap' class).

Fire control - Signaal WM28/41, (Turkish, Nigerian ships). Signaal WM22, (Indonesia 'Singa' class). Philips 9LV 200, (Kuwait).

Sonars: Signaal PMS 32 (Some Indonesian 'Singa' units).

AIR SUPPORT

SINGA (NAV 1)

Helicopters: Platform for Nurtanio NBO 105C
(Indonesian 'Kakap' class only).

KEY RECOGNITION FEATURES

- Long forecastle with 3 in or Bofors SAK 57 mm/70 gun mounting or Bofors 40 mm/60 ('A' position).
- Low freeboard.
- Rounded, short superstructure forward of midships stepped down at after end. (Longer superstructure in Ghanaian and Kuwait units)
- Raised helicopter platform extending aft from superstructure in Indonesia 'Kakap' class.
- Short, square profile lattice mainmast at after end of superstructure.
- Surface search radome atop mainmast, (Not Ghanaian, kuwaiti or Indonesian 'Kakap' units).
- SSM launchers in 'V' formation on afterdeck. (No missiles, Ghana, Indonesia, Nigeria).
- 35 mm/70 mounting right aft ('Y' position). (40 mm/70, Ghana and Indonesian 'Singa' but absent in Indonesian 'Kakap' class.) Twin Breda 40 mm/70 turret in this position in Kuwaiti and Nigerian units.

Note: The Turkish 'Yildiz' class is based on the 'Dogan' class hull. Turkish 'Kiliç' class a variant of 'Yildiz' with very tall and solid enclosed mast at aft end of bridge superstructure with angl;ed step down to long quarterdeck.

Sukanya

SUJATA

Country: INDIA, SRI LANKA
Country of origin: SOUTH KOREA
Ship type: PATROL FORCES
Class: SUKANYA (OPV)
Active: 6 India, 1 Sri Lanka.

INDIA - Name (Pennant Number): SUKANYA (P 50), SUBHADRA (P 51), SUVARNA (P 52), SAVITRI (P 53), SHARADA (P 55), SUJATA (P 56).
SRI LANKA - Name (Pennant Number): SAYURA (ex-*Saryu*) (P 620, ex-P 54).

SPECIFICATION

Displacement, full load, tons: 1,890.
Length, feet (metres): 331.7 (101.1) oa.
Beam, feet (metres): 37.4 (11.5).
Draught, feet (metres): 14.4 (4.4).
Speed, knots: 21.
Range, miles: 5,800 at 15 kts.

ARMAMENT

Guns: 3 – Bofors 40 mm/60; 4 – 12.7 mm machine-guns.
A/S mortars: 4 - RBU 2500 16-tube trainable launchers.

RADARS

Surface search –Racal Decca 2459.
Navigation –Bharat 1245.

AIR SUPPORT

Helicopters: 1 HAL SA 319B Chetak (Alouette III) (ASW).

KEY RECOGNITION FEATURES

- High maindeck dropping down to low freeboard, midships.
- Raised platform immediately forward of bridge.
- High main superstructure, with prominent bridge wings, forward of midships.
- Massive tall enclosed mainmast atop central superstructure.
- Prominent tall rounded funnel midships.
- Large e square helicopter hanger, with aft, very long helicopter landing area over open quarterdeck.

Note: Based on 'Ulsan' frigate design.

Note 2: One unit transferred by India to Sri Lankan service and recommissioned on December 9, 2000.

Note 3: Three units of this class operated by Indian coastguard – *Samar* (42), *Sangram* (43) and *Sarang* (44), with one more building. More heavily armed and with a telescopic hanger.

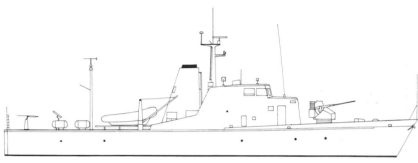

SIBARU

Country: INDONESIA

Country of origin: AUSTRALIA

Ship type: PATROL FORCES

Class: SIBARU (ATTACK) (PC)

Active: 8

Name (Pennant Number): SIBARU (ex-*Bandolier*) (847), SILIMAN (ex-*Archer*) (848), SIGALU (ex-*Barricade*) (857), SILEA (ex-*Acute*) (858), SIRIBUA (ex-*Bombard*) (859), SIADA (ex-*Barbette*) (862), SIKUDA (ex-*Attack*) (863), SIGUROT (ex-*Assail*) (864).

SPECIFICATION

Displacement, full load, tons: 146.

Length, feet (metres): 107.5 (32.8).

Beam, feet (metres): 20 (6.1).

Draught, feet (metres): 6.1 (2.2).

Speed, knots: 21.

Range, miles: 1,200 at 13 kts.

ARMAMENT

Guns: 1 – Bofors 40 mm/60. 1 – 12.7 mm machine-gun.

RADARS

Surface search – Decca 916

KEY RECOGNITION FEATURES

- Sweeping low freeboard maindeck from stem to stern.
- 40 mm gun open mounting on forecastle.
- Bridge superstructure steps up from forecastle and is angled down aft.
- Short pole mainmast at aft end of superstructure.
- Tall angled funnel immediately aft of mainmast.

Note: Two similar craft with pennant numbers 860 and 861 were built locally in 1982/83 but have not been seen for some years.

Peacock / Jacinto

EMILIO JACINTO

Country: IRISH REPUBLIC, PHILIPPINES
Country of origin: UNITED KINGDOM
Ship type: PATROL FORCES
Class: PEACOCK/P41/JACINTO (PG/FS)
Active: 2 Irish Republic (PG), 3 Philippines (FS)
IRISH REPUBLIC - Name (Pennant Number):
ORLA (ex-*Swift*) (P 41), CIARA (ex-*Swallow*) (P 42)
PHILIPPINES - Name (Pennant Number): EMILIO
JACINTO (ex-*Peacock*) (PS 35, ex-P 239),
APOLINARIO MABINI (ex-*Plover*) (PS 36, ex-P
240), ARTEMIO RICARTE (PS 37, ex-P 241).

SPECIFICATION

Displacement, full load, tons: 712, (Irish units).
    763, (Philippines ships).
Length, feet (metres): 204.1 (62.6).
Beam, feet (metres): 32.8 (10).
Draught, feet (metres): 8.9 (2.7).
Speed, knots: 25.
Range, miles: 2,500 at 17 kts.

ARMAMENT

Guns: 1 - OTO MELARA 3 in (76 mm)/62 Compact;
    4 - FN 7.62 mm machine-guns, (plus 2 - 12.7
    mm machine-guns, Irish ships).

RADARS

Surface search - Kelvin Hughes Mk IV, (Irish ships).
Navigation - Kelvin Hughes Type 1006,
    (Philippines). Kelvin Hughes 500A, (Irish ships).

KEY RECOGNITION FEATURES

- Low bow, low freeboard.
- 3 in gun mounting ('A' position).
- Superstructure amidships, stepped down aft of bridge.
- Lattice mainmast atop mid-superstructure.
- Squat, square-section funnel with sloping top atop after end of superstructure.
- Slender crane jib aft of funnel.

Hetz (Saar 4.5)

HETZ CLASS

Country: ISRAEL

Country of origin: ISRAEL

Ship type: PATROL FORCES

Class: HETZ (SAAR 4.5) (PGF)

Active: 6

Name (Pennant Number): ROMAT, KESHET, HETZ (ex-*Nirit*), KIDON, TARSHISH, YAFFO

SPECIFICATION

Displacement, full load, tons: 488.
Length, feet (metres): 202.4 (61.7).
Beam, feet (metres): 24.9 (7.6).
Draught, feet (metres): 8.2 (2.5).
Speed, knots: 31.
Range, miles: 3,000 at 17 kts.

ARMAMENT

Missiles: SSM – 4 - Harpoon plus 6 - IAI Gabriel II. SAM - Israeli Industries Barak I (vertical launch or pack launchers).

Guns: 1 - OTO MELARA 3 in (76 mm)/62 Compact; 2 - Oerlikon 20 mm; 1 - GE/GD Vulcan Phalanx; 2 or 4 - 12.7 mm (twin or quad) machine-guns.

Decoys: Elbit Deseaver 72-barrel chaff/IR launchers.

RADARS

Air/surface search - Thomson-CSF TH-D 1040 Neptune.
Fire control - Elta EL/M-222 1 GM STGR.

KEY RECOGNITION FEATURES

- Long sleek hull, low freeboard.
- Vulcan Phalanx CIWS mounting ('A' position) with distinctive domed top.
- Short superstructure well forward of midships.
- Massive enclosed angled mainmast at after end of superstructure.
- Neptune air/surface search radar aerial atop mainmast.
- Harpoon SSM tubular launchers aft of superstructure and forward of after mounting. Gabriel II box launchers immediately aft.
- 3 in gun mounting right aft.

Note: Easily confused with the Saar 4 class. Nirit upgrade continues on Saar 4 to convert into Saar 4.5. *Yaffo* latest conversion in July, 1998.

Note 2: Two 'Aliya' Class (Saar 4.5), (*Aliya* and *Geoula*) operated by Israel. Of same basic hull design with substantially different weapons fits (CIWS in the eyes of the ships) and substantial slab-side superstructure aft forming helicopter hangar.

Cassiopea

CASSIOPEA

Country:	ITALY
Country of origin:	ITALY
Ship type:	PATROL FORCES
Class:	CASSIOPEA (OPV)
Active:	4

Name (Pennant Number): CASSIOPEA (P 401), LIBRA (P 402), SPICA (P 403), VEGA (P 404)

SPECIFICATION
Displacement, full load, tons: 1,475.
Length, feet (metres): 261.8 (79.8).
Beam, feet (metres): 28.7 (11.8).
Draught, feet (metres): 11.5 (3.5).
Speed, knots: 20.
Range, miles: 3,300 at 17 kts.

ARMAMENT
Guns: 1 OTO MELARA 3 in (76 mm)/62; 1 - Breda Oerlikon 25 mm/90. 2 – 12.7 mm machine-guns.

RADARS
Surface search – SMA SPS-702(V)2.
Navigation –SMA SPN-748(V)2.
Fire control – Selenia SPG-70 (RTN 10X).

AIR SUPPORT
Helicopters: 1 Agusta-Bell 212 (ASW).

KEY RECOGNITION FEATURES
- Raked bows with continuous mmaindeck line from stem to helicopter deck above quarterdeck.
- 3 in gun mounting on raised platform ('A' position).
- High square superstructure midships.
- Large enclosed mainmast atop central superstructure supporting surface search radar aerial.
- Angled funnel with two black exhausts side by side atop.
- Thin pole mast aft of funnel with ship's board on davits outboard.

Commandante OPV

COMMANDANTE BORSINI (on trials)

Giorgio ghiglione

Country: ITALY
Country of origin: ITALY
Ship type: PATROL FORCES
Class: 1500 (OPV)
Building: 6
Name (Pennant Number): COMMANDANTE CIGALA FULGOSI (P 490), COMMANDANTE BORSINI (P 491), COMMANDANTE SIRIO (P409), BETTICA (P 492), COMMANDANTE FOSCARI (P 493), ORIONI (410).

SPECIFICATION

Displacement, full load, tons: 1,520.
Length, feet (metres): 291 (88.7).
Beam, feet (metres): 40 (12.2).
Draught, feet (metres): 15.1 (4.6).
Speed, knots: 26.
Range, miles: 3,500 at 14 kts.

ARMAMENT

Guns: 1 - OTO MELARA 3 in (76 mm)/62 Compact; 2 - Oerlikon 25 mm/90 or 2 - 7.62 mm machinge-guns.

RADARS

Surface search – SPS-703
Navigation –SPS-753.
Fire control – SPG-76 (RTN 30X).

AIR SUPPORT

Helicopters: 1 Agusta-Bell 212 (ASW).

KEY RECOGNITION FEATURES

- High forecastle with raked bows..
- 3 in gun mounting on raised platform ('A' position).
- High stealthy square main superstructure midships with square funnel at forward end of helicopter hanger.
- Squat enclosed mainmast atop central superstructure supporting surface search radar aerial.
- Short helicopter operating platform aft.

Note: Two of class built for Transport Ministry, but operated by Navy. No helicopter hanger in these hulls.

Province (Nyayo / Dhofar) Oman

NYAYO

Country: KENYA, OMAN
Country of origin: UNITED KINGDOM
Ship type: PATROL FORCES
Class: PROVINCE (NYAYO, DHOFAR) (PCFG)
Active: 2 Kenya ('Nyayo' class), 4 Oman ('Dhofar' class)
KENYA - Name (Pennant Number): NYAYO (P 3126), UMOJA (P 3127).
OMAN - Name (Pennant Number): DHOFAR (B 10), AL SHARQIYAH (B 11), AL BAT'NAH (B 12), MUSSANDAM (B 14)

SPECIFICATION

Displacement, full load, tons: 394, (Oman). 430, (Kenya).
Length, feet (metres): 186 (56.7).
Beam, feet (metres): 26.9 (8.2).
Draught, feet (metres): 7.9 (2.4).
Speed, knots: 40.
Range, miles: 2,000 at 18 kts.

ARMAMENT

Missiles: SSM – 8 - Aerospatiale MM 40 Exocet, (Oman). 4 - OTO MELARA/Matra Otomat Mk 2 (2 twin), (Kenya).
Guns: 1 - OTO MELARA 3 in (76 mm)/62 Compact; 2 - Breda 40 mm/70 (twin); 2 - 12.7 mm machine-guns, (Oman). 1 - OTO MELARA 3 in (76 mm)/62 Compact; 2 - Oerlikon/BMARC 30 mm GCM-A02 (twin); 2 - Oerlikon/BMARC 20 mm A41A, (Kenya).

Decoys: 2 - Wallop Barricade 3-barrel launchers, (Oman). 2 Wallop Barricade 18-barrel launchers, (Kenya).

RADARS

Air/surface search - Plessey AWS 4 or AWS 6.
Navigation - Racal Decca TM 1226C, (Oman). Decca AC 1226, (Kenya).
Fire control – Philips 9LV 307, (Oman). Marconi/Ericsson ST802, (Kenya).

KEY RECOGNITION FEATURES

- Short forecastle, 3 in gun mounting ('A' position).
- High superstructure forward of midships. Superstructure is flush with craft's sides.
- Lattice mainmast centrally sited atop superstructure supporting AWS 4/6 air/surface search radar aerial.
- Two quadruple Exocet SSM launchers on maindeck aft of superstructure. Both launchers angled slightly forward. Forward launcher port side and after one starboard, (Oman). 4 Otomat box launchers aft of superstructure in Kenyan units.
- 40 mm/70 gun mounting right aft, (Oman). Twin 30 mm gun in same position in Kenyan boats.
Note: Mast structures in Omani ships are different, dependent on radars fitted.

La Combattante I

ALFAHAHEEL

Country: KUWAIT
Country of origin: FRANCE
Ship type: PATROL FORCES
Class: LA COMBATTANTE I (UM ALMARADIM) (PCFG)
Active: 8
Name (Pennant Number): UM ALMARADIM (P 3711), OUHA (P 3713), FAILAKA (P 3715), MASKAN (P 3717), AL-AHMADI (P 3719), ALFAHAHEEL (P 3721), AL YARMOUK (P 3723), GAROH (P 3725).

SPECIFICATION

Displacement, full load, tons: 245.
Length, feet (metres): 137.8 (42) oa.
Beam, feet (metres): 26.9 (8.2).
Draught, feet (metres): 5.9 (1.8).
Speed, knots: 30.
Range, miles: 1,350 at 14 kts.

ARMAMENT

Missiles: SSM – BAe Sea Skua (2 twin). SAM – Sadral sextuple launcher, Mistral.
Guns: 1 - OTOBreda 40 mm/70; 1 - Giat 20 mm M 621; 2 - 12.7 mm machine-guns.
Decoys: 2 - Dagaie Mk 2 chaff launchers.

RADARS

Air/surface search – Thomson-CSF MRR
Navigation – Racal Decca
Fire control – BAe Seaspray Mk 3.

KEY RECOGNITION FEATURES

- Continuous maindeck from stem to stern.
- Angled, slab-sided superstructure with very tall sturdy enclosed mast with tall, slim pole atop, aft of midships. Whip aerial above bridge.
- 40 mm/70 gun mounting immediately forward of bridge superstructure.
- Sadral/Mistral SAM sextuple launcher atop superstructure immediately aft of mast.
- Sea Skua SSM box launchers right aft.

GEMPITA

Country: MALAYSIA
Country of origin: SWEDEN
Ship type: PATROL FORCES
Class: SPICA-M (HANDALAN) (PCFG)
Active: 4
Name (Pennant Number): HANDALAN (3511), PERKASA (3512), PENDEKAR (3513), GEMPITA (3514)

SPECIFICATION

Displacement, full load, tons: 240.
Length, feet (metres): 142.6 (43.6).
Beam, feet (metres): 23.3 (7.1).
Draught, feet (metres): 7.4 (2.4) (screws).
Speed, knots: 34.5.
Range, miles: 1,850 at 14 kts.

ARMAMENT

Missiles: SSM - 4 - Aerospatiale MM 38 Exocet.
Guns: 1 - Bofors 57 mm/70; 1 Bofors 40 mm/70.

RADARS

Surface search - Philips 9GR 600.
Navigation – Racal Decca 1226.
Fire control - Philips 9LV 212.

KEY RECOGNITION FEATURES

- 57 mm/70 gun mounting ('A' position).
- Main superstructure just forward of midships with tall lattice mainmast at after end.
- 9LV 212 fire control radar aerial atop bridge.
- 9GR 600 surface search radar aerial atop mainmast.
- 2, twin Exocet SSM launchers aft of bridge pointing forward and outboard in crossover formation forward pair to port after pair to starboard.
- 40 mm/70 gun mounting aft of SSM launchers on afterdeck.

Note: Bridge further forward than in the original Swedish design to accommodate Exocet SSMs.

Note 2: Croatian and Yugoslav navies operate 'Koncar' class PCFGs, designed by the Naval Institute in Zagreb based on the 'Spica I' design. Bridge amidships like the Malaysian boats.

Note 3: The Swedish Navy's 'Norrköping class PCFGs were developed from the original 'Spica' class. See separate entry.

Note 4: Trinidad and Tobago operates two Type CG 40 PCs, with similar hulls to the 'Spica' design, but with the bridge amidships.

Musytari

MARIKH

Country: MALAYSIA
Country of origin: SOUTH KOREA
Ship type: PATROL FORCES
Class: MUSYTARI (OPV)
Active: 2
Name (Pennant Number): MUSYTARI (160), MARIKH (161).

SPECIFICATION
Displacement, full load, tons: 1,300.
Length, feet (metres): 246 (75).
Beam, feet (metres): 35.4 (10.8).
Draught, feet (metres): 12.1 (3.7).
Speed, knots: 22.
Range, miles: 5,000 at 15 kts.

ARMAMENT
Guns: 1 – Cruesot-Loire 3.9 in (100 mm)/55 Mk 2 compact. 2 – Emerson Electric 30 mm (twin).

RADARS
Air/Surface search – Signaal DA05.
Navigation – Racal Decca TM 1226.
Fire control - Philips 9LV.

AIR SUPPORT
Helicopters: Platform for 1 medium helicopter – suitable for Sikorsky S-61A Nuri army support helicopter.

KEY RECOGNITION FEATURES
- Sharp bows with continuous maindeck to just aft of midships, then sharp break down to helicopter flight deck.
- 3.9 in gun mounting ('A' position).
- Main superstructure with prominent bridge wings, deck atop.
- Two lattice masts, larger atop bridge superstructure.
- 30 mm gun mounting at aft end of superstructure.
- Ships boat on davits at break in maindeck.

Azteca

IGNACIO ZARAGOZA

Country: MEXICO
Country of origin: UNITED KINGDOM
Ship type: PATROL FORCES
Class: AZTECA (PC)
Active: 30

Name (Pennant Number): ANDRÉS QUINTANA ROO (ex-AZTECA) (PC 201, ex-P01), MATIAS DE CORDOVA (ex-GUAYCURA) (PC 202, EX-P02), MANUEL RAMOS ARIZE (ex-NAHUATL) (PC 204, ex-P03), JOSE MARIA IZAZAGA (ex-TOTORAN) (PC 204, ex- P04), JUAN BAUTISTA MORALES (ex-PAPAGO) (PC205, ex-P05), IGNACIO LÓPEZ RAYÓN (ex-TARAHUMARA) (PC 206, ex-P06), MANUEL CRESCENCIO REJON (ex-TEPEHUAN) (PC 207, ex-P07), JUAN ANTONIO DE LA FUENTE (ex-Mexica) (PC 208, ex-P08), LEON GUZMAN (ex-ZAPOTECA) (PC 209. ex-209), IGNACIO RAMIREZ (ex-HAUSTELA) (PC 210, ex-210), IGNACIO MARISCAL (ex-MAZAHUA) (PC211, ex-P11), HERIBERTO JARA CORONA (ex-HUICHOL) (PC212, ex-P12), JOSE MARIA MATA ex-SERI) (PC213, ex-P13), COLIMA (ex-YACQUI) (PC214, ex-P14), JOSE JOAQUIN FERNANDEZ DE LIZARDI (ex-TIAPANECO) (PC215, ex-P15), FRANCISCO J. MUGICA (ex-TARASCO) (PC216, ex-P16), PASTOR ROUAIX (ex-ACOLHUA) (PC217, ex-P17), JOSE MARIA DEL CASILLO VELASCO (ex-OTOMI) (PC218, ex-P18), LUIS MANUEL ROJAS (ex-MAYO) (PC219, ex-P19), JOSE NATIVIDAD MACIAS (ex-PIMAS) (PC220, ex-P20), IGNACIO ZARAGOZA (ex-CHONTAL) (PC 222, ex-P22), TAMAULIPAS (ex-MAZATECO) (PC223, ex-P23), YUCATAN (ex-TOLTECA) (PC224, ex-P24), TABASCO (ex-MAYA) (PC225, ex-P25), VERACRUZ (ex-COCHIMIE) (PC226, ex-P26), CAMPECHE (ex-CORA) (PC227, ex-P27), PUEBLA (ex-TOTONACA) (PC228, ex-P28), MARGARITA MAZA DE JUAREZ) (ex-MIXTECO) (PC229, ex-P29), LEONA VICARIO (ex-OLMECA) (PC230, ex-P30), JOSEFA ORITZ DE DOMINGUEZ (ex-TIAHUICA) (PC 231, ex-P31)

SPECIFICATION

Displacement, full load, tons: 148.
Length, feet (metres): 112.7 (34.4).
Beam, feet (metres): 28.3 (8.7).
Draught, feet (metres): 7.2 (2.2).
Speed, knots: 24.
Range, miles: 1,500 at 14 kts.

ARMAMENT

Guns: 1 - Bofors 40 mm/70; 1 - Oerlikon 20 mm or 1 - 7.62 mm machine-gun.

RADAR

Surface search – Kelvin Hughes.

KEY RECOGNITION FEATURES

- Continuous maindeck from stem to stern, high freeboard.
- 40 mm/70 gun mounting ('A' position).
- Rounded, low profile central superstructure.
- Small rounded mast and funnel combined at after end of superstructure with radar aerial at its forward end.
- 20 mm gun mounting on afterdeck.

ERLE   *H.M Steele*

Country: NORWAY
Country of origin: NORWAY.
Ship type: PATROL FORCES
Class: HAUK (PCFG)
Active: 14
Name (Pennant Number): HAUK (P 986), ØRN (P
987), TERNE (P 988), TJELD (P 989), SKARV (P 990),
TEIST (P 991), JO (P 992), LOM (P 993), STEGG (P
994), FALK (P 995), RAVN (P 996), GRIBB (P 997),
GEIR (P 998), ERLE (P 999)

SPECIFICATION

Displacement, full load, tons: 160.
Length, feet (metres): 120 (36.5).
Beam, feet (metres): 20.3 (6.2).
Draught, feet (metres): 5.9 (1.8).
Speed, knots: 32.
Range, miles: 440 at 30 kts.

ARMAMENT

Missiles: SSM – 6 - Kongsberg Penguin Mk 2 Mod
5.
SAM - Twin Simbad launcher for Matra Sadral.
Guns: 1 - Bofors 40 mm/70.
Torpedoes: 2 - 21 in (533mm) tubes. FFV Type
613.
Decoys: Chaff launcher

RADARS

Surface search/navigation – 2 - Racal Decca TM
1226.

KEY RECOGNITION FEATURES

- Low profile, compact craft.
- 40 mm/70 gun open mounting ('A'
  position).
- Low superstructure centred just forward of
  midships.
- Forward pointing single torpedo tubes
  outboard of 'A' mounting, port and
  starboard.
- Short lattice mainmast atop after end of
  superstructure.
- 20 mm/20 gun mounting immediately aft
  of superstructure surrounded by high
  circular armoured breakwater.
- Distinctive Penguin SSM launchers
  mounted on afterdeck, 2 port, 2 starboard,
  angled outboard.

Note: Swedish 'Kaparen' class similar to
'Hauk' class. See separate entry.
Note 2: Penguin SSMs sometimes not
embarked.

Dvora/HAI OU

Taiwan

TAIWAN DVORA/HAI OU

Country: PARAGUAY, SRI LANKA, TAIWAN
Country of origin: ISRAEL
Ship type: PATROL FORCES
Class: DVORA (HAI OU) (PCFG)
Active: 2 Paraguay ('Modified Hai Ou' class), 3 Sri Lanka ('Dvora' class), 58 'Hai Ou' class, Taiwan.
Planned: 4 Paraguay
PARAGUAY - Name (Pennant Number): CAPITAN ORTIZ (P 06), TENIENTE ROBLES (P 07).
SRI LANKA - Name (Pennant Number): P 260 (ex-P 420, ex-P 453), P 261 (ex-P 421, ex-P 454), P 262 (ex-P 422, ex-P 455).
TAIWAN - Name (Pennant Number): FABG 7-12, FABG 14-21, FABG 23-30, FABG 32-39, FABG 41-64.

SPECIFICATION

Displacement, full load, tons: 47.
Length, feet (metres): 70.8 (21.6).
Beam, feet (metres): 18 (5.5).
Draught, feet (metres): 3.3 (1). (5.8 (1.8), Sri Lanka).
Speed, knots: 36.
Range, miles: 700 at 32 kts.

ARMAMENT

Missiles: SSM - 2 - Hsiung Feng I, (Taiwan only).
Guns: 1 - CS 20 mm Type 75; 2 - 12.7 mm machine-guns, (Paraguay and Taiwan). 2 - Oerlikon 20 mm and 2 - 12.7 mm machine-guns, (Sri Lanka).
Decoys: 4 - Israeli AV2 chaff launchers, (Taiwan only)

RADARS

Surface search - Marconi LN 66, (Taiwan). Anritsu 72 1UA, (Sri Lanka)
Fire control - RCA R76 C5.

KEY RECOGNITION FEATURES

- Low, rounded bridge structure with square profile lattice mainmast at after end. (Paraguay boats have tall, slim enclosed mast).
- Surface search and fire control radar aerials atop mainmast.
- SSM launcher athwartships immediately aft of mainmast, (Taiwan units only).
- 20 mm gun mounting forward of bridge, (Sri Lanka).
- 20 mm gun mounting right aft, (Sri Lanka, Taiwan).
Note: The first Taiwanese series had an enclosed mainmast and the missiles were nearer the stern. Second Taiwanese series changed to a lattice mainmast and moved the missiles further forward allowing room for 20 mm mounting.
Note 2: See Super Dvora entry.
Note 3: At least two more to be transferred by Taiwan to Paraguay.

SANTILLANA

Peruvian Navy

Country: PERU
Country of origin: FRANCE
Ship type: PATROL FORCES
Class: VELARDE (PR-72P) (CM/PCFG)
Active: 6
Name (Pennant Number): VELARDE (CM 21),
SANTILLANA (CM 22), DE LOS HEROS (CM 23),
HERRERA (CM 24), LARREA (CM 25), SANCHEZ
CARRILLON (CM 26)

SPECIFICATION

Displacement full load, tons: 560.
Length, feet (metres): 210 (64).
Beam, feet (metres): 27.4 (8.4).
Draught, feet (metres): 5.2 (2.6).
Speed, knots: 37.
Range, miles: 2,500 at 16 kts.

ARMAMENT

Missiles: SSM - 4 - Aerospatiale MM 38 Exocet.
   SAM – SA-N-10 launcher may be fitted on the
   stern.
Guns: 1 - OTO MELARA 3 in (76 mm)/62 Compact;
   2 - Breda 40 mm/70 (twin).

RADARS

Surface search - Thomson-CSF Triton.
Navigation - Racal Decca 1226.
Fire control - Thomson-CSF Castor II.

KEY RECOGNITION FEATURES

- Unusual, downturned forward end of
  forecastle.
- 3 in gun mounting ('A' position).
- High rounded main superstructure forward
  of midships.
- Large lattice mainmast atop central
  superstructure supporting Triton surface
  search radar aerial.
- Castor II fire control radar aerial atop
  bridge.
- 4 Exocet SSM launchers aft of
  superstructure. Forward pair angled to
  starboard, after pair to port.
- 40 mm/70 gun twin mounting right aft.
- Note: Morocco operates two PR 72 class
  ('Okba') PCs and Senegal, one PR 72M PC
  that are similar in appearance, although
  smaller in dimensions and displacement.

Barzan (Vita/Super Vita)

HUWAR

Country:	QATAR, GREECE
Country of origin:	UNITED KINGDOM
Ship type:	PATROL FORCES
Class:	BARZAN (VITA), SUPER VITA (PGFG)
Active:	4 Qatar (Vita)
Building:	3 Greece, (Super Vita)
Planned:	4 Greece (Super Vita)

QATAR - Name (Pennant Number): BARZAN (Q04), HUWAR (Q05), AL UDEID (Q06), AL DEEBEL (Q07).

GREECE - Name (Pennant Number): ROUSSEN (P67), DANIOLOS (P68), KRISTALLIDES (P69).

SPECIFICATION

Displacement, full load, tons: 376, (Qatar units). 580, (Greek hulls).

Length, feet (metres): 185.7 (56.3), Qatar. 203.4 (62), Greece.

Beam, feet (metres): 29.5 (9) Qatar. 31.2 (9.5), Greece.

Draught, feet (metres): 8.2 (2.5). 8.5 (2.6), Greece.

Speed, knots: 35.

Range, miles: 1,800 at 12 kts.

ARMAMENT

Missiles: 8 – Exocet MM 40 Block II. SAM – Matra Sadral sextuple launcher for Mistral, Qatar. RAM, Greece.

Guns: 1 - OTO MELARA 3 in (76 mm)/62 Super Rapid. 1 – Signaal Golakeeper 30 mm GIWS; 2 - 12.7 mm machine-guns, Qatar. 2 OTOBreda 30 mm, Greece.

Decoys: CSEE Dagaie Mk 2 chaff/IR flares, Qatar. Sippilan Alex, Greece.

RADARS

Air/surface search – Thomson-CSF MRR, Qatar. Thomson-CSF MW 08, Greece.

Navigation – Kelvin Hughes 1007, Qatar. Litton Marine Bridgemaster, Greece.

Fire control – Signaal STING.

KEY RECOGNITION FEATURES

- Low bow, low freeboard with slope down to afterdeck.
- 3 in gun mounting ('A' position).
- Low superstructure amidships, stepped down aft of bridge. (Greek units will have bridge raised above superstructure.)
- Bridge with prominent all-round windows.
- Squat, chunky enclosed mainmast with complex aerials, atop mid-superstructure with angled tall polemast at aft.
- 4 Exocet SSM launchers aft of superstructure. Forward pair angled to starboard, after pair to port.
- Separate deck house with chaff launcher atop, aft of SSM launchers in Qatar ships. No chaff launcher in Greek hulls.
- Goalkeeper CIWS right aft in Qatar units.
- RAM box launcher right aft in Greek units.

Turya

TURYA (RUSSIA)

Country· RUSSIA, VIETNAM
Country of origin: RUSSIA
Ship type: PATROL FORCES
Class: TURYA (TYPE 206M) (PC/PTH)
Active: 2 Russia, 5 Vietnam
RUSSIA - Name (Pennant Number): 300, 373.
VIETNAM - Name (Pennant Number): HQ 331-335

SPECIFICATION

Displacement, full load, tons: 250.
Length, feet (metres): 129.9 (39.6).
Beam, feet (metres): 24.9 (7.6), (41 (12.5) over foils).
Draught, feet (metres): 5.9 (1.8), (13.1 (4) over foils).
Speed, knots: 40 foilborne.
Range, miles: 600 at 35 kts., foilborne, 1,450 at 14 kts., hullborne.

ARMAMENT

Guns: 2 – USSR 57 mm/80 (twin, aft); 2 – USSR 25 mm/80 (twin, fwd); 1 - 14.5 mm machine-gun in Russian hulls..
Torpedoes: 4 - 21 in (533 mm) tubes. Type 53. (Not in all Vietnamese units)
Depth charges: 2 racks. (1 rack in Russian hulls).

RADARS

Surface search - Pot Drum.
Navigation – SRN 207.
Fire control - Muff Cob.
Sonars: Foal Tail VDS, (not in all Vietnamese units).

KEY RECOGNITION FEATURES

- Blunt bow, short forecastle with 25 mm/80 gun twin mounting ('A' position).
- Angular central superstructure with raised open bridge just aft of enclosed bridge.
- Lattice mainmast aft of bridge with surface search radar aerial atop.
- Two torpedo tubes on maindeck each side of central superstructure, angled outboard, (not in all Vietnamese units).
- Pedestal supporting Muff Cob fire control radar aerial atop after end of superstructure.
- Prominent 57 mm/80 gun mounting right aft ('Y' position).

Note: Superstructure has similar 'ribbed' appearance as 'Stenka' class. Hull is derived from 'Osa' class.

Note 2: Seychelles has a decommissioned hulk *Zoroaster* of this class.

Al Siddiq

OQBAH

H & L van Ginderen Collection

Country: SAUDI ARABIA

Country of origin: USA

Ship type: PATROL FORCES

Class: AL SIDDIQ (PCFG)

Active: 9

Name (Pennant Number): AL SIDDIQ (511), AL FAROUQ (513), ABDUL AZIZ (515), FAISAL (517), KHALID (519), AMYR (521), TARIQ (523), OQBAH (525), ABU OBAIDAH (527)

SPECIFICATION

Displacement, full load, tons: 495.

Length, feet (metres): 190.5 (58.1).

Beam, feet (metres): 26.5 (8.1).

Draught, feet (metres): 6.6 (2).

Speed, knots: 38.

Range, miles: 2,900 at 14 kts.

ARMAMENT

Missiles: SSM - 4 - McDonnell Douglas Harpoon (2 twin) launchers.

Guns: 1 - FMC/OTO MELARA 3 in (76 mm)/62 Mk 75 Mod 0; 1 - GE/GD 20 mm 6-barrel Vulcan Phalanx CIWS; 2 - Oerlikon 20 mm/80; 2 - 81 mm mortars; 2 - 40 mm Mk 19 grenade launchers.

Decoys: 2 - Loral Hycor SRBOC 6-barrel Mk 36 fixed chaff/IR launchers.

RADARS

Surface search - ISC Cardion SPS 55.

Fire control - Sperry Mk 92.

KEY RECOGNITION FEATURES

- High bow with sloping forecastle.
- 3 in gun mounting ('A' position).
- High central superstructure flush with ship's side.
- Large distinctive radome atop bridge roof.
- Slim tripod mainmast amidships.
- Angular, black-capped funnel with exhausts protruding at top aft of mainmast.
- Whiplash aerials above bridge and at aft end of superstructure.
- Crossover Harpoon SSM tubular launchers on afterdeck, after 2 trained to port, forward 2 to starboard.
- Vulcan Phalanx CIWS mounting with distinctive white dome right aft.

Fearless

DAUNTLESS

Suttler/Steele

Country: SINGAPORE
Country of origin: SINGAPORE
Ship type: PATROL FORCES
Class: FEARLESS (OPV)
Active: 12
Name (Pennant Number): FEARLESS (94), BRAVE (95), COURAGEOUS (96), GALLANT (97), DARING (98), DAUNTLESS (99), RESILIENCE (82), UNITY (83), SOVEREIGNTY (84), JUSTICE (85), FREEDOM (86), INDEPENDENCE (87).

SPECIFICATION

Displacement full load, tons: 500.
Length, feet (metres): 180.4 (55).
Beam, feet (metres): 28.2 (8.6).
Draught, feet (metres): 8.9 (2.7).
Speed, knots: 20.

ARMAMENT

Missiles: SAM - Matra Simbad twin launchers for Mistral..
Guns: 1 - OTO MELARA 3 in (76 mm)/62Super Rapid; 4 – CIS 50 12.7 mm machine-guns.
Decoys: 2 – GEC Marine Shield III sextuple fixed chaff launchers.

RADARS

Surface search and fire control – Elta EL/M-2228(X)
Navigation – Kelvin Hughes 1007.
Sonars: Thomson Sintra TSM 2362 Gudgeon hull-mounted, active attack. Towed array in Brave.

KEY RECOGNITION FEATURES

- High bow with sloping forecastle, with low flush-sided superstructure, low freeboard afterdeck.
- 3 in gun mounting ('A' position).
- Enclosed mainmast amidships with tall pole mast atop.
- Prominent white radome at aft end of superstructure.
- Simbad twin launcher right aft.
Note: Simbad SAM launcher replaced by towed array in *Brave*. Other craft may be similarly converted.
Note 2: *Sovereignty* has deck crane to facilitate special forces operations.
Note 3: Fearless has new EW radome on mainmast.

Serviola

VIGÍA

Çamil Busquests I Vilanova

Country: SPAIN
Country of origin: SPAIN
Ship type: PATROL FORCES
Class: SERVIOLA (OPV)
Active: 4
Name (Pennant Number): SERVIOLA (P 71),
CENTINELA (P 72), VIGIA (P 73), ATALAYA (P 74)

SPECIFICATION

Displacement, full load, tons: 1,147.
Length, feet (metres): 225.4 (68.7)
Beam, feet (metres): 34 (10.4)
Draught, feet (metres): 11 (3.4)
Speed, knots: 19.
Range, miles: 8,000 at 12 kts.

ARMAMENT

Guns: 1 - US 3 in (76 mm)/50 Mk 27; 2 - 12.7
machine-guns.

RADARS

Surface search - Racal Decca 2459.
Navigation - Racal Decca ARPA 2690 BT.

AIR SUPPORT

Helicopters: Platform for 1 Agusta AB-212,
(surface search).

KEY RECOGNITION FEATURES

- High bow with break in profile forward of superstructure.
- High central freeboard adjacent to superstructure.
- 3 in gun mounting ('B' position).
- Tall, angular central superstructure.
- High, wide bridge set well aft from forward end of superstructure.
- Lattice mainmast atop after end of bridge.
- Large angular funnel at after end of superstructure, with wedge shaped, black smoke deflector atop.
- Large flight deck aft of superstructure.

Note: Mexico operates 6 'Uribe' class PGs, ordered to a 'Halcón' design with twin funnels and lengthy open quarterdeck beneath a helicopter deck – similar ships to the 5 operated by the Argentine Prefectura Naval. Mexico also operates 4 larger 'Holzinger' class which is a modified Halcón design.

Note 2: Other 'Serviola' equipment fits could include four Harpoon SSM, Meroka CIWS, Sea Sparrow SAM or a Bofors 375 mm ASW rocket launcher.

Kaparen

KAPAREN

Country: SWEDEN
Country of origin: NORWAY
Ship type: PATROL FORCES
Class: KAPAREN (PCFG)
Active: 8
Name (Pennant Number): KAPAREN (P 159),
VÄKTAREN (P 160), SNAPPHANEN (P 161),
SPEJAREN (P 162), STYRBJÖRN (P 163),
STARKODDER (P 164), TORDÖN (P 165), TIRFING (P
166)

SPECIFICATION

Displacement, full load, tons: 170.
Length, feet (metres): 120 (36.6).
Beam, feet (metres): 20.7 (6.3).]
Draught, feet (metres): 5.6 (1.7).
Speed, knots: 36.

ARMAMENT

Missiles: SSM – 6 – Kongsberg Penguin Mk 2.
Guns: 1 – Bofors 57 mm/70 Mk 1. 57 mm
    illuminant launchers on either side of
    mounting.
Torpedoes: 4 – 15.75 in (400 mm). Swedish
    Ordnance Type 43/45 ASW.
A/S mortars: 4 – Saab Elma 9-tube launchers.
Depth charges: 2 racks.
Mines: 24.

RADARS

Surface search - Skanter 16 in Mk 009.
Fire control - Philips 9LV 200 Mk 2.
Sonars: Simrad SA 950 (P 159-166) or SQ 3D/SF;
    hull-mounted. Simrad ST 570 VDS.

KEY RECOGNITION FEATURES

- Long forecastle with 57 mm/70 gun
  mounting ('A' position).
- Low profile, rounded midships
  superstructure.
- Short, tripod mainmast aft of bridge.
- Surface search radar aerial atop mainmast.
- 9LV 200 fire control radar aerial atop after
  end of bridge.
- Forward pointing SSM launchers on
  afterdeck, angled outboard, port and
  starboard.
- Short lattice aftermast with pole mast atop.
- Mine rails running from after end of bridge
  superstructure with an extension over the
  stern. (Cannot be used with missiles in place.)
Note: Norwegian 'Hauk' class similar. See
    separate entry.

Norrköping

NORRKÖPING

Country: SWEDEN
Country of origin: SWEDEN
Ship type: PATROL FORCES
Class: NORRKÖPING (PCFG)
Active: 6
Name (Pennant Number): NORRKÖPING (R 131),
NYNÄSHAMN (R 132), PITEÅ (R 138), LULEÅ (R
139), HALMSTAD (R 140), YSTAD (R 142)

SPECIFICATION

Displacement, full load, tons: 230.
Length, feet (metres): 143 (43.6).
Beam, feet (metres): 23.3 (7.1).
Draught, feet (metres): 7.4 (2.4).
Speed, knots: 40.5.
Range, miles: 500 at 40 kts.

ARMAMENT

Missiles: SSM – 8 - Saab RBS 15.
Guns: 1 - Bofors 57 mm/70 Mk 1, launchers for
57 mm illuminants on side of mounting.
Torpedoes: 6 - 21 in (533 mm) tubes (2-6 can be
fitted at the expense of missile armament);
Swedish Ordnance Type 613.
Mines: Minelaying capability.
Decoys: 2 Philips Philax fixed chaff/IR launchers.

RADARS

Air/surface search - Ericsson Sea Giraffe 50HC.
Fire control - Philips 9LV 200 Mk 1.

KEY RECOGNITION FEATURES

- Exceptionally long forecastle with 57
  mm/70 gun mounting just aft of midway
  between bows and bridge.
- Narrow superstructure centred well aft of
  midships.
- Complex lattice mainmast atop mid-
  superstructure.
- Sea Giraffe air/surface search radar aerial
  atop mainmast.
- 9LV 200 fire control radar aerial atop
  bridge roof.
- Single torpedo tubes outboard of gun
  mounting, port and starboard.
- Afterdeck can be fitted with any one of
  several combinations of torpedo tubes and
  SSM launchers.
- Note: Similar to the original 'Spica' class from
  which they were developed. See separate
  entry.

Jin Chiang

Country: TAIWAN
Country of origin: TAIWAN
Ship type: PATROL FORCES
Class: JIN CHIANG (PGG)
Active: 12
Planned: 12
Name (Pennant Number): JIN CHIANG (603), TAN CHIANG (605), HSIN CHIANG (606), FENG CHIANGE (607) (FONG CHIANG (608), TSENG CHIANG (609), JING CHIANG (610), HSIAN CHIANG (611), TSI CHIANG (612) PO CHIANG (614), CHAN CHIANG (615) CHU CHIANG (617).

SPECIFICATION

Displacement, full load, tons: 680.
Length, feet (metres): 201.4 (61.4).
Beam, feet (metres): 31.2 (9.5).
Draught, feet (metres): 9.5 (2.9).
Speed, knots: 25.
Range, miles: 4,150 at 15 kts.

ARMAMENT

Missiles: 4 – Hsiung Feng 1.
Guns: 1 – Bofors 40 mm/70; 1 – CS 20 mm Type 75. 2 – 12.7 mm machine-guns.
Depth charges: 2 racks.
Mines: 2 rails for Mk 6.

RADARS

Air/Surface search – Marconi LN66
Navigation – Racal Decca Bridgemaster.
Fire control – Hughes HR-76C5.
Sonars: Simrad, search/attack.

KEY RECOGNITION FEATURES

- High bows, angled forecastle, with superstructure flush with ship's side; low freeboard afterdeck.
- 40 mm/70 gun mounting forward of bridge.
- Prominent, angular superstructure, midships, with large square funnel aft.
- Substantial lattice mainmast, topped by pole mast, aft of bridge, supporting air/surface search and navigation radar aerials.
- Note: Looks like enlarged version of Taiwanese *Sui Chiang* class.

Castle

DUMBARTON CASTLE

Country: UNITED KINGDOM
Country of origin: UNITED KINGDOM
Ship type: PATROL FORCES
Class: CASTLE (OPV)
Active: 2
Name (Pennant Number): LEEDS CASTLE (P 258), DUMBARTON CASTLE (P 265)

SPECIFICATION
Displacement, full load, tons: 1,427.
Length, feet (metres): 265.7 (81).
Beam, feet (metres): 37.7 (11.5).
Draught, feet (metres): 11.8 (3.6).
Speed, knots: 19.5.
Range, miles: 10,000 at 12 kts.

ARMAMENT
Guns: 1 - DES/MSI DS 30B 30 mm/75.
Decoys: 2 or 4 - Plessey Shield 102 mm 6-tube chaff launchers.

RADARS
Surface search - Plessey Type 944.
Navigation - Kelvin Hughes Type 1006.

AIR SUPPORT
Helicopters: Platform for operating Westland Sea King or Lynx.

KEY RECOGNITION FEATURES
- High bow, long sweeping forecastle, high freeboard.
- 30 mm/75 gun mounting forward of bridge ('B' position).
- Prominent, angular midships superstructure, lower at forward end.
- High bridge set well aft from bows.
- Substantial enclosed mainmast, topped by pole mast, amidships supporting surface search and navigation radar aerials.
- Large flight deck aft.

Island

NELSON

Country: UNITED KINGDOM, TRINIDAD & TOBAGO

Country of origin: UNITED KINGDOM

Ship type: PATROL FORCES

Class: ISLAND (OPV)

Active: 3 UK, 1 Trinidad and Tobago.

UNITED KINGDOM - Name (Pennant Number):
ANGLESEY (P 277), GUERNSEY (P 297),
LINDISFARNE (P 300)

TRINIDAD & TOBAGO - Name (Pennant
Number): NELSON (ex-*Orkney*) (CG 20, ex-P 299).

SPECIFICATION

Displacement, full load, tons: 1,260.

Length, feet (metres): 195.3 (59.5) oa.

Beam, feet (metres): 36 (11).

Draught, feet (metres): 15 (4.5).

Speed, knots: 16.5.

Range, miles: 7,000 at 12 kts.

ARMAMENT

Guns: 1 – BMARC/Oerlikon 20 mm GAM-B01 or
DES/MSI DS 30B 30 mm/75 Mk 1. 2 – 7.62 mm
machine-guns can be fitted in all ships.

RADARS

Navigation - Kelvin Hughes Type 1006.

KEY RECOGNITION FEATURES

- High bow profile with break down to lower
  level forward of bridge, high freeboard.
- Tall, substantial superstructure just aft of
  midships.
- 40 mm gun mounting on unusual raised
  barbette at after end of forecastle ('B'
  mounting position).
- Short, tripod mainmast atop mid-
  superstructure.
- Prominent funnel, with sloping after end,
  atop superstructure aft of mainmast.
- 2 small crane jibs at after end of
  superstructure, port and starboard.

Note: Also operated by Bangladesh as a
training ship *Shaheed Ruhul Amin*, (ex-
Jersey), A 511, (ex-P 295).

Note 2: Scottish Fisheries Protection Agency
operates the unarmed OPV *Westra*, similar
to 'Island' class.

Cyclone

Country: UNITED STATES OF AMERICA

Country of origin: USA

Ship type: PATROL FORCES

Class: CYCLONE (PCF)

Active: 13

Name (Pennant Number): TEMPEST (PC 2), HURRICANE (PC 3), MONSOON (PC 4), TYPHOON (PC 5), SIROCCO (PC 6), SQUALL (PC 7), ZEPHYR (PC 8), CHINOOK (PC 9), FIREBOLT (PC 10), WHIRLWIND (PC 11), THUNDERBOLT (PC 12), SHAMAL (PC 13) TORNADO (PC 14)

SPECIFICATION

Displacement, full load, tons: 334, (360, PC 2, 8, 13, 14).

Length, feet (metres): 170.3 (51.9). (179,(54.6) PC 2, 8, 13, 14).

Beam, feet (metres): 25.9 (7.9).

Draught, feet (metres): 7.9 (2.4)

Speed, knots: 35.

Range, miles: 2 500 at 12 kts.

ARMAMENT

Missiles: SAM - 1 sextuple Stinger mounting

Guns: 1 - Bushmaster 25 mm Mk 38; 1 - Bushmaster 25 mm/87 Mk 96 (aft); 4 - 12.7 mm machine-guns; 2 - 40 mm Mk 19 grenade launchers (interchangeable with MGs).

Decoys: 2 - Mk 52 sextuple chaff launchers and/or Wallop Super Barricade Mk 3.

RADARS

Surface search - 2 Sperry RASCAR.

Navigation - Raytheon SPS-64(V)9.

Sonars: Wesmar; hull-mounted.

KEY RECOGNITION FEATURES

- Short forecastle with sloping forward edge to main superstructure.
- 25 mm gun mounting ('A' position).
- Raised bridge, with all round windows, set well aft from bows.
- Continuous maindeck from stem to stern.
- Superstructure built in three distinct sections with catwalks between the tops of each section.
- Large lattice mainmast at after end of bridge supporting RASCAR surface search radar aerial atop.
- 25 mm gun mounting atop after section of superstructure ('X' position).

Note: The design is based on the Vosper Thornycroft 'Ramadan' class, modified to meet US Navy requirements, with one inch thick armour on the superstructure.

Note 2: *Cyclone*, first of class, transferred to US Coast Guard in 2000.

CHINOOK

AMPHIBIOUS FORCES

Polnochny

Country: ALGERIA, AZERBAIJAN, BULGARIA,
EGYPT, INDIA, LIBYA, RUSSIA, SYRIA, UKRAINE,
VIETNAM

Country of origin: RUSSIA

Ship type: AMPHIBIOUS FORCES

Class: POLNOCHNY GROUP A (TYPE 770) (LSM)

Active: 2 Bulgaria, 3 Egypt, 1 Vietnam

BULGARIA - Name (Pennant Number): SIRIUS
(ex-*Ivan Zagubanski*) (701), ANTARES (702).

EGYPT - Name (Pennant Number): 301, 303, 305.

VIETNAM - Name (Pennant Number): HQ 512

Class: POLNOCHNY GROUP B (TYPE 771) (LSM)

Active: 1 Algeria, 2 Azerbaijan, 1 Russia, 3 Syria,
2 Vietnam

ALGERIA - Name (Pennant Number): 471.

AZERBAIJAN - Name (Pennant Number):
(None available).

RUSSIA - Name (Pennant Number):
(None available).

SYRIA - Name (Pennant Number): 1-114, 2-114,
3-114.

VIETNAM - Name (Pennant Number): HQ 511,
HQ 513.

Class: POLNOCHNY GROUP C (TYPE 773) (LSM)

Active: 1 India, 1 Ukraine

INDIA - Name (Pennant Number):
SHARBAH (L 17),

UKRAINE - Name (Pennnan Number):
KIROVOGRA (ex-SOK 137) U 401.

Class: POLNOCHNY GROUP D (TYPE 773U) (LSM)

Active: 4 India, 1 + 2 reserve, Libya.

INDIA - Name (Pennant Number): CHEETAH (L 18),
MAHISH (L 19), GULDAR (L 21), KUMBHIR (L 22).

LIBYA - Name (Pennant Number): IBN AL
HADRAMI (112), IBN UMAYAA (116), IBN AL FARAT
(118).

SPECIFICATION

Displacement, full load, tons: 800, (Group A).
834, (Group B). 1,150, (Group C). 1,305 (Group
D).

Length, feet (metres): 239.5 (73), (A). 246.1, (75),
(B). 266.7 (81.3), (C/D). 275.3 (83.9) Libya D).

Beam, feet (metres): 27.9 (8.5), (A). 31.5 (9.6),
(B). 31.8 (9.7), (C/D).

Draught, feet (metres): 5.8 (1.8), (A). 7.5 (2.3), (B).
7.9 (2.4), (C/D).

Speed, knots: 19, (A); 18, (B/C).

Range, miles: 1,000 at 18 kts. (Groups A and B);
2,000 at 12 kts. (Group C).

ARMAMENT

Missiles: SAM - 4 SA-N-5 Grail quad launchers (B
and C, Russia and Ukraine only).

Guns: 30 mm/65 (twin), (A). 2 or 4 30 mm (1 or
2 twin) (B). 30 mm/65 (2 twin) (C). 2 140 mm
18-barrel rocket launchers (A, B and C).

Mines: Capacity to lay 100, (Libya 'D' only).

RADARS

Surface search - Spin Trough. (Bulgaria 'A', Russia,
Syria, Vietnam 'B', Ukraine 'C'); Decca, (Egypt
'A'). Radwar SRN-745, (Libya, 'D').

Navigation – Don 2 (B) or Don 2 or Krivach (SRN
745), (India 'C').

Fire control - Drum Tilt. (Not Bulgaria).

AIR SUPPORT

Helicopters: Platform only in Group D.

POLNOCHNY

KEY RECOGNITION FEATURES

- This class varies in appearance to quite a large degree between groups and countries. Below are general common features.
- High bow with long deck aft to superstructure well aft of midships.
- Squared profile lower superstructure with bridge superstructure atop.
- Mainmast (lattice or tripod) at central superstructure.
- Low profile funnel aft of mainmast.
- Step down at after end of superstructure to short afterdeck.
- Have bow ramps only.
- Group D has a helicopter landing platform amidships.

Note: Poland operates 1 modified Polnochny C, *Grunwald* (811), converted into an amphibious command vessel.

Newport

Country: AUSTRALIA, BRAZIL, CHILE, MALAYSIA, MOROCCO, SPAIN, TAIWAN, UNITED STATES OF AMERICA

Country of origin: USA

Ship type: AMPHIBIOUS FORCES

Class: NEWPORT CLASS (LPA/LST)

Active: 2 Australia, 1 Brazil, 1 Chile, 1 Malaysia, 1 Morocco, 2 Spain, 2 Taiwan, 1 USA

In reserve: 4 USA

Planned: 1 Taiwan

AUSTRALIA - Name (Pennant Number): KANIMBLA (ex-*Saginaw*) (L 51, ex-LST 1188), MANOORA (ex-*Fairfax County*) (L 52, ex-LST 1193).

BRAZIL - Name (Pennant Number): MATTOSO MAIA (ex-*Cayuga*) (G 28, ex-LST 1186).

CHILE - Name (Pennant Number): VALDIVIA (ex-*San Bernardino*) (93 (ex-LST 1189)

MALAYSIA - Name (Pennant Number): SRI INDERAPURA (ex-*Spartanburg County*) (1505, ex-LST 1192).

MOROCCO - Name (Pennant Number): SIDI MOHAMMED BEN ABDALLAH (ex-*Bristol County*) (407, ex-LST 1198).

SPAIN - Name (Pennant Number): HERNÁN CORTÉS (ex-*Barnstaple County*) (L 41, ex-LST 1197), PIZARRO (ex-*Harlan County*) (L 42, ex-LST 1196).

TAIWAN - Name (Pennant Number): CHUNG HO (ex-*Manitowic*) (232, ex-LST 1180), CHUNG PING (ex-*Sumter*) (233, ex-LST 1181), ––– (ex-*Schenectady*) (––, ex-LST 1185).

USA - Name (Pennant Number): FREDERICK (LST 1184).

SPECIFICATION

Displacement, full load, tons: 8,450. 8,750, (Australia). 8,550, (Spain).

Length, feet (metres): 552.3 (168.2).

Beam, feet (metres): 69.5 (21.2).

Draught, feet (metres): 17.5 (5.3).

Speed, knots: 20.

Range, miles: 14,000 at 15 kts. (Australia) 2,500 at 14 kts.

ARMAMENT

Guns: 1 - General Electric/General Dynamics 20mm Vulcan Phalanx Mk 15 can be fitted in Australian hulls. 2 - 12.7 machine-guns. 1 - Vulcan Phalanx CIWS (remainder) and 8 - 12.7 mm machine-guns, (Brazil). Additionally, 2 - Oerlikon 20mm/85 and 4 - 12.7 mm machine-guns, (Spain).

Decoys: 2 - SRBOC Mk 36 chaff/IR launchers. (Australia).

RADARS

Surface search - Kelvin Hughes 1007. (Australia). Raytheon SPS-10F, (Brazil, Spain). Raytheon SPS-67 (Chile, Malaysia, Morocco, Taiwan, USA).

Navigation - Kelvin Hughes. (Australia). Raytheon SPS-64(V)6 and Furuno FR 2120, (Brazil). Marconi LN66, (Chile, Malaysia, Morocco, Spain, Taiwan, USA).

AIR SUPPORT

Helicopters: 4 - Army Black Hawk or 3 Sea Kings or 1 Chinook, (Australia). Platform only, remainder.

CHUNG HO

KEY RECOGNITION FEATURES

- Distinctive twin derrick arms supporting bow ramp. (Absent from Australian hulls).
- Australian ships have high forecastle dropping to long flight deck forward of bridge superstructure, with flight deck right aft. Superstructure is slab-sided.
- Vulcan Phalanx atop bridge in other hulls.
- Long forecastle with high, distinctive superstructure set well aft
- High freeboard.
- Tall pole mainmast atop main superstructure supporting air/surface search and surface search radar aerials.
- Short lattice platform forward of tall rounded funnel
- Large crane derrick aft of funnel.

Note: Substantial difference in appearance of Australian hulls after conversion.

Ceará

RIO DE JANEIRO

Country: BRAZIL
Country of origin: USA
Ship type: AMPHIBIOUS FORCES
Class: CEARÁ (THOMASTON) (LSD)
Active: 2
Name (Pennant Number): CEARÁ (ex-*Hermitage*) (G 30,ex-LSD 34), RIO DE JANEIRO (ex-*Alamo*) (G 31,ex-LSD 33).

SPECIFICATION

Displacement, full load, tons: 12,150.
Length, feet (metres): 510 (155.5).
Beam, feet (metres): 84 (25.6).
Draught, feet (metres): 19 (5.8).
Speed, knots: 22.5.
Range, miles: 10,000 at 18 kts.

ARMAMENT

Guns: 6 – USN 3 in (76 mm)/50 (3 twin) Mk. 33.

RADARS

Surface search – Raytheon SPS-10FF
Navigation - Raytheon CRP 3100.

AIR SUPPORT

Helicopters: Platform for Super Puma.

KEY RECOGNITION FEATURES

- Long forecastle, stepped up to high, distinctive superstructure. Tall communications mast half way on forecastle.
- High freeboard. Superstructure flush with ship's sides.
- Tall pole mainmast atop main superstructure supporting air/surface search and surface search radar aerials with full pole mast at aft end.
- Two large 50-ton capacity crane derricks aft of midships.
- Tall thin rounded funnels.

Note: Well dock 391 x 48 (119.2 x 14.6 m).

Foudre

FOUDRE

Country: FRANCE
Country of origin: FRANCE
Ship type: AMPHIBIOUS FORCES
Class: FOUDRE (TYPE TCD 90/LSD)
Active: 2
Name (Pennant Number): FOUDRE (L 9011), SIROCO (L 9012)

SPECIFICATION

Displacement, full load, tons: 12,400. (17,200 flooded).
Length, feet (metres): 551 (168).
Beam, feet (metres): 77.1 (23.5).
Draught, feet (metres): 17 (5.2), (30.2 (9.2) flooded).
Speed, knots: 21.
Range, miles: 11,000 at 15 kts.

ARMAMENT

Missiles: SAM - 2 - Matra Simbad twin launchers, Mistral.
Guns: 1 - Bofors 40 mm/60 (Foudre); 2 - Giat 20F2 20 mm; 3 - Breda/Mauser 30 mm/70 (Siroco)

RADARS

Air/surface search - Thomson-CSF DRBV 21A Mars.
Surface search - Racal Decca 2459.
Navigation - 2 - Racal Decca RM 1229.

AIR SUPPORT

Helicopters: 4 - Aerospatiale AS 332F Super Puma or 2 Aerospatiale SA 321G Super Frelon.

KEY RECOGNITION FEATURES

- Short forecastle with high, distinctive superstructure set well forward.
- High freeboard.
- 40 mm/60 gun mounting immediately forward of bridge (Foudre) or 30 mm/70 (Siroco).
- Large complex lattice mainmast atop main superstructure supporting air/surface search and surface search radar aerials.
- 2 Syracuse SATCOM domes, on pedestals, on after outboard edges of superstructure.
- 2 Simbad/Mistral SAM launchers at base of mainmast.
- Long flight deck aft of superstructure.
- Large crane derrick at after end of well deck.
- 2 - 20 mm gun mountings, port and starboard, aft of crane.
Note: Designed to take a mechanised regiment of the Rapid Action Force and act as a logistic support ship.
Note 2: Well dock 122 x 14.2 x 7.7 m, can dock a 400 ton ship.
Note 3: 30 mm guns to replace existing 40 mm and 20 mm in Foudre.

Mistral

MISTRAL (Computer generated image)

Country: FRANCE
Country of origin: FRANCE
Ship type: AMPHIBIOUS FORCES
Class: MISTRAL (LHD/NTCD)
Active: 0
Building: 2
Name (Pennant Number): MISTRAL (L 9013), TONNERRE (L 9014).

SPECIFICATION
Displacement, full load, tons: 20,000.
Length, feet (metres): 653 (199).
Beam, feet (metres): 105 (32).
Draught, feet (metres): 26 (8).
Speed, knots: 19.
Range, miles: 11,000 at 15 kts.

ARMAMENT
Missiles: SAM - 2 - Matra Simbad sextuple launchers; Mistral.
Guns: 2 - 30 mm; 4 - 12.7 mm machine-guns.

RADARS
Air/surface search - Thomson- CSF MMR 3D
Navigation –2 Racal Decca.

AIR SUPPORT
Helicopters: 16-NH 90 or Eurocopter Cougar tactical trooplift.

KEY RECOGNITION FEATURES
- Blunt bows, with continuous deck from stem to stern..
- High distinctive bridge structure offset on starboard side of ship, aft of midships.
- Two large enclosed masts atop superstructure, with angled funnel integral part of aft mast.
- Flight deck length of ship.
- 2 medium-sized crane derricks aft at well deck.
Note: Two LCACs or four of a new class of LCM can be carried.

Ouragan

OURAGAN

Country: FRANCE
Country of origin: FRANCE
Ship type: AMPHIBIOUS FORCES
Class: OURAGAN (TCD/LSD)
Active: 2
Name (Pennant Number): OURAGAN (L 9021), ORAGE (L 9022)

AIR SUPPORT

Helicopters: 4 - Aerospatiale SA 321G Super Frelon or Super Pumas or 10 - Aerospatiale SA 319B Alouette III.

SPECIFICATION

Displacement, full load, tons: 8.500. (15.000. flooded).
Length, feet (metres): 488.9 (149).
Beam, feet (metres): 75.4 (23).
Draught, feet (metres): 17.7 (5.4) (28.5 (8.7),flooded).
Speed, knots: 17.
Range, miles: 9,000 at 15 kts.

ARMAMENT

Missiles: SAM - 2 - Matra Simbad twin launchers; Mistral.
Guns: 2 - 4.7 in (120 mm) mortars; 2 - Bofors 40 mm/60; 2 - Breda/Mauser 30 mm/70; 4 - 12.7 mm machine-guns.

RADARS

Air/surface search - Thomson-CSF DRBV 51A.
Navigation - 2 - Racal Decca 1226.

KEY RECOGNITION FEATURES

- Very high freeboard section forward of midships.
- High distinctive bridge structure offset on starboard side of ship, well forward of midships.
- Large pole mainmast supporting radar aerials atop bridge roof.
- Flight deck aft of bridge.
- 2 medium-sized crane derricks aft at well deck.
- Small, black-capped funnel adjacent forward crane.

Note: Three LCVPs can be carried.
Note 2: Typical loads: 18 Super Frelon or 80 Alouette III helicopters or 120 AMX 13 tanks or 84 DUKWs or 340 vehicles or 12 - 50 ton barges. 400 ton ship can be docked.

Jason

CHIOS

Country: GREECE
Country of origin: Greece
Ship type: AMPHIBIOUS FORCES
Class: JASON (LST)
Active: 5
Name (Pennant Number): CHIOS (L 173), SAMOS (L 174), LESBOS (L 176), IKARIA (L 175), RODOS (L 177)

SPECIFICATION

Displacement, full load, tons: 4,400.
Length, feet (metres): 380.5 (116).
Beam, feet (metres): 50.2 (15.3).
Draught, feet (metres): 11.3 (3.4).
Speed, knots: 16.

ARMAMENT

Guns: 1 - OTO MELARA 76 mm/62 Mod 9 Compact; 2 - Breda 40 mm/70 (2 twin) Compact. 4 - Rheinmetall 20 mm (2 twin).

RADARS

Surface search – Thomson-CSF Triton.
Navigation - Kelvin Hughes Type 1007
Fire control - Thomson-CSF Pollux.

AIR SUPPORT

Helicopters: Platform for 1 medium.

KEY RECOGNITION FEATURES

- High forecastle with 76 mm/62 gun mounting at mid-point on raised platform
- Break, down from forecastle, to extensive well deck.
- High superstructure aft of well deck.
- Large tripod mainmast atop bridge roof supporting radar aerials.
- Distinctive twin funnels, side-by-side, at after end of superstructure. Funnels of square section, black-capped, with sloping tops.
- Large raised helicopter platform aft with stern overhang.

Note: Bow and stern ramps, drive-through design.

Frosch I

TELUK BERAU

Country: INDONESIA
Country of origin: GERMANY
Ship type: AMPHIBIOUS FORCES
Class: FROSCH I (TYPE 108) (LSM)
Active: 12
Name (Pennant Number): TELUK GILIMANUK (ex-*Hoyerswerda*) (531, ex-611), TELUK CELUKAN BAWANG (ex-*Hagenow*) (532 ex-632), TELUK CENDRAWASIH (ex-*Frankfurt/Oder*) (533 ex-613), TELUK BERAU (ex-*Eberswalde-Finow*) (534 ex-634), TELUK PELENG (ex-*Lübben*) (535 ex-631), TELUK SIBOLGA (ex-*Schwerin*) (536 ex-612), TELUK MANADO (ex-*Neubrandenburg*) (537 ex-633), TELUK HADING (ex-*Cottbus*) (538 ex-614), TELUK PARIGI (ex-*Anklam*) (539 ex-635), TELUK LAMPUNG (ex-*Schwedt*) (540 ex-636), TELUK JAKARTA (ex-*Eisenhüttenstadt*) (541 ex-615), TELUK SANGKULIRANG (ex-*Grimmen*) (542 ex-616)

SPECIFICATION
Displacement full load, tons: 1,950.
Length, feet (metres): 321.5 (98).
Beam, feet (metres): 36.4 (11.1).
Draught, feet (metres): 9.2 (2.8).
Speed, knots: 18.

ARMAMENT
Guns: 1 – 40 mm/60; 4 - 37mm (2 twin), 4 – 25 mm (2 twin).

Mines: Can lay 40 mines through stern doors.
Decoys: 2 – PK 16 chaff launchers.

RADARS
Air/surface search - Strut Curve.
Navigation - TSR 333.

KEY RECOGNITION FEATURES

- Wide bow ramp at forward end of forecastle with very distinctive wide, flat-topped bows.
- Crane at mid-foredeck.
- Large, stepped, slab-sided superstructure well aft of midships giving very high freeboard.
- Distinctive vertical-ribbed appearance to main superstructure.
- Large double-pole mainmast atop mid-superstructure supporting air/surface search and navigation radar aerials.

Note: Former East German Navy ships transferred, unarmed, from Germany in August 1993.

Note 2: Two Frosch II class (*Teluk Cirebon*, ex-*Nordperd*, and *Teluk Sabang*, ex-*Südperd*, serve with the Indonesian Navy as support ships, (AK/AR).

San Giorgio

SAN GIUSTO

Country: ITALY

Country of origin: ITALY

Ship type: AMPHIBIOUS FORCES

Class: SAN GIORGIO (LPDs)

Active: 3

Name (Pennant Number): SAN GIORGIO (L 9892), SAN MARCO (L 9893), SAN GIUSTO (L 9894)

SPECIFICATION

Displacement full load, tons: 7,665. (7,950, *San Giusto*).

Length, feet (metres): 437.2 (133.3). (449.5 (137), *San Giusto*).

Beam, feet (metres): 67.3 (20.5).

Draught, feet (metres): 17.4 (5.3).

Flight deck, feet (metres): 328.1 x 67.3 (100 x 20.5)

Speed, knots: 21.

Range, miles: 7,500 at 16 kts.

ARMAMENT

Guns: 1 - OTO MELARA 3 in (76 mm)/62, (Compact *San Giusto*); 2 - Oerlikon 20 mm or 25 mm. 2 - 12.7 mm machine-guns.

RADARS

Surface search - SMA SPS-702.

Navigation - SMA SPN-748.

Fire control - Selenia SPG-70 (RTN 10X).

AIR SUPPORT

Helicopters: 3 - Agusta-Sikorsky SH-3D Sea King or EH 101 Merlin, or 5 - Agusta-Bell AB 212.

KEY RECOGNITION FEATURES

- Short forecastle with break up to aircraft carrier type flight deck, which continues to stern.
- Clean profile, high freeboard.
- 3 in gun mounting ('B' position).
- High, angular, square profile island superstructure sited starboard side, midships.
- Pole mainmast atop central island superstructure.
- 3 LCVPs carried in davits, 2 port side opposite island superstructure, 3rd starboard side forward of island superstructure.
- Small, square profile, raked funnel atop island superstructure.

Note: Bow ramp (except for amphibious landings. Stern docking well 20.5 x 7 m. Fitted with a 30 ton lift and 2 40 ton travelling cranes for LCMs.

Note 2: *San Giusto* displaces 285 tons heavier, is of similar design except for a slightly longer island and different LCVP davit arrangement. Also no bow doors and therefore no beaching capability.

Osumi

OSUMI

Country: JAPAN
Country of origin: JAPAN
Ship type: AMPHIBIOUS FORCES
Class: OSUMI (LPD/LST)
Active: 2
Building: 1
Name (Pennant Number): OSUMI (LST 4001), SHIMOKITA (LST 4002), KUNISAKI (LST 4003).

SPECIFICATION

Displacement, standard, tons: 8,900.
Length, feet (metres): 584 (178).
Beam, feet (metres): 84.6 (25.8).
Draught, feet (metres): 19.7 (6).
Flight deck, feet (metres): 426.5 x 75.5 (130 x 23).
Speed, knots: 22.

ARMAMENT

Guns: 2 - GE/GD Vulcan Phalanx Mk 15 CIWS.

RADARS

Air search – Mitsubishi OPS-14C.
Surface search – JRC OPS-28D
Navigation – JRC OPS-20.

AIR SUPPORT

Helicopters: Platform for 2 Kawasaki/Boeing CH-47J Chinook.

KEY RECOGNITION FEATURES

- Short forecastle with sharp break up to aircraft carrier style flight deck, continuous to stern.
- Angular island sited starboard side, amidships.
- Enclosed pyramid mainmast with OPS-14C air search radar on projecting gantry forward.
- Square black funnel at aft end of superstructure with projecting exhausts and pole aerials.
- Large crane immediately aft of funnel.
- Vulcan Phalanx CIWS on platforms forward and aft of superstructure.

Note: Through deck and stern docking. Military lift – 330 troops; 2 LCAC; 10 Type 90 tanks or 1,400 tons cargo.

Rotterdam/Galicia

ROTTERDAM

Country: NETHERLANDS, SPAIN

Country of origin: NETHERLANDS

Ship type: AMPHIBIOUS FORCES

Class: ROTTERDAM/GALICIA (LPD/ATS)

Active: 1 Netherlands, 2 Spain

Planned: 1

NETHERLANDS - Name (Pennant Number):
ROTTERDAM (L 800) JOHAN DE ZWITT (-)

SPAIN - Name (Pennant Number): GALICIA
(L 51), CASTILLA (L 52)

SPECIFICATION

Displacement, full load, tons: 12,750,
Netherlands. 16,500 (Netherland LPD2)13,815,
Spain.

Length, feet (metres): 544.6 (166), Netherlands.
524.9 (160), Spain.

Beam, feet (metres): 82 (25), 87 (26.5) Netherlands
LPD2, 580.9 (177) Netherlands LPD2.

Draught, feet (metres): 19.3 (5.9).

Flight deck, feet (metres): 183.7 x 82 (56 x 25),
Netherlands. 196.9 x 82 (60 x 25), Spain.

Speed, knots: 19.

Range, miles: 6,000 at 12 kts.

ARMAMENT

Guns: 2 - Signaal Goalkeeper 30 mm CIWS.
4 - Oerlikon 20 mm, Netherlands. 1 Bazán
20mm/120 12-barrel Meroka; 4 - Oerlikon
20mm, Spain.

Decoys: 4 - SRBOC chaff launchers.

RADARS

Air/surface search - Signaal DA08, Netherlands.
Surface search -Signaal Scout/Kelvin Hughes
ARPA.

Navigation - 2 sets.

AIR SUPPORT

Helicopters: 6 - NH 90 or 4 EH 101 Merlin or Sea
King, Netherlands. 6 AB 212 or 4 SH-3D Sea
Kings, Spain.

KEY RECOGNITION FEATURES

- Very short forecastle with sharp break up
  to very tall superstructure, slab-sided and
  flush with ship's sides.
- Goalkeeper CIWS mounted on forecastle
  immediately forward of superstructure,
  (Netherlands only).
- Bridge projects forward of superstructure.
- Two thin rectangular funnels atop
  superstructure, port and starboard,
  midships, with pole aerials.
- Large enclosed mainmast above bridge,
  with air/surface search radar atop. Two
  spherical SATCOM domes outboard of this
  mast.
- Second enclosed mast between funnels.
- Second Goalkeeper CIWS mounted on aft
  edge of superstructure. In Spanish ships,
  20mm Meroka.
- Curved section "cut out" of aft
  superstructure to accommodate ship's
  boats and crane derrick.
- Long flight deck aft over dock.

Note: The UK is building two 16,160 ton LSLs,
Lyme Bay and *Largs Bay* based on the
Rotterdam design.

Ivan Rogov

MITROFAN MOSKALENKO

Country: RUSSIA
Country of origin: RUSSIA
Ship type: AMPHIBIOUS FORCES
Class: IVAN ROGOV (YEDNOROG) (TYPE 1174) (LPD)
Active: 1
Name (Pennant Number): MITROFAN MOSKALENKO

SPECIFICATION

Displacement, full load, tons: 14,060.
Length, feet (metres): 516.7 (157.5).
Beam, feet (metres): 80.2 (24.3)
Draught, feet (metres): 21.2 (6.5). (27.8 (8.5), flooded).
Speed, knots: 19.
Range, miles: 7,500 at 14 kts.

ARMAMENT

Missiles: SAM - SA-N-4 Gecko twin launcher. 2 - SA-N-5 Grail quad launchers.
Guns: 2 - 3 in (76mm)/60 (twin); 1 -122 mm BM-21 (naval) rocket launcher; 2 - 20-barrel rocket launchers; 4 - 30 mm/65 AK 630.
Decoys: 16 - PK 10 and 4 - PK 16 chaff launchers.

RADARS

Air/surface search –Top Plate A
Navigation - 2 Don Kay or 2 Palm Frond.
Fire control - Owl Screech; 2 Bass Tilt; Pop Group.
Sonars: Mouse Tail VDS.

AIR SUPPORT

Helicopters: 4 Kamov Ka-29 Helix B (assault).

KEY RECOGNITION FEATURES

- Raised forecastle with 3 in gun twin mounting ('A' position).
- Long tank deck aft to very large superstructure, well aft of midships.
- Curved leading edge to high main superstructure with large pyramid mainmast atop supporting Top Plate A air/surface search radar aerial
- Lattice mast atop after end of superstructure.
- 4 - 30 mm/65 gun mountings, 2 port, 2 starboard, outboard of mainmast and one deck down.
- Gecko SAM launcher at after end of superstructure.
- Short helicopter landing platform right aft with open quarterdeck below.
- Note: Has bow ramp with beaching capability leading from a tank deck. Stern doors open into a docking bay.
- Note 2: Helicopters can enter the hangar from both front and rear.
- Note 3: Two Pacific Fleet units paid off in 1996 and 1997. One may be transferred to Indonesia.

Ropucha

ROPUCHA II

Country: RUSSIA, UKRAINE

Country of origin: RUSSIA

Ship type: AMPHIBIOUS FORCES

Class: ROPUCHA I (TYPE 775), ROPUCHA II (TYPE 775M) (LST)

Active: 13 'Ropucha I', 3 'Ropucha II' – Russia. 1 'Ropucha I' - Ukraine

RUSSIA – Name (Pennant Number): Ropucha I – 012, 016, 027, 142, 156, 158, 102, 110, 125, 127, 055, 066, 070. Ropucha II – 130, 151, 077.

UKRAINE - Name (Pennant Number): KONSTANTIN OLSHANSKY (ex-BDK 56) (U 402).

SPECIFICATION

Displacement, full load, tons: 4,400.

Length, feet (metres): 369.1 (112.5). (370.7 (113), Ukraine).

Beam, feet (metres): 49.2 (15.9). (47.6 (14.5), Ukraine).

Draught, feet (metres): 12.1 (3.7). (11.5 (3.6), Ukraine).

Speed, knots: 17.5.

Range, miles: 6,000 at 12 kts.

ARMAMENT

Missiles: SAM - 4 - SA-N-5 Grail quad launchers (in at least two Russian ships and Ukraine unit).

Guns: 4 - 57 mm/80 (2 twin) (Ropucha I). 1 - 76 mm/60 (Ropucha II). 2 - 30 mm/65 AK 630 (Ropucha II). 2 - 122 mm BM-21 (naval) (in some). 2 - 20-barrel rocket launchers.

Mines: 92 contact type. (Russia and Yemen only).

RADARS

Air/surface search - Strut Curve (Ropucha I) or Cross Dome (Ropucha II).

Navigation - Don 2 or Kivach. (Nayada, Yemen unit).

Fire control - Muff Cob (Ropucha I). Bass Tilt (Ropucha II).

Sonars: Mouse Tail VDS can be carried in Russian ships.

KEY RECOGNITION FEATURES

- Unusual squared-off forward end to forecastle.
- 57 mm/80 (Ropucha I) or 76 mm/60 gun mounting (Ropucha II) at forward end of superstructure.
- Large superstructure centred aft of midships.
- Pole mast atop bridge roof.
- Large lattice mainmast atop mid-superstructure.
- Very wide square section funnels aft of mainmast.

Note: A 'roll-on-roll-off' design with a tank deck running the whole length of the ship.

Note 2: All have very minor differences in appearance. (See Guns and Missiles sections.)

Note 3: At least five Russian ships have rocket launchers at the after end of the forecastle.

Note 4: 1 Ropucha II has a masthead radar dome.

Note 5: Ropucha 139, in Yemen service, is an alongside hulk.

Endurance

ENDURANCE

Country: SINGAPORE
Country of origin: SINGAPORE
Ship type: AMPHIBIOUS FORCES
Class: ENDURANCE (LPD/LST)
Active: 4
Name (Pennant Number): ENDURANCE (L 207),
RESOLUTION (L 208), PERSISTENCE (L 209),
ENDEAVOUR (L 210)

SPECIFICATION

Displacement, full load, tons: 8,500.
Length, feet (metres): 462.6 (141).
Beam, feet (metres): 68.9 (21).
Draught, feet (metres): 16.4 (5).
Speed, knots: 15.
Range, miles: 10,400 at 12 kts.

ARMAMENT

Missiles: 2 – Matra Simbad twin launchers for
  Mistral.
Guns: 1 – OTOBreda 76 mm/62 Super Rapid. 5 –
  12.7 mm machine-guns.
Decoys: 2 – GEC Marine Shield III 102 mm
  sextuple fixed chaff launchers.

RADARS

Air/surface search –Ericsson.
Navigation – Kelvin Hughes Type 1007.

AIR SUPPORT

Helicopters: 2 Super Pumas.

KEY RECOGNITION FEATURES

- High forecastle with sharp down, forward
  of superstructure, continuous to very long
  flight deck, over short open quarterdeck.
- 76 mm gun on raised platform immediately
  forward of bridge.
- Thin angled funnels, port and starboard, at
  aft end of bridge, supporting catwalks.
- Fat pyramidal platform supporting radar
  aerial atop bridge.
- Tall pyramidal enclosed mast aft end of
  superstructure.
- Two large cranes immediately aft of
  funnels.
Note: Through deck and stern docking.
  Military lift – 350 troops; 18 tanks, 20
  vehicles, 4 LCVP.

Albion

ALBION (artist's impression)

Country: UNITED KINGDOM
Country of origin: UNITED KINGDOM
Ship type: AMPHIBIOUS FORCES
Class: ALBION (LPD)
Building: 2
Name (Pennant Number): ALBION (L 14), BULWARK (L 15).

SPECIFICATION

Displacement, full load, tons: 19,560.
Length, feet (metres): 577.4 (176).
Beam, feet (metres): 98.1 (29.9).
Draught, feet (metres): 22 (6.7).
Speed, knots: 20.
Range, miles: 8,000 at 15 kts.

ARMAMENT

Guns: 2 – 20 mm (twin). 2 Goalkeeper CIWS.
Decoys: 8 – Sea Gnat launchers and DLH offboard decoys.

RADARS

Air/surface search –Siemens Plessey Type 996.
Surface search –E/F band
Navigation – 2 Racal Marine Type 1007.

AIR SUPPORT

Helicopters: Platform for 3 - EH Industries EH 101 Merlin. Chinook capable.

KEY RECOGNITION FEATURES

- Short forecastle with angular raised platform with Goalkeeper CIWS atop.
- Vertical forward face to bridge superstructure. Open walkway around bridge.
- Pyramid enclosed fore mast with search radar atop and navigation/aircraft control radar on projecting gantry forward.
- Two square funnels on starboard side of superstructure with projecting exhausts.
- Massive enclosed mainmast with air/surface search radar atop and SATCOM domes on gantries on either side.
- Third enclosed pyramid mast at aft end of superstructure.
- Large crane immediately aft of superstructure.
- Flight deck over short open quarterdeck.

Note: Will have well docks and stern gates and with side ramp access as well.

Ocean

OCEAN

Country: UNITED KINGDOM
Country of origin: UNITED KINGDOM
Ship type: AMPHIBIOUS FORCES
Class: OCEAN (LPH)
Active: 1
Name (Pennant Number): OCEAN (L 12).

SPECIFICATION

Displacement, full load, tons: 21,758.
Length, feet (metres): 667.3 (203.4) oa.
Beam, feet (metres): 112.9 (34.4).
Draught, feet (metres): 21.3 (6.6).
Flight deck, feet (metres): 557.7 x 104 (170 x 31.7).
Speed, knots: 19.
Range, miles: 8,000 at 15 kts.

ARMAMENT

Guns: 3 - GE/GD Vulcan Phalanx Mk 15 CIWS. 8 – Oerlikon/BMARC 20 mm GAM-B03 (4 twin).
Decoys: 8 – Sea Gnat 130 mm/102 mm launchers and DLH offboard decoys.

RADARS

Air/surface search –Plessey Type 996.
Surface search/aircraft control – 2 Kelvin Hughes Type 1007.

AIR SUPPORT

Helicopters: 12 Sea King HC Mk 4/EH 101 Merlin plus 6 Lynx (or Apache by 2005).

KEY RECOGNITION FEATURES

- Aircraft carrier style flight deck, continuous to stern.
- Vulcan Phalanx CIWS positioned in eyes of ship and on sponsons projecting, port and starboard, at stern
- Thin, angular island sited starboard side, amidships.
- Prominent bridge angled out over flight deck.
- Enclosed pyramid foremast atop bridge, with surface search radar on projecting gantry forward.
- Square angled black funnel midway atop superstructure, with projecting exhausts and pole aerials.
- Massive enclosed pyramidal mainmast at aft end of superstructure with air/surface radar atop. SATCOM dome on gantries projecting inboard and forward.
- Large crane aft of superstructure on starboard side.
Note: Based on Invincible CVS hull design. Military lift – 4 LCVP Mk 5 on davits; 2 Griffon hovercraft, 40 vehicles and equipment for most of a marine commando.

OGDEN

Country: UNITED STATES OF AMERICA

Country of origin: USA

Ship type: AMPHIBIOUS FORCES

Class: AUSTIN (LPD)

Active: 11

Name (Pennant Number): AUSTIN (LPD 4), OGDEN (LPD 5), DULUTH (LPD 6), CLEVELAND (LPD 7), DUBUQUE (LPD 8), DENVER (LPD 9), JUNEAU (LPD 10), SHREVEPORT (LPD 12), NASHVILLE (LPD 13), TRENTON (LPD 14), PONCE (LPD 15)

SPECIFICATION

Displacement, full load, tons: 17,244.

Length, feet (metres): 570 (173.8).

Beam, feet (metres): 100 (30.5).

Draught, feet (metres): 23. (7).

Speed, knots: 21.

Range, miles: 7,700 at 20 kts.

ARMAMENT

Guns: 2 - GE/GD 20 mm/76 Vulcan Phalanx Mk 15; 2 - 25 mm Mk 38; 8 -12.7 mm machine-guns.

Decoys: 4 Loral Hycor SRBOC 6-barrel Mk 36.

RADARS

Air search - Lockheed SPS-40B/C.

Surface search - Norden SPS-67.

Navigation – Raytheon SPS-64(V)9.

AIR SUPPORT

Helicopters: Up to 6 Boeing CH-46D/E Sea Knight can be carried. Hangar for only 1 light (not in LPD 4).

KEY RECOGNITION FEATURES

- High bow with wire aerial structure on forecastle.
- Large superstructure forward of midships creating very high freeboard.
- Two Vulcan Phalanx CIWS mountings, 1 forward end of main superstructure, the other atop superstructure, immediately aft of mainmast.
- Large tripod mainmast atop mid-superstructure.
- Unusual tall, slim twin funnels. Starboard funnel well forward of port one.
- Crane derrick between funnels.
- Long flight deck aft with telescopic hangar. (No hangar in LPD 4)

Note: Enlarged version of 'Raleigh' class now paid off.

Note 2: There are structural variations in the positions of guns and electronic equipment in different ships of the class.

Note 3: LPD 7-13 have an additional bridge and are fitted as flagships.

Note 4: *Coronado* (AGF 11, ex-LPD 11) former class member, converted into command ship role.

Blue Ridge

BLUE RIDGE

Country: UNITED STATES OF AMERICA
Country of origin: USA
Ship type: AMPHIBIOUS FORCES
Class: BLUE RIDGE (LCC)
Active: 2
Name (Pennant Number): BLUE RIDGE (LCC 19), MOUNT WHITNEY (LCC 20)

SPECIFICATION

Displacement, full load, tons: 19,648 (LCC 19), 19,760 (LCC 20).
Length, feet (metres): 636.5 (194).
Beam, feet (metres): 107.9 (32.9).
Draught, feet (metres): 28.9 (8.8).
Speed, knots: 23.
Range, miles: 13,000 at 16 kts.

ARMAMENT

Guns: 2 - GE/GD 20 mm/76 Vulcan Phalanx Mk 15.
Decoys: 4- Loral Hycor SRBOC 6-barrel Mk 36. SLQ-25 Nixie torpedo decoy.

RADARS

Air search - ITT SPS-48C; Lockheed SPS-40E.
Surface search - Raytheon SPS-65(V)1.
Navigation - Marconi LN66; Raytheon SPS-64(V)9.

AIR SUPPORT

Helicopters: 1 Sikorsky SH-3H Sea King.

KEY RECOGNITION FEATURES

- Vulcan Phalanx CIWS mountings in eyes of the ship and right aft on specially built platform.
- Numerous communications aerials and masts along length of maindeck, including tall lattice mast mid-way between bows and superstructure.
- Small superstructure amidships.
- Pole mainmast atop superstructure.
- Large, distinctive SPS-48C air search 3D radar aerial aft of mainmast atop superstructure.
- Twin, angled exhausts at top after end of superstructure.
- Very unusual flared hull midships section to protect stowages for LCPs and LCVPs.
- Large communications aerial mast mid-afterdeck.
- Tall, enclosed pyramid structure topped by white dome, further aft.

Note: Hull design similar to 'Iwo Jima' class.

Tarawa

PELELUI

Country: UNITED STATES OF AMERICA	
Country of origin: USA	
Ship type: AMPHIBIOUS FORCES	
Class: TARAWA (LHA)	
Active: 5	

Name (Pennant Number): TARAWA (LHA 1), SAIPAN (LHA 2), BELLEAU WOOD (LHA 3), NASSAU (LHA 4), PELELIU (ex-*Da Nang*) (LHA 5)

SPECIFICATION

Displacement, full load, tons: 39,967.
Length, feet (metres): 834 (254.2).
Beam, feet (metres): 131.9 (40.2).
Draught, feet (metres): 25.9 (7.9).
Flight deck, feet (metres): 820 x 118.1 (250 x 36).
Speed, knots: 24.
Range, miles: 10,000 at 20 kts.

ARMAMENT

Missiles: SAM - 2 GDC Mk 49 RAM.
Guns: 6 - Mk 242 25 mm automatic cannons; 2 - GE/GD 20 mm/76 Vulcan Phalanx Mk 15; 8 - 12.7 mm machine-guns.
Decoys: 4 - Loral Hycor SRBOC 6-barrel Mk 36; SLQ-25 Nixie torpedo decoy; NATO Sea Gnat. SLQ-49 chaff buoys.

RADARS

Air search –ITT SPS-48E; Lockheed SPS-40E; Hughes Mk 23 TAS.
Surface search - Raytheon SPS-67(V)3.

Navigation - Raytheon SPS-64(V)9.
Fire control - Lockheed SPG-60; Lockheed SPQ-9A.

AIR SUPPORT

Fixed wing aircraft: Harrier AV-8B VSTOL aircraft in place of helicopters as required.
Helicopters: 9 - Sikorsky CH-53D Sea Stallion or 26 Boeing CH-46D/E Sea Knight.

KEY RECOGNITION FEATURES

- Similar outline to *Wasp* class but higher profile island with prominent crane aft of superstructure.
- Vulcan Phalanx CIWS mounting on platform at forward end of island.
- 2 masts atop island, slightly taller lattice mast forward and complex pole mast aft.
- SPS-52D air search 3D radar aerial atop after end of island, (forward end of island in *Wasp* class).
- 1 RAM SAM launcher on platform, below flight deck at stern, starboard side; second above bridge offset to port.
- Second CIWS mounting, below flight deck, at stern, port side.

Note: Floodable docking well beneath the after elevator (268 ft long and 78 ft wide) capable of taking four LCUs.

San Antonio

SAN ANTONIO (artist's impression)

Country: UNITED STATES OF AMERICA
Country of origin: USA
Ship type: AMPHIBIOUS FORCES
Class: SAN ANTONIO (LPD)
Building: 4
Planned: 8
Name (Pennant Number): SAN ANTONIO (LPD 17), NEW ORLEANS (LPD 18), MESA VERDE (LPD 19), GREEN BAY (LPD 20), ––– (LPD 21), ––– (LPD 22).

SPECIFICATION

Displacement, full load, tons: 25,300.
Length, feet (metres): 683.7 (208.4).
Beam, feet (metres): 104.7 (31.9)
Draught, feet (metres): 23 (7).
Speed, knots: 22.

ARMAMENT

Missiles: SAM - Mk 41 VLS for 2 octuple cell Evolved Sea Sparrow. 2 - GDC Mk 31 Mod 1 RAM.
Guns: 2 – 30 mm Mk 46; 4 - 12.7 mm machine-guns.
Decoys: 6 - Mk 53 Mod 4 Nulka and chaff launcher; SLQ-25A Nixie torpedo decoy.

RADARS

Air search - ITT SPS-48E.
Surface search/navigation – Raytheon SPS-73(V)3.
Fire control – Lockheed SPQ-9B

AIR SUPPORT

Helicopters: 2 - Sikorsky CH-53E Super Stallion or 4 CH-46E Sea Knight or 2 MV-22 Osprey or 4 UH-1.

KEY RECOGNITION FEATURES

- Short forecastle with VLS SAM forward of bridge.
- Massive tall "stealthy" superstructure, flush with ship's sides.
- Two black-capped funnels with four black exhausts, offset port and starboard atop island.
- Two massive pyramidal Advanced Enclosed Mast Systems atop superstructure.
- Crane between funnels.
- Flight deck aft with two hangers.
Note: Well deck and stern gate arrangements similar to 'Wasp' class.

Wasp

Bohomme Richard

Country: UNITED STATES OF AMERICA

Country of origin: USA

Ship type: AMPHIBIOUS FORCES

Class: WASP (LHD)

Active: 7

Building: 1

Planned: 1

Name (Pennant Number): WASP (LHD 1), ESSEX (LHD 2), KEARSARGE (LHD 3), BOXER (LHD 4), BATAAN (LHD 5), BONHOMME RICHARD (LHD 6), IWO JIMA (LHD 7).

SPECIFICATION

Displacement, full load, tons: 40,532.

Length, feet (metres): 844 (257.3) oa.

Beam, feet (metres): 140.1 (42.7) oa.

Draught, feet (metres): 26.6 (8.1).

Flight deck, feet (metres): 819 x 106 (249.6 x 32.3).

Speed, knots: 22.

Range, miles: 9,500 at 18 kts.

KEY RECOGNITION FEATURES

- Effectively aircraft carrier style with continuous flight deck.
- Large starboard side island amidships.
- Two black-capped funnels, fore and aft atop island.
- 2 - Sea Sparrow SAM box launchers, 1 at forward end of island, the other right aft on overhanging transom. RAM SAM also fitted forward of Sea Sparrow on superstructure and at stern.)
- Two similar pole masts atop island, after one slightly the taller of the two.
- Vulcan Phalanx CIWS mountings, 1 atop bridge, 1 other on each quarter.
- 2 aircraft elevators, one to starboard and aft of the island and one to port amidships.

Note: Stern doors with well deck of 267 x 50 ft to accommodate up to three LCACs.

Note 2: Vehicle storage is available for five M1A1 main battle tanks, 25 LAV-25 APCs, eight M 198 155 mm howitzers, 68 trucks, 10 logistic vehicles and several service vehicles.

ARMAMENT

Missiles: SAM - 2 - Raytheon GMLS Mk 29 octuple launchers; Sea Sparrow. 2 - GDC Mk 49 RAM.

Guns: 2 or 3 - GE/GD 20 mm Vulcan Phalanx Mk 15; 3 –Boeing Bushmaster 25 mm Mk 38; 4 or 8 - 12.7 mm machine-guns.

Decoys: 4 or 6 - Loral Hycor SRBOC 6-barrel Mk 36; SLQ-25 Nixie torpedo decoy; NATO Sea Gnat; SLQ-49 chaff buoys.

RADARS

Air search - ITT SPS-48E; Raytheon SPS- 49(V)9; Hughes Mk 23 TAS.

ESSEX

Surface search - Norden SPS-67.
Navigation – SPS-64(V)9.
Fire control – 2 Mk 95.

AIR SUPPORT

Fixed wing aircraft: 6-8 AV-8B Harriers or up to
  20 in secondary role.
Helicopters: Capacity for 42 Boeing CH-46E Sea
  Knight. Capability to support Bell AH-1W
  SuperCobra, Sikorsky CH-53E Super Stallion,
  Sikorsky CH-53D Sea Stallion, Bell UH-1N Twin
  Huey, AH-1T SeaCobra, and Sikorsky SH-60B
  Seahawk.

Whidbey Island/Harpers Ferry

Country: UNITED STATES OF AMERICA

Country of origin: USA

Ship type: AMPHIBIOUS FORCES

Class: WHIDBEY ISLAND (LSD)

Active: 8

Name (Pennant Number): WHIDBEY ISLAND (LSD 41), GERMANTOWN (LSD 42), FORT McHENRY (LSD 43), GUNSTON HALL (LSD 44), COMSTOCK (LSD 45), TORTUGA (LSD 46), RUSHMORE (LSD 47), ASHLAND (LSD 48).

Class: HARPERS FERRY (LSD-CV)

Active : 4

Name (Pennant Number): HARPERS FERRY (LSD 49), CARTER HALL (LSD 50), OAK HILL (LSD 51), PEARL HARBOR (LSD 52)

KEY RECOGNITION FEATURES

- Short forecastle with wire aerial structure on forecastle.
- High superstructure well forward of midships.
- Large lattice mainmast atop mid-superstructure.
- 2 Vulcan Phalanx CIWS mountings atop main superstructure, 1 on bridge roof, 1 immediately forward of funnel. (1 CIWS immediately forward of bridge in Harpers Ferry class).
- RAM SAM box launchers atop bridge and at aft end of superstructure in 'Harpers Ferry' class.
- Large funnel with sloping after profile at after end of superstructure.
- 1 or 2 large cranes aft of funnel.
- Long afterdeck.

Note: Based on the earlier 'Anchorage' class. 'Harpers Ferry' class cargo-carrying variants.

Note 2: Well deck measures 440 x 50 ft (134.1 x 15.2 m) in the LSD but is shorter in the Cargo Variant (CV).

Note 3: Approximately 90% commonality between the two variants.

SPECIFICATION

Displacement, full load, tons: 15,726 (LSD 41-48), 16,740 (LSD 49 onwards)

Length, feet (metres): 609.5 (185.8).

Beam, feet (metres): 84 (25.6).

Draught, feet (metres): 20.5 (6.3).

Speed, knots: 22.

Range, miles: 8,000 at 18 kts.

HARPERS FERRY

ARMAMENT

Missiles: SAM - 1 or 2- GDC Mk 49 RAM.
Guns: 2 - GE/GD 20 mm/76 Vulcan Phalanx Mk 15; 2 - 25 mm Mk 38; 8 - 12.7 mm machine-guns.
Decoys: 4 - Loral Hycor SRBOC 6-barrel Mk 36 and Mk 50; SLQ-25 Nixie towed torpedo decoy.

RADARS

Air search - Raytheon SPS-49(V)5.
Surface search - Norden SPS-67V.
Navigation - Raytheon SPS-64(V)9.

AIR SUPPORT

Helicopters: Platform only for 2 Sikorsky CH-53D Sea Stallion.

MINE

WARFARE

FORCES

Lerici

Country: AUSTRALIA, ITALY, MALAYSIA, NIGERIA, THAILAND

Country of origin: ITALY

Ship type: MINE WARFARE FORCES

Class: LERICI (MAHAMIRU) (MHC/MSC)

Active: 4 Italy, 4 Malaysia ('Mahamiru' class), 2 Nigeria

ITALY - Name (Pennant Number): LERICI (M 5550), SAPRI (M 5551), MILAZZO (M 5552), VIESTE (M 5553).

MALAYSIA - Name (Pennant Number): MAHAMIRU (11), JERAI (12), LEDANG (13), KINABALU (14)

NIGERIA - Name (Pennant Number): OHUE (M 371), MARABA (M 372).

Class: GAETA (HUON), (LAT YA) (MHC/MSC)

Active: 5 Australia ('Huon' class), 8 Italy, 2 Thailand ('Lat Ya' class)

Building: 1 Australia

AUSTRALIA - Name (Pennant Number): HUON (82), HAWKESBURY (83), NORMAN (84), GASCOYNE (85), DIAMANTINA (86), YARRA (87).

ITALY - Name (Pennant Number): GAETA (M 5554), TERMOLI (M 5555), ALGHERO (M 5556), NUMANA (M 5557), CROTONE (M 5558), VIAREGGIO (M 5559), CHIOGGIA (M 5560), RIMINI (M 5561)

THAILAND - Name (Pennant Number): LAT YA (633), THA DIN DAENG (634).

MILAZZO

SPECIFICATION

Displacement, full load, tons: 620. (697 *Gaeta* onwards). 610 (Malaysian ships). 540, (Nigerian). 680 (Thailand). 720, (Australia).

Length, feet (metres): 164. (50), (172.1 (52.5) *Gaeta* class, and Australia, Thailand). 167.3 (51), Malaysian and Nigerian ships).

Beam, feet (metres): 32.5 (9.9).

Draught, feet (metres): 8.6 (2.6). (9.2 (2.8), Malaysian and Nigerian ships). (9.8 (3), Australia).

Speed, knots: 15.

Range, miles: 2,500 at 12 kts.

ARMAMENT

Guns: 1 - Oerlikon 20 mm/70 or 2 Oerlikon 20 mm/70 (twin) (*Gaeta* class), (Italy). 1 - MSI DS 30B 30 mm/75, (Australia, Thailand). 1 - Bofors 40 mm/70 (Malaysian ships). 2 - Emerson Electric 30 mm (twin); 2 - Oerlikon 20 mm GAM-B01 (Nigeria).

Countermeasures: Minehunting – 1 - MIN 77 or MIN Mk 2 (*Gaeta* class) ROV; 1 - Pluto mine destruction system. Minesweeping - Oropesa Mk 4 wire sweep, (Italy). 2 - Bofors SUTEC Double-Eagle Mk 2 mine disposal vehicles; ADI Oropesa mechanical sweep, (Australia). Thomson-CSF IBIS II minehunting system; 2 - Improved PAP 104 ROVs, Oropresa 'O' Mis-4 mechancial sweep, (Malaysia). 2 Pluto systems; Oropesa 'O' Mis-4 and IBIS V control system, (Nigeria). Atlas MWS 80-6 minehunting system; magnetic, acoustic and mechanical sweeps; 2 - Pluto Plus ROVs, (Thailand).

Decoys: 2 - Super Barricade chaff launchers, (Australia only).

RADARS

Navigation - SMA SPN-728V(3), (Italy). Kelvin Hughes 1007, (Australia). Racal Decca 1226; Thomson-CSF Tripartite III, (Malaysia,). Racal Decca 1226, (Nigeria). Atlas Elektronik 9600M (ARPA), (Thailand).

Sonars: FIAR SQQ-14(IT) VDS (lowered from keel forward of bridge), (Italy). Thomson-Sintra TSM 2022, minehunting, (Malaysia, Nigeria). GEC Marconi Type 2093 VDS, (Australia). Atlas Elektronik DSQS-11M, hull-mounted, active, (Thailand).

KEY RECOGNITION FEATURES

- High bow, high freeboard. Sloping break, aft of funnel, down to sweep deck.
- 20 mm/70 mounting ('A' position). (40 mm/70 in Malaysian ships, 30 mm (twin) mounting in Nigerian ships. MSI DS 30B 30 mm in Australian and Thai ships).
- High bridge superstructure with forward sloping bridge windows.
- SATCOM dome atop aft end of bridge in Australian ships.
- Tapered funnel with unusual, wedge shaped, smoke deflector atop.

Note: Two types easily distinguished by large pole mainmast sited immediately aft of bridge (Lerici) and immediately forward of funnel (Gaeta).

Note 2: 12 of much larger, modified Lerici design built by the USA as 'Osprey' class. See separate entry.

Note 3: South Korea's 'Swallow' class similar to 'Lerici'.

Note 4: Italian ships fitted with telescopic crane for launching Callegari diver boats.

Tripartite

Country: BELGIUM, FRANCE, INDONESIA,
NETHERLANDS, PAKISTAN

Country of origin: INTERNATIONAL

Ship type: MINE WARFARE FORCES

Class: TRIPARTITE MINEHUNTERS (FLOWER, ÉRIDAN,
PULAU RENGAT, ALKMAAR, MUNSIF) (MHC)

Active: 7 Belgium ('Flower' class, 13 France
('Éridan' class), 2 Indonesia ('Pulau Rengat' class),
12 Netherlands ('Alkmaar' class), 3 Pakistan
('Munsif' class)

BELGIUM - Name (Pennant Number): ASTER (M
915), BELLIS (M 916), CROCUS (M 917), LOBELIA
(M 921), MYOSOTIS (M 922), NARCIS (M 923),
PRIMULA (M 924)

FRANCE - Name (Pennant Number): ÉRIDAN (M
641), CASSIOPÉE (M 642), ANDROMÈDE (M 643),
PÉGASE (M 644), ORION (M 645), CROIX DU SUD
(M 646), AIGLE (M 647), LYRE (M 648), PERSÉE (M
649), SAGITTAIRE (M 650), VERSEAU (ex-Iris) M
651), CÉPHÉE (ex-Fuchsia), (M 652), CAPRICORNE
(ex-Dianthus) (M 653).

INDONESIA - Name (Pennant Number): PULAU
RENGAT (711), PULAU RUPAT (712).

NETHERLANDS - Name (Pennant Number):
HAARLEM (M 853), HARLINGEN (M854),
SCHEVENINGEN (M 855), MAASSLUIS (M 856),
MAKKUM (M 857), MIDDELBURG (M 858),
HELLEVOETSLUIS (M 859), SCHIEDAM (M 860),
URK (M 861), ZIERIKZEE (M 862), VLAARDINGEN
(M 863), WILLEMSTAD (M 864).

PAKISTAN - Name (Pennant Number): MUNSIF
(ex-Sagittaire) (M 166), MUHAFIZ (M 163),
MUJAHID (M 164).

SPECIFICATION

Displacement, full load, tons: 595, (605, French
ships), (568, Indonesian ships).

Length, feet (metres): 168.9 (51.5).

Beam, feet (metres): 29.2 (8.9).

Draught, feet (metres): 8.5 (2.6), Dutch ships. 8.2
(2.5), Belgian, Indonesian and French. 9.5 (2.9),
Pakistani.

Speed, knots: 15.

Range, miles: 3,000 at 12 kts.

ARMAMENT

Guns: 1 - DCN 20 mm/20. 1 - 12.7 machine-gun,
(Belgium). 1 - Giat 20F2 20 mm, (France,
Netherlands, Pakistan). 1 - 12.7 mm machine-
gun, (France, Pakistan). 2 - Rheinmetall 20 mm

(Indonesia. Matra Simbad/Mistral SAM launcher
may be added for patrol duties or a third 20
mm gun).

Countermeasures: MCM - 2 - PAP 104 remote-
controlled mine locators. Mechanical sweep
gear (medium depth). (OD3 mechanical sweep
gear, AP-4 acoustic sweep; Double Eagle ROV
from 2001, France). (Elesco MKR 400 acoustic
sweep, MRK 960 magnetic sweep, Pakistan).
(OD3 Oropesa mechanical sweep; Fiskars F-82
magnetic sweep and SA Marine AS 203
acoustic sweeps; 2 - PAP 104 Mk 4 ROV,
Indonesia). OD3 mechanical sweep,
Netherlands.

RADARS

Navigation - Racal Decca 1229, (Belgium, France,
Pakistan, M 166). Kelvin Hughes 1007, Pakistan,
M 163-164. Racal Decca TM 1229C (Indonesia,
Netherlands).

CROCUS

Sonars: Thomson-Sintra DUBM 21A/B or 21D;
hull-mounted, (Thomson-Sintra TSM 2022,
Indonesia), minehunting.

KEY RECOGNITION FEATURES

- High bow and high freeboard.
- Continuous maindeck aft to break down to low freeboard quarterdeck.
- 20 mm/20 gun mounting ('A' position).
- Low superstructure from forecastle aft to quarterdeck.
- Pole mainmast atop after end of bridge.
- Squat, tapered, black-capped funnel with sloping top, atop superstructure.
- Small crane on quarterdeck.
- SATCOM on pole aft end of superstructure, (some Dutch ships).

Note: There are differences in design between Indonesian ships and the European Tripartite hulls.
Deckhouses and general layout are different as the Indonesian units are required to act as
minehunters, minesweepers and patrol ships.

Kingston

KINGSTON

Country: CANADA
Country of origin: CANADA
Ship type: MINE WARFARE FORCES
Class: KINGSTON (MCDV/MCM)
Active: 12
Name (Pennant Number): KINGSTON, (700), GLACE BAY (701), NANAIMO (702), EDMONTON (703), SHAWINIGAN (704), WHITEHORSE (705), YELLOWKNIFE (706), GOOSE BAY (707), MONCTON (708), SASKATOON (709), BRANDON, (710), SUMMERSIDE (711).

SPECIFICATION

Displacement, full load, tons: 962.
Length, feet (metres): 181.4 (55.3).
Beam, feet (metres): 37.1 (11.3).
Draught, feet (metres): 11.2 (3.4).
Speed, knots: 15.
Range, miles: 5,000 at 8 kts.

ARMAMENT

Guns: 1 – Bofors 40mm/60 Mk 5c. 2 – 12.7 mm machine-guns.

Countermeasures: MCM – 1 or 3 modular payloads. (a) Indal Technologies SLQ-38 (single and double Oropesa sweeps), (b) route survey system; (c) Mine inspection, Sutec ROV.

RADARS

Surface search – Kelvin Hughes 6000
Naviagtion – Kelvin Hughes I-band.
Sonars: MacDonald Dettwiler towed side scan, active.

KEY RECOGNITION FEATURES

- Long forecastle, with continuous maindeck to aft of stepped superstructure, then sharp drop down to sweep deck.
- All round windows to bridge.
- Thick pole mast atop bridge
- Two angled, thin funnels, port and starboard, aft of superstructure.
- Crane derrick between funnels.

Frankenthal

ROTTWEIL

Country: GERMANY
Country of origin: GERMANY
Ship type: MINE WARFARE FORCES
Class: FRANKENTHAL (TYPE 332) (MHC)
Active: 12
Name (Pennant Number): FRANKENTHAL (M 1066), WEIDEN (M 1060), ROTTWEIL (M 1061), BAD BEVENSEN (M 1063), BAD RAPPENAU (M 1067), GRÖMITZ (M 1064), DATTELN (M 1068), DILLINGEN (M 1065), HOMBURG (M 1069), SULZBACH-ROSENBERG (M 1062), FULDA (M 1058), WEILHEIM (M 1059).

SPECIFICATION

Displacement full load, tons: 650.
Length, feet (metres): 178.8 (54.5).
Beam, feet (metres): 30.2 (9.2).
Draught, feet (metres): 8.5 (2.6).
Speed, knots: 18.

ARMAMENT

Missiles: SAM - 2 - Stinger quad launchers.
Guns: 1 - Bofors 40 mm/70, (being replaced by Mauser 27 mm).

RADARS

Navigation – Raytheon SPS-64.
Sonars: Atlas Elektronik DSQS-11M; hull-mounted.

KEY RECOGNITION FEATURES

• High freeboard forward with break down to maindeck level amidships.
• 40 mm/70 gun mounting ('A' position).
• Tall, substantial superstructure stepped down aft of midships.
• Small pole aerial atop bridge.
• Tall, slim, tripod mainmast amidships.
• Small crane on quarterdeck.
Note: Same hull, similar superstructure as 'Ensdorf' class, Type 352.
Note 2: Similar in appearance to 5 – strong 'Kulmbach' class converted minehunters (M 1091, 1095, 1096, 1097, 1099) and 5 strong 'Ensdorf' converted minesweepers (M 1090, 1092, 1093, 1094, 1098)
Note 3: Equipped with 2 - STN Systemtechnik Nord Pinguin-B3 drones with sonar and TV cameras.

Ensdorf

ENSDORF

Country:	GERMANY
Country of origin:	GERMANY
Ship type:	MINE WARFARE FORCES
Class:	ENSDORF (TYPE 352) (MHC)
Active:	5

Name (Pennant Number): HAMELN (M 1092), PEGNITZ (M 1090), SIEGBURG (M 1098), ENSDORF (M 1094), AUERBACH (M 1093).

SPECIFICATION

Displacement full load, tons: 635.
Length, feet (metres): 178.5 (54.4).
Beam, feet (metres): 30.2 (9.2).
Draught, feet (metres): 8.2 (2.5).
Speed, knots: 18.

ARMAMENT

Missiles: SAM - 2 Stinger quad launchers.
Guns: 2 - Mauser 27 mm.
Mines: 60.
Decoys: 2 - Silver Dog chaff rocket launchers.

RADARS

Surface search/fire control - Signaal WM 20/2.
Navigation - Raytheon SPS-64.
Sonars: STN ADS DSQS-15A mine avoidance, active.

KEY RECOGNITION FEATURES

- Very similar profile to 'Frankenthal' class with main distinguishing differences as follows: -
- Latticed, pyramid shaped mainmast atop bridge roof supporting WM20/2 surface search/fire control radome.
- Mauser 27 mm turret mounting forward of bridge.

Note: Five hulls of 'Hameln' class converted to minesweepers 2000-2001. Can control up to four remotely controlled minesweeping drones ('Seehund'). Sea Fox C ROV for mine disposal. Double Oropesa mechanical sweep. Very similar to 'Kulmbach' class, M 1091, 1095, 1096, 1097, 1099.

Kulmbach

KULMBACH

Country: GERMANY
Country of origin: GERMANY
Ship type: MINE WARFARE FORCES
Class: KULMBACH (TYPE 333) (MHC)
Active: 5
Name (Pennant Number): ÜBERHERRN (M 1095), LABOE (M 1097), KULMBACH (M 1091), PASSAU (M 1096), HERTEN (M 1099).

SPECIFICATION

Displacement full load, tons: 635.
Length, feet (metres): 178.5 (54.4).
Beam, feet (metres): 30.2 (9.2).
Draught, feet (metres): 8.2 (2.5).
Speed, knots: 18.

ARMAMENT

Missiles: SAM - 2 Stinger quad launchers.
Guns: 2 - Mauser 27 mm.
Mines: 60.
Decoys: 2 - Silver Dog chaff rocket launchers.

RADARS

Surface search/fire control - Signaal WM 20/2.
Navigation - Raytheon SPS-64.
Sonars: Atlas Elektronik DSQS-11M hull-mounted.

KEY RECOGNITION FEATURES

- Very similar profile to 'Frankenthal' class with main distinguishing differences as follows: -
- Latticed, pyramid shaped mainmast atop bridge roof supporting WM20/2 surface search/fire control radome.
- Mauser 27 mm turret mounting forward of bridge.
- Mauser 27 mm turret aft of superstructure.

Note: Five hulls of 'Hameln' class converted to minehunters 1999-2001. Very similar to 'Ensdorf' class, M 1090, 1092, 1093, 1094, 1098 Disposal Sea Fox 1 used for inspection and Sea Fox C ROV for mine disposal.

Natya I

NATYA I

Country: INDIA, LIBYA, RUSSIA, SYRIA, UKRAINE, YEMEN

Country of origin: RUSSIA

Ship type: MINE WARFARE FORCES

Class: NATYA I (TYPE 266M) (PONDICHERRY) (AKVAMAREN) (MSO)

Active: 12 India ('Pondicherry' class), 4 Libya, 9 Russia ('Akvameren'), 1 Syria, 2 Ukraine, 1 Yemen

Building: 1 Russia

INDIA - Name (Pennant Number): PONDICHERRY (M 61), PORBANDAR (M 62), BEDI (M 63), BHAVNAGAR (M 64), ALLEPPEY (M 65), RATNAGIRI (M 66), KARWAR (M 67), CANNANORE (M 68) CUDDALORE (M 69), KAKINADA (M 70), KOZHIKODA (M 71), KONKAN (M 72).

LIBYA - Name (Pennant Number): AL ISAR (ex-*Ras El Gelais*) (111), AL TIYAR (ex-*Ras Hadad*) (113), RAS AL FULAIJAH (117), RAS AL MASSAD (123).

RUSSIA - Name (Pennant Number): POLEMETCHIK (834), NAVODCHIK (824), MOTORIST (806), VALENTINE PIKUL (770), SVYAZIST (610), DESANTNIK (719), SEMEN ROSHAL (718), MACHINIST (855), ZARYAD (738).

SYRIA - Name (Pennant Number): 642.

UKRAINE - Name (Pennant Number): ZHOVTI VODY (ex-ZENITCHIK) U310, CHERSARY (ex-RAZVEDCHIK) U311.

YEMEN - Name (Pennant Number): 201

SPECIFICATION

Displacement, full load, tons: 804.
Length, feet (metres): 200.1 (61).
Beam, feet (metres): 33.5 (10.2).
Draught, feet (metres): 9.8 (3).
Speed, knots: 16.
Range, miles: 3,000 at 12 kts.

ARMAMENT

Missiles: SAM - 2 - SA-N-5/8 Grail quad launchers (in some Russian and Indian ships).

Guns: 4- 30mm/65 AK 306 (2 twin) or 2- 30mm/65 AK 630; 4- 25mm/80 (2 twin), (Russian). 4- 30mm/65 (2 twin); 4- 25mm/60 (2 twin), (Remainder).

A/S mortars: 2 - RBU 1200 5-tubed.

Mines: Indian, Libyan and Yemeni ships can carry 10.

Countermeasures: MCM-1 or 2-GKT-2 contact sweeps; 1-AT-2 acoustic; 1 TEM-3 magnetic sweep.

RADARS

Surface search - Don 2 or Low Trough.
Fire control - Drum Tilt (not in all).
Sonars: MG 79/89 hull-mounted; minehunting, (Russian). MG 69/79 remainder.

KEY RECOGNITION FEATURES

- High bow, short forecastle with slender mast at forward end.
- 30 mm/65 gun mounting ('A' position).
- Continuous maindeck aft to break down to sweep deck.
- Main superstructure well forward of midships.
- Large lattice mainmast atop after end of superstructure supporting distinctive radar aerial.
- Black-capped funnel with sloping top aft of midships.
- Ship's boat in davits, starboard side just forward of funnel.
- 30 mm/65 gun mounting ('X' position).
- Distinctive hydraulic gantries right aft (in some).

Note: Some have Gatling 30 mm guns.

Note 2: At least one Libyan hull painted in green striped camouflage in 1991. Others may have blue hulls.

Kondor II

FORTUNA

Country:	INDONESIA, LATVIA, URUGUAY
Country of origin:	GERMANY
Ship type:	MINE WARFARE FORCES
Class:	KONDOR II (TYPE 89) (MSC/PC)
Active:	9 Indonesia, 2 Latvia, 3 Uruguay

INDONESIA - Name (Pennant Number): PULAU ROTE (ex-*Wolgast*) (721 ex-V 811), PULAU RAAS (ex-*Hettstedt*) (722 ex- 353), PULAU ROMANG (ex-*Pritzwalk*) (723 ex-325), PULAU RIMAU (ex-*Bitterfeld*) (724 ex-332, ex-M 2672), PULAU RONDO (ex-*Zerbst*) (725 ex 335), PULAU RUSO (ex-*Oranienburg*) (726 ex-341), PULAU RANGSANG (ex-*Jüterbog*), (727 ex-342), PULAU RAIBU (ex-*Sömmerda*) (728 ex-311, ex-M 2670), PULAU REMPANG (ex-*Grimma*) (729 ex-336).

LATVIA - Name (Pennant Number): VIESTURS (ex-*Kamenz*) (M 01 ex-351), IMANTA (ex-*Röbel*) (M 02 ex-324).

URUGUAY - Name (Pennant Number): TEMERAIRO (ex-*Riesa*) (31), FORTUNA (ex-*Bernau*) (33), AUDAZ (ex-*Eisleben*) (34).

SPECIFICATION

Displacement standard, tons: 310.
Length, feet (metres): 186 (56.7).
Beam, feet (metres): 24.6 (7.5).
Draught, feet (metres): 7.9 (2.4).
Speed, knots: 17.
Range, miles: 2,000 at 14 kts.

ARMAMENT

Guns: 6 - 25 mm/80 (3 twin), (Indonesia).
    2 - Wrobel 23 mm (twin), 2 - FK20 20 mm,
    (Latvia). 1 - Bofors 40 mm/60, (Uruguay).
Mines: 2 rails, (Indonesia, Uruguay only).

RADARS

Surface search – Racal Decca (Latvia).
Navigation - TSR 333 or Raytheon 1900.
Sonars: Bendix AQS-17(V) VDS, (Indonesia).

KEY RECOGNITION FEATURES

- Low freeboard with continuous maindeck from stem to stern.
- 23/25 mm twin turret on barbette immediately forward of bridge, (Indonesia and Latvia). 40mm/70 in same position, Uruguayan units,
- High, stepped, smooth contoured superstructure centred well forward of midships.
- Sturdy pole mainmast immediately aft of bridge, supporting radar aerials.
- Squat, square sectioned funnel with sloping top sited midships.
- 2 - 25mm/80 twin gun mountings mounting on sponsons aft of funnel in Indonesian ships. (Absent, Uruguayan units). Latvia has 2 – 20 mm cannon side by side in same position.
- Small square structure on afterdeck.
- Sweep gear right aft.
- Kondor II some 16 ft longer than Kondor I.
- Kondor I has square profile funnel with sloping top. Kondor II has rounded funnel with wedge shaped smoke deflector at its after edge.

Note: Malta operates 3 Kondor I (P 30, P 31, P 29), as coastal patrol craft. Cape Verde operates 1 Kondor 1 as a coastal patrol craft. Tunisian coastguard operates 5 Kondor I class as patrol craft.

Hatsushima

HATSUSHIMA CLASS

Country: JAPAN

Country of origin: JAPAN

Ship type: MINE WARFARE FORCES

Class: HATSUSHIMA (MHC/MSC)

Active: 11

Class: UWAJIMA (MHC/MSC)

Active: 8

Name (Pennant Number): Hatsushima class -
NUWAJIMA (MSC 662), ETAJIMA (MSC 663),
KAMISHIMA (MSC 664), HIMESHIMA (MSC 665),
OGISHIMA (MSC 666), MOROSHIMA (MSC 667),
YURISHIMA (MSC 668), HIKOSHIMA (MSC 669),
AWASHIMA (MSC 670), SAKUSHIMA (MSC 671).
Uwajima class - UWAJIMA (MSC 672), IESHIMA
(MSC 673), TSUKISHIMA (MSC 674), MAEJIMA
(MSC 675), KUMEJIMA (MSC 676), MAKISHIMA
(MSC 677), TOBISHIMA (MSC 678), YUGESHIMA
(MSC 679) NAGASHIMA (MSC 680).

SPECIFICATION

Displacement, full load, tons: 510.

Length, feet (metres): 180.4 (55), (189.3 (57.7)
MSC 670 on).

Beam, feet (metres): 30.8 (9.4).

Draught, feet (metres): 7.9 (2.4).

Speed, knots: 14.

ARMAMENT

Guns: 1 - JM-61 20 mm/76 Sea Vulcan 20.

RADARS

Surface search - Fujitsu OPS-9 or OPDS-39 (MSC
674 onwards).

Sonars: Nec/Hitachi ZQS 2B or ZQS 3 (MSC 672
onwards); hull-mounted; minehunting.

KEY RECOGNITION FEATURES

- Continuous deck from bow aft to break
adjacent to funnel, down to lower deck
level.
- Small bridge superstructure well forward of
midships.
- Tall tripod mainmast midships.
- Tall, black-capped cylindrical funnel aft of
mainmast at deck break.
- Slender aftermast forward of sweep deck.
- Sweeping gantries at after end of sweep
deck.

TSUNOSHIMA

Country: JAPAN
Country of origin: JAPAN
Ship type: MINE WARFARE FORCES
Class: SUGASHIMA (MSC)
Active: 5
Building: 5
Planned: 1
Name (Pennant Number): SUGASHIMA (MSC 681), NOTOJIMA (MSC 682), TSUNOSHIMA (MSC 683), NAOSHIMA (MSC 684), TOYOSHIMA (MSC 685), UKUSHIMA (MSC 686), IZUSHIMA (MSC 687), --- (MSC 688) ---(MSC 689), --- (MSC 690).

SPECIFICATION
Displacement, full load, tons: 510.
Length, feet (metres): 180.1 (54.9).
Beam, feet (metres): 30.8 (9.4).
Draught, feet (metres): 8.2 (2.5).
Speed, knots: 14.

ARMAMENT
Guns: 1 - JM-61 20 mm/76 Sea Vulcan 20.

RADARS
Surface search - OPDS-39B
Sonars: Hitachi/Thomson/Marconi GEC Type 2093 VDS.

KEY RECOGNITION FEATURES
- Continuous deck from bow aft to curved break just aft of funnels, down to lower deck level.
- Small bridge. Set well back from forward edge of superstructure.
- Tall tripod mainmast midships.
- Twin, tall, black-capped angled thin funnels, with pole aerials, aft of mainmast, just forward of deck break.
- Sweeping gantries at after end of sweep deck.
Note: Hull is similar to 'Uwajima' class, but upper deck is extended aft to provide greater stowage.
Note 2: PAP 104 Mk 5 ROVs carried. ADI Dyad minesweeping gear fitted.

Oksøy

KARMØY

Country: NORWAY
Country of origin: NORWAY
Ship type: MINE WARFARE FORCES
Class: OKSØY/ALTA (MHC/MSC)
Active: 9
Name (Pennant Number): MHC - OKSØY (M 340), KARMØY (M341), MÅLØY (M 342), HINNØY (M 343). MSC -ALTA (M 350), OTRA (M 351), RAUMA (M 352), ORKLA (M 353), GLOMMA (M 354)

SPECIFICATION

Displacement, full load, tons: 375.
Length, feet (metres): 181.1 (55.2).
Beam, feet (metres): 44.6 (13.6).
Draught, feet (metres): 8.2 (2.5)
Speed, knots: 20.5.
Range, miles: 1,500 at 20 kts.

ARMAMENT

Missiles: SAM – Matra Sadral; twin launcher; Mistral.
Guns: 1 or 2 – Rheinmetall 20 mm. 2 - 12.7 mm machine-guns.
Countermeasures: Minehunters - 2 Pluto submersibles. Minesweepers - Mechanical and influence sweeping equipment.

RADARS

Navigation - 2 Racal Decca.
Sonars: Thomson Sintra/Simrad TSM 2023N; hull-mounted (minehunters). Simrad Subsea SA 950; hull-mounted (minesweepers).

KEY RECOGNITION FEATURES

- Unusual blunt, flat-fronted bow.
- Twin-hulled.
- Flat, uncluttered forecastle forward of stepped, substantial superstructure.
- Bridge just forward of midships set atop superstructure.
- Lattice mainmast atop after end of bridge.
- Unusual, square section twin funnels at after end of main superstructure.
- Deck aft of funnels drops down to small sweep deck.
- Distinctive, modern design ship with clean, smooth lines and high freeboard.

KATONG

Country: SINGAPORE, SWEDEN
Country of origin: SWEDEN
Ship type: MINE WARFARE FORCES
Class: LANDSORT (BEDOK) (MHC)
Active: 4 Singapore ('Bedok' class), 7 Sweden
SINGAPORE - Name (Pennant Number): BEDOK
(M 105), KALLANG (M 106), KATONG (M 107),
PUNGGOL (M 108).
SWEDEN - Name (Pennant Number): LANDSORT
(M 71), ARHOLMA (M 72), KOSTER (M 73), KULLEN
(M 74), VINGA (M 75), VEN (M 76), ULVÖN (M 77)

SPECIFICATION

Displacement, full load, tons: 360.
Length, feet (metres): 155.8 (47.5).
Beam, feet (metres): 31.5 (9.6).
Draught, feet (metres): 7.3 (2.2).
Speed, knots: 15.
Range, miles: 2,000 at 12 kts.

ARMAMENT

Missiles: SAM – Saab Manpads.
Guns: 1 - Bofors 40 mm/70 Mod 48. 2 - 7.62 mm
machine-guns. (4 - 12.7 mm machine-guns in
Singapore ships).
A/S mortars: 4 Saab Elma 9-tube launchers,
(Sweden only).
Mines: 2 rails (Singapore only).

Decoys: 2 Philips Philax launchers can be carried,
(Sweden only).
Countermeasures: MCM - Fitted for mechanical
sweeps for moored mines, magnetic and
acoustic sweeps. 2 PAP 1-4 Mk 5 ROVs
embarked in Singapore ships. (Sutec or Double
Eagle ROV; possible to operate 2 - unmanned
magnetic and acoustic sweepers, Sweden).

RADARS

Navigation - Thomson-CSF Terma, (Sweden).
Norcontrol DB 2000, (Singapore).
Sonars: Thomson-CSF TSM-2022; hull-mounted;
minehunting.

KEY RECOGNITION FEATURES

- High freeboard with continuous maindeck
  from stem to stern.
- Main superstructure forward of midships
  with step down to sweep deck.
- Bridge set atop mid-superstructure.
- 40 mm/70 gun mounting ('B' position).
- Sturdy pole mainmast at after end of main
  superstructure with twin funnels at its base.
Note: Bofors Sea Trinity CIWS trial in
  Sweden's *Vinga* vice 40 mm/70.

Hunt

EUROPE (GREECE)

Country:	UNITED KINGDOM, GREECE
Country of origin:	UNITED KINGDOM
Ship type:	MINE WARFARE FORCES
Class:	HUNT (MSC/MHC)
Active:	11 UK, 2 Greece

UK - Name (Pennant Number): BRECON (M 29), LEDBURY (M 30), CATTISTOCK (M 31), COTTESMORE (M 32), BROCKLESBY (M 33), MIDDLETON (M 34), DULVERTON (M 35), CHIDDINGFOLD (M 37), ATHERSTONE (M 38), HURWORTH (M 39), QUORN (M 41).

GREECE - Name (Pennant Number): EUROPE (ex-*Bicester*) (M 62, ex-M 36), KALLISTO (ex-*Berkeley*) (M 63, ex-M 40).

SPECIFICATION

Displacement, full load, tons: 750.
Length, feet (metres): 197 (60) oa.
Beam, feet (metres): 32.8 (10).
Draught, feet (metres): 9.5 (2.9) (keel).
Speed, knots: 15.
Range, miles: 1,500 at 12 kts.

ARMAMENT

Guns: 1 - DES/MSI DS 30B 30 mm/75; 2 - Oerlikon/BMARC 20 mm GAM-CO1; 2 - 7.62 mm machine-guns.
Countermeasures: 2 - PAP 104/105 remotely controlled submersibles; MS 14 magnetic loop; Sperry MSSA Mk 1 towed acoustic generator; conventional K 8 Oropesa sweeps.
Decoys: 2 Wallop Barricade Mk III.

RADARS

Navigation - Kelvin Hughes Type 1006 or 1007.
Sonars: Plessey Type 193M Mod 1; hull-mounted; minehunting. Mil Cross mine avoidance sonar; hull-mounted. Type 2059 addition to track PAP 104/105.

KEY RECOGNITION FEATURES

- High freeboard maindeck.
- Continuous maindeck aft to sloping break down to sweep deck.
- 30 mm/75 gun mounting mid-forecastle.
- Midships superstructure has high bridge at forward end.
- Tapered, enclosed mainmast amidships.
- Navigation radar aerial atop bridge roof.
- Large, black-capped funnel aft of mainmast.
- Large structure on afterdeck housing various minehunting and minesweeping equipment.

Sandown

PEMBROKE

Country: UNITED KINGDOM. SAUDI ARABIA
Country of origin: UNITED KINGDOM
Ship type: MINE WARFARE FORCES
Class: SANDOWN (AL JAWF) (MHC)
Active: 3 Saudi Arabia ('Al Jawf'), 11 United Kingdom
SAUDI ARABIA - Name (Pennant Number): AL JAWF (420), SHAQRA (422) AL KHARJ (424).
UNITED KINGDOM - Name (Pennant Number): SANDOWN (M 101), INVERNESS (M 102), WALNEY (M 104), BRIDPORT (M 105), PENZANCE (M 106), PEMBROKE (M 107), GRIMSBY (M 108), BANGOR (M 109), RAMSEY (M 110), BLYTHE (M 111), SHOREHAM (M 112).

SPECIFICATION

Displacement, full load, tons: 484, (480, Saudi Arabia).
Length, feet (metres): 172.2 (52.5). (172.9 (52.7), Saudi Arabia).
Beam, feet (metres): 34.4 (10.5).
Draught, feet (metres): 7.5 (2.3). (6.9 (2.1), Saudi Arabia).
Speed, knots: 13.
Range, miles: 3,000 at 12 kts.

ARMAMENT

Guns: 1 - DES/MSI 30 mm/75 DS 30B, (UK). 2 Electronics & Space Emerlec 30 mm (twin), (Saudi Arabia).

Decoys: 2 - Loral Hycor SRBOC Mk 36 Mod 1 6-barrel chaff launcher, (Saudi Arabia). 2 Barricade fitted for deployment in UK hulls.
Countermeasures: ECA mine disposal system; 2 PAP 104 Mk 5.

RADARS

Navigation - Kelvin Hughes Type 1007.
Sonars: Marconi Type 2093 VDS; mine search and classification.

KEY RECOGNITION FEATURES

- Short, sloping forecastle with 30 mm/75 gun mounting ('A' position).
- Long superstructure extending from forecastle to small quarterdeck.
- Most of superstructure is flush with ship's side giving a slab-sided effect.
- Bridge sited atop superstructure just forward of midships.
- Navigation radar aerial atop bridge roof.
- Tapered, enclosed mainmast amidships, with short pole mast atop.
- Square profile, black-capped funnel with sloping top, aft of mainmast.

Note: Spain operates four 'Segura' class minehunters, based on the 'Sandown' class. A further two are being built.

CHIEF

Country: UNITED STATES OF AMERICA
Country of origin: USA
Ship type: MINE WARFARE FORCES
Class: AVENGER (MCM/MSO/MHO)
Active: 14
Name (Pennant Number): AVENGER (MCM 1),
DEFENDER (MCM 2), SENTRY (MCM 3), CHAMPION
(MCM 4), GUARDIAN (MCM 5), DEVASTATOR
(MCM 6), PATRIOT (MCM 7), SCOUT (MCM 8),
PIONEER (MCM 9), WARRIOR (MCM 10),
GLADIATOR (MCM 11), ARDENT (MCM 12),
DEXTROUS (MCM 13), CHIEF (MCM 14)

SPECIFICATION
Displacement, full load, tons: 1,312.
Length, feet (metres): 224 (68.3).
Beam, feet (metres): 38.9 (11.9).
Draught, feet (metres): 12.2 (3.7).
Speed, knots: 13.5.

ARMAMENT
Guns: 2 - 12.7 mm Mk 26 machine-guns.
Countermeasures: MCM – 2- SLQ-48; includes
ROV mine neutralisation system; SLQ-37(V)3
magnetic/acoustic influence sweep; Oropesa
SLQ-38 Type 0 Size 1; mechanical sweep.

RADARS
Surface search - ISC Cardion SPS-55.
Navigation – Raytheon SPS-64(V)9 or LN66.

Sonars: General Electric SQQ-30
(Raytheon/Thomson-Sintra SQQ-32 (MCM 10
on and being retrofitted) VDS; minehunting.

KEY RECOGNITION FEATURES
- High bow, sloping forecastle.
- Continuous maindeck profile from bow aft,
  with two breaks down aft of main
  superstructure.
- High superstructure extending from
  forecastle to sweep deck.
- Large, distinctive tripod mainmast on
  bridge roof with short pole mast atop.
- Very large tapered funnel aft of midships
  with sloping top and flat, sloping after end.
- Sweep cable reels and floats on sweepdeck.
- Unusually large for MCM craft.

Note: Japan operates 3 'Yaeyama' class MSOs
(*Yaeyama* (MSO 301), *Tsushima* (MSO 302)
and *Hachijou* (MSO 303), which appears to
be a derivative of the 'Avenger' class. Hulls
are slightly smaller, with a full load
displacement of 1,275 tons. There is only
one break in the maindeck down to the
sweeping deck and the lattice mainmast is
at the aft end of the superstructure. There
is also a small radome atop the bridge roof
in these vessels.

Osprey

HERON

Country: UNITED STATES OF AMERICA
Country of origin: USA
Ship type: MINE WARFARE FORCES
Class: OSPREY (MHC)
Active: 12

Name (Pennant Number): OSPREY (MHC 51), HERON (MHC 52), PELICAN (MHC 53), ROBIN (MHC 54), ORIOLE (MHC 55), KINGFISHER (MHC 56), CORMORANT (MHC 57), BLACK HAWK (MHC 58), FALCON (MHC 59), CARDINAL (MHC 60), RAVEN (MHC 61), SHRIKE (MHC 62)

SPECIFICATION

Displacement full load, tons: 959.
Length, feet (metres): 187.8 (57.2).
Beam, feet (metres): 35.9 (11).
Draught, feet (metres): 9.5 (2.9).
Speed, knots: 10.
Range, miles: 1,500 at 10 kts.

ARMAMENT

Guns: 2 - 12.7 mm machine-guns.
Countermeasures: MCM – Alliant SLQ-48 ROV mine neutralisation system ROV. Degaussing DGM-4.

RADARS

Surface search – Raytheon SPS-64(V)9 or SPS-73
Navigation - R4 1XX.
Sonars: Raytheon/Thomson-Sintra SQQ-32(V)3 VDS;minehunting.

KEY RECOGNITION FEATURES

- Continuous maindeck from bow, aft to break down to low freeboard afterdeck.
- Main superstructure extending from forecastle to break.
- High bridge at forward end of superstructure with unusual outward-sloping bridge windows.
- Bulky, square section, tapered funnel at after end of superstructure with wedge shaped smoke deflector Rad-Haz screen atop.
- Narrow, square section enclosed mainmast immediately forward of funnel.
- Large crane deck on afterdeck.
Note: Modified design based on 'Lerici' class, with much larger hull.

SUBMARINES

Kilo

Country: ALGERIA, CHINA, INDIA, IRAN, POLAND, ROMANIA, RUSSIA

Country of origin: RUSSIA

Ship type: SUBMARINES

Class: KILO/KILO 4B (VASHAVYANKA) (TYPE 877E/877K/877M) (SINDHUGHOSH) (SSK)

Active: 2 Algeria (Type 877E), 4 China (Type 877EKM/636), 10 India ('Sindhughosh' class, Type 877EM), 3 Iran (Type 877EKM), 1 Poland (Type 877E), 1 Romania (Type 877E), 9 Russia (Type 877,877K,877M)

ALGERIA - Name (Pennant Number): RAIS HADJ MUBAREK (012), EL HADJ SLIMANE (013)

CHINA - Name (Pennant Number): 364, 365, 366, 367.

INDIA - Name (Pennant Number): SINDHUGHOSH (S 55), SINDHUDHVAJ (S 56), SINDHURAJ (S 57), SINDHUVIR (S 58) SINDHURATNA (S 59), SINDHUKESARI (S 60), SINDHUKIRTI (S 61), SINDHUVIJAY (S 62), SINDHURAKSHAK (S 63), SINDHUSHASTRA (S 65).

IRAN - Name (Pennant Number): TAREQ (901), NOOR (902), YUNES (903).

POLAND - Name (Pennant Number): ORZEL (291).

ROMANIA - Name (Pennant Number): DELFINUL (521).

RUSSIA - Name (Pennant Number): None available.

SINDHUDHVAJ

SPECIFICATION

Displacement, surfaced, tons: 2,325.

Displacement, dived, tons: 3,076.

Length, feet (metres): 238.2 (72.6). (242.1 (73.8), China, Russia, Kilo 4B). (243.8. (74.3), Poland).

Beam, feet (metres): 32.5 (9.9).

Draught, feet (metres): 21.7 (6.6).

Speed, knots: 10 surfaced; 17 dived

Range, miles: 6,000 at 7 kts, surfaced; 400 at 3 kts. dived.

ARMAMENT

Missiles: SLCM – Novator Alfa Klub SS-N-27
(3M-54E1), (Indian boats). SAM – SA-N-8
Gremlin portable launcher, (India). SA-N-5/8
(Russia). 8 – SA-N-5 (Strela 2M) portable
launcher, (Poland).

Torpedoes: 6 - 21 in (533 mm) tubes.
Combination of TEST 71/96 and 53-65. (TEST-
71ME, Algeria only).

Mines: 24 in lieu of torpedoes.

RADARS

Surface search - Snoop Tray MRP-25. (Racal
Decca Bridgemaster, Poland).

Sonars: MGK-400 Shark Teeth/Shark Fin; hull-
mounted. Mouse Roar MG-519; hull-mounted

Type 209

Country: ARGENTINA, BRAZIL, CHILE, COLUMBIA, ECUADOR, GREECE, INDIA, INDONESIA, SOUTH KOREA, PERU, TURKEY, VENEZUELA.

Country of origin: GERMANY

Ship type: SUBMARINES

Class: TYPE 209 (TYPES 1100, 1200, 1300, 1400 and 1500) (SALTA, TUPI, THOMSON, PIJAO, GLAVKOS, SHISHUMAR, CAKRA, CHANG BOGO, ANGAMOS, CASMA, ATILAY, PREVEZE, SABALO) (SSK)

Active: 1 Argentina ('Salta,' Type 1200), 4 Brazil ('Tupi' class, Type 1400), 2 Chile ('Thomson' class. Type 1300), 2 Colombia ('Pijao' class, Type 1200), 2 Ecuador (Type 1300), 8 Greece ('Glavkos' class, Types 1100 and 1200), 4 India ('Shishumar' class, Type 1500), 2 Indonesia ('Cakra' class, Type 1300), 9 South Korea ('Chang Bogo' class, Type 1200), 6 Peru ('Casma' class, Type 1200), 6 Turkey'Atilay' class, (Type 1200), 4 Turkey 'Preveze' class, (Type 1400) Turkey, 2 Venezuela ('Sabalo'class, Type 1300).

Building: 4 Turkey (Type 1400).

ARGENTINA - Name (Pennant Number): SALTA (S 31).

BRAZIL - Name (Pennant Number): TUPI (S 30), TAMOIO (S 31), TIMBIRA (S 33), TAPAJÓ (ex-Tapajós) (S 33).

CHILE - Name (Pennant Number): THOMSON, (20), SIMPSON (21).

COLOMBIA - Name (Pennant Number): PIJAO (SO 28), TAYRONA (SO 29).

ECUADOR - Name (Pennant Number): SHYRI (S 101, ex-S 11), HUANCAVILCA (S 102, ex-S 12).

GREECE - Name (Pennant Number): GLAVKOS (S 110), NEREUS (S 111), TRITON (S 112), PROTEUS (S 113), POSEIDON (S 116), AMPHITRITE (S 117), OKEANOS (S 118), PONTOS (S 119).

INDIA - Name (Pennant Number): SHISHUMAR (S 44), SHANKUSH (S 45), SHALKI (S 46), SHANKUL (S 47).

INDONESIA - Name (Pennant Number): CAKRA (401), NANGGALA (402).

SOUTH KOREA - Name (Pennant Number): CHANG BOGO (061), YI CHON (062), CHOI MUSON (063), PAKUI (065), LEE JONGMU (066) JEONGUN (067) LEE SUNSIN (068), NADAEYONG (069), LEE OKKI (071)

PERU - Name (Pennant Number): ANGAMOS (ex-Casma) (SS 31), ANTOFAGASTA (SS 32), PISAGUA (SS 33), CHIPANA (SS 34), ISLAY (SS 35), ARICA (SS 36).

PAKUI (SOUTH KOREA)

TURKEY - Name (Pennant Number): 'Atilay' class – ATILAY (S 347), SALDIRAY (S 348), BATIRAY (S 349), YILDIRAY (S 350), DOGANAY (S 351), DOLUNAY (S 352). 'Preveze' class – PREVEZE (S 353), SAKARYA (S 354), 18 MART (S 355), ANAFARTALAR (S 356), GÜR (S 357), ÇANAKKALE (S 358) BURAKREIS (S359).

VENEZUELA - Name (Pennant Number): SÁBALO (S 31, ex-S 21), CARIBE (S 32, ex-S 22).

SPECIFICATION

Displacement, surfaced, tons: 980 (Turkey 'Atilay' class) 1,100 (Greece, South Korea). 1,180, (Colombia). 1,185 (Peru). 1,248 (Argentina). 1,260 (Chile). 1,285, (Ecuador, Indonesia, Venezuela). 1,400 (Brazil). 1,454 (Turkey 'Preveze' class). 1,660 (India).

Displacement, dived, tons: 1,185 (Turkey 'Atilay' class). 1,285 (Colombia, Greece, South Korea). 1,290 (Peru). 1,390, (Chile, Ecuador, Indonesia). 1,440 (Argentina). 1,550, (Brazil). 1,586(Turkey 'Preveze' class). 1,600 (Venezuela). 1,850, (India).

Length, feet (metres): 183.4 (55.9), (Argentina, Columbia, Greece). 183.7 (56), (South Korea, Peru). 195.2 (59.5), (Chile, Ecuador, Indonesia). 200.1 (61), (Venezuela). 200.8 (61.2), (Brazil, Turkey 'Atilay' class). 203.4 (62), (Turkey, 'Preveze' class). 211.2 (64.4), India.

Beam, feet (metres): 20.5 (6.3), (Argentina,

Columbia, Ecuador). 20.3 (6.2) (Chile, Greece, Brazil, Indonesia, South Korea, Peru, Turkey, (both classes), Venezuela). 21.3 (6.5), (India).

Draught, feet (metres): 17.9 (5.5). 19.7 (6), (India).

Speed, knots: 11 surfaced; 21.5 dived

ARMAMENT

Missiles: McDonnell Douglas Sub-Harpoon. (Greece and Turkey, 'Preveze' class only). SSM also fitted to planned Indian boats S 48, S 49.

Torpedoes: 8 - 21 in (533 mm) bow tubes. AEG SUT SST 4 Mod 1 (Argentina, Chile, Columbia Ecuador, India, Turkey 'Atilay' class, Venezuela). Mod 0, (Greece, Indonesia). Marconi Mk 24 Tigerfish Mod 1/2 (Brazil, Turkey, 'Preveze' class). SystemTechnik Nord (STN) SUT Mod 2, (South Korea). Whitehead A184, (Peru).

Mines: External 'strap-on' type for 24, (India). 28 in lieu of torpedoes, (South Korea).

RADARS

Surface search - Thomson-CSF Calypso II/III (all, except Turkey 'Atilay' class). S 63B, (Turkey, 'Atilay' class)

Navigation – Thomson-CSF Calypso II, (Argentina). Terma Scanter, (Brazil, Venezuela).

Sonars: Atlas Elektronik CSU 83-90 (DBQS-21), (Greece S 110-113). CSU 83/1, (Brazil, India. South Korea, Turkey, 'Preveze' class). Atlas

Elektronik PRS-3-4; passive ranging. Atlas Elektronik CSU 3-4 (Argentina, Chile, Ecuador, Greece (S 116-119), Peru, Turkey, 'Atilay' class, Venezuela); hull-mounted. CSU 3-2 (Indonesia). Atlas Elektronik TAS-3 towed array, (Turkey, 'Preveze' class). Atlas Elektronik PRS-3-4, (Greece, Indonesia). Krupp Atlas PSU 83-55, (Colombia). Thomson Sintra DUUX 2C, (Argentina, Ecuador, Greece, Peru, Venezuela). DUUX 5 (India). DUUG 1 D (Argentina)

KEY RECOGNITION FEATURES

- Blunt bow profile with bow mounted diving planes not visible.
- Round top to casing.
- Low, long fin mounted on raised part of the casing on some, with blunt profile forward and sloping profile aft.
- Fin has vertical leading and after edges.
- Rudder just visible right aft.
- Type 1300/1400/1500 and South Korean Type 1200 have more streamlined curves to hull, without raised portion around fin.

Note - These are a single hull design with two ballast tanks and forward and after trim tanks.

Collins

COLLINS CLASS

Country:	AUSTRALIA
Country of origin:	SWEDEN
Ship type:	SUBMARINES
Class:	COLLINS (KOCKUMS TYPE 471) (SSK)
Active:	5
Building:	1

Name (Pennant Number): COLLINS (73), FARNCOMB (74), WALLER (75), DECHAINEUX (76), SHEEAN (77), RANKIN (78)

SPECIFICATION

Displacement, surface, tons: 3,051.
Displacement, dived, tons: 3,353.
Length, feet (metres): 255.2 (77.8).
Beam, feet (metres): 25.6 (7.8).
Draught, feet (metres): 23. (7).
Speed, knots: 10 surfaced; 10 snorting; 20 dived.
Range, miles: 9,000 at 10 kts. (snort).

ARMAMENT

Missiles: SSM - McDonnell Douglas Sub-Harpoon.
Torpedoes: 6 - 21 in (533 mm) forward tubes;
  Gould Mk 48 Mod 4.
Mines: 44 in lieu of torpedoes.
Decoys: 2 - SSE torpedo decoys.

RADARS

Navigation – Kelvin Hughes Type 1007.
Sonars: Thomson-Sintra Scylla bow and flank
  arrays. GEC-Marconi Kariwara (73-74) or
  Thomson Marconi Narama or Allied Signal TB
  23 passive towed array.

KEY RECOGNITION FEATURES

- Blunt bow with prominent pod.
- Low, slim fin with forward edge sloping slightly aft.
- Unusual, flat extension to the top after end of the fin.
- Conventional diving planes low down on fin.
- Rounded top to casing.
- X rudders visible above waterline, aft.

VICTORIA

Country: CANADA

Country of origin: UNITED KINGDOM

Ship type: SUBMARINES

Class: UPHOLDER (Type 2400) (SSK)

Active: 4

Name (Pennant Number): VICTORIA (ex-*Unseen*) (876, ex-S 41), WINDSOR (ex-*Unicorn*) (877, ex-S 43), CORNERBROOK (ex-*Ursula*) (878, ex-S 42), CHICOUTIMI (ex-*Upholder*) (879, ex-S 40).

RADARS

Navigation – Kelvin Hughes Type 1007

Sonars: Thomson Sintra Type 2040 hull-mounted, passive. BAE Type 2007 flank array, passive. Hermes Electronics/MUSL towed array.

SPECIFICATION

Displacement, surfaced, tons: 2,168.
Displacement, dived, tons: 2,455.
Length, feet (metres): 230.6 (70.3).
Beam, feet (metres): 25 (7.6).
Draught, feet (metres): 17.7 (5.5).
Speed, knots: 20 dived, 12 surfaced.

ARMAMENT

Torpedoes: 8 - 21 in (533 mm) bow tubes; Gould Mk 48 Mod 4 dual purpose.
Decoys: 2 – SSE launchers.

KEY RECOGNITION FEATURES

- Blunt bow with prominent pod.
- Tall rounded fin, midships, with two bulges atop at aft end.
- Rounded top to casing
- Casing slopes down more steeply at its after end.
- Tall rudder with sloping forward edge and vertical after edge.

HAN 404

Country: CHINA
Country of origin: CHINA
Ship type: SUBMARINES
Class: HAN (Type 091) (SSN)
Active: 5
Name (Pennant Number): (401), (402), (403), (404), (405).

SPECIFICATION

Displacement, surfaced, tons: 4,500.
Displacement, dived, tons: 5,550.
Length, feet (metres): 321.5 (98). (347.8 (106), 403 onwards).
Beam, feet (metres): 32.8 (10).
Draught, feet (metres): 24.2 (7.4).
Speed, knots: 25 dived, 12 surfaced.

ARMAMENT

Missiles: SSM - YJ8-2 (Eagle Strike) (C-801).
Torpedoes: 6 - 21 in (533 mm) bow tubes; Yu-3 (SET-65E) and Yu-1 (Type 63-51) combination.

RADARS

Surface search – Snoop Tray.
Sonars: Trout Cheek, hull-mounted, active/passive search and attack; DUUX-5.

KEY RECOGNITION FEATURES

- Fin sited well forward of midships with diving planes at its forward edge, just above mid-height.
- Fin has vertical forward edge, top sloping down towards after end and sloping after edge, curved at the bottom.
- Tall rudder with sloping forward edge and vertical after edge.
- YJ 8-2 (C-801) SSM tubes fitted aft of the fin.

Agosta/Agosta B

AGOSTA

Country: FRANCE, PAKISTAN, SPAIN

Country of origin: FRANCE

Ship type: SUBMARINES

Class: AGOSTA /AGOSTA B (HASHMAT, GALERNA) (SSK)

Active: 1 France, 2 Pakistan ('Hashmat' class), 2 Pakistan ('Khalid' class, 'Agosta B'), 4 Spain ('Galerna' class)

Building: 1 Pakistan

FRANCE - Name (Pennant Number): OUESSANT (S 623).

PAKISTAN - Name (Pennant Number): Agosta class - HASHMAT (ex-*Astrant*) (S 135), HURMAT (ex-*Adventurous*) (S 136). Agosta B - KHALID (S 137), SAAD (S 138), HAMZA (ex-GHAZI) (S 139).

SPAIN - Name (Pennant Number): GALERNA (S 71), SIROCO (S 72), MISTRAL (S 73), TRAMONTANA (S 74).

SPECIFICATION

Displacement, surfaced, tons: 1,230, (France). 1,490, Pakistan). 1,510, (Pakistan, Agosta B). 1,490, (Spain).

Displacement, dived, tons: 1,760, (France) 1,740 (Pakistan, Agosta, and (Spain). 1,760, (Pakistan, Agosta B).

Length, feet (metres): 221.7 (67.7).

Beam, feet (metres): 22.3 (6.8).

Draught, feet (metres): 17.7 (5.4).

Speed, knots: 12 surfaced, 20 dived.

Range, miles: 8,500 at 9 kts. snorting; 350 at 3.5 kts. dived.

ARMAMENT

Missiles: SSM - Aerospatiale SM 39 Exocet; launched from 533 mm tubes, (Agosta B). McDonnell Douglas Sub-Harpoon, (Pakistan Agosta).

Torpedoes: 4 - 21 in (533 mm) bow tubes. ECAN F17P Mod 2. (ECAN L5 Mod 3/4 Spain).

Mines: Stonefish, (Pakistan). Up to 19, (Spain).

RADARS

Search - Thomson-CSF DRUA 33. (Agosta)

Surface search – Kelvin Hughes 1007 (Agosta B)

Sonars: Thomson-Sintra DSUV 22; DUUA 2D; DUUA 1D; DSUV 62A towed array, (France). Thomson-Sintra TSM 2233D, (Pakistan). Thomson-Sintra DSUV 22, DUUA 2A/2B, DUUX 2A/5, SAES Solarsub towed passive array. (Spain).

KEY RECOGNITION FEATURES

- Blunt, bull-nose bow with sonar pod atop forward end of casing.
- Wide fin with rounded surfaces. Fin has vertical leading edge with straight, sloping after edge. Distinctive protrusion at top after end of fin.
- Bow-mounted diving planes.
- Flat top to casing.
- Rudder has steeply sloping forward edge.

Note - French boat is test bed for the Project Barracuda SSN new equipment.

L'Inflexible

L'INFLEXIBLE

Country: FRANCE	
Country of origin: FRANCE	
Ship type: SUBMARINES	
Class: L'INFLEXIBLE (SNLE/SSBN)	
Active: 2	
Name (Pennant Number): L'INDOMPTABLE (S 613), L'INFLEXIBLE (S 615)*	

*One of this class will pay off as each of the successor *Le Triomphant* SNLE-NG/SSBNs commissions.

SPECIFICATION

Displacement, surfaced, tons: 8,080.
Displacement, dived, tons: 8,920.
Length, feet (metres): 422.1 (128.7).
Beam, feet (metres): 34.8 (10.6).
Draught, feet (metres): 32.8 (10)
Speed, knots: 20 surfaced; 25 dived.
Range, miles: 5,000 at 4 kts. on auxiliary propulsion only.

ARMAMENT

Missiles: SLBM - 16 Aerospatiale M4/TN 71. SSM - Aerospatiale SM 39 Exocet, launched from 533 mm torpedo tubes.

Torpedoes: 4 - 21 in (533 mm) tubes. ECAN L5 Mod 3 and ECAN F17 Mod 2.

RADARS
Navigation - Thomson-CSF DRUA 33.
Sonars: Thomson-Sintra DSUX 21, passive bow and flank arrays. DUUX 5. DSUV 61; towed array.

KEY RECOGNITION FEATURES

- Streamlined fin with diving planes at forward end towards its top.
- Large, flat-topped casing atop main pressure hull, housing the SLBM tubes.
- Slim, rounded fin with diving planes forward and protrusion at after end.
- Casing extends well aft of the fin and slopes down more steeply at its after end.
- Square-topped rudder with slightly sloping forward edge, right aft.

Rubis

AMÉTHYSTE

Country: FRANCE
Country of origin: FRANCE
Ship type: SUBMARINES
Class: RUBIS AMÉTHYSTE (SSN)
Active: 6
Name (Pennant Number): RUBIS (S 601), SAPHIR (S 602), CASABIANCA (S 603), ÉMERAUDE (S 604), AMÉTHYSTE (S 605), PERLE (S 606)

SPECIFICATION
Displacement, surfaced, tons: 2,410.
Displacement, dived, tons: 2,670.
Length, feet (metres): 241.5 (73.6).
Beam, feet (metres): 24.9 (7.6).
Draught, feet (metres): 21 (6.4).
Speed, knots: 25.

ARMAMENT
Missiles: SSM - Aerospatiale SM 39 Exocet, launched from 533 mm torpedo tubes.
Torpedoes: 4 - 21 in (533 mm) tubes. ECAN L5 Mod 3 and ECAN F17 Mod 2.
Mines: Up to 32 FG 29 in lieu of torpedoes.

RADARS
Navigation – Kelvin Hughes Type 1007.
Sonars: Thomson-Sintra DMUX 20 multi-function; DSUV 62C; towed array.

KEY RECOGNITION FEATURES
- Rounded, smooth lined hull.
- Small, prominent pod atop casing forward of fin.
- Rounded top to casing.
- Slim fin forward of midships with vertical leading edge and sloping after edge. Top of the fin is slightly rounded in profile and slopes down at the after end.
- Diving planes sited near the top of the fin at its leading edge.
- Rudder, right aft, has sloping forward edge.

Le Triomphant

LE TÉMÉRAIRE

Country: FRANCE

Country of origin: FRANCE

Ship Type: SUBMARINES

Class: LE TRIOMPHANT (SNLE-NG/SSBN)

Active: 2

Building: 2

Name (Pennant Number): LE TRIOMPHANT (S 616), LE TÉMÉRAIRE (S 617), LE VIGILANT (S 618), LE TERRIBLE (S 619)

SPECIFICATION

Displacement, surfaced, tons: 12,640.

Displacement, dived, tons: 14,335.

Length, feet (metres): 453 (138).

Beam, feet (metres): 41 (12.5).

Draught, feet (metres): 41 (12.5).

Speed, knots: 25 dived.

ARMAMENT

Missiles: SLBM – 16 Aerospatiale M45/TN 75. SSM – Aerospatiale SM 39 Exocet.

Torpedoes: 4 - 21 (533 mm) tubes; ECAN L5 Mod 3.

RADARS

Search – Dassault.

Sonars: Thomson-Sintra DMUX 80 passive bow and flank arrays. Towed array.

KEY RECOGNITION FEATURES

- Very thin, tall fin with large diving planes at forward end towards its top.
- Rounded casing with flattened top with SLBM tubes aft of fin.
- Casing slopes down steeply at aft end to square-topped rudder.

U17 (Old pennant number)

Country: GERMANY
Country of origin: Germany
Ship type: SUBMARINES
Class: TYPE 206A (SSK)
Active: 12
Name (Pennant Number): U 15 (S 194), U 16 (S 195), U 17 (S 196), U 18 (S 197), U 22 (S 171), U 23 (S 172), U 24 (S 173), U 25 (S 174), U 26 (S 175), U 28 (S 177), U 29 (S 178), U 30 (S 179)

SPECIFICATION

Displacement, surfaced, tons: 450.
Displacement, dived, tons: 498.
Length, feet (metres): 159.4 (48.6).
Beam, feet (metres): 15.1 (4.6).
Draught, feet (metres): 14.8 (4.5).
Speed, knots: 10 surfaced; 17 dived.
Range, miles: 4,500 at 5 kts. surfaced.

ARMAMENT

Torpedoes: 8 - 21 in (533 mm) bow tubes. STN Atlas DM 2A3.

Mines: GRP container secured outside hull each side containing 12 each, in addition to normal torpedo or mine armament.

RADARS

Surface search - Thomson-CSF Calypso II.
Sonars: Thomson-Sintra DUUX 2; Atlas Elektronik DBQS-21D.

KEY RECOGNITION FEATURES

- Distinctive, bulbous bow narrowing down to slim casing.
- Large, bulky, irregular shaped fin with vertical forward edge, rounded at top. Fin is stepped at its after end with sloping after edge down to casing.
- Round top to casing of which very little is visible aft of the fin.
- Bow-mounted diving planes not visible.

Note - Unusual GRP mine containers are secured either side of the hull, forward of the fin.

Dolphin

DOLPHIN CLASS

Michael Nitz

Country: ISRAEL
Country of origin: GERMANY
Ship type: SUBMARINES
Class: DOLPHIN (TYPE 800) (SSK)
Active: 3.
Name (Pennant Number): DOLPHIN (-),
LEVIATHAN (-), TEKUMA (-).

SPECIFICATION

Displacement, surfaced, tons: 1,640.
Displacement, dived, tons: 1,900.
Length, feet (metres): 188 (57.3).
Beam, feet (metres): 22.5 (6.8).
Draught, feet (metres): 20.3 (6.2).
Speed, knots: 11 snorting; 20 dived
Range, miles: 8,000 surfaced at 8 kts., 420 dived
at 8 kts.

ARMAMENT

Missiles: SSM/SLCM – Sub Harpoon UGM-84C.
SAM – Fitted for Triten anti-helicopter system.

Torpedoes: 4 - 25.6 in (650 mm) and 6 – 21 in
(533 mm) bow tubes. STN Atlas DM24A4
Seehecht.
Mines: In lieu of torpedoes.

RADARS

Search/navigation – Elta.
Sonars: Atlas Elektronik CSU 90. Atlas Elektronik
PRSW-3. FAS-3 flank array.

KEY RECOGNITION FEATURES

- Blunt, rounded bow.
- Diving planes flush with top of casing, aft
  of bow, with sonar dome between planes.
- Flat top to casing.
- Low profile, slim fin with sloping, tapering
  edges.
- Short visible casing aft of fin

Sauro

SAURO

Country: ITALY

Country of origin: ITALY

Ship type: SUBMARINES

Class: SAURO (TYPE 1081)/IMPROVED SAURO (SSK)

Active: 2 'Sauro' and 4 'Improved Sauro'.

Name (Pennant Number): 'Sauro' - FECIA DI COSSATO (S 519), LEONARDO DA VINCI (S 520), GUGLIELMO MARCONI (S 521). 'Improved Sauro' – SALVATORE PELOSI (S 522), PRIMO LONGOBARDO (S 524), GIANFRANCO GAZZANA PRIAROGGIA (S 525).

SPECIFICATION

Displacement, surfaced, tons: 1,456, (Sauro). 1,476 (Improved Sauro. 1,653, S 524-5).

Displacement, dived, tons: 1,631, (Sauro). 1,662 (Improved Sauro, 1,862, S 524-5).

Length, feet (metres): 210 (63.9). (211.2 (64.4), Improved Sauro; 217.8 (66.4), S 524-5).

Beam, feet (metres): 22.5 (6.8).

Draught, feet (metres): 18.9 (5.7). (18.4 (5.6), Improved Sauro).

Speed, knots: 11 surfaced; 12 snorting; 19 dived

Range, miles: 11,000 surfaced at 11 kts., 250 dived at 4 kts.

ARMAMENT

Torpedoes: 6 - 21 in (533 mm) bow tubes. 12 Whitehead A184.

RADARS

Search/navigation - SMA BPS-704.

Sonars: Selenia Elsag IPD 70/S. Selenia Elsag MD 100/100S.

KEY RECOGNITION FEATURES

- Blunt, rounded bow.
- Three sets of diving planes, one at bow, one on fin and one aft.
- Flat top to casing.
- Low profile, slim fin with vertical forward edge and sloping after edge. Diving planes just under midway up fin.
- Rudder visible right aft with vertical leading edge ('Sauro' – slopes in 'Improved Sauro') and sloping after edge.

Harushio

HARUSHIO

Country: JAPAN
Country of origin: JAPAN
Ship type: SUBMARINES
Class: HARUSHIO (SSK)
Active: 7
Name (Pennant Number): HARUSHIO (SS 583), NATSUSHIO (SS 584), HAYASHIO (SS 585), ARASHIO (SS 586), WAKASHIO (SS 587), FUYUSHIO (SS 588), ASASHIO (SS 589)

SPECIFICATION

Displacement, standard, tons: 2,450. (2,560 SS 589).
Displacement, dived, tons: 2,750, (2,850, SS 589).
Length, feet (metres): 252.6 (77). (255.9 (78), SS 589).
Beam, feet (metres): 32.8 (10).
Draught, feet (metres): 25.3 (7.7).
Speed, knots: 12 surfaced; 20 dived

ARMAMENT

Missiles: SSM - McDonnell Douglas Sub-Harpoon, fired from torpedo tubes.
Torpedoes: 6 - 21 in (533 mm) tubes. Japanese Type 89.

RADARS

Surface search - JRC ZPS 6.
Sonars: Hughes/Oki ZQQ 5B; hull-mounted. ZQR 1 towed array similar to BQR 15.

KEY RECOGNITION FEATURES

- Low profile bow.
- Rounded top to casing.
- Only short amount of casing visible forward of fin which is sited well forward of midships.
- Tall fin, tapered from forward to aft with vertical leading and after edges.
- Diving planes on fin at leading edge, just below mid-height.
- Curved, hump-back profile to hull.
- Rudder visible right aft with sloping forward edge.

Note - The slight growth in all dimensions and same basic shape suggests a natural progression from the 'Yuushio' class (active 6).

Oyashio

OYASHIO CLASS

Country: JAPAN

Country of origin: JAPAN

Ship type: SUBMARINES

Class: OYASHIO (SSK)

Active: 5

Building: 4

Name (Pennant Number): OYASHIO (SS 590), MICHISHIO (SS 591), UZUSHIO (SS 592), MAKISHIO (SS 593), ISOSHIO (SS 594), NARUSHIO (SS 595), –- (SS 596) –- (SS 597).

SPECIFICATION

Displacement, standard, tons: 2,700.
Displacement, dived, tons: 3,000.
Length, feet (metres): 268 (81.7).
Beam, feet (metres): 29.2 (8.9).
Draught, feet (metres): 25.9 (7.9).
Speed, knots: 12 surfaced; 20 dived

ARMAMENT

Missiles: SSM - McDonnell Douglas Sub-Harpoon, fired from torpedo tubes.
Torpedoes: 6 - 21 in (533 mm) tubes. Japanese Type 89.

RADARS

Surface search - JRC ZPS 6.
Sonars: Hughes/Oki ZQQ 5B/6; hull-mounted. ZQR 1 towed array similar to BQR 15.

KEY RECOGNITION FEATURES

- Low profile bow.
- Rounded top to casing with prominent low sonar dome above bow.
- Only short amount of casing visible forward of fin, which is sited well forward of midships.
- Tall fin, tapered from forward to aft with vertical leading and sloping after edges.
- Diving planes on fin at leading edge, around mid-height.
- Rudder visible right aft with sloping forward edge.

Yuushio

AKISHIO

Country:	JAPAN
Country of origin:	JAPAN
Ship type:	SUBMARINES
Class:	YUUSHIO (SSK)
Active:	6

Name (Pennant Number): OKISHIO (TSS, ex-SS 576), HAMASHIO (SS 578), AKISHIO (SS 579), TAKESHIO (SS 580), YUKISHIO (SS 581), SACHISHIO (SS 582)

SPECIFICATION

Displacement, standard, tons: 2,200. (2,250, SS 578-58. 2,300, SS 576).
Displacement, dived, tons: 2,450.
Length, feet (metres): 249.3 (76).
Beam, feet (metres): 32.5 (9.9).
Draught, feet (metres): 24.3 (7.4).
Speed, knots: 12 surfaced; 20 dived

ARMAMENT

Missiles: SSM - McDonnell Douglas Sub-Harpoon, fired from torpedo tubes.
Torpedoes: 6 - 21 in (533 mm) tubes. Japanese Type 89.

RADARS

Surface search - JRC ZPS 6.
Sonars: Hughes/Oki ZQQ 5B; hull-mounted. ZQR 1 towed array similar to BQR 15.

KEY RECOGNITION FEATURES

- Low profile bow.
- Rounded top to casing.
- Only short amount of casing visible forward of fin, sited well forward of midships.
- Very tall fin, tapered from forward to aft with vertical leading and after edges.
- Diving planes on fin at leading edge, just below mid-height.
- Curved, hump-back profile to hull.
- Rudder visible right aft with sloping forward edge.
Note - The same basic shape as 'Harushio' class.

WALRUS CLASS

Country:	NETHERLANDS
Country of origin:	NETHERLANDS
Ship type:	SUBMARINES
Class:	WALRUS (SSK)
Active:	4

Name (Pennant Number): WALRUS (S 802), ZEELEEUW (S 803), DOLFIJN (S 808), BRUINVIS (S 810).

SPECIFICATION

Displacement, surfaced, tons: 2,465.
Displacement, dived, tons: 2,800.
Length, feet (metres): 223.1 (67.7).
Beam, feet (metres): 27.6 (8.4).
Draught, feet (metres): 23 (7).
Speed, knots: 12 surfaced; 20 dived.
Range, miles: 10,000 at 9 kts. snorting

ARMAMENT

Missiles: SSM - McDonnell Douglas Sub-Harpoon.
Torpedoes: 4 - 21 in (533 mm) tubes. Honeywell
    Mk 48 Mod 4.

RADARS

Surface search - Signaal/Racal ZW07.
Sonars: Thomson-Sintra TSM 2272 Eledone
    Octopus; hull-mounted. GEC Avionics Type
    2026; towed array. Thomson-Sintra DUUX 5.

KEY RECOGNITION FEATURES

• Low bow with small pod at forward end of casing.
• Flat top to casing.
• Large slender fin with leading edge sloping slightly aft and vertical after end.
• Diving planes at extreme forward edge of fin and just above mid-height.
• X rudders just visible right aft.

Note - These are improved 'Zwaardvis' class, upon which the Taiwanese 'Hai Lung' class (active 2) is based.

Ula

UTSIRA

Country: NORWAY	
Country of origin: NORWAY	
Ship type: SUBMARINES	
Class: ULA (SSK)	
Active: 6	

Name (Pennant Number): ULA (S 300), UREDD (S 305), UTVAER (S 303), UTHAUG (S 304), UTSTEIN (S 302), UTSIRA (S 301)

SPECIFICATION

Displacement, surfaced, tons: 1,040.
Displacement, dived, tons: 1,150.
Length, feet (metres): 193.6 (59).
Beam, feet (metres): 17.7 (5.4).
Draught, feet (metres): 15.1 (4.6).
Speed, knots: 11 surfaced; 23 dived.
Range, miles: 5,000 at 8 kts.

ARMAMENT

Torpedoes: 8 - 21 in (533 mm) bow tubes. AEG DM 2A3.

RADARS

Surface search - Kelvin Hughes 1007.
Sonars: Atlas Elektronik CSU 83. Thomson-Sintra flank array.

KEY RECOGNITION FEATURES

- Blunt, high bow. Flat-topped casing slopes down from bow to water level right aft.
- Diving planes sited at bow, not visible.
- Fin sited just aft of midships.
- Fin is unusually low in profile with vertical leading edge and sharp, sloping after edge with notch cut out at mid-point.
- X rudders just visible right aft.

Daphné

BARRACUDA

Country: PAKISTAN, PORTUGAL, SOUTH AFRICA, SPAIN

Country of origin: FRANCE

Ship type: SUBMARINES

Class: DAPHNÉ (HANGOR, ALBACORA, DELFIN) (SSK)

Active: 4 Pakistan ('Hangor' class), 2 Portugal ('Albacora' class), 2 South Africa, 4 Spain ('Delfin' class)

PAKISTAN - Name (Pennant Number): HANGOR (S 131), SHUSHUK (S 132), MANGRO (S 133), GHAZI (ex-*Cachalote*) (S 134).

PORTUGAL - Name (Pennant Number): BARRCUDA (S 164), DELFIM (S 166).

SOUTH AFRICA - Name (Pennant Number): UMKHONTO (ex-*Emily Hobhouse*) (S 98), ASSEGAAI (e- *Johanna van der Merwe*) (S 99).

SPAIN - Name (Pennant Number): DELFÍN (S 61), TONINA (S 62), MARSOPA (S 63), NARVAL (S 64).

SPECIFICATION

Displacement, surfaced, tons: 869.
Displacement, dived, tons: 1,043.
Length, feet (metres): 189.6 (57.8).
Beam, feet (metres): 22.3 (6.8).
Draught, feet (metres): 15.1 (4.6).
Speed, knots: 13.5 surfaced; 16 dived.
Range, miles: 4,500 at 5 kts. surfaced; 3,000 at 7 kts. snorting.

ARMAMENT

Missiles: SSM – McDonnell Douglas Sub-Harpoon (Pakistan only).

Torpedoes: 12 - 21.7 in (550 mm) (8 bow, 4 stem) tubes.

Mines: Stonefish, (Pakistan only). (12 can be carried in lieu of torpedoes, Spain).

RADARS

Search - Thomson-CSF Calypso II, (South Africa). Thomson-CSF DRUA 31, (Pakistan). Kelvin Hughes Type 1007, (Portugal). DRUA 31 or 33A, (Spain).

Sonars: Thomson-Sintra DSUV 2; DUUX 2 or UEC, (South Africa).TSM 2233D, DUUA 1 (Pakistan). DSUV 2; DUUA 2, (Portugal). DSUV 22; DUUA 2A, (Spain).

KEY RECOGNITION FEATURES

- Pointed bow, flat fronted in profile.
- Flat, elongated sonar atop casing at bow.
- Slim fin with vertical leading edge and sloping after edge.
- Flat top to casing.
- Bow-mounted diving planes and rudder not visible.

Akula I/II

AKULA

Country: RUSSIA	
Country of origin: RUSSIA	
Ship type: SUBMARINES	
Class: AKULA I/II (BARS) (TYPE 971/971M) (SSN)	
Active: 7 Akula I; 3 Akula II.	
Building: 2 Akula I.	

Name (Pennant Number): Akula I – MAGADAN (ex-NARWHAL), WOLF (K 461), KUZBASS (ex-Morzh), LEOPARD (K 328) TIGR (K 154), SAMARA (ex-Drakon), NERPA (K 267). Akula II – VEPR (K 157), GEPARD (K 335), COUGAR (K 337).

SPECIFICATION

Displacement, surfaced, tons: 7,500.
Displacement, dived, tons: 9,100. (9,500 Akula II).
Length, feet (metres): 360.1 (110) oa.
Beam, feet (metres): 45.9 (14).
Draught, feet (metres): 34.1 (10.4).
Speed, knots: 10 surfaced; 28 dived.

ARMAMENT

Missiles: SLCM – Raduga SS-N-21 Sampson (RKV-500 Granat) fired from 533 mm tubes. SAM – SA-N-5/8 Strela portable launcher. A/S – Novator SS-N-15 Starfish fired from 533 mm tubes. SS-N-16 Stallion fired from 650 mm tubes; with 200 kT nuclear warhead or Veder Type 40 torpedoes.

Torpedoes: 4 - 21 in (533 mm) and 4 - 25.6 in (650 mm) tubes.

RADARS

Surface search - Snoop Pair or Snoop Half with back-to-back aerials on same mast as ESM.
Sonars: Shark Gill (Skat MGK-503); hull-mounted. Mouse Roar MG-519; hull-mounted. Skat 3 towed array.

KEY RECOGNITION FEATURES

- Blunt, bull-nosed bow.
- Large diameter hull, flat-topped aft of fin.
- Very distinctive, long low profile fin, unusually long sloping edge aft with smoothly rounded hydrodynamic lines moulded into the casing.
- Retractable diving planes not visible.
- Large stern pod (towed array dispenser) on rudder.
- **Note** - Has the same broad hull as 'Sierra' class.
- **Note 2** - A number of non-acoustic sensors have begun to appear on the fin leading edge and on the forward casing of later Akulas.

Delta IV

DELTA IV

Country: RUSSIA
Country of origin: RUSSIA
Ship type: SUBMARINES
Class: DELTA IV (DELFIN) (TYPE 667BDRM) (SSBN)
Active: 7
Name (Pennant Number): VERCHOTURE (K 51) ,
EKATERINGBURG (K 84) , VLADMIR (K 64) , TULA
(K 114), BRIANSK (K 117), KARELIA (K 18),
NOVOMORSKOVSK (K 407).

SPECIFICATION

Displacement surfaced, tons: 10,800.
Displacement dived, tons: 13,500.
Length, feet (metres): 544.6 (166) oa.
Beam, feet (metres): 39.4 (12).
Draught, feet (metres): 28.5 (8.7).
Speed, knots: 14 surfaced; 24 dived

ARMAMENT

Missiles: SLBM – Makeyev SS-N-23 (RSM 54)
Skiff with 4-10 MIRVed 100 kT warheads. A/S –
Novator SS-N-15 Starfish with 200 kT warhead
or Type 40 torpedo.
Torpedoes: 4 - 21 in (533 mm).

RADARS

Surface search - Snoop Tray MRP-25.

Sonars: Shark Gill (Skat MGK-503); hull-mounted.
Mouse Roar MG-519; hull-mounted. Pelamida
towed array.

KEY RECOGNITION FEATURES

- Blunt, rounded, low bow.
- Low profile fin sited well forward.
- Large diving planes on fin at leading edge,
  about mid-height.
- Very large and distinctive raised flat-
  topped missile casing aft of the fin with its
  forward end moulded round after edge of
  fin. Missile casing runs straight for
  approximately half the distance to the
  stern where it smoothly tapers away.
- Rudder, with sloping forward edge, just
  visible right aft.

Note - Delta IV differs from III by being
about 20 ft longer oa. and has a pressure-
tight fitting on the after end of the missile
tube housing. 6 Delta III 'Kalmar' class are
active; the 2 operational Delta I 'Murena'
class SSBNs were expected to pay off in
the near future.

Oscar II

OSCAR II

Country: RUSSIA

Country of origin: RUSSIA

Ship type: SUBMARINES

Class: OSCAR II (ANTYEY) (TYPE 949A) (SSGN)

Active: 6

Name (Pennant Number): KRASNOYARSK (K 173), SMOLENSK (K 410), CHELIABINSK (K 442), OREL (ex-*Severodvinsk*) (K 266), OMSK (K 186), ST GEORGE THE VICTORIOUS (ex-*Tomsk*) (K 512).

SPECIFICATION

Displacement, surfaced, tons: 13,900.

Displacement, dived, tons: 18,300.

Length, feet (metres): 505.2 (154).

Beam, feet (metres): 59.7 (18.2).

Draught, feet (metres): 29.5 (9).

Speed, knots: 15 surfaced; 28 dived.

ARMAMENT

Missiles: SSM – 24 Chelomey SS-N-19 Shipwreck (Granit). Warhead 750 kg HE or 500 kT nuclear. A/S – Novator SS-N-15 Starfish fired from 533 mm tubes. Novator SS-N-16 Stallion fired from 650 mm tubes; payload Type 45 Veder torpedo or Vodopad 200 kT nuclear weapon.

Torpedoes: 4 - 21 in (533 mm) and 4 - 25.6 in (650 mm) tubes. Type 53 and Type 65.

RADARS

Surface search - Snoop Pair (Albatros) or Snoop Half.

Sonars: Shark Gill (Skat MGK-503); hull-mounted; Shark Rib flank array; Mouse Roar MG-519; hull-mounted; Pelamida towed array.

KEY RECOGNITION FEATURES

- Blunt, rounded low bow.
- Exceptionally large diameter hull with rounded top.
- Low, smooth profile fin forward of midships.
- Fin is tapered at the leading and after edges.
- Three windows at either side of top leading edge of fin.
- Retractable diving planes, not visible.
- Large rudder right aft.

Note – Much shorter and much larger diameter than Delta IV.

Note 2 - SSM missile tubes are in banks of 12 either side and external to the 8.5 m diameter pressure hull.

Note 3 - All have a tube on the rudder fin as in Delta IV which may be used for dispensing a thin line towed sonar array.

Victor III

VICTOR III

Country: RUSSIA	
Country of origin: RUSSIA	
Ship type: SUBMARINES	
Class: VICTOR III (SCHUKA) (TYPE 671RTM) (SSN)	
Active: 6	

Name (Pennant Number): - (B244), - (B292), - (B388), OBNINSK (B138), DANIL MOSKOVOSKIY (B414), TAMBOY (B448).

SPECIFICATION

Displacement, surfaced, tons: 4,850.
Displacement, dived, tons: 6,300.
Length, feet (metres): 351.1 (107).
Beam, feet (metres): 34.8 (10.6).
Draught, feet (metres): 24.3 (7.4).
Speed, knots: 10 surfaced; 30 dived.

ARMAMENT

Missiles: SLCM - SS-N-21 Sampson (Granat) fired from 533 mm tubes. A/S – Novator SS-N-15 Starfish fired from 533 mm tubes. SS-N-16 Stallion fired from 650 mm tubes; payload Veder Type 40 torpedo or Vodopad 200 kT nuclear warhead.

Torpedoes: 4 - 21 in (533 mm) and 2 - 25.6 in (650 mm) tubes.
Mines: Can carry 36 in lieu of torpedoes.

RADARS

Surface search - Snoop Tray (MRP-25).
Sonars: Shark Gill (Skat MGK-503); hull-mounted. Shark Rib flank array. Mouse Roar MG-519; hull-mounted. Skat 3 towed array.

KEY RECOGNITION FEATURES

- Low, blunt bow.
- Retractable, hull-mounted diving planes.
- Large diameter, bulbous hull with a low profile.
- Rounded top to casing.
- Relatively small, rounded fin with slightly sloping leading edge and shallow sloping after edge.
- Distinctive, large, streamlined pod, housing towed array dispenser, mounted on rudder.

Typhoon

TYPHOON

Country: RUSSIA

Country of origin: RUSSIA

Ship type: SUBMARINES

Class: TYPHOON (AKULA) (TYPE 941) (SSBN)

Active: 2

Name (Pennant Number): (TK 17), SEVERSTAL (TK20).

SPECIFICATION

Displacement, surfaced, tons: 18,500.
Displacement, dived, tons: 26,500.
Length, feet (metres): 562.7 (171.5) oa.
Beam, feet (metres): 80.7 (24.6).
Draught, feet (metres): 42.7 (13).
Speed, knots: 12 surfaced; 25 dived.

ARMAMENT

Missiles: SLBM – 20 Makeyev SS-N-20 (RSM 52/3M20) Sturgeon with 10 MIRVeD warheads of 200 kT. SAM - SA-N-8 Gremlin capability when surfaced. A/S – Novator SS-N-15 Starfish fired from 533 mm tubes, payload, 200 kT Vodopad nuclear warhead or Veder Type 40 torpedo.
Torpedoes: 6 - 21 in (533 mm).
Mines: Could be carried in lieu of torpedoes.

RADARS

Surface search - Snoop Pair (Albatros).
Sonars: Shark Gill (Skat MGK-503); hull-mounted. Shark Rib flank array; Mouse Roar MG-519; hull-mounted; Pelamida towed array.

KEY RECOGNITION FEATURES

- Easily identified, the largest submarine built.
- Blunt, bull-nosed bows with huge cylindrical hull.
- Flat top to casing.
- Streamlined fin, with windows at the top forward edge, sited well aft of midships.
- The fin has a relatively low profile with the lower part being larger and rounded where it moulds onto the main casing.
- In profile the leading edge to the fin is vertical and the after edge has a slight slope.
- Retractable diving planes are not visible.
- The very large rudder at the after end gives this class an unmistakable profile.
- Missile tubes are mounted forward of the fin.

Sjöormen

CONQUEROR

Country: SINGAPORE
Country of origin: SWEDEN
Ship type: SUBMARINES
Class: SJÖORMEN (A 12) (SSK)
Active: 4
Name (Pennant Number): CHALLENGER
(ex-*Sjöbjörnen*), CENTURION (ex-*Sjöormen*),
CONQUEROR (ex-*Sjölejonet*), CHIEFTAIN
(ex-*Sjöhunden*)

SPECIFICATION

Displacement, surfaced, tons: 1,130.
Displacement, dived, tons: 1,210.
Length, feet (metres): 167.3 (51).
Beam, feet (metres): 20 (6.1).
Draught, feet (metres): 19 (5.8).
Speed, knots: 12 surfaced; 20 dived.

ARMAMENT

Torpedoes: 4 - 21 in (533 mm) bow tubes. FFV
Type 613; 2 - 16 in (400 mm) tubes. FFV
Type 431.

RADARS

Navigation - Terma.
Sonars: Plessey Hydra; hull-mounted.

KEY RECOGNITION FEATURES

- Low, blunt bow.
- Low profile hull with smooth, sloping forward and after ends.
- Rounded top to casing.
- Bulky fin with unusual curves to leading edge. Vertical after edge, slightly flared at bottom.
- Fin-mounted diving planes sited at centre of fin and well below mid-height.
Note - Albacore hull. Twin-decked.

Gotland

UPPLAND

Country:	SWEDEN
Country of origin:	SWEDEN
Ship type:	SUBMARINES
Class:	GOTLAND (A 19) (SSK)
Active:	3

Name (Pennant Number): GOTLAND (-),
UPPLAND (-), HALLAND (-).

SPECIFICATION

Displacement, surfaced, tons: 1,240.
Displacement, dived, tons: 1,490.
Length, feet (metres): 198.2 (60.4).
Beam, feet (metres): 20.3 (6.2).
Draught, feet (metres): 18.4 (5.6).
Speed, knots: 10 surfaced, 20 dived.

ARMAMENT

Torpedoes: 4 - 21 in (533 mm) bow tubes; FFV
Type 613/62. 2 - 15.75 in (400 mm) bow tubes;
Swedish Ordnance Type 432/451.
Mines: Capability for 48 in external girdle or 12
Type 47 swim-out mines in lieu of torpedoes.

RADARS

Navigation – Terma Scanter.
Sonars: STN/Atlas Elektronik CSU 90-2, hull-
mounted.

KEY RECOGNITION FEATURES

- Blunt, bull-nosed rounded bow.
- Flat top to casing.
- Slim fin amidships with slightly sloped
  base, forward and aft.
- Diving plans midway up centre of fin.

Västergötland

ÖSTERGOTLAND

Country: SWEDEN
Country of origin: SWEDEN
Ship type: SUBMARINES
Class: VÄSTERGÖTLAND (A 17) (SSK)
Active: 4
Name (Pennant Number): VÄSTERGÖTLAND (-),
HÄLSINGLAND (-), SÖDERMANLAND (-),
ÖSTERGÖTLAND (-).

SPECIFICATION

Displacement, surfaced, tons: 1,070.
Displacement, dived, tons: 1,143.
Length, feet (metres): 159.1 (48.5).
Beam, feet (metres): 20 (6.1).
Draught, feet (metres): 18.4 (5.6).
Speed, knots: 10 surfaced; 20 dived.

ARMAMENT

Torpedoes: 6 - 21 in (533 mm) tubes. FFV Type
613; 3 - 15.75 in (400 mm) tubes. FFV Type
431/451.

RADARS

Navigation - Terma.
Sonars: Atlas Elektronik CSU 83; hull-mounted.

KEY RECOGNITION FEATURES

- Rounded bow, small pod atop forward
  casing.
- Smooth, symmetrical casing with rounded
  top.
- Large, distinctive fin with sloping top at
  forward edge.
- Fin is slightly flared out (in profile) for the
  lower one third of its height.
- Fin-mounted diving planes, aft from
  forward edge below mid-height.
Note - Single hulled, with an X type
  rudder/after hydroplane design.

Swiftsure

SWIFTSURE CLASS

Country: UNITED KINGDOM
Country of origin: UNITED KINGDOM
Ship type: SUBMARINES
Class: SWIFTSURE (SSN)
Active: 5
Name (Pennant Number): SOVEREIGN (S 108), SUPERB (S 109), SCEPTRE (S 104), SPARTAN (S 105), SPLENDID (S 106)

SPECIFICATION

Displacement, standard, tons: 4,400.
Displacement, dived, tons: 4,900.
Length, feet (metres): 272 (82.9).
Beam, feet (metres): 32.3 (9.8).
Draught, feet (metres): 28 (8.5).
Speed, knots: 30+ dived

ARMAMENT

Missiles: SLCM – Hughes Tomahawk Block III. SSM - McDonnell Douglas UGM-84B Sub-Harpoon.
Torpedoes: 5 - 21 in (533 mm) bow tubes. Marconi Spearfish/Marconi Tigerfish Mk 24 Mod 2.
Mines: Can be carried in lieu of torpedoes.

RADARS

Navigation - Kelvin Hughes Type 1007.
Sonars: Marconi/Plessey Type 2074; hull-mounted, active/passive search and attack. Marconi 2072 flank array.
Ferranti Type 2046; towed array. Thomson-Sintra Type 2019 PARIS or THORN EMI 2082 passive intercept and ranging; Marconi Type 2077 short-range classification, active.

KEY RECOGNITION FEATURES

- Submarine has hump-backed appearance in profile.
- The pressure hull maintains its diameter for most of the hull length.
- Retractable, hull-mounted diving planes.
- Prominent, slender sonar pod atop casing forward of fin.
- Fin mounted just forward of midships. Fin has vertical leading and after edges and is tapered to point at after end.
- Slopes steeply down at after end of hull compared with shallow slope at forward end.
- Large, flat-topped rudder with sloping forward edge at after end of casing.

Trafalgar

TALENT

Country:	UNITED KINGDOM
Country of origin:	UNITED KINGDOM
Ship type:	SUBMARINES
Class:	TRAFALGAR (SSN)
Active:	7

Name (Pennant Number): TRAFALGAR (S 107), TURBULENT (S 87), TIRELESS (S 88), TORBAY (S 90), TRENCHANT (S 91), TALENT (S 92), TRIUMPH (S 93)

SPECIFICATION

Displacement, surfaced, tons. 4,740
Displacement, dived, tons: 5,208.
Length, feet (metres): 280.1 (85.4).
Beam, feet (metres): 32.1 (9.8).
Draught, feet (metres): 31.2 (9.5).
Speed, knots: 32 dived.

ARMAMENT

Missiles: SLCM – Hughes Tomahawk Block IIIC.
SSM - McDonnell Douglas UGM-84B Sub-Harpoon Block IC.
Torpedoes: 5 - 21 in (533 mm) bow tubes.
Marconi Spearfish/Marconi Tigerfish Mk 24 Mod 2.
Mines: Can be carried in lieu of torpedoes.

RADARS

Navigation - Kelvin Hughes Type 1007.
Sonars: Marconi 2072; hull-mounted flank array.

Plessey Type 2020 or Marconi/Plessey 2074 or Ferranti/Thomson Sintra 2076 passive/active search and attack; hull-mounted. Ferranti Type 2046 towed array. Thomson-Sintra Type 2019 PARIS or THORN EMI 2082 passive intercept and ranging. Marconi Type 2077 short range classification, active.

KEY RECOGNITION FEATURES

- Long, low hull with almost identical sloping profiles at the forward and after ends of the pressure hull.
- Rounded top to casing.
- Retractable, forward, hull-mounted diving planes.
- Prominent, slender sonar pod atop casing just forward of fin.
- Fin is mounted forward of midships. Fin has vertical leading and after edges and is tapered to point at after end.
- Large, flat-topped rudder at after end of casing.

Note - The pressure hull and outer surfaces are covered with conformal anechoic noise reduction coatings.

Note 2 - Strengthened fins for under ice operations.

Vanguard

VENGEANCE

Country: UNITED KINGDOM
Country of origin: UNITED KINGDOM
Ship type: SUBMARINES
Class: VANGUARD (SSBN)
Active: 4
Name (Pennant Number): VANGUARD (S 28),
VICTORIOUS (S 29), VIGILANT (S 30), VENGEANCE
(S 31)

SPECIFICATION

Displacement, dived, tons: 15,900.
Length, feet (metres): 491.8 (149.9).
Beam, feet (metres): 42 (12.8).
Draught, feet (metres): 39.4 (12).
Speed, knots: 25 dived.

ARMAMENT

Missiles: SLBM - Lockheed Trident 2 (D5) with up
to 8 MIRVed nuclear warheads of 100-120 kT.
Torpedoes: 4 - 21 in (533 mm) tubes. Marconi
Spearfish.

RADARS

Navigation - Kelvin Hughes Type 1007.
Sonars: Marconi Type 2054; hull-mounted sonar
suite. Marconi/Ferranti Type 2046 towed array.
Type 2043 hull-mounted, active; Type 2082
passive intercept and ranging.

KEY RECOGNITION FEATURES

- Casing slopes down forward of fin to
waterline.
- Slim, tapered fin well forward of midships.
- Hull-mounted diving planes approximately
midway between fin and bow.
- Large, distinctive, flat-topped casing aft of
fin, dropping down steeply at its after end.
Casing houses SLBMs.
- Large rudder with curved top.
Note - The outer surface of the submarine is
covered with conformal anechoic noise
reduction coatings.

Ohio

MARYLAND

Country: UNITED STATES OF AMERICA
Country of origin: USA
Ship type: SUBMARINES
Class: OHIO (SSBN)
Active: 18
Name (Pennant Number): OHIO (SSBN 726), MICHIGAN (SSBN 727), FLORIDA (SSBN 728), GEORGIA (SSBN 729), HENRY M JACKSON (SSBN 730), ALABAMA (SSBN 731), ALASKA (SSBN 732), NEVADA (SSBN 733), TENNESSEE (SSBN 734), PENNSYLVANIA (SSBN 735), WEST VIRGINIA (SSBN 736), KENTUCKY (SSBN 737), MARYLAND (SSBN 738), NEBRASKA (SSBN 739), RHODE ISLAND (SSBN 740), MAINE (SSBN 741), WYOMING (SSBN 742), LOUISIANA (SSBN 743).

SPECIFICATION
Displacement, surfaced, tons: 16,600.
Displacement, dived, tons: 18,750.
Length, feet (metres): 560 (170.7).
Beam, feet (metres): 42 (12.8).
Draught, feet (metres): 36.4 (11.1).
Speed, knots: 24 dived.

ARMAMENT
Missiles: SLBM - Lockheed Trident I (C4) (726-733). Up to 8 MIRVed nuclear warheads of 100 kT. Lockheed Trident II (D5) up to 12 MIRVed nuclear warheads of 100-475 kT. (734 onwards).

Torpedoes: 4 - 21 in (533mm) Mk 68 bow tubes. Gould Mk 48 ADCAP.
Decoys: 8 launchers for Emerson Electric Mk 2; torpedo decoy.

RADARS
Surface search/navigation/fire control – BPS-15A/H.
Sonars: IBM BQQ-6 passive search. Raytheon BQS-13; spherical array for BQQ-6. AMETEK BQS-15 active/passive for close contacts.
Western Electric BQR-15 (with BQQ-9 signal processor) passive towed array. Raytheon BQR-19 active, for navigation.

KEY RECOGNITION FEATURES
- Very long, low profile pressure hull.
- Hull steeply sloped at the forward end with a long shallow slope down to the rudder aft.
- Comparatively small, slim fin sited well forward with vertical leading and after edges. After end of fin is tapered.
- Long, slender fin-mounted diving planes at mid-height.

Los Angeles

Country: UNITED STATES OF AMERICA

Country of origin: USA

Ship type: SUBMARINES

Class: LOS ANGELES (SSN)

Active: 51

Name (Pennant Number): LOS ANGELES (SSN 688), PHILADELPHIA (SSN 690), MEMPHIS (SSN 691), BREMERTON (SSN 698), JACKSONVILLE (SSN 699), DALLAS (SSN 700), LA JOLLA (SSN 701), CITY OF CORPUS CHRISTI (SSN 705), ALBUQUERQUE (SSN 706), PORTSMOUTH (SSN 707), MINNEAPOLIS-SAINT PAUL (SSN 708), HYMAN G. RICKOVER (SSN 709), AUGUSTA (SSN 710), SAN FRANCISCO (SSN 711), HOUSTON (SSN 713), NORFOLK (SSN 714), BUFFALO (SSN 715), SALT LAKE CITY (SSN 716), OLYMPIA (SSN 717), HONOLULU (SSN 718), PROVIDENCE (SSN 719), PITTSBURGH (SSN 720), CHICAGO (SSN 721), KEY WEST (SSN 722), OKLAHOMA CITY (SSN 723), LOUISVILLE (SSN 724), HELENA (SSN 725), NEWPORT NEWS (SSN 750), SAN JUAN (SSN 751), PASADENA (SSN 752), ALBANY (SSN 753), TOPEKA (SSN 754), MIAMI (SSN 755), SCRANTON (SSN 756), ALEXANDRIA (SSN 757), ASHEVILLE (SSN 758), JEFFERSON CITY (SSN 759), ANNAPOLIS (SSN 760), SPRINGFIELD (SSN 761), COLUMBUS (SSN 762), SANTA FE (SSN 763), BOISE (SSN 764), MONTPELIER (SSN 765), CHARLOTTE (SSN 766), HAMPTON (SSN 767), HARTFORD (SSN 768), TOLEDO (SSN 769), TUCSON (SSN 770), COLUMBIA (SSN 771), GREENEVILLE (SSN 772), CHEYENNE (SSN 773)

KEY RECOGNITION FEATURES

- Blunt bow, very low profile pressure hull.
- Hull profile tapers gently and consistently down to water level from bow to stern.
- Slender fin, with vertical leading and after edges, is sited well forward of midships.
- Fin-mounted diving planes at mid-height. Diving planes have distinct swept wing appearance. (See Note 3).
- Tall rudder right aft with sloping forward edge.

Note - From SSN 719 onwards, all are equipped with the Vertical Launch System that places 12 launch tubes esternal to the pressure hull behind the BQQ-5 spherical array forward.

Note 2 - From SSN 751 onwards the class have acoustic tile cladding to augment the 'mammalian' skin which up to then had been the standard USN outer casing coating.

Note 3 - From SSN 751 onwards the forward diving planes are hull-fitted forward instead of on the fin.

Note 4 - The towed sonar array is stowed in a blister on the side of the casing.

Note 5 - Five of the class are fitted with Dry Dock shelters on the aft casing for special forces operation (SSN 688, 690, 700, 701). Four others are being fitted to operate Advanced Swimmer Delivery System dry submersibles, (SSN 772, 762, 766, 768).

LOS ANGELES CLASS

SPECIFICATION

Displacement, standard, tons: 6,082.
Displacement, dived, tons: 6,927.
Length, feet (metres): 362 (110.3).
Beam, feet (metres): 33 (10.1).
Draught, feet (metres): 32.3 (9.9).
Speed, knots: 32 dived.

ARMAMENT

Missiles: SLCM – GDC/Hughes Tomahawk (TLAM-N). SSM – GDC/Hughes Tomahawk (TASM). McDonnell Douglas Harpoon.
Torpedoes: 4 - 21 in (533 mm) tubes midships. Gould Mk 48 ADCAP.
Mines: Can lay Mk 67 Mobile and Mk 60 Captor mines.
Decoys: Emerson Electric Mk 2; torpedo decoy.

RADARS

Surface search/navigation/fire control - Sperry BPS 15H/16.
Sonars: IBM BQQ-5D/E passive/active search and attack. BQG-5D (flank array, SSN 710 and SSN 751 onwards). TB 23/29 thin line array or TB 16 and TB 93 passive towed array. AMETEK BQS-15 active close range; MIDAS (mine and ice avoidance system) (SSN 751 on).

Seawolf

Country: UNITED STATES OF AMERICA

Country of origin: USA

Ship type: SUBMARINES

Class: SEAWOLF (SSN)

Active: 2

Building: 1

Name (Pennant Number): SEAWOLF (SSN 21), CONNECTICUT (SSN 22), JIMMY CARTER (SSN 23).

SPECIFICATION

Displacement, surfaced, tons: 8,080.
Displacement, dived, tons: 9,142.
Length, feet (metres): 353 (107.6).
Beam, feet (metres): 42.3 (12.9).
Draught, feet (metres): 35.8 (10.9).
Speed, knots: 39 dived.

ARMAMENT

Missiles: SLCM – Hughes Tomahawk (TLAM-N) land attack. SSM – GDC/Hughes Tomahawk (TASM) anti-ship.
Torpedoes: 4 – 26 in (660mm) Gould Mk 48 ADCAP.
Mines: 100 in lieu of torpedoes.

RADARS

Navigation – BPS-16.
Sonars: BQQ-5D suite with bow spherical active/passive array and wide aperture passive flank arrays. TB 16 and TB 29 surveillance and tactical towed arrays. BQS-24 active close range detection.

KEY RECOGNITION FEATURES

- Long, low profile pressure hull.
- Characteristic integral rounded curve upwards from forward casing to low slim fin with notch above. After end of fin is tapered
- Casing flattened with a short, sharp slope down to the rudder aft.

SEAWOLF

NATO STANAG DESIGNATORS FOR SHIPS

Designator	Reporting title	Description
AA	Auxiliary type ship, general	General designator for all naval auxiliary type ships
AH	Hospital ship	Ship 40 m or more providing hospital services
AP	Personnel transport	Ship of 120 m or over to transport troops and their supplies
CA	Cruiser, gun	A cruiser with 6 in guns or larger as main armament and carries no missiles
CC	Cruiser, general	Cruisers of 150 m and over
CG	Cruiser, guided missile	Cruiser having guided missiles as main armament
CGH	Cruiser, guided missile, Helicopter	Guided missile cruiser with helicopter operational capability
CGN	Cruiser, guided missile, nuclear	As CG but with nuclear propulsion
CV	Aircraft carrier	Designator for aircraft carriers and multi-role aircraft carriers
CVG	Aircraft carrier, guided missile	Aircraft carrier fitted with surface-to-air guided missiles
CVH	Aircraft carrier, VSTOL/helicopter	Carrier not fitted with arrest gear/catapult, operating VSTOL and/or helicopters which is not an amphibious or mine warfare vessel
CVN	Aircraft carrier, nuclear	As CV but with nuclear propulsion
CVS	Aircraft carrier, ASW	Carrier capable of operating VSTOL and/or helicopters in sustained ASW operations
DD	Destroyer, general	General designator for destroyer type ships in range of c.95 to 140 m
DDE	Destroyer, escort (Canada)	
DDG	Destroyer, guided missile	Destroyer fitted with surface-to-air guided missiles
DDH	Destroyer, helicopter (Canada)	
FF	Frigate/corvette general	General designator for frigate. Ship of 75 to 150 m. Generally lighter surface armament than DD
FFG	Frigate, guided missile	Frigate fitted with surface-to-air guided missiles
FFH	Frigate, helicopter	Frigate carrying helicopters
FFT	Frigate	Frigate which can be used as a training platform
FS	Corvette	Small escort of 60 to 100 m
FSG	Corvette (guided missile)	
LCC	Amphibious command ship	Command ship for amphibious taskforce and landing assault operations
LCM	Landing craft, mechanised	Landing craft of 15 to 25 m capable of carrying one tank or 50-200 troops. Must have landing ramp
LCP	Landing craft, personnel	Landing craft of 7.5 to 30 m suitable for only personnel
LCU	Landing craft, utility	All purpose landing craft of 25 to 55 m capable of handling 2-3 tanks or 300-450 troops. Must have landing ramp
LCVP	Landing craft, vehicle, personnel	Similar to LCP but capable of carrying light vehicle in place of troops
LHA	Amphibious general assault ship	Large general purpose amphibious assault ship for landing an assault force from helicopters or landing craft. Must have internal stowage, ramp and flooded well
LHD	Amphibious assault ship, multi-purpose	Large multi-purpose amphibious ship for landing an assault force from helicopters, landing craft or amphibious vehicles. Can also conduct missions with VSTOL aircraft and ASW helicopters
LL	Amphibious vessel, general	General designator for amphibious vessels
LPA	Amphibious transport, personnel	Ship capable of carrying 1300-1500 troops and landing them in its own landing craft
LPD	Amphibious transport, dock	Capable of carrying 1000 troops up to 9 LCM. Must have helicopter platform
LPH	Amphibious assault ship	Large helicopter carrier for landing circa 1800 troops with its own aircraft
LSD	Landing ship, dock	Primarily tank and vehicle carrier, also capable of carrying 150-400 troops
LSM	Landing ship, medium	Of 45 to 85m capable of beaching to land troops and tanks
LST	Landing ship, tank	Of 85 to 160m to transport troops, vehicles and tanks for amphibious assault. Must have bow doors and/or ramps
MM	Mine warfare vessels, general	General designator for mine warfare vessels
MCM	Mine countermeasures vessel	Minehunter with mechanical and influence sweep capability
MH(I)(C)(O)	Minehunter, general	Fitted with equipment to hunt mines (Inshore) (Coastal) (Ocean). Ship of 25 to 60 m with enhanced minehunting capability. May also carry sweep gear and mine clearance divers
MHS	Minehunter and sweeper, general	Ship designed to sweep mines
MLC	Minelayer (coastal)	
MSC	Minesweeper, coastal	Of 40 to 60 m
MSO	Minesweeper, ocean	Of 46 m or more
OPV	Offshore patrol vessel	
PC(F)	Patrol craft, general (fast).	General designator for patrol vessels
PG	Patrol ship, general	Of 45 to 85 m not designed to operate in open ocean. Must have at least 76 mm armament
PG (F) (G)	Patrol or gunship (fast) (guided missile)	
PHM	Patrol combatant, guided missile	High speed (hydrofoil) craft with SSM capability
PT (H)	Patrol/torpedo boat (hydrofoil)	High speed (35 kts) of 20 to 30 m. Anti-surface torpedo equipped.
SS	Submarine, general	General designator for submarines
SSA	Submarine, missile	Submarines fitted with underwater-to-surface guided missiles
SSBN	Submarine, ballistic missile, nuclear	Primary strategic nuclear submarine armed with ballistic missiles
SSGN	Submarine, attack, surface missile, nuclear	Nuclear submarine fitted with underwater or surface to surface missiles
SSK	Submarine, patrol	Non-nuclear long range patrol submarine may have anti-surface or anti-submarine role
SSN	Submarine, attack, nuclear	Nuclear attack submarine with both anti-submarine and anti-surface capability

Note: It should be noted that not all countries conform to the NATO STANAG codings for their ships. There are a number of ships in this publication whose designations will not be found in the above list (e.g. France).

GLOSSARY

AAW	Anti-air warfare.
ACDS	Advanced combat direction system.
ACV	Air cushion vehicle.
AEW	Airborne early warning.
AIP	Air independent propulsion
ANV	Advanced naval vehicle.
ARM	Anti-radiation missile
A/S, ASW	Anti-submarine (warfare).
ASDS	Advanced Swimmer Delivery System
ASM	Air-to-surface missile.
ASROC/SUBROC	Rocket-assisted torpedo.
ASV	Anti-surface vessel.
AUSS	Advanced Unmanned Search System
AUV	Autonomous Undersea Vehicle
AX/TD	Training ship.
BPDMS	Base point defence missile system
Cal./Calibre	Diameter of a gun barrel; also used for measuring the length of the barrel.
CIWS	Close-in weapons system.
CH	Helicopter cruiser.
cp	Controllable pitch propellers.
DC	Depth charge
DCT	Depth charge thrower.
DE	Destroyer escort, (Japan).
DDK	Destroyer. (Japan).
DDS	Dry Dock Shelter (mounted on aft casing of US SSNs for special forces operations)
DP	dual purpose.
Displacement	The weight of water displaced by a ship's hull when floating.
DSV	Deep submergence vehicle
DSRV	Deep submergence recovery vehicle.
ECM	Electronic countermeasures.
ECCM	Electronic counter-counter measures.
EHF	Extremely high frequency.
ELF	Extremely low frequency.
ELINT	Electronic intelligence.
ESM	Electronic support measures.
EW	Electronic warfare.
FAC	Fast attack craft.
FLIR	Forward looking infra-red radar.
FRAM	Fleet rehabilitation and modernisation programme.
fwd	forward
FY	fiscal year.
GCCS	Global Command and Control System
GFCS	Gun fire control system.
GML5	Guided missile launch system.
GPS	Global positioning system.
GRP	Glass reinforced plastic
GWS	Guided weapons system.
HE	High explosive
HF	High frequency.
IFF	Identification friend/foe.
IRST	Infra-red search and track.
kT	Kiloton. (Explosive power equivalent to 1,000 tons of TNT).
kts	Knots.(Speed of 1 nautical mile per hour)
LAMPS	Light airborne multipurpose system (helicopter).
LAMS	Local area missile system
LCA	Landing craft – assault.
LCAC	Landing craft – air cushion.
LCL	Landing craft – logistic, (UK).
LCM	Landing craft – mechanised load.
LCP	Landing craft – personnel.
LCT	Landing craft – tank.
LCU	Landing craft – utility.
LCVP	Landing craft – vehicles and personnel.
LF	Low frequency.
LMCR	Liquid metal cooled reactor
LRMP	Long-range maritime patrol.
LSM	Landing ship, medium.
MAD	Magnetic anomaly detector.
MCM/MCMV	Mine countermeasures/mine countermeasures vessel.

MF	Medium frequency.
MFCS	Missile fire control system.
MG	Machine gun.
MIDAS	Mine and ice avoidance system.
MIRV	Multiple, independently targetable re-entry vehicle. (Nuclear warhead).
MRV	Multiple re-entry vehicle. (nuclear warhead).
MSC	US Military Sealift Command.
MSC	Coastal minesweeper.
MW	Megawatt.
NBC	Nuclear, biological and chemical warfare.
nm	Nautical miles.
NTDS	Naval tactical direction system.
NTU	New threat upgrade.
oa	Overall length between extremities.
OPV	Offshore patrol vessel
OTH	Over the horizon.
PAAMS	Principal anti-air missile system
PAN	Aircraft carrier, nuclear-powered, (France).
PDMS	Point defence missile system.
PWR	Pressurised water reactor.
RAM	Rolling Airframe Missile.
RAM	Radar absorbent material.
RAS	Replenishment at sea.
RBU	Russian anti-submarine rocket launcher.
Ro–ro	Roll-on/roll-off.
ROV	Remote operated vehicle.
SAM	Surface-to-air missile.
SAR	Search and rescue.
SATCOM	Satellite communications.
SDV	Swimmer delivery vehicle.
SES	Surface effect ships.
SHF	Super high frequency.
SINS	Ship's inertial navigation system.
SLBM	Submarine-launched ballistic missile.
SLCM	Ship(submarine)-launched cruise missile.
SLEP	Service Life Extension Programme.
SNLE/SNLE-NG	Sous-Marins Nucléaires Lanceurs d'Engins. (French version of SSBN). NG stands for Nouvelle Génération.
SRBOC	Super rapid blooming offboard chaff.
SSDE/SSE	Submerged signal and decoy ejector.
SSM	Surface-to-surface missile.
SSTDS	Surface Ship Torpedo Defence System.
STIR	Surveillance Target Indicator Radar.
SURTASS	Surface Towed Array Surveillance System.
SUWN	Surface-to-underwater missile launcher.
SWATH	Small waterplane area twin hull.
TACAN	Tactical air navigation system.
TACTASS	Tactical Towed-Acoustic Sensor System.
TAS	Target Acquisition System.
TASM	Tomahawk anti-ship missile
TASS	Towed Array Surveillance System.
TBMD	Theatre ballistic missile defence
TCD	Landing ship, dock. (France).
TLAM	Tomahawk Land Attack Missile with HE warhead
TLAM–N	Tomahawk Land Attack Missile - Nuclear
ULF	Ultra-high frequency.
UUV	Unmanned Undersea Vehicle
VDS	Variable depth sonar.
Vertrep	Vertical replenishment.
VLF	Very low frequency.
VLS	Vertical launch system.
VSTOL	Vertical or short take-off/landing (aircraft).
WIG	Wing-in-ground effect (aircraft).
wl	Water line. (measurement of length between extremities on the water-line.)

INDEX

INDEX

INDEX